The Military in South American Politics

George Philip

Routledge
Taylor & Francis Group

First published in 1985
by Croom Helm Ltd

This edition first published in 2024 by Routledge
4 Park Square, Milton Park, Abingdon, Oxon, OX14 4RN

and by Routledge
605 Third Avenue, New York, NY 10017

Routledge is an imprint of the Taylor & Francis Group, an informa business

Publisher's Note
The publisher has gone to great lengths to ensure the quality of this reprint but points out that some imperfections in the original copies may be apparent.

Disclaimer
The publisher has made every effort to trace copyright holders and welcomes correspondence from those they have been unable to contact.

A Library of Congress record exists under LCCN: 85016635

ISBN: 978-1-032-86818-9 (hbk)
ISBN: 978-1-003-52954-5 (ebk)
ISBN: 978-1-032-86842-4 (pbk)

Book DOI 10.4324/9781003529545

THE MILITARY IN SOUTH AMERICAN POLITICS

GEORGE PHILIP

CROOM HELM

London • Sydney • Dover, New Hampshire

© 1985 George Philip
Croom Helm Ltd, Provident House, Burrell Row,
Beckenham, Kent, BR3 1AT
Croom Helm Australia Pty Ltd, Suite 4, 6th Floor,
64-76 Kippax Street, Surry Hills, NSW 2010, Australia

British Library Cataloguing in Publication Data

Philip, George D. E.
    The military in South American politics.
    1. Latin America – Armed forces – Political
activity
    I. Title
    322'.5'098   UA619
    ISBN 0-7099-2082-2

Croom Helm, 51 Washington Street, Dover,
New Hampshire 03820, USA

Library of Congress Cataloging in Publication Data

Philip, George D. E.
    The military in South American politics.

    Bibliography: p.
    Includes index.
    1. South America – Politics and Government – 20th
Century. 2. Civil-military Relations – South America –
History – 20th Century. 3. South America – Armed Forces –
Political Activity – History – 20th Century. I. Title.
F2237.P49   1985   322'.5'098   85-16635
ISBN 0-7099-2082-2 (U. S.)

Printed and bound in Great Britain by
Biddles Ltd, Guildford and King's Lynn

The Military in South American Politics

First published in 1985, *The Military in South American Politics* analyses the nature of military involvement in politics in Latin America. The author presents many original arguments in the course of his discussion of the key issues. These include: the civil-military system, whereby the military exert power and influence even when they are not in government; how this system and also military professionalism have developed over time; how the "corporatist" ethic of South America military differs from the "partisan" ethic of the military in Central American and Caribbean countries and the consequences of this; how there are different types of coups; how the military find it difficult to disengage; how the military often intervene to exercise the principle of "guardianship" in order to preserve the fabric of society and economy which, in South America, are remarkably stable despite the many coups. Throughout, the author draws on examples from all Latin American countries from the middle of the nineteenth century onwards and summarises the existing literature to support his rich and convincing arguments. The book concludes with a summary of the arguments and with a discussion of trends and the prospects for "real" democratisation. It is a must read for students and researchers of Latin American politics and military studies.

CONTENTS

Preface

Introduction

Chapter		Page
1	Modernisation, Mass Society Theory and the Middle Class Military	1
2	Reactions against "Modernisation"; Dependency, Bureaucratic Authoritarianism and the State	26
3	The Military Institution; Some Comparisons from Central America and the Caribbean	54
4	From Status to Institution; Early Professionalisation and its Consequences	84
5	The Military Institution in Politics; The First Wave	116
6	Military Politics in the Post-War Decades	149
7	South American Military Institutions; A View Inside	177
8	Dilemmas of Military Regimes	200
9	The Brazilian Regimes since 1964	213
10	Military Governments and Military Failures in Argentina	246
11	Military Radicalism and After in Peru	275
12	Chile under Pinochet	306
13	Some Other Cases; Bolivia, Ecuador and Uruguay	325
14	The Military in South American Politics	356
References		372
Index		390

PREFACE

This book stems very largely from my experience of teaching Latin American politics at the LSE and London Institute of Latin American Studies. I owe a debt of gratitude to all those who argued with me during this time, and especially to Ian Roxborough with whom I shared a political sociology class for six years. I should also thank Chris Clapham, Ian Campbell and all those who attended the ECPR Panel on the military at Freiburg in 1983, and those who commented on my paper at the PSA in Canterbury in 1982. More specifically, I also wish to thank Dudley Ankerson for his helpful comments on my Argentine chapter.

Acknowledgement is also due to the British Council, the London School of Economics and the Central Research Fund at Senate House, who all helped finance my trips to South America while this work was in progress.

George Philip

INTRODUCTION

At a topical level, this book attempts to
tackle what must be a very common question from
people approaching South American politics from
outside. Given the Continent's reputation for
political instability and acute social conflict,
why is political breakthrough (or breakdown) so
rare? Cuba and Nicaragua have had Marxist-Leninist
revolutions, and other Central American countries
are facing major domestic insurgencies; in South
America, however, the only successful revolution
this century occurred in Bolivia in 1952. This was
an event on altogether a far less significant
scale. Countries outside South America in which
the military has taken an active role have often
had military-led revolutions, usually headed by
junior officers or NCOs, in which the discipline of
the institution - and the power of senior officers
- has been broken. Examples include Nasser's
Egypt, the Ethiopian Revolution, Jerry Rawlings'
movement in Ghana and the Portuguese upheavals of
1974-75. Nothing of this kind has happened in
South America, although Batista did lead a
successful sergeant's revolt in Cuba. For a period
(mainly 1925-45) South America did experience
junior officers' movements but these were far from
being socially, and still less politically,
revolutionary. Moreover, an outside observer might
find it hard to understand how military
institutions in South America have been able to
continue with an active political role, and not
always an unpopular one, even after the spectacular
failure of particular military governments. The
cases of Peru after 1977-78, Argentina after 1982,
and Bolivia after 1980-81 spring immediately to
mind (and may be contrasted with the effective
settling of accounts with a failed military
government in Greece after 1974). Civilian
political parties and movements in South America
have had to pay a far higher price for political
failure than has the military.
Taken together, these questions suggest a
paradox. The military in South America may be
successful in a deeper sense, even if military
governments persistently end in failure. It is
almost as if high rates of political turnover act
as a safeguard against fundamental political

change. There have been twenty changes of
government in Argentina since 1936, but no
Revolution; in Nicaragua during this time, changes
of regime were very few, but a Revolution occurred.
It may then be that the military's inability to
institutionalise politics in South America, and the
complete failure of particular military governments
and their policies, are less significant in the
long run than the military's ability to protect its
own institutional discipline and, through this, to
guarantee the political order against
disintegration or "subversion".

This line of enquiry is not the usual one in
the literature. Stability is more commonly defined
in a narrower sense. Criteria have included the
ability of a military government to maintain itself
in office for a substantial period[1], its ability
to avoid serious internal conflict and maintain a
degree of policy coherence[2], its ability to
acquire "legitimacy" or Gramscian hegemony[3], and
its ability to "institutionalise" itself in
political-system terms[4]. These questions are not
without interest but do not go to the root of the
matter. A disunited, transitory, non-hegemonic (in
Gramsci's sense) and unpredictable regime may yet
succeed in protecting the social order in the
short-term by repression and, in the longer term
(in Burke's words), by acting mobbishly in order to
make its opponents moderate. The Argentine
military over the past generation and the Perez
Jiménez regime in Venezuela are perhaps cases in
point.

General theoretical approaches to military
politics in South America are both more badly
needed and, at the same time, more difficult to
write than in the past. During the 1960s, a number
of studies were published (some of which will be
reviewed in Chapter 1) at a time when sufficient
detailed work was not available to back-up (or
refute) the often ambitious generalisations
attempted. During the 1970s, ambitious theory
generally left the military alone and concentrated
its efforts elsewhere (as we shall see in Chapter
2), while at the same time a vast amount of good
quality empirical work was becoming available. The
material, in a sense, seems to have drowned the
questions.

The synthesis being attempted here has its
intellectual roots in comparative politics. For a
student of South America, the role of the military

may appear normal, even predictable. To a
comparative theorist, it appears odd. South
America in general, and Argentina in particular,
are notoriously cases where theories of comparative
politics fail.[5] If this failure is due to the
inherent limitations of the comparative method,
then the quest being undertaken here is doomed
from the start. If, however, it is because the
intricacies of South American politics have not
been fully appreciated, and because the right
questions have not been asked, then the reader is
encouraged to follow the attempt that follows.

NOTES

[1]   S. E. Finer, <u>The Man on Horseback</u>, Concluding
      sector (1975 edition, Penguin).
[2]   A. Stepan, <u>The Military in Politics; changing
      patterns in Brazil</u>, (Princeton U.P., 1971).
[3]   J. Linz, "The Future of an Authoritarian
      Situation or the Institutionalization of an
      Authoritarian Regime; the case of Brazil", in
      A. Stepan Ed., <u>Authoritarian Brazil</u>, (Yale
      U.P.; 1973) and G. O'Donnell, "Tensions in the
      Bureaucratic-Authoritarian State and the
      Question of Democracy" 285-319, in D. Collier
      Ed., <u>The New Authoritarianism in Latin
      America</u>, (Princeton U.P.; 1979).
[4]   S. P. Huntington, <u>Political Order in Changing
      Societies</u>, (Yale U.P.: 1968).
[5]   A point made by G. Ionescu in his Introduction
      to the special issue on Brazil and Argentina in
      <u>Comparative Politics</u>, Spring 1984.

Chapter 1

MODERNISATION, MASS SOCIETY THEORY AND THE MIDDLE
CLASS MILITARY

Serious study of the political role of the
Latin American military dates back only to the
1960s.[1] It began, as serious study so often
does, with a series of assumptions based upon
general notions of politics which reflected the
climate of the times more than the state of the
art.[2] These assumptions, which tended to inform
the work of earlier scholars, have often been
reflected also in the work of their critics. It
has often happened, and not only in this particular
case, that the development of an academic
discipline was disproportionately influenced by the
assumptions and concerns current at the time of its
serious initiation. For this reason it is worth
exploring briefly the intellectual climate in the
United States in the early 1960s.

It is a generally acknowledged although
sometimes regretted fact that the United States
has had a preponderant influence in the development
of political science in general, and in the
political science of Latin America in particular.
This influence has sometimes been direct, sometimes
indirect and sometimes reactive - as with the
influential dependency school. The decisive
intellectual climate for our purposes, then, was
that of the Kennedy-Johnson years. The major
agenda-setting events were, at the beginning, the
Cuban revolution and, subsequently, the Vietnam
war. These formed an essential backdrop to the
main academic debates.

The Kennedy administration's Latin American
policy was substantially shaped by its need to
respond to the Cuban Revolution. The fact that the
overthrown Batista was a military dictator led it
to become a central part of Washington's thinking

that military dictatorships in Latin America encouraged Marxist revolutions whereas civilian governments did not. Thus Kennedy gave strong support to the elected Acción Democrática government in Venezuela (a country with a long previous history of military rule) and strongly opposed the Trujillo dictatorship in the Dominican Republic, even conniving at the assassination of the dictator in 1961. Although this pro-civilian policy was not followed with total consistency throughout Latin America, it was the commonly accepted wisdom both in the Administration and within liberal academic circles that military rule was a bad thing, not only in moral terms but also in terms of immediate US interests.

The Cuban setback aside, the early 1960s was a good time for liberal optimists in the United States. In Latin America dictatorships had been overthrown or fallen from power in Peru (1956), Colombia (1957), Venezuela (1958), as well as the Dominican Republic (in 1961); most of the Continent was then governed by civilians. Outside Latin America, Washington could believe that its own brand of liberal democracy was the wave of the future. It was being plausibly asserted that in Western Europe there was an "end of ideology" in which the working classes and their political parties would give up militant class politics and socialist ideologies in return for affluence and a guaranteed place in the political and social system. In Africa and Asia, many former European colonies had achieved independence under formally democratic constitutions and it was still too early for hope to turn into disillusionment. Some writers even talked of the likely "convergence" of the Soviet with the US systems of government as embourgeoisement influenced not just West European workers but even the Soviet system itself. The enemy heartland was to be melted with consumer goods. Less optimistic about the USSR, but highly confident about the political benefits of affluence, Walt Rostow argued that developing countries would eventually "take off" into mature and mass consumption societies. If, during the dangerous "take off" stage, the threat of Communism could be averted, then democratic welfare capitalism would spread along with growing affluence. "Take off", like the "end of ideology" and "embourgeoisement" became catchphrases among liberal optimists of the period.

2

LIBERALS AND NEO-REALISTS

It is not surprising that this mood of optimism influenced the first academic debate of note within the United States about the role of military involvement in Latin America. This debate took place between liberals who expected that military intervention in Latin America would tend to die out and neo-realists who saw it as something continuing and progressive. Lieuwen was the most notable exponent of the first view and, as he later recalled, "it appeared to the post-World War II generation, despite the chronic temporary military intervention, that democracy, social justice and greater economic equality were inexorable trends that were firmly tied to the modernisation-industrialisation process."[3] This is a pure statement of what might be called the Kennedy-orthodoxy that, in Robert Packenham's words, "all good things go together".[4] In political terms, this permitted a sense of unity between the liberal intellectual community and harder-boiled policy-makers. It was possible and necessary to oppose both Communism and military dictatorship, both economic nationalism and under-development. There is much that was morally attractive in this vision, but equally there can be no doubt that it was descriptively inadequate. There was soon to be a parting of the ways between the liberal optimists and the hard-headed realists.[5]

Against this view, there came to be presented what might be called the neo-realist school of John Johnson (in Latin America) as well as writers such as Shils and Pye in other parts of the world (notably South East Asia). This school tended to see the role of the military in politics as potentially constructive. The superior quality of military organisation, as opposed to that of civilians, would - it was argued - enable them to develop management, including political management, qualities which were in short supply elsewhere. In the long run, effective management could help promote develement which would in turn facilitate a return to democracy. Johnson was more circumspect and had greater respect for historical tradition than did some of the "Asian" writers but he was clearly sympathetic towards the military and anxious to influence US policy away from what he saw as an excessively pro-civilian bias.

More specifically, Johnson argued that the
military in mid-twentieth century Latin America
identified with the urban middle class and
suggested that it might take power in order to
pursue "populist" policies (of the kind attempted
by Vargas and Perón) with middle class backing.
Johnson did correctly forecast that military rule
would become more common than was the case in Latin
America in the early 1960s. Yet Johnson proved
scarcely more accurate as a prophet than his
liberal opponents. Writing after the falls of
Odría in Peru and Pérez Jiménez in Venezuela,
but before the rise of Videla, Pinochet etc.
Johnson did not believe that the military could
afford to deploy very much coercive power against
civil society. Rather, he suggested, the forces of
economic development would increase the level of
social mobilisation and so reduce the coercive
aspects of the state. He thus argued that "as the
suppression of the popular will becomes
increasingly difficult, soldier-statesmen will be
forced, more often than in the past, to test their
political conclusions and will be driven to seek a
broader base for their power."[6]
The idea that "suppression of the popular
will" was likely to become difficult as economic
development continued was a crucial tenet of
modernisation theory. Its intellectual basis lay
in the argument that economic growth changed social
conditions - increasing levels of urbanisation,
education and the size of the middle class and
creating a 'critical mass' for reformist political
parties and means of mass communication. These
developments were seen as both inevitable and
wholly benign in their consequences.
The debate between liberals and neo-realists
was conducted over a narrow area within this broad
framework of agreement. It was simply that the
neo-realists asserted that military rule had a part
to play in the process of modernisation, a
proposition denied by the liberals. Both views
should have been criticised more, both at the time
and subsequently, for over-stressing such universal
themes as "development" at the expense of more
specific local and historical factors. In Isiah
Berlin's terminology, this was the vision of
hedgehogs rather than foxes.[7] The world, and
even Latin America, is too big to be taken in at a
glance. Yet the later opponents, as well as the
supporters, of modernisation theory were too often

willing to accept its global vision. Later
dependency writers merely sought to turn
modernisation theory on its head, arguing for a
different universal theme, this time that of the
"exploitation" of the developing by the developed
countries. Even O'Donnell[8], whose influential
writings on bureaucratic-authoritarianism will be
discussed in the next chapter, took over this
essential premise of modernisation theory
uncriticised and so passed it on to a different set
of intellectual and political circles.

It is always possible for a theory which is in
some way conceptually inadequate to yield
interesting empirical propositions. The neo-
realist school, however, has not been a great
success even according to this rather less
demanding criterion. A cross sectional study of
countries ruled by the military conducted by
Nordlinger[9] suggests that military rulers are
neither more nor less adept than civilian rulers at
increasing local GNP, but that they are less likely
to carry out significant socio-economic reform. A
later study by Jackman[10], which uses Nordlinger's
data and criticises his methodology, concludes that
"military governments have no unique effects on
social change, regardless of level of economic
development." Meanwhile McKinlay and Cohen[11]
show that military regimes by no means guarantee
political stability; "no less than 48 per cent of
them last fewer than two years and only 21 of them
last longer than five years." Nobody has yet (as
far as I know) sought a correlation between
military regimes and the successful conduct of war;
such a correlation might turn out to be strikingly
negative. According to the three most obvious
measures of "success", therefore - economic
management, political stability and military
victory - military governments do not perform
better than democratic ones.

These studies seem to show convincingly that
the neo-realist view is untenable in general terms,
although two important qualifications must be made.
One is that it is only possible to compare military
regimes with civilian governments which exist (or
existed); potential civilian regimes kept out by
the military cannot be included. One might expect
these latter regimes to have had systematically
different features from regimes which the military
were willing to tolerate. This might slightly
improve the neo-realist argument if patently

incompetent civilian regimes were disproportionately kept out - although one might
counter-argue that the existence of military rule
itself corrupts the process of civilian politics in
countries subjected to it and thus tends to worsen
the performance of civilian governments in
alternating civil-military systems. This problem
will be considered again in Chapter 3 as will a
further point which also tends to confuse the
issue; where is a distinction to be drawn between
military and civilian regimes? In some parts of
the world, though not so often in South America,
this question does indicate a very real
difficulty. [12]

The liberal hypothesis, that military rule
becomes less likely as countries develop, is far
more difficult to deal with cross-sectionally
because the question of which countries to include
cannot easily be resolved. Thus, if one considers
all rich non-Communist countries, none is presently
governed by the military or appears in any imminent
danger of a military coup. Moreover, if one
considers the cases of Greece, Spain and Portugal,
there is at least a superficial justification for
the hypothesis that modernisation and democratisation go together. But what is one to make of
comparatively rich developing countries such as
Argentina, Chile and Uruguay? One answer is to
say, as Finer does[13], that the level of political
culture in these countries, though quite high, is
still not high enough to prevent the military from
intervening. Indeed, he argues, precisely because
the level of civilian organisation is high in these
countries (although "civil institutions are not
nearly so powerful, or so respectfully regarded, as
at the 'developed' level"[14]), so military rule is
more brutal than in countries where political
culture is lower. However, Finer's argument seems
to lack empirical basis. It is not at all clear
that Argentina lacks either political organisation
or political consciousness in comparison with (say)
post-1974 Portugal, contemporary Italy or turn-of-
the-Century Britain. O'Donnell[15] concludes his
survey of public opinion in Argentina in 1966 by
describing it as "a politically informed
population, conscious of the inefficiency of
government, sceptical about political parties,
hostile in their inter-sectoral perceptions and
aware of the zero-sum character of national
wealth." It is also perhaps worth remembering that

in 1930 Argentina was one of the half-dozen richest
countries in the world and that, prior to the
military coup of that year, liberal opinions were
to be heard to the effect that Argentina was too
developed for a military takeover to be
conceivable.[16] Equally Chilean politics was
scarcely under-organised in 1972-3 whatever other
difficulties the political system may have faced.

Moreover, even if we were to give Finer the
benefit of this empirical doubt, one would still
have to conclude that concepts of modernisation or
development (whether directly or mediated through
the notion of political culture) had little or no
explanatory significance in Argentina, Turkey or
any poorer country; they could say only what we
know already, which is that military rule is
possible under certain circumstances in all
countries poorer or less developed than Argentina.
However, such competetive democracies as exist in
the Third World - Venezuela, Colombia, Costa Rica,
India, and perhaps a few others - occur both in
relatively wealthy and relatively poor states.
Finer's other point, that military regimes in
relatively affluent Third World countries are
necessarily more brutal than in poorer ones
similarly lacks empirical basis[17]; it is merely
that urban brutality is more evident than brutality
in rural areas, and that urban techniques of
control must rely less heavily on social and
implicit controls which so often serve
dictatorships in rural areas. Without wishing to
become involved in ghoulish comparisons, it is far
from clear that any recent South American dictatorship has been more brutal than Hernández Martínez
in El Salvador in and after 1932, than Idi Amin in
Uganda or than the Guatemalan military since 1978.

The same observations could also be applied to
an equal but opposite theory to Finer, namely that
of O'Donnell who argues that "political authoritarianism, not political democracy, is the more
likely concomitant of the highest levels of modernisation."[18] This last hypothesis has received
empirical support from some cross-sectional
studies[19] but findings again seem to depend
crucially upon what is being compared. O'Donnell
specifically confines his theory to late-developing
countries presently part of the Third World; he is
also concerned with dictatorship rather than
specifically with military rule. O'Donnell's
specific arguments will be considered in detail in

chapter 2; the point is merely being made here that both Finer's and O'Donnell's plainly incompatible hypotheses can both appear plausible, depending on what is being compared with what. If one takes all non-Communist countries, military rule occurs in only the relatively less developed ones. If one takes only the Third World, no such trend exists. If one takes the Southern Cone of South America during the 1970s, there is some plausibility for the modernisation-dictatorship argument; outside this region and time frame, the equation largely fails. Nor do historic time-paths make the going any easier. In 1965 the most affluent South American countries (Venezuela, Uruguay, Chile and Argentina) were ruled by civilians, while Spain and Portugal were ruled by the military and Greece had still to experience its last military intervention. Without the advantage of hindsight, it is not always easy to say what develops into what.

The conclusion being drawn here, then, is that the liberal-modernisation hypothesis was in the early 1960s a bad guide to the future of Latin America and that it is not useful in general application - which is not to say that it can convincingly be refuted or that it is entirely without value. Now, however, it is much more promising to turn from universal single-factor explanations to a study of particular types of civil-military system.

MASS SOCIETY AND THE MILITARY

An important implication of the modernisation approach was that, at least in the more developed South American countries, one was dealing with a kind of politics in which drastic suppression was politically unfeasible. This led more pessimistic writers, who shared some but not all of the "modernisation" assumptions, to fear anarchy rather than dictatorship from rapid social transformation. Thus Kenworthy developed an influential paradigm of Latin American politics which suggested that governments "reigned" but "did not rule" ("one must explicitly isolate government from power ... National government provides the area for decision making but it is possible that those chosen for high governmental roles contribute no more to decisions than a referee does to the score of a football game."[20]) More influentially, Huntington devised his notion of "praetorianism" due to his fear that "order" in the third world was in the process of breaking down.[21] One may note in passing that the US government's continuing difficulty in imposing order upon a particular part of the Third World, despite the commitment of over 500,000 troops, must have played a major part in convincing US observers of the potential "ungovernability" of the Third World as a whole.

Huntington draws heavily on what might be seen as the pessimistic face of modernisation theory - namely "mass society" theory. Following Durkheim and Kornhauser[22], who both emphasised the disruptive potential of rapid social change, Huntington argues that "It is not the absence of modernity but the efforts to achieve it which produce political disorder."[23] For Huntington, there were two keys to an understanding of the political role of the military in Latin America, as in other developing areas. The first was that, like many developing areas, Latin America suffered from an absence of effective political institutions. (One important reason was the original preference of the post-independence leaders of the continent for idealistic imported constitutions rather than realistic ones which related to the existing post-independence social reality.) This led to the development of what Huntington described as a praetorian society, defined as follows:

> Social forces confront each other nakedly ... Each group employs means which reflect its particular nature and capabilities. The wealthy bribe; students riot; workers strike; mobs demonstrate and the military coup.[24]

A praetorian society comes into existence when popular demands or, what in Huntington's view is effectively the same thing, popular participation comes to exceed the "output" capacity of the country's political institutions. "The relationship between social mobilisation and political instability seems reasonably direct ... In the absence of strong and adaptable political institutions ... increases in participation mean instability and violence."[25] Where institutions are weak and political demands excessive, a country faces the danger of "political decay" which is a kind of semi-anarchy.

These countries have held elections, but they are clearly not democracies ... They have had authoritarian rulers, but they are not effective dictatorships like the communist states. At other times they have been dominated by highly personalistic, charismatic rulers or by military juntas. They are unclassifiable in terms of any particular governmental form because their distinguishing characteristic is the facility and fleeting-ness of all forms of authority.[26]

Huntington's second point is that the military, whose political role stems from this institutional weakness, suffers from an ambivalence toward popular mobilisation (which, in Huntington's view, results from the familiar "modernisation" process - urbanisation, education, trade union organisation, newspaper circulation etc.) which it shares with the civilian middle class. The role of the military is therefore to open the door to the middle class and close it to the lower classes; this essential ambivalence, and the military's own unwillingness to divert power away from itself, makes it unable to develop political institutions and thus to arrest political decay. Instead, the military - faced with increasing popular mobilis-ation - would in all probability come to adopt a narrowly reactionary position. In his well known words:

As society changes, so does the role of the military. In the world of oligarchy, the soldier is a radical; in the middle class world, he is a participant and arbiter; as mass society looms on the horizon, he becomes the conservative guardian of the existing order. Thus, paradoxically but understand-ably, the more backward a society is, the more progressive the role of the military; the more advanced a society becomes, the more conservative and reactionary becomes the role of the military.[27]

Huntington's analysis, while not free of shortcomings, has added some new and valuable concepts to the study of the military in politics. One particularly valuable point is his antithesis between popular mobilisation and military reaction. From this he derived a classification of military interventions. Under "oligarchic" (or restricted participation) political systems, the military may well launch "breakthrough" coups in order to expand the base of political society; examples include Egypt in 1952, Uruguay in 1903, Brazil in 1930 and El Salvador in 1948 (since his analysis appeared, one might add to the list Peru 1968 and Portugal 1974). When mass mobilisation (or one might add, though he does not, "Marxist subversion") poses a threat, then the military will launch a "veto" coup aimed at keeping the dangerous civilian groups out of power (as, for example, in Peru in 1962, Spain in 1936 and Brazil in 1964 - and later, in Chile in 1973). At other times, the military will play a role within the parameters of the existing political system, either remaining behind the scenes or intervening as an arbitrator (or, as Huntington puts it, a "guardian") - as in Brazil between 1945 and 1964 and post-independence Nigeria. Interventions in such cases will be justified by the need to avoid "corruption" in the workings of the system rather than by opposition to the system itself.

This is not only a worthwhile insight, it also provides a possible basis for classification of different types of military coup and military regime. Classification of this kind breaks completely with modernisation theory because of its recognition that there are different types of military-political action and so different types of military regime. A single universal explanation is no longer enough.

There are, however, some serious weaknesses in Huntington's analysis. One major objection is that, even if one accepts that there is an inverse relation between the degree of radicalism present within civil society and that present within the military, it does not necessarily follow that the military will necessarily become more reactionary over time. It is simplistic to assert that popular mobilisation relates directly to "the process of development" and to nothing else (Huntington, it is true, does at one point mention that unrest may be precipitated by economic recession but does not build on this). Popular participation may indeed be related to such factors as literacy, size of urban population, etc. but one can imagine (and indeed discover) societies which are highly agitated and mobilised although only a minority of the population actively participates in politics

11

(Peru in 1931 may serve as an example[28]) and, on the other hand, societies which enjoy mass participation but little social polarisation (Venezuela since 1958 as an example[29]). Moreover, following Kornhauser, Huntington argues that rapid modernisation is even more damaging to political order than gradual modernisation.[30] There is, however, some empirical support for the argument that, in some cases at least, rapid and successful growth can be politically demobilising. Thus Fitch finds of post-war Ecuador that

> The new economic prosperity promoted a substantial lessening of tensions between the coastal oligarchy, the traditional landowning aristocracy of the sierra, and the increasingly numerous members of the urban middle class. With the increased opportunities for elite mobility outside of the political system and the rapid increase in the number of bureaucratic positions resulting from the doubling of public expenditures, control over the government ceased to be such a highly salient issue.[31]

In Peru, similarly, economic growth after 1948 helped ease the extreme political tensions of the 1945-48 period and substantially changed the balance of politics.[32] When one considers Venezuela also, the conclusion seems to be that the behaviour of commodity markets predict the likelihood of political instability in at least some South American countries much more accurately than does the rate of "modernisation".

The military, in most cases, is far more concerned with popular militancy than participation - remaining in barracks in post-1958 Venezuela but taking over the government in Peru in and after 1931. It follows that the relationship between the degree of modernisation and the likelihood and type of military intervention, on which Huntington rested so much of his argument, is much less clear than Huntington suggests. Huntington offers little evidence for his assertion except for a cross-sectional study (his use of cross-sectional studies is in any case excessive and one major methodological weakness of the book) and a few historical illustrations. It is also remarkable that, although discussing the Argentine "veto coup" of 1930, he has nothing to say about the subsequent

role of the Argentine military in the rise of
Perón.
   If the time-path part of Huntington's
hypothesis becomes untenable so also does the view
that it is the final fate of all weakly-
institutionalised societies to end with a
reactionary military in power. Popular de-
mobilisation is, under certain circumstances, no
less a possibility than popular mobilisation - so,
if we accept the rest of the argument, the military
can move Left at certain times just as it can move
Right at others. At other times it can stay out of
government altogether. In Peru, for example, the
radical coup of 1968 came after the conservative
one of 1948 and in Argentina Perón came after the
conservative military rulers of the 1930's. Indeed
a writer who considered only the Peruvian
military's hostility to Apra and its subsequent
reformism and also the behaviour of the Argentine
military between 1930 and 1945 might conclude that
it was the role of the military "to close the door
to the middle class and open it to the lower
classes".
   Another major criticism of Huntington is that
he overstates the importance of the formally
political. The original mass society theorists
were concerned with the effect of social change on
a variety of social institutions. By restricting
consideration to narrowly political factors,
Huntington appears to commit what might be called
the liberal fallacy according to which society is
naturally atomised. Class and class solidarity
play little part in his analysis; neither do
religion or ethnicity. Yet it is these which often
play a far more active part in holding societies,
and a fortiori third world societies, together
than political institutions as such.
   Admittedly, conceptual sharpness is an asset
in presentation and Huntington's memorable
descriptive accounts of political behaviour in a
praetorian society do much to justify the use of
the concept. Nevertheless, the costs of ignoring
non-institutional bases of social action can be
seen from Huntington's treatment of Chile. On p.
80 Chile is described as a civic (i.e. non-
praetorian society) and yet that country
subsequently went through a period of intense
social polarisation followed by a harsh military
dictatorship. There was, it is true, some increase
in the size of the Chilean electorate and in

"modernisation" generally between 1967 (when the book was written) and 1973, but this was plainly not enough to explain the magnitude of the political change; the main and obvious cause of the political crisis was the victory of a Marxist candidate in presidential elections. The logic of class conflict (some might prefer to say factional conflict) thus proved stronger than that of political institutionalisation.

If countries such as Chile and Uruguay, given a clean bill of political health by most observers in the 1960's[33] could be subjected to military rule, then can any South American country, in principle, be said to be free of the possibility? If not, then concepts such as praetorianism fail to distinguish between, but merely lump together, all the countries in the third world. Yet omnibus concepts of this type, as we saw with modernisation, are not particularly useful. In any case, third world societies are not all as chaotic or anarchic as examples drawn from the more extreme cases might suggest. If one compares politics in Brazil with Uganda, Brazil appears a haven of stability and a model of respect for the civic order. Above all if one argues, against Huntington, that political institutions are of no more than secondary importance in comparison with those social institutions capable of attracting primary loyalty (ethnicity, religion and perhaps class), then the weakness of the former proves nothing about the weakness of the latter. It is almost a commonplace in South America that social stability lies side by side with the expendability of formal political systems and written constitutions. It will not do to confuse them both under the category of "praetorianism".

To sum up, then, Huntington's general theory of social change and political decay in developing countries is seriously inadequate. Despite its superficial sophistication, it contains no more than a generalised pessimism which may be an antidote to, but is not an advance upon, the generalised optimism of some earlier writers. It has been suggested that this swing from optimism to pessimism reflects specific US government experiences, with the Dominican Republic and Vietnam on the one hand, and with domestic assassinations, conflicts and fears of ungovernability on the other.[34] Nevertheless, despite the shortcomings of this general framework,

Huntington's specific insights on the importance of
order to the military, and the interaction of this
concern with the politics of social mobilisation
can provide the beginning of a system of
classification which leads away from single-factor
explanations of third world politics.

THE MIDDLE CLASS MILITARY

Another idea which appears in Huntington's
work is that the military somehow represents the
interests of the civilian middle class. It is
best, however, to consider this idea in the context
of the work of another influential social
scientist of the period - the Argentinian Jose
Nun.[35] The context in which it emerged was that
of new military coups in Brazil in 1964 and
Argentina in 1966. These were certainly not
progressive or "modernising" in the sense according
to which these words had previously been understood
although they were aggressively developmentalist.
Could they, however, be considered middle class?
        Nun began his argument by making the point
that, within the Latin American context, military
rule did not vary positively with the level of
economic development. Both rich and poor Latin
American countries experienced military rule at
times (Nun was thinking primarily of Argentina
here, but the 1973 military coups in Chile and
Uruguay strengthen this point further). Yet it did
not follow at all that it was the same kind of
military, or the same kind of political role, which
led the military to intervene in the various Latin
American countries with vastly different histories
and levels of development. This point holds, a
fortiori of military intervention in Argentina
and (say) a newly independent West African country.
For this reason, it was mistaken to treat military
intervention and military rule as if they were
identical in all cases; on the contrary, they were
society- specific. Moreover, argued Nun, it would
be wrong to assume (as many earlier writers tacitly
did) that military intervention came from outside
political society, as if it were analogous to
invasion by Martians. On the contrary, the roots
of military intervention had to be understood as
lying within society and changing in parallel with
society.
        Nun developed his argument further by
considering the consequences of military

professionalism. At the time, there was an
influential view (which had explicitly been argued
by Huntington[36]) that a professional military -
in other words one with a recognisable career
structure, promotion on merit, a specific identity
and a role in society - would become too
specialised, too strongly oriented to its primary
defence role, to want to take a direct interest in
politics. Professionalisation, in this
conventional view, reduced the likelihood of
military rule. In Nun's view, however,
professionalisation did not reduce the likelihood
of military intervention in politics; rather, it
reinforced the political role which the military
was already playing. "Professonalisation is
therefore the means by which the armed forces are
incorporated into a determined place in the
structualisation of society as a whole."[37]
Following a series of historical sketches of
the various South American countries Nun concluded
that

> Military intervention does not threaten the
> middle-class (as in the liberal model), nor is
> it a substitute for its absence (as in the
> developmentalist model); it tends to represent
> that class and compensate for its inability to
> establish itself as a well-integrated
> hegemonic group.[38]

Military intervention as a response to an
absence of middle class hegemony (in the Gramscian
sense) is a notion which recurs frequently in
discussions of military rule; if it is to be
valuable, however, it must be non-tautologous. In
other words, there must be evidence for the lack of
"hegemony" which does not consist simply in the
fact that military rule is prevalent. This could
perhaps be done (as we shall see briefly in the
concluding sector) but Nun makes no serious effort
to do it.
There is much of value in Nun's account but it
is open to two further criticisms. The first is
that the term "middle class" is either vague or
misconceived. Nun deliberately rejects the idea
that the South American military is
pro-bourgeois[39] because (or so it appears from a
somewhat ambiguous passage) he does not accept that
South America has a real "bourgoisie" but rather a
more-or-less parasitic middle class consuming the

export earnings of a land-owning oligarchy. This might perhaps do in the case of Uruguay but is misleading in the case of Argentina and hopelessly wide of the mark for Brazil. (The question of social stratification needs more space than it can be given here.) Nun's critics have also argued that, even if they were to accept that the military was middle class, the category is too broad to be useful (it must include the intelligentsia, government employees, the private sector etc.) and might account for almost every conceivable form of military-political behaviour. Nun might reply to this that he was concerned, not to set out a blueprint for military behaviour in politics, but rather to explain its continued existence in countries such as Argentina where it might, according to either the "liberal" or "development-alist" perspectives, appear anomalous. What is being argued, then, is not that the middle class is necessarily a homogenous group but rather that it proved unable - in contrast to British, French or US experience - to assert a distinctive political identity sufficiently attractive to secure for itself the political leadership of democratic society. Thus even in Argentina, with its substantial middle class, its high level of urbanisation and Mediterranean standard of living, military rule continued to be commonplace because the country lacked middle class "hegemony" and not because it lacked a middle class. This in turn, according to Nun, relates to patterns of economic change in Latin America. There is certainly something in this point, but Nun does not sufficiently bring it out.

The second criticism relates directly to this last point. In Nun's account, civil-military links are not sufficiently explored. Nun asserts that the military's professional identity (the nature of which he does not question) does not prevent it from assuming a social and political role. This much, indeed, one might accept. He also does well to quote a passage by Imaz which has since become famous:

> The appeal to the armed forces as a source of legitimation - quite apart from all the other explanations given - has become a tacit rule of the Argentine political game. It is a rule that no one explicitly invokes but from which all political groups have benefited at least

once. Publicly they would all deny the existence of such a rule, but in reality it can never be ignored by Argentine politicians who, at one time or another during this quarter of a century, have all gone to knock on the door of the barracks.[40]

Here, as we shall see, is the key to a great deal of military-political behaviour but Nun unfortunately gives this point little attention and his positive evidence for a military-middle class link is based almost exclusively on the matter of social origins. He quotes Imaz[41] to the effect that most Argentine generals (to judge from the sample studied) came from upper middle class backgrounds, and cites other work to the effect that the same was true of Chile, Brazil and Mexico. Major empirical studies of the matter subsequent to (and in some cases encouraged by) Nun's essay tend to confirm the hypothesis that a middle class background was typical of most military officers.[42] Although intuitively not surprising, this finding did falsify at least some earlier assertions that the military recruited mainly from the oligarchy. The usual requirement that youths wishing to become officer cadets must have completed secondary education at least and the impossibility of promotion from the ranks have combined to put a career as military officer beyond the reach of most, if not all, of the sons of the poor. Meanwhile, the sons of the wealthy can enjoy many lucrative and high status positions without the disagreeable necessity of submitting to military hardship and discipline for (as we shall see in more detail below) an officer's career in South America is by no means a sinecure.

One may briefly note, however, one fact of some significance. Almost all of these surveys considers the military itself to be a middle class occupation; they did not always highlight the important fact that a significant proportion of military officers - and an even more significant proportion of the more successful ones - had military fathers or brothers. Astiz does, however, find that 18% of senior officers in his sample are sons of military men, including NCOs, but makes no strong comment on this very high figure and concludes in agreement with Nun's "middle class origins" hypothesis.[43] Figures on Ecuador and Brazil, to be considered further below, suggests that the figure for Ecuador is around 20% while the figure for Brazil is higher still - around 33%.

This suggests a significant, although not an overwhelming, caste element in South American officer corps; in fact, raw recruitment figures almost certainly understate the real importance of caste because military sons or brothers are more likely to be successful than the average intake. Impressionistic evidence suggests that family groups have, at times, played a major part in military-political involvement. Thus, to take a few examples, Ernesto Geisel owed his adoption as President of Brazil (1974-79) in large part to the patronage of his brother Orlando who was Minister of War under the previous regime. In Peru, Morales Bermúdez (military president of Peru 1975-80) was the grandson of a military president and the son of a (murdered) military governor of Trujillo; Mariscal Benavides (President of Peru 1933-39) had a military son who was a government minister under, and briefly a rival to, General Velasco in Peru (1968-69); the Velasco government also at one time contained the two brothers Barandiarán as Cabinet Ministers, one was an air force and the other an army general. Again in Peru, General Ernesto Montagne - Prime Minister under Velasco and an important semi-reformist officer - was the son of a prominent military reformist briefly gaoled under Odría.

To provide some further examples, the Menendez family, prominent figures in the Argentine military, led two unsuccessful military coup attempts, one in 1951 and the other in 1979, while a third family member surrendered to British troops at Port Stanley in June 1982 (this family, one might conclude, was more notorious than successful). General Alvarez (President of Uruguay since 1981) had a brother, also in active service, killed by Tupamaru guerrillas during the 1970s. General Pinochet in Chile was son of a Colonel who had been politically active, and extremely Right-wing, during the 1920s. These cases are by no means trivial, particularly when one considers the general importance attached to family in Latin America, and they suggest that social origins - even if these are taken to have serious explanatory value - do not link senior military officers only with civil society.

What is in question, however, is not so much the fact of middle class origin but rather its importance in determining political behaviour. It is not difficult to cast doubt on this hypothesis. For one thing, the military is, <u>par excellence</u> a channel of social mobility. Social origin may be one thing; social destiny will be another. There is a good deal more to be said on this point which will be considered again in Chapter 5. Moreover, it is probable (in many if not most cases) that professional, or at any rate institutional, norms will outweigh social origins. As counter evidence, it is clear that youths who wish to join the military tend to be different from the rest of their class and generation; the desire to embark upon a military career is by no means universal even among the Latin American middle class. We do not, unfortunately, have reliable data on how, in South American cases, this difference between those who do and who do not wish to become officers is expressed in terms of political outlook; Swedish data[44] suggests, however, that such political differences can be significant. Moreover, those who do apply to join are not necessarily selected for officer training. It seems reasonable to suppose that those whom existing officers do select share certain distinctive characteristics even more strongly than those who apply; it is also likely that strong emotional ties to "civil society" would constitute a handicap to selection. Finally officer cadets are trained and indoctrinated with military values.

CONCLUSION

To sum up this chapter, then, we have been concerned with four general theories relating to the behaviour of the military in Latin America. These four - the liberal theory, neo-realism, the middle class military, and the praetorian society - were all influential at the time and have continued to be discussed since. They all sought to be general in their application and none devoted much attention to two factors which will feature heavily in forthcoming discussion - namely the nature of the military institutions themselves and the particular socio-economic problems which faced, and which continue to face, South America. As we shall see, the idea - explicitly rejected by Nun and Huntington - that developments within the military institution can be crucial in explaining its political role is not so easily dismissed.

Similarly, the general assumption (welcomed by the liberal theorists, viewed with apprehension by "mass society" theorists such as Huntington) that Latin American countries, like those elsewhere in the Third World, were "modernising" - perhaps even "modernising rapidly" - was subjected to sustained attack in subsequent years and is now seen to require heavy qualification.

All four approaches are flawed, then, largely because they assume a homogeneity in Latin America (or even in the Third World) which does not in fact exist. Liberal theories ("all good things go together") were brutally exposed by the repressive military dictatorships which took power in Latin America since 1964; they had largely been abandoned by the mid-1970s. "Neo-realist" theories, apart from their inherent implausibility, have not been confirmed despite considerable empirical testing. It is quite clear that not all military organisations are equally capable, or incapable, in either military or political terms and also that broad terms such as "developmentalism" do not adequately describe what particular military or civilian governments do. Similarly Huntington's notion of praetorianism is too general and all-embracing to be of much use. Some countries are more "praetorian" than others. Moreover, if we accept that Huntington's notion of praetorianism does have descriptive merit for extreme cases, we have nevertheless to conclude that countries can move very rapidly between a praetorian and civic culture - so the notion is largely without predictive value. Contingency takes over.

These difficulties together stem from what might be called the Anna Karenina fallacy (after the opening words of the famous novel). This asserts that "All rich countries are rich in different ways; poor countries, however, are all poor (all modernising, all dependent etc.) in the same way." As Griffin[45] has pointed out, this interpretation robs poor countries of their diversity and sense of identity and, for this reason, does no service. It also, in its more liberal variants, creates a false "born again" optimism that a country can emerge from its past as though this had never been.

Finally, if one regards the military as being "middle class" in its attributes and behaviour, there is a problem of misplaced precision (what is the middle class?) together with an empirical

21

problem (what does one say when the military in power comes into conflict with sections of the middle class?) and a behavioural problem (why should the military want to act in this way?). If the officer corps is as highly institutionalised as its training and life experience suggests it should be, then how can it be expected to act in the interests of a civilian class (and one, moreover, from which many joined the officer corps precisely in order to escape)? The notion of a middle-class military seems at first sight to break away from the single-dimensionality of the other concepts explained, but upon examination it fails to provide very much enlightenment.

The reader may wonder, following the argument just presented, whether an acceptable basis for generalisation about military-political behaviour can be found at all. Partial theory certainly is possible, but it is absolutely necessary to separate out a specific search for determinants of military behaviour from general feelings about the state of the world, or the state of the third world. Moreover, an essential basis for a successful theory of military-political behaviour must concern itself with how military institutions actually work, and must seek some behavioural plausibility in what the military does. This, necessarily, must involve a proper concern for the differences between as well as the similarities of different patterns of military organisation and different types of political society. To be fair to the writers considered in this chapter, far more detailed information on the military in South America (and elsewhere) is now available and so there is far less need to resort to heroic assumption than was the case during the 1960s.

NOTES

1   Lyle McAllistair "Recent Research and Writings on the Role of the Military in Latin America", Latin American Research Review, Vol. 11 (Fall, 1966), pp. 5-36, is largely dismissive of most work appearing before the early 1960s.
2   Donal Cruise O'Brien "Modernization, Order and the Erosion of a Democratic Ideal", Journal of Development Studies, Vol. 8, (1971-72).
3   E. Lieuwen "The Problem of Military Government", pp. 1-16, in R. Wesson Ed. New

Military Politics in Latin America, (Hoover Institution, Stanford U.P.; 1982), p. 10.

4   R. A. Packenham, *Liberal America and the Third World*, (Princeton; 1973).

5   A rather similar process, in the field of development economics, is described in A. Hirschman "The Rise and Decline of Development Economics", *Essays in Trespassing; Economics to Politics and Beyond*, (Cambridge U.P.; 1981).

6   J. Johnson, "The Military in South America" in Johnson Ed., *The Role of the Military in Underdeveloped Countries*, p. 127.

7   Isiah Berlin, "The Hedgehog and the Fox", 22-82 in *Russian Thinkers*, (Pelican; 1979).

8   G. O'Donnell, *Modernisation and Bureaucratic Authoritarianism; Studies in South American Politics*, (Berkeley; 1973).

9   E. Nordlinger, "Soldiers in Mufti", *APSR*, Vol. 64, No. 4, (December 1970).

10 R. W. Jackson, "Politics in Uniform: military governments and social change in the Third World", *APSR*, Vol. 70, No. 4, December 1976.

11 Quoted in S. E. Finer, "The mind of the military", *New Society*, 7 August 1975.

12 The point is well made by A. Perlmutter, "The Comparative Analysis of Military Regimes; formations, aspirations and achievements", *World Politics*, Vol. 33, No. 1, October 1980.

13 S. E. Finer, *The Man on Horseback*, Postscript to 1975 Edition, (Penguin).

14 *Ibid.*, p. 244.

15 G. O'Donnell, "Permanent Crisis and the Failure to Create a Democratic Regime; Argentina 1955-66", in J. Linz and A. Stepan, *Latin America; The Breakdown of Democratic Regimes*, (Johns Hopkins; 1978).

16 A. Rouquie takes pleasure in quoting some of these opinions in his *Pouvoir Militaire et Societe Politique en Republique Argentine*, (Paris; 1976).

17 Finer, *op. cit.*, p. 244.

18 O'Donnell, *Modernisation and Bureaucratic Authoritarianism*, pp. 93-94.

19 D. Geller, "Economic Modernization and Political Stability in Latin America", pps. 33-50, *Western Political Quarterly*, March 1982.

20 E. Kenworthy, "Coalitions and Political Development in Latin America", pps. 119-30 in

E. Groennings <u>et al</u>, Eds. <u>The Study of Coalition Behaviour; theoretical perspective and cases from four continents</u>, (New York; 1970), pp. 103-40.

21 S. P. Huntington, <u>Political Order in Changing Societies</u>, (Yale U.P.; 1968).
22 W. Kornhauser, <u>The Politics of Mass Society</u>, (Free Press; 1959).
23 Huntington, <u>Political Order</u>, p. 41.
24 <u>Ibid.</u>, p. 47.
25 <u>Ibid.</u>, p. 47.
26 <u>Ibid.</u>, p. 81.
27 <u>Ibid.</u>, p. 81.
28 On Peru, see S. Stein, <u>Populism in Peru</u>, (Wisconsin U.P.; 1980).
29 E. Arroyo, "Elections and Negotiation; democracy in Venezuela", (PhD, London; 1983).
30 Huntington, <u>Political Order</u>, p. 46.
31 J. S. Fitch, <u>The Military Coup d'Etat as a Political Process; Ecuador 1948-66</u>, (Johns Hopkins; 1977), p. 150.
32 G. Philip, <u>The Rise and Fall of the Peruvian Military Radicals 1968-76</u>, (Athlone; 1978).
33 Uruguay, like Chile, is described as a "modern" political system in G. Almond and D. Coleman, <u>The Politics of the Developing Areas</u>, (Princeton U.P.; 1960). However M. J. Finch disputes this interpretation in "Three Perspectives on the Crisis in Uruguay", pp. 173-90, <u>Journal of Latin American Studies</u>, Vol. 3, Pt. 2, (November 1971).
34 Donal Cruise O'Brien in <u>JDS</u>, Vol. 8.
35 Jose Nun, "The Middle Class Military Coup Revisited", pp. 49-87 in A. Lowenthal Ed. <u>Armies and Politics in Latin America</u>, (Holmes and Meier; 1977).
36 S. P. Huntington, <u>The Soldier and the State</u>.
37 Nun in <u>Armies and Politics</u>, p. 76.
38 <u>Ibid.</u>, p. 112.
39 <u>Ibid.</u>, p. 77.
40 J. de Imaz, <u>Los que Mandan</u>, quoted in Nun, pp. 103-4.
41 J. de Imaz, <u>Los que Mandan</u>, (Buenos Aires; 1964).
42 Studies include A. Astiz, "The Argentine Armed Forces; their role and political involvement", <u>Western Political Quarterly</u>, Vol. 5, No. 2, (December 1969), A. Stepan, <u>The Military in</u>

Politics; changing patterns in Brazil, (Princeton 1971), and J. S. Fitch, <u>The Military Coup d'Etat as a Political Process.</u>
[43] Astiz, <u>WPQ</u> 5, 2, pp. 868-9.
[44] Quoted in Finer in <u>New Society</u>, 7 August 1975.
[45] K. Griffin introduction to <u>Underdevelopment in Spanish America</u>, (Oxford U.P.; 1969).

Chapter 2

REACTIONS AGAINST "MODERNISATION"; DEPENDENCY,
BUREAUCRATIC AUTHORITARIANISM AND THE STATE

Modernisation theory set the agenda for much
subsequent discussion. Nowhere was this more true
than in the reaction against it. One important
strand of this reaction accepted two crucial
features of the modernisation approach - the modal
pattern, and the emphasis on economic change as the
key to social and political change. This
acceptance is perhaps not surprising since both of
these features are essential tenets of Marxism and
can be made to fit more effectively into an openly
Marxist theory of social change than into the
liberal optimism of the 1960s.

In any case, at the end of the 1960s, a new
paradigm, which came to be known as "dependency
theory", came into existence. Although this new
paradigm dealt only by implication with the
political role of the South American military, it
is worth discussing some of the central ideas
behind dependency theory in broad terms because of
its influence over the intellectual climate which
was, for a time, very considerable indeed.

Dependency theory itself evolved out of a
reappraisal of Marxist thought with respect to
Latin America. Two factors had provoked this
reappraisal. The Cuban Revolution, which had taken
almost everybody by surprise at the time, seemed to
show that socialist revolution was indeed possible
in Latin America - there was no need to wait for a
capitalist transformation of the continent and to
encourage moderate reform in the meantime. (Up
until then official Communist Parties, perhaps
influenced by Baran[1], tried to give their support
to a "progressive national bourgeoisie" in its
supposed conflict with "imperialism and the
oligarchy"). The Cuban Revolution seemed to

suggest, instead, that successful industrialisation
was neither necessary for Socialism, nor did it
necessarily facilitate it. Both of these views
were heretical to classical Marxism and both were
tied up with a re-casting of Marxism (in Asia as
well as Latin America) away from a theory of
working class action in the developed countries
toward a theory of peasant revolutionary movements
in the Third World. (The Vietnam War was of
obvious importance here and one might also note
that Marxist intellectuals in the United States
had, by this time, largely given up on their own
working classes).

This reappraisal had a significance which was
not purely intellectual. During the 1960s the
Cubans made a number of efforts to export their
type of Revolution to the rest of Latin America,
and in doing so presented an ideological case for
revolution as against mere reform. The best known
example of this presentation was Debray's
Revolution in the Revolution?, a book largely
concerned with political tactics and making the
positive case for the feasibility of Revolution.
Cuban sympathisers, however, also vigorously
presented a negative case, to discredit reform and
to suggest that Revolution was the only alternative
to Right-wing repression. The Brazilian
sociologist Theotonito Dos Santos achieved a brief
notoriety with his claim that Latin America faced
"revolution or fascism".

The second factor in the emergence of
"dependency theory" was a wave of pessimism about
the economic prospects facing Latin America - a
wave fuelled by the economic crisis prior to the
military takeover in Brazil (1962-64). It became a
conventional view (for which there was something to
be said) that the industrialisation strategy known
as import-substituting-industrialisation (ISI),
commonly adopted throughout Latin America after
1945, had run into decisive crisis and become
"exhausted".[2] This strategy had itself been
based on two main assumptions. First, following
the work of Prebisch, it was the conventional
wisdom among Latin American economists that the
price of raw material and mineral exports would
tend to fall relative to the price of manufactured
goods - and it was indeed true that such prices had
tended to fall in the decade following the Korean
War (the mineral prices boom induced by the Vietnam
War still lay in the future). Secondly, it was

pessimistic about the possibility of Latin American countries moving successfully - as Japan and some other Asian countries were doing - into the export of labour-intensive manufactured goods. If these assumptions were justified, Latin America faced an almost permanent balance of payments problem because it would have to export increasing quantities of raw materials in order to import the same volume of manufactures.

In fact the strategy of ISI involved the continuation of what had been common practice (faute de mieux) during the 1930-45 period, namely market-oriented industrialisation aimed at replacing imports. The "first stage" was to be the production of consumer goods, then consumer durables and intermediate goods (such as steel and petrochemicals) and finally capital goods, by which time each Latin American market would, it was hoped, be largely autonomous. It was indeed the case that many Latin American countries undertook a fairly rapid and superficially successful process of industrialisation between 1945 and 1960. However, by the early 1960s, problems were beginning to show (with difficulties already very apparent in Argentina and Uruguay, and becoming increasingly obvious in Brazil) and critics were beginning to find their voice. On the liberal Right it was argued that it was an error to de-emphasise exports and to over-protect inefficient consumer industries; this combination would lead to misallocation of resources and to balance of payments crisis. On the "structuralist" Left it was noted that foreign capital (largely through multi-national corporations) was playing a major part in the industrialisation process and was repatriating (or would eventually repatriate) the easy profits that resulted from manufacturing behind tariff walls; this would deprive Latin American economies of much needed capital and stunt further development.[3] (It is a marked feature of early Dependency writing that capital movements received far more attention than the production or exchange of goods.) Furthermore, existing patterns of industrialisation relied on capital-intensive techniques which created too few job opportunities for an expanding workforce and it also relied, for its final demand, on a highly unequal distribution of income which similarly distorted production decisions.[4] Some writers also suggested that absence of demand itself might eventually abort the process of economic growth; "underconsumptionism" was canvassed as an explanation for impending economic crisis, particularly in the case of Brazil.[5]

In retrospect the mid-1960s wave of pessimism about the Latin American economies appears to have been greatly exaggerated (at least by the standards of the early 1980s) despite the fact that many of the specific points of criticism mentioned above were essentially valid. From the mid-1960s, indeed, the main Latin American countries enjoyed at least a decade of rapid growth based on a mixture of policies including greater direct state intervention, some development of manufacturing exports (notably in Brazil), expanded supply of raw material and mineral exports - often at favourable international prices - and (last but by no means least) a great expansion of foreign borrowing. In normal circumstances the economic difficulties faced by several Latin American countries in the early 1960s could hardly have justified the abrupt switch in prevailing sentiment from heady optimism to extreme pessimism that in fact occurred. Political factors - support for Cuba, disgust at the military takeover in Brazil and, within the US, disillusionment with the Alliance for Progress and with foreign intervention in Vietnam and the Dominican Republic - powerfully underpinned economic perceptions. Nevertheless it became a common view that further economic development in Latin America would not come easily and more extreme writers argued that it would not come at all. It seemed, therefore, that social scientists in previous years had been altogether too sanguine about the possibilities of economic development, too naive about "modernisation" and for ideological reasons unwilling to give due weight to the negative impact of foreign capital and "US imperialism".

Dependency theory, under these circumstances, took modernisation theory and turned it in its head.[6] It was quite wrong, its proponents argued, to assume that every country had an autonomous status with respect to its own economic development - in the world economy, no country was an island. Yet the pattern of international action was essentially harmful to poor and weak countries. It was their role to be exploited - to be kept underdeveloped in order that others might develop. At the beginning, Latin America had been plundered

29

by the Spaniards and Portuguese who had destroyed
its indigenous civilisation and looted its silver
and precious metals. Later Latin America was to be
exploited by the British, who destroyed the less
competitive indigenous industries of the continent
and forced Latin America into the strait-jacket of
becoming raw material export economies. Later
again, it was the turn of the Americans - operating
mainly through the multi-national corporation -
to extract surplus from Latin America, originally
from its oil and minerals and later from the
manufacturing sectors. Yet the story was not
simply one of international plunder. In each era,
the dominant metropolitan powers had brought into
existence a class of allies in the "satellite"
countries whose own private interests - though
certainly not the interest of the country as a
whole - lay in siphoning off a small share of the
surplus finally earmarked for the metropolitan
power. (It was therefore quite wrong to believe
that there was a "progressive national bourgeoisie"
which should be supported in its efforts to develop
a national capitalism against "feudalism",
"imperialism" or "the oligarchy". This - reformist
- solution led nowhere; the domestic bourgeoisie,
far from being the ally of autonomous development
strategies, was their deadly enemy). Indeed, in
Frank's[7] version of dependency theory, the only
chance Latin American economies had of developing
in a "normal" way came when calamity overtook the
metropolitan powers; thus it was that Latin America
had managed partial industrialisation in 1930-53
(during Depression, War and Korean War).
Subsequently, the United States had reasserted its
grip and stifled independent Latin American
capitalism; further development would occur through
socialism or not at all.

Not all dependency writers were as apocalyptic
as Frank whose own rather extreme formulations were
soon discredited on both theoretical and empirical
grounds (his own case studies in Capitalism and
Underdevelopment present conclusions wildly at
variance with the historical evidence); indeed,
differences among those who accepted the basic
premises of the Dependency approach soon became
almost as marked as their similarities of
viewpoint. Dependency theory conveyed a powerful
emotional appeal and gave rise to an enormous
literature among supporters, critics and

revisionists who accepted some basic premises of this approach but sought to reinterpret it in varying ways. It was the latter group which, ultimately, proved most influential.[8] One important element in their critique was that it was too dramatic to talk about the "development of underdevelopment"[9]; as became obvious later in the 1960s, it was wrong to assert that Latin America faced (or had in the past faced) perpetual stagnation. It was, however, equally as wrong to assume that "autonomous growth" was possible; to illustrate this point, one only has to consider the way in which Latin American growth rates have been influenced during the past decade by the tactics of the international banks - tactics which related far more to changes in the world outside Latin America than to any developments originating within the area itself. Revisionist dependency writers thus developed the concept of "dependent development"[10] - which involved a measure of growth, considerable inequality, and a series of close connections between domestic and international capital which greatly limited the political freedom of government policy in dependent countries.

The dropping of the easy assumption that economic growth in poor countries is automatic (or, in other words, that all developing countries are in fact developing) represents a clear gain for political analysis. Another clear improvement is the dependency writers' introduction of the international economy and its logic, and the dropping of the notion that "development within one country" was inevitably a feasible option. However, it is probable that the balance of economic analysis swung too far both in emphasising the importance of international conditions and in overstating their malign effects.[11]

In addition to questions relating to the accuracy of dependentista perceptions of the international economy, it soon became clear as well (not least because of the decisive defeat of Castroist guerrillas throughout South America) that dependency theory lacked a serious class analysis and a satisfactory view of state institutions. Without such an analysis, any Marxist theory of political action was inevitably incomplete; moreover, the idea that "imperialism and the bourgeoisie" could be overthrown in South America by a mass popular uprising was plainly fantasy - as insurrectionary groups found to their cost.

(Central America, for reasons to be considered in the next chapter, is quite a different matter.) To move from morality tale ("Latin America is perpetually exploited" etc.[12]) to a serious analysis of politics and policymaking required some far more specific discussion of particular realities than early dependency writers were prepared to consider.

There have been a number of detailed critiques of dependency theory whose content does not need to be reproduced here.[13] One fundamental objection should however be noted. From a purely academic standpoint, dependency theory in most cases - though not always in the hands of revisionists - remained highly aggregative and modal. This aggregation and modality was held to centre on the uniformity of world-wide economic processes. Yet both commonsense and such serious empirical work as was conducted within the dependency school (mainly by revisionists) suggest that there were and are considerable variations according to time and place. The dependency analysis is undoubtedly helpful in certain circumstances but it does not necessarily tell a global story. All under-developed countries may be poor (although some formerly underdeveloped countries are no longer so poor) but not all in the same way or to the same extent, and the international economy cannot always be held clearly responsible.

BUREAUCRATIC-AUTHORITARIANISM

Perhaps the most influential recent attempt to relate economic change to political outcome throughout Latin America was made by a writer by no means clearly within the "dependency" tradition, namely Guillermo O'Donnell. O'Donnell is a complex writer who has produced interesting contributions on a variety of topics but we are here concerned with his theory of bureaucratic-authoritarianism, an ambitious attempt to sustain the view that modernisation in late developing countries (later[14] defined to include Mexico and Greece as well as the larger South American countries) has an "elective affinity" with authoritarian rule.

Thus O'Donnell used the phrase "bureaucratic-authoritarianism" to describe politics under both the civilian government of Mexico and the long-term military rulers of Argentina after 1966 and Brazil after 1964 (to which category were later added those of Chile and Uruguay following military coups in these countries in 1973). According to O'Donnell, three main factors underlay this form of authoritarianism. There was the "exhaustion" of ISI (see above) which turned politics from a positive-sum game into a zero-sum game and also convinced policy-making elites that certain necessarily unpopular economic changes would have to be made to create the possibility of renewed growth. (These included classic deflation, a greater concentration of capital and a reduced amount of protection for local industries). Authoritarianism, in O'Donnell's view, was designed to prevent unmanageable popular opposition to these various changes.

The second factor was the activation of the popular sector. The earlier phase of ISI, argued O'Donnell, was at least compatible with an expansion of popular participation and a limited positive redistribution of income, a combination which could be expressed in shorthand form as "populism". However, these newly activated groups (peasants, trade unionists, much of the middle class, in some cases small employers) needed to be brought under control if they were not to frustrate the economic changes which were to be brought in from above following the "exhaustion" of ISI and the need to develop a new development strategy. At times, indeed, these "populist" groups were successful in mobilising against and delaying the implementation of these changes. (There is a broad resemblance here between O'Donnell's account and Huntington's notion of mass praetorianism.) Finally, bureaucratic-authoritarianism also related, in O'Donnell's scheme, to a great increase in the autonomy and power of economic technocrats. These technocrats, who included the "new professionals" within the military discovered earlier by Stepan, Einaudi and, in a previous work, O'Donnell[15] (see below, chapter 7) had, according to O'Donnell, an even lower tolerance for lower class political activism than did the traditional upper classes.

O'Donnell's argument, then, was that a coalition of capitalists, technocrats and the military launched military coups in Brazil (1964) and Argentina (1966) in order to overcome the political-economic crisis associated with the "exhaustion of ISI". The more severe the crisis, the greater the threat perception uniting the

supporters of military rule, and the more cohesive
and decisively victorious the Right-wing coalition.
Thus the Onganía government in Argentina, which did
not follow a major crisis, eventually fell apart;
the military regime in Brazil, which did, was able
to last longer.

What does bureaucratic-authoritarianism
actually consist of? O'Donnell argues (here I am
drawing from his more concise reformulation of
bureaucratic-authoritarianism in a subsequent
article[16]) that it is "first and foremost,
guarantor and organizer of the domination exercised
through a class structure subordinated to the upper
fractions of a highly oligopolized and trans-
nationalized bourgeoisie"[17]. It is "in
institutional terms" made up of an alliance of
coercive and technocratic agencies. It is a system
of political exclusion involving a denial of the
rights of citizenship (e.g. free organisation,
association and speech) to the people. It promotes
high and growing levels of social inequality and an
"increased transnationalisation of the productive
structure" (shades of dependency theory here). And
it is technocratically rational.

Despite some Marxist elements in the theory,
O'Donnell is on the whole eclectic. He is also
something of a system-builder with a number of
writings, supplementary to his original work,
adding or (less often) removing parts from his
earlier construction. However, it would appear
that the theory is an ingenious amalgam of three
different approaches; economic determinism,
Huntington's notion of mass praetorianism (see
chapter 1 above for a further discussion of this)
and Linz' work on authoritarianism.[18] When
discussing O'Donnell then, it is useful to "unpack"
these elements and to deal with them separately.

Logically O'Donnell's argument from economics
to politics must involve three stages. First, he
must correctly specify the pattern of economic
change involved which must be recognisably similar
in all cases. Secondly, this pattern must lead to
recognisably similar political formations in all,
or at least most, of the countries considered.
Finally, these political formations must be
recognisably distinctive; the term bureaucratic
authoritarianism was deliberately chosen to suggest
that the type of dictatorship imposed was sharply
different from earlier patterns. Each of these
propositions has come under attack.

The variable which O'Donnell selects as crucial to the pattern of modernisation is "capital deepening" - that is to say a connecting process between the development of a capital goods industry and a worsening capital/output ratio. This is quite distinct from what are generally accepted to have been the precipitating economic factors behind the most notorious post-1964 military coups in South America - hyper-inflation and (in most cases) a difficult balance of payments proposition. Critics have disputed the idea that there is any clear evidence of capital deepening associated with these authoritarian regimes. Sierra finds of Brazil that there was indeed a process of capital deepening in the late 1950s; in the decade following the military coup, i.e. 1964-74, "instead of deepening the economy was 'undeepened' at least in relative terms".[19] In the case of Mexico, no serious attempt had been made to set up a sophisticated capital goods industry as late as 1982.[20] Moreover, the military regimes of the 1970s, Argentina, Chile and Uruguay, made no attempt at "capital deepening" - rather their aim was to restructure and trim back the manufacturing sector as a whole according to principles of comparative advantage. These last three cases did of course occur after O'Donnell formulated his initial hypothesis, but they do nothing to confirm it.

If one drops the notion of deepening, then one is left with essentially a Huntingtonian hypothesis that the beginnings of serious industrialisation in Latin America were associated with a deliberate policy (called "populism" by O'Donnell) which aimed to increase urban mobilisation. In the longer run, however, this mobilisation ran up against the "structural" ability of Latin American economies to cope with popular demands, and began to create alarm, or "threat", among the dominant classes (including the military and the technocracy) who responded by imposing authoritarian control. As a rough generalisation, this view has something to commend it but the link with economic change, in this revised hypothesis, has become very weak.

Even if we try to find an alternative economic variable around which to recast the hypothesis, difficulties remain. For one thing, it is far from clear that what O'Donnell calls bureaucratic-authoritarian regimes (Brazil since 1964, Chile and Uruguay since 1973, and Argentina 1966-73, and

1976-83) have pursued identical economic policies.[21] It is true that four of these governments (Brazil 1964, Uruguay and Chile 1973, and Argentina 1976) all faced major inflation and balance of payments crises when they took office, and all of them responded by adopting "typical" IMF policies which constrained their ability to attract popular support (assuming that they had wanted to do so in the first place). Yet too much should not be read into pursuit of orthodox deflationary policies in these cases; policies of a very similar kind have been pursued by a wide variety of governments in many different parts of the world (including Labour governments in Britain and a Socialist government in France) many of which are far from authoritarian and would bitterly resent being labelled Right-wing. Moreover, the fact that hyper-inflation was allowed to develop in these cases says far more about the overthrown civilian governments than about the incoming military regimes. In many other respects the policies adopted by these various authoritarian governments were strikingly different. To take just one example, the Brazilian regime expanded the state sector in the economy whereas the Chilean regime (at any rate until 1981) sought to reduce it to the minimum. Finally, although all of these economies (along with almost all others in Latin America) suffered severely during the world recession of 1981-83, some were managed quite successfully over quite a long period (this was certainly true of Brazil) while others (e.g. post-1976 Argentina) were very poorly managed by any standard.

O'Donnell's final argument, that bureaucratic-authoritarianism is a distinctive type of politics also raises questions. O'Donnell himself talks about the bureaucratic-authoritarian <u>state</u> but his own definition of the word "state" raises methodological problems to be considered in the next section. Cardoso, as we shall see, prefers to describe b/a as a regime[22], but one cannot meaningfully discuss the specific political organisation of a regime in terms of development needs, popular threats or economic policies. Indeed, the problems of creating and maintaining a stable authoritarian regime in South America are not trivial[23] and involve questions well beyond those considered by O'Donnell.

It is not even clear that there is a bureaucratic-authoritarian type of regime which

differs seriously from the ordinary
authoritarianism sketched out by Linz.[24] While
accepting that military rule in highly urbanised
societies is likely to be different in some
important ways from rule in predominantly rural
ones, it is not so clear that there is a
fundamental difference of type. Cammack[25] has
argued that the b/a regime of post-1964 Brazil has
come to rely heavily on clientelist politics,
particularly in rural areas and small towns, and
has, in this sense, not been particularly
bureaucratic at all. Another recent study of
regional politics in Brazil has shown that
policymaking has in practice been far less
"rational" and far more influenced by political
considerations than appeared on paper.[26]
Similarly, the Pinochet regime in Chile adopted a
personalist and plebiscitary style by no means at
odds with that of past military dictators. His
revealing, if chilling, comment to an interviewer
that "not a leaf falls in Chile without my knowing
about it" puts him in familiar company among Latin
American dictators, not excluding such fictional
figures as El Señor Presidente. Quite apart
from the fact there are certain historical
continuities in the form of rule adopted by these
various military regimes, it is also true that
there have been significant differences between
them.[27]

SOME METHODOLOGICAL CONSIDERATIONS

Finally, there is the inevitable question of
methodology. O'Donnell's work consists, in large
measure, of a relentless construction of ideal
types. However, Remmer and Merkx point out that[28]
"Ideal types may be highly suggestive yet they
present two characteristic problems. First they
aggregate several variables, tending to obscure the
relationships among those variables and leading to
the need for unspecifiable circumlocutions such as
'elective affinities' between variables. Second,
the relationship between empirical reality and the
ideal type becomes problematic; the latter is
neither a hypothesis to be tested against the facts
nor an empirical generalisation based upon them."
In addition to these general difficulties relating
to all ideal types are specific problems relating
to economic determinism.

As we have seen, O'Donnell's work on bureaucratic-authoritarianism is an ingenious construct but its central hypotheses either fail empirically or are insufficiently specific to be empirically applicable. The main reason for the empirical problems is that the approach is both general and economistic. A comparative economic determinism is a methodological horror and "modal patterns" do not come to grips either with diversity within Latin America or with the distinctive histories of particular countries. It might be possible to sustain an argument that the political evolution of a single country (or series of them) can be related credibly through patterns of economic change and social formation. An earlier work by Cardoso and Faletto can be said to indicate this possibility.[29] Cammack, committed to a broadly economistic view of politics, concludes his study of O'Donnell's work by stating that "the search for a single 'regime type' or 'modal pattern' has been misguided ... if the historical structural method is to be of service, it must renew its commitment to theoretically informed accounts of individual cases and build upon the specific features and relationships of such historical cases as a prelude to meaningful comparison."[30]

The alternative to single-country or multiple-path analysis can be sought through a comparative study of institutions or political systems. There are, even here, major differences between (e.g.) churches and armies in different countries but there is at least a basis for comparison and one might find some common factors of importance. A protean entity such as "bureaucratic authoritarianism" cannot be said to provide a basis either for contrast or comparison.

It would be somewhat misleading, however, to treat the work of the dependency writers and O'Donnell purely as empirical hypothesis without relating their standpoint to the particular metaphysic which they have adopted. This metaphysic itself requires some discussion.

The easiest place to begin is by analysing some different treatments of the notion of "the state". Broadly speaking (and without pursuing the vast and complex literature that exists on the topic beyond the limited scope of this discussion) there are two generally accepted ways of approaching this topic. The first, largely derived

from Max Weber, is to see the state as a set of
institutions (military, police, bureaucracy,
judiciary etc.) or alternatively as a set of people
occupying these institutions. To study the state
from this perspective is to see how these positions
are filled (by election, ascription, promotion
etc.), by whom they are filled, and what are the
characteristics (social origin, social contacts,
mental outlook etc.) of those who fill them.[31]
This is the subject matter of mainstream political
science. In studying regimes in this way, the
methodology is fairly straightforward although
there is always a problem of evidence. We need to
know who fills state positions (under military
regimes, for example, are they senior officers,
junior officers, retired officers, civilians with
military backing?) and how these jobs are assigned,
whom key office-holders associate with on a day-
to-day basis (other officers or civilians? what
kind of civilians?), what they read and what their
mental outlook and policy preferences are.

There is, however, a second view of the state
which has come to be known as "structuralist" (the
former view being known as "instrumentalist").
This has roots in classical Marxism but is now
identified particularly with Althusser and
Poulantzas.[32] That is not to say, however, that
all Marxist accept it.[33] It appears in fact to
owe more to the earlier, more Hegelian, phase of
Marx's thought than to the later more economistic
phase which was interpreted and influenced by
Engels. It also, in one of the ironies of
intellectual history, bears some similarity to the
structural-functionalism of US political sociology
circa 1955. In any case - and this is crucial -
this view is monist and idealist; it assumes that
social reality represents a coherent whole which
can be grasped philosophically rather than
primarily through experience; it is not, therefore,
empirical in any very demanding sense (which is not
to deny that it may have important empirical
implications). In the hands of O'Donnell and many
of the dependency writers, it defines the state as
the relationships of power which maintain the
capitalist system. The state is, by definition
therefore, always placed at the disposal of
dominant groups and acts to preserve the system of
domination as a whole. (The state may, however,
have to move against the interests of particular
sections of the dominant class in order to maintain

the position of the rest of that class; it may,
moreover, have to become "relatively autonomous" in
order to do this.[34] These concessions to greater
realism, however, still fail to relate this theory
of history to direct historical experience.) An
important implication of this view is that
political power as such cannot be observed or
measured outside the total social environment of
which it is part (as it can be, indeed must be, in
the "instrumentalist" view of the state). It
therefore becomes a meaningless exercise to try and
"allocate" power to particular social or political
groups - the military, political parties, the
bourgeoisie, the trade unions or whatever. The
whole dimension of power (i.e. who is powerful, who
is not and under what circumstances) becomes lost,
with the result that some important techniques of
political analysis (such as Lenin's own important
question, ("who/whom?") become unusable.

O'Donnell is quite explicit on this point.
"The state is fundamentally a social relationship
of domination or, more precisely, one aspect - as
such comprehensible only analytically - of the
social relations of domination."[35] His state,
then, is "comprehensible only analytically" and so
cannot be fully appreciated empirically. There
are, it is true, "certain objective manifestations
of the state"[36], such as governments. "Yet the
true meaning and consequences of these can be
understood only in terms of their being the
objective manifestations of certain aspects of the
system of domination in society."[37] Government,
in other words, is real only in as far as it is
"rational" but it must be rational because it is
real. This plainly Hegelian conception is itself
quite safe from empirical refutation but the price
of occupying this safe haven is that the theory can
only set out the logic which is implicit within
itself and which may have little or no relationship
with the real world outside (or, more precisely, it
is flexible enough to meet any real world
experience which might arise but can treat the
world of experience only as the proverbial drunk
treats a lamp-post - as a source of support rather
than illumination). It follows then, that such a
conception can, by definition, explain only that
which accords to itself. On all other matters it
must be silent.

Such a metaphysic can, however, appear in
empirical garb if it is equipped with a master key,

a Zeitgeist, of which human history is merely cast as the expression; for O'Donnell the master key is the logic of capital accumulation in the various countries subjected to bureaucratic-authoritarian rule (not, however, capitalism on a world scale which is an alternative master key offered by other writers).

Seen in this way, there can be no such thing as empirical refutation - the notion itself becomes meaningless. If one were to demonstrate that these various bureaucratic regimes were in fact quite different, O'Donnell might reply that this difference did no more than underline the difference between "state" and "regime" (as we shall see, Cardoso has attempted an explanation of this type). It is, however, somewhat mystifying that he writes clearly of a b/a <u>state</u> which he proceeds to define in terms ("a system of political exclusion"[38]) which seem more apposite to a discussion of regime. O'Donnell's problem is, however, that regimes cannot fully be comprehended in relation to one or two developmentalist variables; their functioning is plainly more complex than this as any serious empirical analysis would bring out. As Cammack states, "the tasks allocated to the bureaucratic-authoritarian state are so narrow and transitional in nature that they provide no clue as to what the long term nature of the regime might be once the immediate crisis has passed."[39]

Moreover, even if we leave aside purely philosophical objections to this formulation, there is something absurd about the notion that development strategy (i.e. a state-directed pattern of capital accumulation) should determine politics. A classical Marxist would argue that class struggle was important and that "development strategies" were adopted more to legitimise dominant class interests than for any other reason; there is indeed much truth in this evaluation. A dependency writer would say that development strategies were crucially shaped by changing conditions in the world economy (about which O'Donnell has curiously little to say). "Development strategies" are in any case a matter of bitter dispute between rival factions of economists, whose political success depends far more on fashion and far less on scientific experiment than they would like to admit. Such disputes are frequently conducted within "bureaucratic-authoritarian" regimes and not rarely influence the direction and tactics of these regimes. Thus even if O'Donnell had been successful in showing, which as we have seen he was not, that "bureaucratic-authoritarian" regimes did carry out development strategies in ways identical with each other but quite different from those of their civilian predecessors, this would only emphasise that development strategies, like theories of the state, are more often a matter of fashion than science. Any theory, and there are many beside that of O'Donnell, which treats "development strategy" of being of prime causal significance in Latin American politics is behaviourally odd as well as empirically untenable.

O'Donnell is, of course, far more than just another metaphysician inhabiting what Ayer has called "the ruins of absolute idealism"[40], but there is, as we have just seen, a strand in his work that at best makes for quite unnecessary confusion and obscurity and at worst sharply devalues the quality of his empirical work. One might, as a brief aside, also mention that variants of Hegelian developmentalism in which "the state" is given metaphysical properties, in order to reflect the logic of capital rather than - as in the accounts of most European Marxist structuralists - that of class, are not rare in Latin America.[41] One need hardly repeat that such approaches are hopelessly unequal to the task of understanding social and political reality in Latin America. Their widespread adoption can perhaps be attributed to the psychological effects of some very severe defeats suffered by the Left in the Southern Cone of South America during the past dozen years just as the original spread of Hegelianism owed much to the disappointment felt by intellectuals at the betrayal and defeat of the French Revolution.[42]

CARDOSO AND BUREAUCRATIC-AUTHORITARIANISM

The same strand of Hegelian developmentalism has also created problems in the work of one of the leading dependency writers, Cardoso, who together with O'Donnell has been one of the main figures in South American social science during the past decade. Although it is not possible here to discuss his work in detail, it is worth briefly considering an aspect of his writing which relates to the debate on bureaucratic-authoritarianism and is thus concerned, on a comparative theoretical basis, with authoritarian government and the state.[43] In this work, Cardoso himself adopts BA as an organising concept within which to present some of his own observations. The result oddly parallels the work of O'Donnell; the insights are interesting and a lot can be learned from them, but the methodology is unclear and the conceptual approach unsatisfactory.

Cardoso begins by explicitly accepting the term "bureaucratic-authoritarianism" and stresses that a crucial element in its nature is the distinction "between the <u>caudillismo</u> of the old Latin American militarism (as in the case of Paraguay) or family-based <u>caudillismo</u> (as in the case of Nicaragua) and the more institutional control of power by the officer corps as a whole which exists in some other countries."[44] Therefore bureaucratic-authoritarianism is a product of "new style" military rule which will be discussed in the next chapter; Cardoso, therefore, unlike O'Donnell does not view Mexico as bureaucratic-authoritarian.

Cardoso then goes on to try to define state and regime, an exercise which as we shall see later involves him in some difficulty. He is clear, however, that we are concerned with bureaucratic-authoritarian regimes (and not with an ideal type as O'Donnell originally stipulated) and is therefore able to consider differences between the various governments considered to be bureaucratic-authoritarian. This is an advance in realism but, as we shall see, it creates a serious conceptual difficulty. Cardoso is distinctive in being one of the first writers to predict that these BA regimes might have some success (Marxist critics earlier vied with each other in the outspokenness with which they predicted doom and destruction for both these regimes and the economies which they sought to reorganise; O'Donnell also on balance expected them to fail - no doubt Cardoso's different prediction relates to his greater emphasis on the Brazilian rather than the Argentine case). Cardoso, following Linz, focusses his discussion mainly on the nature of the authoritarian regime, in particular its internal unity and its points of contact with civil society.[45]

Cardoso thus begins his analysis by stating that BA regimes have greatly increased centralisation and have rested power on a coalition of the "technocratic bureaucracy and on the only real party, the armed forces."[46] He then looks for sources of tension within the BA regime. He finds one source in the possible conflict between the military and the techno-bureaucracy itself. Thus, "the success of the regime depends in part on the type of delegation of military authority to the executive that is adopted."[47] Cardoso notes (correctly) that the succession period has repeatedly proved difficult for the Brazilian regime since 1964. He then goes on to argue that any autonomous political action from outside the system is likely to create grave problems for maintaining the precarious balance within the regime itself. He then, in an important innovation, goes on to argue that it is characteristic of the state to seek to control and coopt civil society directly, not through corporatist controls (or, at least, not mainly through these) but through giving an appearance of representation to civilian interests. Here, in brief, is the theory of bureaucratic rings.

These rings work as follows. Those who control the state select various people to participate in the decision-making system; these come from and appear to represent the main interest groups of civil society. Yet real representation is discouraged or even made impossible by the use of repression. Those who, coming from civil society, do succeed in entering the decision-making process, will not necessarily represent (or represent only) the group from which they have been selected. They may well, instead, come to represent mainly themselves. Yet "thanks to this mechanism, civil servants can 'defuse' any pressure simply by dispensing opportunities to participate by their own selective means."[48] One result of this will be the creation of "bureaucratic rings" - clusters of essentially particularistic interests grouped around various parts of the state bureaucracy, held together immediately by clientelism and co-optation and ultimately by the reality of state power. These "rings" may then enter into political competition with each other, and with outsiders, and are likely to acquire a group consciousness which is neither a class consciousness nor an identification with the "state elite" as such.

In his historical analysis, Cardoso largely follows O'Donnell. BA regimes come to power at a time of acute fear and tension; they seek, first, to suppress elements within civil society which worry them and then to recreate civil society in their own interest. This objective would be feasible to the extent that the institutions of civil society were relatively weak (e.g. it would be easier in Brazil with its weak parties and unions than in Argentina where Peronism was far stronger at both levels). However, success in recreating the political system was by no means guaranteed given the essential unpopularity of what the BA regimes were attempting to do in economic terms (of which more later). Even so, these regimes retained a degree of tactical flexibility. The Brazilian regime, Cardoso notes acidly, has "made a rather original contribution to modern forms of authoritarianism by creating a party system almost exclusively based on the opposition."[49] In any case, rule purely through repression, possible always in the short-term, was a long-term impossibility and it was always likely that declining repression would see an increase in disunity within the regime itself.

Cardoso then goes on to consider the socio-economic base of BA rule. Here he makes another point of very considerable importance. One of the most notable trends in almost all South American economies since 1945 has been an increase in the direct economic role of the public sector. In Brazil by the mid-1970s the state had become responsible for around one half of all fixed investment. Apart from acquiring a greatly enhanced economic role, the state thus produced a set of state company managers who controlled an impressive volume of cash and fixed assets and evolved something of a distinctive state company outlook. How is this phenomenon to be evaluated from a socio-economic point of view? If, like Cardoso, one adopts a Marxist perspective, the question is easier to put than it is to answer. Can one talk of a "state bourgeoisie" - an authentic part of the dominant class rather than a mere representative of it? If so, then it seems reasonable to argue that the main socio-economic base of BA regimes lies within itself - a New Class almost in the sense in which the Stalinist elite was so labelled. Such would, in South America at least, be an extreme view but it would be equally as extreme to adopt uncritically a nineteenth century "classical" Marxist view of the relationship between the (organisationally defined) state and civil society. Cardoso does not really answer this point satisfactorily (although he does point out that the public sector economic managers are by no means identical with the political class and may have their differences with it), but he does pose an important question.

As well as excluding from his discussion authoritarian regimes (such as Mexico) not actually run by the "new" military, Cardoso further limits his definition to cases in which "the military intervention occurred in reaction against Leftist movements"[50] - thus excluding Peru post-1968. He justifies this selection in terms of the need to highlight the military characteristics of BA which are given far less attention in O'Donnell's own work; one might note in passing that by accentuating the military's role and also by attributing the militancy of the Left, in significant part, to the effect of the Cuban Revolution, Cardoso finally leaves behind the original "development leads to dictatorship" rationale central to the original development of the BA concept. By bringing military motivations and behaviour more into the forefront, Cardoso again moves in the direction of greater realism. He is right to point out that the military may move into the background once an apparently stable authoritarian regime has been established, but it is always there and is the ultimate guarantor of the system. However, his definition and approach seems essentially pragmatic ("it would be wrong to believe that the formal characteristics I have been discussing will always appear in an orderly and predictable fashion in conjunction with other important features of authoritarian regimes"[51]) and is concerned to discuss and explain common elements in the counter-revolutionary military regimes which took power in several South American countries after 1964.

In the quality of his perception and in the realism of his account, Cardoso has clearly improved on O'Donnell. However, this very realism leads to some serious conceptual problems in view of Cardoso's inability or unwillingness to break free of Hegelian developmentalism; there are obvious inconsistencies in his discussion from which O'Donnell's more coherent formulation is largely free.

Thus Cardoso explicitly adopts a Hegelian concept of the state - but this time in a rather confusing disguise. "The notion of the state refers to the basic alliance, the basic 'pact of domination' that exists among social classes or fractions of dominant classes and the norms which guarantee their dominance over the subordinate strata."[52] Yet, he asserts, "this 'expression' ought to be conceived of in organisational terms"[53] which, he thinks, "avoid(s) metaphysics". It seems that he is attempting to have things both ways - the state ought to be defined as an "expression" but "conceived" as an organisation (or series of organisations). How, one may ask, can one relate to a state defined as an "expression", when it is to be conceived as an organisation? Organisations have some empirical substance; "expressions" - as defined above - do not. How, then, can one demonstrate the existence, much less examine the nature, of the latter by discussing the former? Medieval theologians used to believe that one could prove the ("expressive") existence of God by showing the ("organisational") existence of the Church. This was not convincing then, and has surely not become more convincing since. Cardoso moves on to compound this confusion a little later[54] when he complains about a lack of research on the subject of "the relationship between a dependent capitalist state and different forms of political regime." But what could such research or analysis possibly consist of? The capitalist state, defined in structuralist terms, cannot be empirically determined to exist, let alone explored in any detail. So how can one explore its relationship with "different forms of political regime" (which can indeed be explored in detail, as Cardoso shows in his own discussion)?
Perhaps what Cardoso has in mind is a comparative evaluation of development strategies, involving a political sociology of economic change, class formation, class behaviour, political consequences etc. Yet as was argued above, it is not clear why development strategies should be treated exogenously (and reified as "the state") rather than stemming from existing patterns of social stratification, the nature of the political system, the intellectual climate etc. To express something as "the state", conceived structurally, is to make it an <u>a priori</u> which may be used to explain things but which may not itself be

explained or examined. Intellectual constructions
of this kind do not seem helpful for serious social
science.

That Cardoso is genuinely confused about this
question and has not simply expressed himself badly
seems clear from his further discussion of the
topic. Thus we find[55] that the differences in
economic policy pursued by, on the one hand, the
military government of Peru (1868-80) and, on the
other, those of Brazil, Argentina and Chile, can be
explained through "the character of the state
rather than the regime". Presumably he means that
these were all military governments (i.e. similar
in terms of regime) but that the Peruvian
government was pursuing a different set of
developmentalist objectives. Yet it is not at all
clear empirically that the policies of the Velasco
regime in Peru were motivated by a desire to
maintain a "pact of domination" (an essential part,
as we have seen, of Cardoso's own view of the
state) in any non-tautologous sense (see chapter 11
below for the empirical evidence).

This same difficulty, which stems from trying
to give an essentially tautologous definition of
the state some kind of non-tautologous meaning,
comes up again on the following page[56] when
Cardoso takes it "for granted that all capitalist
states must facilitate and guarantee the process of
capital accumulation." But what are capitalist
states? The proposition is clearly absurd if
applied to particular regimes - Duvalier's Haiti,
Batista's Cuba, Galtieri's Argentina plainly did
not facilitate the process of capital accumulation
in their respective countries. (Even as I write,
some Hegelian developmentalist is probably claiming
that Duvalier's regime reflected the purest logic
of Haitian capitalism - but that way madness lies).
But how can states "facilitate and guarantee"
capitalist development if many regimes plainly do
not - unless the statement is understood as a
metaphysical one totally lacking in empirical
content? But if it is, then how can it possibly be
useful to an understanding of politics?

A CONCLUDING NOTE

Dependency theory and bureaucratic-
authoritarianism were both highly ambitious
intellectual constructs which enjoyed a great deal
of prestige and attracted a great deal of scholarly

attention during the last decade (as also did notions of corporatism which will not be discussed here for reasons of space[57]). Within Latin American studies, the 1970s was the decade of the grand system-builder. Yet the empirical status of these various systems was always ambiguous or hybrid. The works considered in this chapter were by no means unique in marrying uneasily a philosophical idealism which denies the value of historical experience and some plainly empirical, if excessively aggregative and over-ambitious, cross-sectional generalisations.

This is not to say that these writings are altogether without value or without insight. Nevertheless, they do not seem to provide a good basis for continued elaboration or development. Moreover, like most of the works considered in the first chapter, they are strongly biased against institutional studies whether of the military or of other topics. Within the strict internal logic of Hegelian developmentalism (or other types of "structuralism"), institutions do no more than "reflect" or "express" non-tangible abstractions; there is little notion of action, conflict or power. Empirically, moreover, for a time during the 1970s, the ability of military bureaucracies to maintain internal unity and political order appeared unproblematic (however unusual such an outcome might have appeared to students of comparative politics) and there seemed little need to examine their internal dynamics. It should now be clear, however, that these grounds - both theoretical and empirical - for downgrading the study of institutions lack validity.

An institutional study of the political role of the South American military, therefore, can make sense only within a conceptual framework which breaks sharply with Hegelian developmentalist (or indeed more broadly structuralist) orthodoxy. There would be no point in simply seeking to add a military dimension to some over-arching "theory of the state". It is time, instead, to return to a serious study of politics.

NOTES

1 P. Baran, The Political Economy of Growth, (Stanford U.P.; 1957).

2 On this general, rather controversial question, see Maria Conceicao de Tavares, "The Growth and Decline of Import Substitution", Economic Bulletin for Latin America, (March 1964), pp. 1-65; A. Hirschman, "The Political Economy of Import-Substituting Industrialization in Latin America", Quarterly Journal of Economics, 82, no. 1 (February 1968), pp. 2-32; and W. Baer, "Import Substitution and Industrialisation in Latin America; experiences and interpretations", Latin American Research Review, 7, No. 1 (Spring 1972), pp. 95-122.

3 See T. Dos Santos, "The Crisis of Development Theory and the Problem of Dependence in Latin America" reprinted in H. Bernstein Ed. Underdevelopment and Development; the Third World Today, (Penguin; 1973).

4 Dos Santos, Ibid..

5 C. Furtado, Diagnosis of the Brazilian Crisis, (Berkeley; 1965).

6 Important early works are A. G. Frank, Capitalism and Underdevelopment in Latin America, (Penguin; 1967) and, from a very different standpoint, F. H. Cardoso and E. Faletto, Dependencia y Desarrollo en America Latina, (Santiago; 1967).

7 Capitalism and Underdevelopment.

8 See in particular the very worthwhile studies of R. Thorp and G. Bertram, Peru 1890-1977; Growth and Policy in an Export Economy, (McMillan; 1979) and Peter Evans, Dependent Development; the Alliance of Multinational, State and Local Capital in Brazil, (Princeton; 1979).

9 A point specifically made by F. H. Cardoso, "Dependency and Development in Latin America", New Left Review, July/August 1972.

10 Cardoso in New Left Review, 1972, Evans, Dependent Development.

11 For a detailed study of a particular industry, G. Philip, Oil and Politics in Latin America; nationalist movements and state companies, (Cambridge U.P.; 1982).

12 Of which a classic example is E. Galeano, Open Veins of Latin America; five centuries of the pillage of a continent, (Monthly review; 1975).

[13] For reasonably friendly critiques see P. O'Brien, "Dependency; the new nationalism?", Latin American Review of Books, 1973, I. Roxborough, Theories of Underdevelopment, (McMillan; 1979), and G. Palma, "Dependency; a formal theory of underdevelopment or a methodology for the analysis of concrete situations of underdevelopment?", World Development, 6, 1978, (July-August), pp. 881-924.

[14] G. O'Donnell, Modernization and Bureaucratic-Authoritarianism; Studies in South American Politics, (Berkeley; 1973) and "Reflections on the patterns of change in the bureaucratic-authoritarian state", Latin American Research Review, 12, No. 1, (Winter, 1978), pp. 3-38.

[15] G. O'Donnell, "Modernization and Military Coups; theory, comparisons and the Argentine case", in A. Lowenthal, Armies and Politics in Latin America, (Holmes and Meier; 1976), pp. 197-244.

[16] G. O'Donnell, "Tensions in the Bureaucratic-Authoritarian State and the Question of Democracy" in D. Collier Ed., The New Authoritarianism in Latin America, (Princeton; 1979), pp. 285-319.

[17] Ibid., p. 292.

[18] J. Linz, "An Authoritarian Regime; Spain", in E. Allardt and S. Rokkan, Mass Politics, (Free Press; 1970). Linz's work is also discussed in G. Philip, "Military-Authoritarianism in South America; Brazil, Chile, Uruguay and Argentina", Political Studies, (1984), Vol. 22, No. 1, pp. 1-20.

[19] J. Serra, "Three Mistaken Theses Regarding the Connection between Industrialization and Authoritarian Regimes", in D. Collier Ed., The New Authoritarianism in Latin America, (Princeton; 1979), pp. 99-165.

[20] W. Peres, "La Estructura de la Industria Estatal 1965-75", in CIDE, Economia Mexicana, 4, 1982.

[21] Philip in Political Studies, Vol. 23, No. 1, and A. Foxley, Neo-Conservative Experiments in South America, (Stanford; 1983).

[22] F. H. Cardoso, "On the Characterization of Authoritarian Regimes in Latin America", in Collier Ed., The New Authoritarianism, pp. 33-61.

23 See G. Philip, "Military Rule in South America" in C. Clapham and G. Philip Eds., <u>The Political Dilemmas of Military Regimes</u>, (Croom Helm; 1984).

24 Linz in Allardt and Rokkan, <u>Mass Politics</u>.

25 Paul Cammack, "Bureaucratic-Authoritarianism; a dissenting note", in <u>Politics</u>, 2, No. 1, (April 1982), pp. 9-14.

26 A. De Medeiros, "Politics and Intergovernmental Relations in Brazil 1964-82", (PhD, London; 1983).

27 Philip in <u>Political Studies</u>, Vol. 23, No. 1.

28 A. Remmer and G. Merckx, "Bureaucratic Authoritarianism Revisited", <u>Latin American Research Review</u>, Vol. 17, No. 2, (1982), p. 7.

29 Cardoso and Faletto, <u>Dependencia y Desarrollo</u>.

30 P. Cammack, "The Political Economy of Contemporary Military Regimes in Latin America; from bureaucratic authoritarianism to restructuring", (Mimeo, Manchester; 1984).

31 For example, R. Miliband, <u>The State in Capitalist Society</u>, (McMillan; 1969).

32 Particularly in N. Poulantzas, <u>Political Power and Social Classes</u>, (new Left Books; 1973).

33 For a powerful dissent see E. P. Thompson, "The poverty of theory" in <u>The Poverty of Theory</u>, (London; 1980).

34 Poulantzas, <u>Political Power</u>.

35 O'Donnell in Collier Ed., <u>The New Authoritarianism</u>, p. 286.

36 <u>Ibid.</u>, p. 287.

37 <u>Ibid.</u>, p. 287.

38 <u>Ibid.</u>, p. 292.

39 Cammack, "The Political Economy of Contemporary Military Regimes", p. 11.

40 A. Ayer, <u>Philosophy in the Twentieth Century</u>, (Unwin 1982), p. 193.

41 For a helpful discussion of this point see C. Fortin, "The relative autonomy of the state and capital accumulation in Latin America; some conceptual issues", pp. 195-211, in D. Tussie Ed., <u>Latin America in the World Economy</u>, (Gower; 1983).

42 A. Pizzorno, "Introduction" in Pizzorno Ed., <u>Political Sociology</u>, (Penguin; 1975).

43 Cardoso, "On the Characterization of Authoritarian Regimes", in Collier Ed., <u>The New Authoritarianism</u>.

44 <u>Ibid.</u>, p. 35.

[45] Linz, "An Authoritarian Regime; Spain", in Allardt and Rokkan, **Mass Politics**.

[46] Cardoso, op. cit., p. 41.

[47] Ibid., p. 41.

[48] Ibid., p. 43. Compare T. Lowi's critique of Interest Group Liberalism, (Univ. of Chicago; 1970).

[49] Ibid., p. 46.

[50] Ibid., p. 38.

[51] Ibid., p. 45.

[52] Ibid., p. 38.

[53] Ibid., p. 40.

[54] Ibid., p. 40.

[55] Ibid., p. 50.

[56] Ibid., p. 51.

[57] On which see G. Philip, "The Military Institution Revisited", Journal of Latin American Studies, November 1980.

Chapter 3

THE MILITARY INSTITUTION; SOME COMPARISONS FROM
CENTRAL AMERICA AND THE CARIBBEAN

There is certainly nothing new in the idea
that military-political behaviour owes much to the
corporate interest of the military institution
itself. Writers such as Finer have treated this
point as if it were almost axiomatic.[1] There is,
moreover, a great deal of writing specifically on
the South American military which has explicitly
adopted an institutional perspective. Scholars
such as Canton in Argentina[2], Campos Coelho in
Brazil[3] and Villanueva in Peru[4] have made
important contributions together with several
European and North American writers[5]. It should
already be clear that the present author also
favours this perspective.

Nevertheless, there are two immediate problems
with an institutionalist approach. The first is
that there is a good deal of cross-sectional data
which seems to show, in Jackson's words, that "the
simple civilian-military government distinction
appears to be of little use in the explanation of
social change."[6] It is likely, however, that
this finding owes more to the inherent limitations
of the cross-sectional approach than to any
particular truth about the military. To begin
with, empirical comparison of regimes can only deal
with actual governments; a very large potential
category, of potential governments actually vetoed
by the military, cannot be included. It is
intuitively apparent that these (non-existent)
regimes might have behaved quite differently from
those which were actually allowed to take office;
they may well have been vetoed precisely because
they were different. A comparison between military
regimes and civilian regimes acceptable to the
military cannot possibly bring out the full

54

importance of a military-political role. Moreover, civilian regimes acceptable to the military have often had to moderate their behaviour in order to maintain this acceptability; in South America the military, in Burke's words, has often acted mobbishly in order to make its opponents moderate. Attempts to adopt a more sophisticated cross-sectional framework, such as McKinlay and Cohen's efforts to distinguish between military and non-military systems[7], raise serious problems of categorisation; these authors, for example, included Chile and Uruguay as "non-military" systems - correctly in terms of their adopted definition, but surely not usefully. Nor does such a framework fully dispense with the problem of the counter-factual (i.e. of knowing what would have happened in the absence of military involvement). Finally the statistics themselves, used to measure (for example) the relationship between military government and military spending are not always reliable - and in other cases the "obvious" variable is not the most useful one. (For example, as we shall see, the level of military spending in Brazil and Argentina is a very bad guide to the real importance of the military on the economy and society in these countries). None of this is to dismiss the value of cross-sectional work per se, but it does suggest that a more historical and substantive treatment of military politics may have more immediate value.

The second problem with an institutionalist perspective is at first sight more serious. This is that, in Karakatal's words, "there is no such thing as a typical army".[8] To put the matter differently, there may be so much variation between different types of military institution that the whole notion of military-political behaviour becomes meaningless. In some political systems, indeed, it is hard to know where the military ends and civilian politics begins.

It is certainly true that the "militariness" of an army is not something that can simply be assumed.[9] However, it is surely something that can be determined empirically. An obvious distinction can be made between armies in politics that, on the whole, behave like armies and those which do not. To put the matter with slightly more sophistication, military institutions in politics can be distinguished according to their level of unity and differentiation from civil society.[10]

Unity relates to respect for hierarchical structure; it makes a difference whether a military government is led by generals or by master sergeants. Differentiation relates to the internalisation of military values and, more particularly, a strong sense of military solidarity. Differentiation is high when two military officers, of different political persuasions (or religions or tribal backgrounds, where these are important) have more in common with each other than two political allies, one of whom is an officer.

Modern South American militaries are fairly united and highly differentiated. As we shall see from chapters 4 to 6, it was not always thus. However, the fact of this unity and differentiation is one of great political significance even though there are, of course, all kinds of other factors which help to explain particular political situations and outcomes. Not only does the military structure help to explain what the military can and cannot do (without undermining its own discipline), it also has implications for how civilians perceive and react towards the military. In South America, as elsewhere, a kind of political Say's Law operates - the fact of power alters expectations and tends to promote its own acceptability. The fact that the military can take power, repress opponents and appear at least in the short-term to resolve political conflicts or crises, greatly influences the attitude of civilian groups toward the military and leads them to internalise values sympathetic to military rule. In broad outline, therefore, one has the basis of a civil-military system. It is now worth exploring briefly how such a system, in South America, may differ from other systems in which the military also plays an active part.

If one wishes to discuss the nature of any political system, a key question concerns the ultimate loyalty of the coercive establishment. Under different systems, this loyalty may be to elected civilian leadership, to a monarch, to a political party or more broadly based political movement. Within South America, the ultimate loyalty of the military establishment is to its own institutional interest which may seem to lie in direct rule or alternatively in various kinds of relationship with civilian parties or individual leaders. Because the military is (relatively)

highly united and differentiated from civil society
in South America, it maintains itself at arms-
length from specific civilian groups and parties
and retains the ability to play a direct political
role without irrevocably factionalising or losing
its cohesion and discipline. This is a constant
and crucial feature of South American politics,
although the fate of particular governments, and a
fortiori of particular economic policies, will
depend on many variable factors and contingencies.
    Within South America it is often, as we saw in
chapter 2, taken for granted that the military
plays such an ultimate, underpinning, role. In
comparative perspective, however, South American
experience is relatively unusual. One need only
consider the role of the military in Ethiopia, or
most Arab countries, or in West Africa. With
this point in mind, it is worth looking in rather
more detail at the nature of the military in four
cases in Central America and the Caribbean. These
various countries have some similarities with South
America, indeed cultural determinists would claim a
good deal more[11], but their actual forms of
political organisation are quite different. The
four countries include three in which there have
been successful Revolutions (Mexico, Cuba and
Nicaragua) and one (the Dominican Republic) in
which there was a civil war followed by US
intervention. There are undoubtedly factors
bearing greatly upon the political history of these
countries over and above those which will briefly
be considered here. Nevertheless, one brute fact
distinguishes these four cases from the experience
of almost all of South America; in a crisis, the
coercive apparatus of the state failed to cope with
various forms of rebellion. Much of the
explanation for this can be seen in the structure
of the various military institutions.

THE DOMINICAN REPUBLIC[12]

    The Dominican Republic became independent
comparatively late (the 1840s) and went through
a chaotic caudillo period similar to that of
Bolivia or Venezuela rather than the relatively
more stable post-independence period experienced by
Chile or Brazil. The reason appears to have been
similar to that in these South American cases -
namely the absence of a strong oligarchy or Church

capable of exerting a degree of order. The history of the Dominican Republic, however, parts company with that of any South American country after 1916 when (at a time when the Dominican Republic still did not have a national army) US Marines occupied the country. (The US had several times previously discussed the complete annexation of the Dominican Republic whose geographic position put it directly within the US sphere of influence within the Caribbean.)

The US Marines remained in the Dominican for eight years, during which there was a rationalisation of public administration and a considerable expansion of US commercial influence in the area. The US also in common with its policy in other countries which it occupied at this time (Panama, Haiti, Nicaragua) set up a National Guard which quickly turned itself into the strongest power centre in the country. Trujillo, as head of the Guard, took over the government in 1930 and ruled for 31 years before his assassination in 1961.

During these 31 years, the Dominican Republic enjoyed a degree of semi-capitalist development which led to some growth of urban dwellers and, more particularly, the middle class. Local conflicts and regional identities were replaced throughout the country by centralised national concerns. Moreover, Trujillo - by carefully buying out the main foreign interests - made government more lucrative and increased its importance within civil society. All of these changes produced pent-up political demands but, until 1961, there was no means of resolving them.

In 1961 the US connived at the assassination of Trujillo and sought to set up a reformist (Alliance for Progress type) democracy fearing that the island might become "a second Cuba" if the democratic project failed.[13] To cut a long story very short, the US at first supported the reformist President Juan Bosch but soon lost confidence in him and so made no real effort to defend him when he fell victim to a military coup in September 1963. He was replaced by an unpopular and ineffectual military government which survived until April 1965 when there was a military rising (led by "Constitutionalists" - mainly supporters of Bosch); after several days of fighting, it seemed as though the rebels might win a civil war. In order to prevent this, US troops invaded the island on 30 April 1965. The invasion was a military, and to some extent a political, success. Elections were held in 1966 and were won by Balaguer (a former servant of Trujillo who had subsequently distanced himself enough to achieve an independent image).

The political events of April 1965 in the Dominican Republic involved civil war and direct US military intervention demonstrated the vulnerability of the Dominican military and power structure as a whole. Two things stand out that one might reasonably expect to have happened in a wholly praetorian society but which would certainly not have been considered normal in any South American country. One was that the "Constitutionalist" rebels distributed weapons to civilian allies (it was this that lent some plausibility to US fears of a possible "Communist victory" in the fighting - there was certainly no serious suggestion that Bosch or officers supporting him were Communists). The second was that a week of serious fighting was allowed to take place without domestic efforts to halt it; there was no sign of a political solution until the US invasion (which was itself a last-minute decision that the Dominican Republic's military leaders were not expecting). The government was able neither to take decisive action against the rebels nor to resign and allow a newly appointed Junta to negotiate a compromise solution. These courses of action proved impossible, not because the rebels were particularly strong (the rebels themselves, incidentally, had aimed for a quick coup and were as unprepared as anybody else for several days of fighting) but because the state was so weak. A crucial factor here was that the (often only nominally) pro-government officers were incapable of taking any decisive action. In short, events in the Dominican Republic revealed the existence of very deep military factionalism. Instead of coming together in a crisis, as has almost always been the case with South American militaries, the military split apart. A feature of this factionalism, and a contributing factor to it, was the absence of a serious military career structure or sense of "profession"; at the top, position depended on patronage, lower down, promotion could be extremely rapid. One of the leaders of the pro-Bosch coup was a 30 year old Colonel Rafael Fernandez.[14]

Lowenthal has hypothesised that military disunity resulted from an institutional vacuum.[15]

As we have seen, Trujillo governed the Dominican
Republic on highly personalist lines for a period
of thirty years.[16] When he fell, there was no
structure which could keep the competing ambitions
of military officers in check. After Trujillo was
assassinated, his close allies and family members
were quickly removed; a little later, they were
followed by General Echavarria who had masterminded the assassination of Trujillo and was
certainly a candidate to become the new leading
military-political figure in the country. During
the 1960s, almost the entire senior officer corps
was purged, retired or sent abroad.[17] Younger
officers came to the fore, adding a generational
conflict with Trujillista officers to other lines
of cleavage.[18] Thus, it was perhaps natural that
officers would conspire with civilians (and vice-
versa) in order to secure their share of the
spoils. This competition had little to do with
serious political principle or with conflict
between genuine socio-economic interests. Instead,
Lowenthal found of the 1965 rising:

> There does not seem to have been any
> appreciable difference between the top
> military leadership of the two sides with
> respect to previous ideology or degree of
> honesty ... The major distinction was that of
> age and rank; the established leaders were of
> higher rank precisely because they had
> prevailed in previous struggles to reach the
> top.[19]

Here we have, then, a classic praetorian
society. The military behaved as one would expect
under these circumstances; it conspired,
confronted and finally blundered into a civil war
(though no great issues were at stake) which ended
only with open foreign military intervention. In
contrast, however, the military in South America
almost never falls apart due to a botched coup
attempt; it simply closes ranks behind the winning
side while insisting that the principles of
military hierarchy are maintained. Nor does the
military normally arm civilians in order to fight
other officers (Torres refused to do this in
Bolivia in 1971 and made the revealing comment, "If
I do give you weapons, then you will have no
further need of me."). It is also notable,
although in Guatemala rather than South America,

that Arbenz' effort to arm civilians in the face of
a military coup attempt in 1954 precipitated his
downfall.[20] It is perhaps true, given the range
and sophistication of modern weaponry, that arming
civilians might have no more than a symbolic effect
in the face of a military organisation really
determined to take power. What is more important
is the fact that South American armies - while
often disunited on a variety of policy and
personality issues - almost invariably do maintain
the essential minimum of unity in order to avoid a
complete collapse of military authority.

Also interesting, if less spectacular, is the
history of the Dominican military after 1965.
Balaguer, after winning elections in 1966, became
another personalist ruler and largely bought the
loyalty of the army.

> Officers were deeply involved in politics,
> using their positions to protect their
> political, economic and social status. Some
> officers, even generals, did not become
> wealthy and were relatively apolitical, but
> those who had this different concept of a
> military career were few in number and usually
> in the lower ranks.[21]

However, it proved impossible to co-opt everybody
and factional divisions within the Dominican army
remained. In 1978 when the opposition candidate
won the elections, Balaguer's supporters tried a
pre-emptive coup but backed down partly because of
US opposition but largely because factional
disunity again prevented an effective move. When
the opposition candidate (Guzmán) took office, he
began an attempt to "professionalise" the Dominican
army (after first having purged the pro-Balaguer
officers); it is too early to say what the
results of this might be but the Dominican Republic
is still ruled by civilians. Unhappy memories of
1965 have played an important part in keeping the
military out of power and in promoting civilian
rule.

NICARAGUA

A somewhat different pattern of politics
occurred in Nicaragua prior to 1979; this was one
in which the military institution was taken over
and dominated by a single individual. Like the
Dominican Republic, Nicaragua had an unstable and
violent nineteenth century. Its level of military
organisation reflected this. In Millett's
evocative account,

> It would be hard to imagine anything less like
> a fighting force than the Nicaraguan armies.
> Troops were recruited by compulsory
> dragooning, those who sought to escape being
> simply shot down. These men received no
> training, no uniforms, no adequate weapons.
> Identified only by a ribbon bearing their
> party's colour and armed with antiquated
> muskets or simply with machetes they were set
> into combat.[22]

In the 1890s, however, a successful caudillo
(Estrada) emerged and began to organise serious
military training. He set up the Escuela
Politecnica for officer training and imported a
German and several Chilean officers to staff it; he
also, at least in theory, introduced conscription.
This marked only the very beginnings of
professionalism. Nicaragua in 1908 - Millett tells
us[23] - had 23 major generals, 54 brigadier
generals, 174 colonels and 260 Lt. colonels, whose
prime qualification for rank was their "ability to
raise a body of armed local partisans". Even so,
the Nicaraguan army was still strong enough to
defeat Honduras in a war in 1907.

Estrada made the serious mistake of annoying
the US Embassy which ensured his downfall in 1910.
This was followed by a period of armed confusion
rather than any consolidation of an opposing
government and US Marines landed in 1912. Rather
than ruling directly, Washington supported
administration by a Nicaraguan puppet president
who, secure in this support, allowed the army to
decline.

In 1923 the State Department pressed the
Central American republics into signing a treaty
pledging themselves to set up National Guards; the
United States had already been involved in creating

National Guards in the Phillipines, Haiti and the Dominican Republic, and now wanted to repeat this "success" in Central America. In February 1925, therefore, the State Department submitted to the Nicaraguan government a detailed plan for a "constabulary" of 23 officers and 329 men which was to be internally controlled and kept separate from the Ministry of War. This last proposal was part of an attempt to keep the Guard out of politics (although the quis custodiet custodies? problem was not so easily side-stepped) and partly an effort to free it from the peculation practised regularly by the Ministry of War. A retired US officer, Major Calvin Carter, was given the job of setting up the new organisation. After a few false starts, development of the new organisation began in earnest in 1927 under tight US control (Millett writes that "for several years almost all the Guardia's commissioned officers were Americans assigned to that duty by the Navy Department"[24]); even as late as March 1932 there were no more than 39 Nicaraguan citizens serving as Guard officers; all of these were Lieutenants. All other members of the total officer corps of 220 were foreign. In January 1933, when the United States - disappointed by its political failures in Nicaragua - precipitatively withdrew its Marines, no Nicaraguan officer had yet got beyond the rank of Captain.

It may be that, had the United States remained a few years longer, the Nicaraguan National Guard would have assumed some of the more "professional" characteristics of South American armies. Instead, the Guard - while organisationally and technically capable of decisively dominating the country - did not have time to develop a corporate political identity. It was, instead, taken over by a Liberal politician - Anastasio Somoza - who had won the confidence of the United States during the complex political manoeuvering of the 1920's.

Although Somoza's early years as head of the National Guard were characterised by some conflict between himself and the more "professional" officers, whom Somoza did not dare remove immediately, he was ultimately able to consolidate his personal control over the Guard. He used the Guard to eliminate internal opposition - luring the guerrilla leader Sandino into a trap and shooting him. He did not move for national power until 1936 when he launched a bloodless coup against President Sacasa.

For the next forty years, Anastasio Somoza and his two sons ran Nicaragua as a personal fiefdom - almost as a personal <u>hacienda</u>. The Guard, meanwhile, was bought-off. It was given control of a number of "outside" functions, all of them lucrative - these included the sanitation service, the postal service and, most lucratively of all, customs and excise. Meanwhile Guard officers were kept apart from the rest of society as far as possible. Officers had their own system of medical care, their own housing, their own system of jurisdiction and even their own tax system. Corruption was institutionalised.

> Every higher post in the Guardia reportedly has its price tag, representing the amount of money, over and above his salary, which an officer can reasonably expect to make through graft, "gifts" and similar perquisites. Loyalty to Somoza is the major requirement for appointment to any potentially lucrative post.[25]

The Somoza family, or at least its last President, did however overlook one thing. A Guard of this type could not seriously be expected to fight. It even contained some junior officers whose loyalty, as a result of their exclusion from the main advantages of Guard membership, was suspect. In August 1978, when the FSLN's campaign against Tacho Somoza was at its height, the President arrested 85 Guard officers for plotting against him.[26] However, what was in the long run more important was not Somoza's dependence on the Guard but the Guard's dependence on Somoza. "Tacho" Somoza, the last of the dynasty, was a brutal and incompetent figure who decisively alienated the sympathies of the Nicaraguan middle class and many business interests (unlike his father and brother who had both been careful not to push their power to its limit and also to co-opt some support from outside their immediate circle); what was surprising about his downfall was that it took so long. However, the main reason for his survival until 1979 also explains why his overthrow took the form of a Revolution - the moderate opposition was unable to make headway against him in enough time to head off the "Revolutionary" opposition.

At least two years before "Tacho" Somoza was overthrown by the FSLN he had decisively lost the support of Washington and the Nicaraguan Church hierarchy. The middle class had opposed him ever since the 1972 earthquake which had been the occasion for peculation on an even greater scale than had been common in the past. Yet Somoza could rely on the unconditional loyalty of senior Guard officers until the end. Why did they not, as the United States had hoped, overthrow Somoza and negotiate a settlement with the moderate opposition? This might have paved the way for elections and would certainly have helped unite the non-Revolutionary opposition which, in the end, was almost forced to throw in its lot with the Sandinistas.

The answer lies in the nature of the Guard itself. By the 1970's, and indeed long before, it had become the creature of the Somozas. There was no chance of an independent leadership and, indeed, since any overthrow of Somoza would have threatened most of the perks and privileges of the Guard, any serious opposition to Somoza would almost inevitably have found it necessary to confront the Guard as a whole. Moreover, the Guard itself was made up of carefully selected Somoza loyalists; more professional officers remained on the margins of real command. Thus, Somoza was proof against moderate opposition but vulnerable to Revolutionaries who could plausibly present themselves as the only alternative to the dictator.

The Nicaraguan National Guard was in some ways the opposite side of the same coin when compared with Dominican military in 1961-65. After the death of Trujillo (who shared certain characteristics with Somoza), officers in the Dominican Republic lacked a structure within which to reconcile their differences. The result was a tendency toward chronic factionalisation culminating in civil war and foreign intervention. In Nicaragua, the Guard had become so dependent upon the Somoza dynasty that it was incapable of taking political action which might have secured its future. In the one case, there was anarchy, in the other Leviathan, but in both the effect was to undermine the effectiveness of the military.

The South American pattern is quite distinct. Even allowing for the fact that there have been some remarkable despotisms during the course of the century (Gomez in Venezuela, Stroessner in

Paraguay, and one might add Pinochet in Chile), politics has never been allowed to become as personalist or as exclusionary as it was in Nicaragua. South American dictators, like Franco in Spain, have held on to power because they were able to maintain contact with, and the confidence of, a variety of civilian interests. Military establishments in South America have always been willing to support an effective and successful dictator, but have invariably been quicker to leave a sinking ship than the Nicaraguan National Guard proved to be. Indeed, South American militaries have been able to manoeuvre quite adroitly in difficult political and economic circumstances in order to avoid complete isolation from civil society - even (as has happened recently in Argentina) allowing an example to be made of their senior officers in order to avoid being pushed completely into a political corner. In Argentina, perhaps an extreme example, superficial political instability has in some ways been system-maintaining at a deeper level. Thus, there were nine unauthorised changes of government in Argentina since 1936 (not including returns to barracks, or constitutional presidential successions) but no Revolution; there was only one such change of government in Nicaragua during this period - the Nicaraguan Revolution.

Moreover, it has been quite common for military officers in South America to overthrow a military president because he was becoming "totalitarian" (the official reason for the 1955 coup in Argentina) or because of a "cult of personality" (official reason for the 1975 coup in Peru). Military regimes which took power in Brazil after 1964 and Argentina after 1976 were quick to agree on a rotating presidency with a finite term of office and no re-appointment after a term had expired. In earlier cases, this difficulty was often resolved by converting a successful coup leader into a "civilian" President, running regularly for office in more-or-less fixed elections - as with Odría in Peru (1948-56) and, indeed, Stroessner in Paraguay (1954-).

By way of contrast with the Nicaraguan National Guard's attachment to Somoza, it might be worth discussing how the Argentine military overthrew Perón in 1955. Perón had originally been a successful military officer, and conspirator, and in 1946 won elections with support

of some of the military but, decisively, with the
support of public opinion. His presidential period
had by no means been uncontroversial but by 1954 he
had successfully foiled two coup attempts (Menéndez
in 1951 and Suarez in 1952) and had, during nine
years of rule, enjoyed ample opportunity to place
his own men in key positions. He also maintained a
high degree of popular support despite some recent
economic setbacks[27] - which, in a highly
developed society such as Argentina, was a very
significant factor. How, then, did he fall?

There were known opponents of Perón with army
connections (men such as Lonardi and Aramburu) but
these had either retired or been confined to
administrative tasks which did not give them
command of troops. From late 1954[28] Perón began
to lose support from former loyalists, many of them
Catholic officers concerned at Perón's
deteriorating relations with the Church. Moreover,
Perón had never been able to complete his control
of the Navy where, because of the technical
requirements of the service, political loyalty
could not be the only criterion for promotion.
Thus serious conspiracy began in the Navy (where it
had never fully subsided even after the defeat of
the 1951 attempt) where the leader of the
conspiracy, Admiral Torranzo Calderon, had
originally been a Perón loyalist but later changed
his views. By April 1955 the plotters came into
contract with a variety of civilian groups ranging
from conservatives to socialists.

The nascent conspiracy was given force after a
Catholic (i.e. anti-government) demonstration on
June 11 1955 and a pro-government counter
demonstration the next day. In fact, these events
led the coup leaders to declare themselves
prematurely although their hand was forced to some
extent by intimations of discovery.[29] A coup
attempt began on June 16 but it was badly planned
and it failed. It was a fairly violent affair with
the bombing from the air of the Plaza de Mayo,
while civilian supporters of the government were
(unusually for South America) armed against it.

At this point one might again have expected a
failed rebellion to have consolidated Perón's
authority. It did not because of the continued
existence of "sleepers" in the military - men who
were waiting for their opportunity and who had
avoided complicity in the earlier attempt. Thus
although the Navy and Air Force, where active

conspirators were located, suffered purges, the army - which had not moved - remained unscathed. Meanwhile the Navy despite, or because of, purges directed against it was further embittered. By late August, the Navy was conspiring again - with a new leader, Admiral Rojas, who had - like his predecessor - taken no previous part in anti-Perón conspiracies. The army meanwhile remained far less disaffected and its quiescence convinced the Navy to wait for more support. According to Potash "as of late August only three or four of the 90-odd generals on active duty could be described as actively committed to the ouster of Perón".[30] One of these, Aramburu, was also plotting. His plans were, however, interrupted by a "free-lance" coup attempt led on 1 September by General Balaguer, a former Perón loyalist. The failure of this attempt, and fear of discovery, led Aramburu to withdraw temporarily from plotting. This, however, simply led to the emergence of another General, Lonardi, willing to take the lead along with the Navy as support for Perón within the army continued to erode. The revolt began on 16 September; it was far from bloodless but after a somewhat confused three days Perón resigned and went into exile. Perón's surrender was, in fact, quite carefully negotiated by a military Junta of senior officers brought into existence for this purpose once the coup had started.

This coup has been discussed at some length partly because it has been exceptionally well documented and partly because it involved, on the face of it, an almost impossibly difficult undertaking - the removal of a popular President whose military background and nine years in power might have seemed enough to consolidate his rule. Yet seen from the inside one finds a whole series of conspiracies mounted by disaffected officers, one of which finally succeeded. One obvious conclusion to emerge from this is that the power of appointment is not a decisive advantage for an incumbent president in a large South American country; many of Perón's most important opponents were former loyalists. Nor is this fact unusual when one considers other coups - Et tu Brute is a familiar enough cry in South American politics. Another conclusion is that, in the Argentine military though not in the Nicaraguan National Guard, alternative leadership was available - there were (as became even more apparent after 1955) more

leading conspirators than there were leading
positions for them to fill. The sheer size of the
officer corps was an important factor here. A
third conclusion is that the military officers
whose loyalty (or in this case disloyalty) was
decisive were by no means easily identifiable
professional conspirators, but rather formerly
loyal or at least apolitical officers who had
turned against Perón when they believed he had
gone "too far" and demonstrated totalitarian
tendencies as evidenced (in their eyes) by his
conflict with the Church. The loyalty of the
military, even after nine years of Perónist rule,
was no more than conditional - despite careful
efforts made by the President to win over the
military with material and other benefits as well
as by loyalty oaths and various efforts made to
counter the potential threat to Perón posed by the
officer corps - notably the attempt to use NCOs and
the trade unions as means of checking the power of
the officer corps. Finally it is worth noting that
the military conspirators made contact with
civilian politicians known to be opposed to Perón
and that these men, far from throwing up their
hands in horror at the proposed overthrow of a
popularly elected President, were obviously willing
to see the coup go ahead. Even the Radical Party,
itself a victim of a military coup in 1930, was
happy now that the officers were on its side.
These, it should be emphasised, are fairly typical
features of military-political behaviour in South
America but they are set apart from the two Central
American and Caribbean cases we have so far
considered - and also from the Cuban case which
will be considered next.

CUBA

Pre-Revolutionary Cuba is another instructive
contrast with South American patterns of military
politics. Cuba became independent only after the
Spanish-American War of 1898. The country was in
fact "liberated" mainly by US troops with Cubans
playing only an ancillary role. However, after
hostilities with Spain ended the Cuban army became
the centre of a movement seeking independence from
the USA (whose Platt Amendment in 1900 gave it the
right, under US law, to intervene almost at will in
Cuban politics). The first Cuban army was

therefore dismantled by the US Embassy, mainly through bribery, and a new one was built.[31]

The reason for the re-building of the army, then, was to weaken it rather than strengthen it. The US government, and the Cuban civilian establishment, did not want to build up any kind of countervailing power which might subsequently discover the virtues of nationalism. The army was therefore factionalised and serious discipline undermined by politicians in pursuit of party objectives. It thus came to present the familiar picture of a clientelist army dependent upon civilian elites rather than seeking autonomy from them. Nevertheless, as happened so frequently with armies of this kind, it was eventually taken over by a personalist ruler, in this case Machado, who became dictator in Cuba in 1925, and converted the military into a personal machine. However, Machado was "caught in possession" by the Great Depression and forced to make serious budgetary cutbacks which soured his relations with the military. Moreover, his dictatorial excesses led the US to oppose him, particularly after Franklin Roosvelt took over as President in early 1933. The US Ambassador to Havana, Sumner Welles, made it his mission to remove Machado who finally fell in August 1933. This put senior Cuban officers in a serious position; they had supported Machado almost until the end and now felt acutely vulnerable to a backlash. The troops and some junior officers, meanwhile, had openly participated in civilian led action in opposition to Machado. The younger officers now openly demanded purges of their seniors and a reorganisation of the military. Purges did not occur but the senior officers, on the defensive and "hesitating to take any action to impose their authority ... allowed disorder to grow among the troops".[32] On 4 September, a group of sergeants, of whom Batista became the spokesman and later the leader, revolted successfully. Once their movement was underway, they made contact with student opposition leaders and what began as a barracks revolt took on some of the characteristics of a social revolution.

The sergeants revolt illustrated clearly the deep factional divisions within the Cuban army. Senior officers were patronage appointees now rendered largely helpless by the disappearance of their patron. Junior officers were in many cases men of good professional qualifications who had lost out to political loyalists in career terms. As Perez notes,

> The graduates of the cadet classes of 1913, 1914 and 1915, with few exceptions, were all lieutenants on 4 September 1933; no member of the graduating class of 1912, the first produced by the military academy, had reached the rank of major.[33]

On 4 September nearly 20 per cent of the junior officers - 112 captains and lieutenants - joined the sergeants movement; many had been kept in junior positions for a decade or more. If the junior officers' grievances were largely professional, those of the sergeants were largely racial. Sergeants had, it is true, occasionally moved into the officer corps (a channel which the junior officers had succeeded in blocking by law in late August 1933) but many were disqualified from such promotion. In Perez' words, following the sergeants revolt, "a white officer corps, tied to the Island's social elite through consanguity and position, was deposed by a largely non-white, non-commissioned officer corps".[34] The precipitating factor in the revolt was the government's attempt, in late August, to cut sergeants' pay.

This intense factionalism by no means disappeared with the success of the sergeants' revolt. In its immediate aftermath, military discipline weakened still further[35], but those who had led it were obviously eager to consolidate their new position. They were thus willing to follow the lead of Batista (who quickly promoted himself Major) who was able to secure undreamt-of benefits for his military allies, in return being able to count on their support. Consequently, although Batista's later career was by no means free of adventure, he was eventually able to establish decisive control over the army. His ability to re-establish control in this way was also aided by the desire of some of the beneficiaries of the 1933 "revolution" to put an end to further turbulence and to the danger that they, in their turn, might be overthrown either by counter-revolutionaries or by men further to the Left. The importance of military discipline became particularly obvious after the narrow failure of a major counter-revolutionary attempt in November

1933. Batista's final master stroke came after this rebellion when he managed to win the confidence of the US Embassy. Early in 1934, Batista and the army moved in to consolidate the new post-Revolutionary order.

Subsequently, Batista turned the Cuban army into his personal machine and, like his predecessors, deliberately kept it weak and divided in order to protect his own position as its head. Thus secure, he ruled for many years behind the scenes and then launched his own coup in 1952 - a step which soon afterwards led to the emergence of a guerilla movement which, the world now knows, was to have momentous consequences. One of the main reasons for the inability of the Cuban army to combat the rebels lay in its internal divisions between such professional officers as were appointed and Batista's cronies; indeed, an anti-Batista coup attempt, led by professional officers, failed in April 1956. Following this the army was purged extensively and its military capacity even further undermined. Indeed as late as September 1957 Batista had to put down a naval revolt against his rule. Thus the more militarily competent officers increasingly withdrew from active support of Batista who was left only with his close associates to defend him.

There were many contingencies in history but it is interesting to speculate on what might have happened if the military revolt against Batista had succeeded in 1956. Of course if the United States had perceived more clearly what was at stake in Castro's revolt it might have supported Batista more energetically than it did (it is one of history's ironies that in 1957 the State Department was, if anything, supporting Castro while the Cuban Communist Party, long an ally of Batista, was if anything supporting the dictator). Nevertheless after March 1958, when the US imposed an arms embago on Batista, Washington did begin to look around for an intermediary caretaker government which could negotiate a cease-fire with Castro. However, by then army morale was too low and any decisive move might well have brought forward the total collapse of the military institution which, as the world now knows, eventually took place at the end of 1958.

The Cuban case is interesting for a number of reasons, not the least one being that it was the prototype for a good deal of later insurrectionary

activity in Central and South America. Central
American revolutionaries have so far had a great
deal more success than their South American
counterparts who were invariably crushed before
they could mount a serious threat to the
authorities. One important reason for this is
different quality of South American armies.

Indeed, the Cuban army had a number of
distinct features. Most obviously, Cuba
experienced a successful sergeants revolt. In no
South American army has this ever happened. There
have been cases of NCO rebellions notably in Brazil
in 1933 and again in 1963 and of rebellions by
sailors and enlisted men (Chile 1931, Peru 1932,
Brazil 1964) and even of civil-military rebellions
which allied senior and junior officers and NCOs
(Peru 1948, Argentina 1956), but these were
invariably failures. Senior officers, with few
exceptions, closed ranks against the rebels in all
cases. Even the famous <u>tenente</u> (lieutenants)
movement in Brazil in 1922 - led in fact by an army
captain - was quickly defeated and was mainly of
symbolic value. Junior officers movements have
sometimes succeeded in South America but these, as
we shall see, were quite different in their
consequences.

Indeed there is an important sense in which
senior officers can only participate successfully
in South American politics if they keep their
junior officers and, even more so, their NCOs and
enlisted men out, otherwise the cohesiveness of the
military - necessary to any effective political
role and, indeed, its own long-term survival - will
be undermined. In Cuba the successful sergeants
revolt, possible only because of the existing
weakness and factionalisation of the officer corps
(largely the result of previous US intervention),
destroyed the hierarchy upon which military
discipline and organisation depended. Instead,
Batista ran the army as though it were a gang and
he its boss; what mattered to him was personal
loyalty rather than any ability to perform military
tasks. Like Somoza in Nicaragua, he found that
this assured him protection from coups but made him
vulnerable to revolution.

The case of pre-Revolutionary Cuba, like that
of Nicaragua, provides further evidence that it is
generally in the interests of the officer corps as
a whole to keep a check upon their formal leaders.
It is of course true that the emergence of a

Batista or a Somoza would be hard to conceive outside small countries with extremely weak institutional structures which could be ruled like personal fiefdoms. Nevertheless these cases do illustrate the point that the interests of a military-political leader and those of senior military officers can and do conflict, and senior officers do well to prevent the extremes of personal rule - this lesson was well understood by the Argentine military when it moved against Perón. Military opposition to "politics" therefore, in this sense, is by no means purely an instinctive reflex or the result of indoctrination; it is also a rational calculation. A military-president may need the officer corps more than it needs him - but under different circumstances he may not. Similarly, an officer corps may be able to retain its essential independence under a military dictatorship - or, again, it may not. Therein lie some essential political calculations and much of the difference between South American militaries and some of their Central American and Caribbean counterparts.

MEXICO

Mexico provides another interesting comparison with South America.[36] Like Cuba and Nicaragua, but unlike any South American country with the possible exception of Bolivia in 1952, Mexico has undergone a full-scale Revolution in the present century. This began with the overthrow of Porfirio Díaz in 1910 but its roots go back considerably earlier.

After a particularly violent nineteenth century, apparent stability had returned to Mexico under Díaz, effective ruler since 1874. Mexico on the eve of the Revolution provides almost a textbook example of a pre-revolutionary state - autocratic and inefficient, with its army a personal machine rather than an effective fighting force, and with its stagnant political system increasingly out of step with a rapidly changing society. The state, and the army, was manned in its senior ranks by men who had grown old with Díaz himself leaving a younger generation, together with a middle class which had expanded during years of economic prosperity, resentful at the lack of liberty, and restive and anxious for the opening up of the political system and for a widening of access to the state.

The Mexican army in 1910 was perhaps no more factional than others in Latin America at this time; in most of South America the first serious impact of military professionalism only came to be felt around the time of the First World War. What was really distinctive about the Mexican case was that what began as a middle class movement for reform (not, perhaps, altogether dissimilar to similar movements at that time in Argentina and Uruguay) later deepened into a more genuinely Revolutionary conflict involving indigenous peasants and fundamental demands for the reform of land tenure. These escalating conflicts shattered the Mexican army and led to a whole series of regional and national wars.

By 1920 the "Constitutionalists" had emerged triumphant. These were a heterogenous collection of men under arms rather than a group with any clear national purpose. A number of "Generals", including Calles, had no military background at all until the Revolution broke out and they had learned their military skills in the field rather than the academy. Thus although the leaders of the Mexican Revolution during the next two decades were, for the most part, military men they were by no means a military caste. What they had in common was a particular kind of military-political experience rather than military training and organisation per se.

Indeed, in the early 1920s it was not at all clear that Mexico had a military institution as such. A number of regional leaders had local power bases and could rely upon armed men quite independently of the Federal army - such as the Agraristas (essentially armed peasants) who acted as retainers for men such as Cedillo in San Luis Potosi.[37] The Federal army itself was badly organised - so much so that scholars have found difficulty in getting a clear sense of military numbers.[38] There was no uniform system of conscription; only the very poor volunteered while others were pressed into service. Desertion was heavy and difficult to check because few officers could securely identify their men; it was not uncommon for deserters to re-enlist under a different name. Officers were excessive in number (an estimated 14,000 in 1927 as against around 79,000 men) and had little professional formation.

Of a sample of 34 generals serving between 1920 and
1935 only four had a professional qualification
before joining the army; the military college
itself did not open until 1926 and so technically
expert officers could not have reached the top
ranks until the 1940s.[39]
During the 1920s one of the prime concerns of
the Mexican state was to de-mobilise the various
local armies and power centres which had grown up
during the Revolution. This was accomplished in
large part through bribery ("I know of no General"
said President Obregón, "who can withstand a
broadside of 50,000 pesos."); former military
leaders were brought into the formal state
apparatus, or encouraged to take advantages of
lucrative "business opportunities" provided by the
state, or simply paid off with haciendas or other
properties. Indeed this former military leadership
provided the backbone of Mexico's post-
Revolutionary capitalist class. On the other hand,
repression was also sometimes necessary - two major
military revolts, and a number of minor ones, were
put down by the Mexican government after 1920 not
to mention a civil war resulting from the Cristero
rising of 1926. Indeed it was to head off the
threat of a major revolt by Obregón's followers,
after the mysterious assassination of Obregón
himself in 1929, that Calles created the official
revolutionary party in order to incorporate the
various competing military-political factions.
(Party and state, at that time, were virtually
identical.)
What happened, then, was that the
"Constitutionalist" elite formed itself into the
new political and economic order which was
organised, at least ostensibly, along civilian
lines despite the fact that the elite was largely
made up of Generals. Meyer et al conclude that
"despite having military force at their disposal,
officers were uniformed civilians much more than
centurions or praetorians. It has been estimated
that between 1920 and 1935 half of the most
important jobs in the country belonged to them."[40]
The word "belong" was used advisedly.
This military-political order was by no means
democratic; the system was authoritarian with some
Marxist-Leninist trappings (dropped after around
1940) and some important and effectively observed
political procedures. These procedures (the six-
year Presidency, no re-election, etc.), established

after a struggle, continued to operate even after
the composition of the elite changed, after the
Second World War, from Generals to <u>licenciados</u>
(i.e. civilian technocrats) and operators of the
political machine (labour leaders etc.). The
establishment of these political procedures,
moreover, went hand-in-hand with a considerable
expansion in the political base of the
Revolutionary party which successfully incorporated
peasant unions and much of organised labour. Quite
radical social changes were permitted to occur
during the 1930s but within the framework of a
gradually strengthening authoritarian state. This
was also the period in which the last of the
independent military <u>caudillos</u> were brought to
heel or defeated.

Since then there has been a limited re-
professionalisation of the Mexican officer corps
but this has been kept securely under political
control. Military officers have at times been
switched to "political" work (as state governors
etc.) and have thus not been allowed to become
caste conscious. Moreover, partly because the
heroes of the Revolution were always portrayed as
civilians rather than military men, the Mexican
army has lacked prestige in comparison with its
South American counterparts. It has not attracted
politically ambitious youth on the South American
pattern. At the same time the near monopoly of
electoral success enjoyed by the official party
(the PRI) has ensured that the state elite has
become largely a self-perpetuating entity -
promoting technocrats, political operators and
occasionally military men according to their
contacts, qualifications and performance.
Factional political competition, which might easily
have involved a semi-professionalised military, has
not so far taken place to any significant degree
since 1940.

Mexico affords a unique example in Latin
America of a military elite transforming itself
into a political elite and so transferring the
basis of power from the army to the civil state.
There are a few similar cases in the Middle East
and the Horn of Africa.[41] It is obviously
noteworthy that in Mexico, as in Iraq and Ethiopia,
this transformation followed a Revolution (of a
kind successfully avoided by almost all South
American officer corps). The Revolutionary
leadership, once established, could do a good deal

to encourage loyalty by its "stick and carrot" policy but there was from the very beginning an effective basis of coercive support from which it could operate. This support was offered directly to the state rather than mediated through some form of caste loyalty to the military institution as such. It was thus possible to transform it so as to "de-militarise" the system and lay the basis for a highly effective form of political organisation.

By way of contrast, South American military elites regard their primary loyalties as being to their own institution rather than to leadership which might in practice threaten it. Most officers in South America would agree with General Onganía (President of Argentina 1966-70) that "military obedience is ultimately owed and directed to the Constitution and its laws, never to the men or political parties which circumstantially hold power."[42] Mexican generals had never learned such loyalties either to the Porfirian army or to the competing factions which fought out the Revolution. They were thus willing to co-operate in the creation of a state party.

MILITARY INSTITUTIONS COMPARED

In these four cases, then, military institutions were not merely defeated but actually destroyed (or in the case of the Dominican Republic almost destroyed) by Revolutionaries. Moreover, if one considers the history of these countries over a longer period, this overthrow does not appear completely surprising; the military had shown evidence of brittleness and vulnerability well before the final <u>coup de grace</u>. The post-Revolutionary Mexican case, moreover, shows that a post-Revolutionary military elite can, in Latin America no less than elsewhere, transform itself into what is effectively a single-party system. In South America, however, no such events have taken place. There has been no successful NCO movements and no Revolutionary overthrow of the state, except for the somewhat ambiguous case of Bolivia in 1952. South America has certainly suffered from periods of dictatorship but no military institution has reached the state of atrophy and dependence upon a single individual comparable with the Dominican Republic under Trujillo or Nicaragua under the Somoza dynasty.

While one may seek to explain this different
evolution in varying ways, there is descriptive
validity in the point that military institutions in
South America have been able to play a "ballast"
role in the political system - protecting the
system in general rather than governments in
particular - in a way that could not occur in the
four cases considered here. In these later cases
there was no military brake on the factionalisation
which can often accompany military rule; this
factionalism led either to civil war and political
decay, or to the imposition of a rigid Leviathan
which was too brittle to adapt to changing
circumstances, or alternatively, in the case of
Mexico, to the morphology of military rule into a
single party system. In South America no military
institution has lost its identity in this way and,
as we shall see, there are powerful forces
maintaining the discipline and consequent
independence of the military high command.

It was suggested at the beginning of this
chapter that there is a basic distinction to be
made between military institutions which maintain
their unity and differentiation despite political
involvement - outside South America the cases of
Turkey and Indonesia come to mind - and those which
tend to decay during periods of conflict - such as
Ethiopia, Ghana and, for that matter, Greece and
Portugal.[43] A distinction of this kind is, of
course, not an explanation per se. One might very
briefly suggest that military factionalisation is
more likely in very small countries (where senior
military officers are not a "critical mass"), in
countries where military technology and skills are
insufficient to mark a distinction from civil
society, and societies where ethnic, regional or
religious conflicts are particularly pronounced.
This is by no means a full explanation. What we
are concerned with here, however, is the particular
case of South America where the historical
development and political behaviour of the military
need detailed attention.

Before leaving this comparative perspective,
however, two general points will be made about
military institutions which remain united and
differentiated. The first is that this unity and
differentiation will not be maintained without some
kind of effort; there will always be factionalising
forces at work when the military is actively
involved in politics. These will need to be

managed in certain particular, and possibly explicit, ways. These forms of management, or ways of dealing with threats to military "discipline" will themselves become political facts of very considerable importance. Secondly, because the military institution will be defined by its cohesion and discipline it will subjectively acquire a sense of distance from civil society and a distinct corporate interest of its own. What others will come to see as military privileges, officers will tend to see as legitimate and necessary interests. In pursuing these, military institutions are likely to seek wealth and power within the country as a whole and will not be readily relegated to the marginal role which many civilians would prefer them in.

While one can evidently describe the nature of a military (or any other) institution at a particular moment, deeper understanding requires a sense of its historical development. Before moving on to discuss South American militaries' different experiences of rule and political involvement, therefore, it will be useful to look in more detail at their political and institutional formation. The next three chapters will offer a necessarily brief survey of their most important military-political experiences and developments in the years since independence.

NOTES

[1]   S. E. Finer, The Man on Horseback, (Pall Mall; 1962).

[2]   D. Canton, La Politica de los Militares Argentinos 1900-1971, (Buenos Aires; 1971).

[3]   E. Campos Coelho, Em Busca de Identidade: o Exercito e a Politica na Sociedade Brasileira, (Forense, Rio; 1976).

[4]   V. Villanueva, Cien Anos del Ejercito Peruano, (Lima; 1973) and El Caem y la Revolucion de la Fuerza Armada, (IEP, Lima; 1972).

5   Many of these will be discussed below. The most notable writings, however, are A. Stepan, The Military in Politics; Changing Patterns in Brazil (Yale U.P.; 1971), A. Rouquie, Pouvoir Militaire et Societe Politique en Republique Argentine, (Paris; 1976), and R. Potash, The Army and Politics in Argentina, (2 vols., 1928-45 and 1945-62; Stanford U.P.; 1969 and 1982).

6   R. W. Jackson, "Politicians in Uniform", APSR, Vol. 70, no. 4 (December 1976), p. 1097.

7   R. D. McKinlay and A. S. Cohen, "Performance and Instability in Military and Non-Military Regime Systems", APSR, Vol. 70, no. 3, (September 1976).

ε   B. Karakatal, "The Military in Turkish Politics", in C. Clapham and G. Philip (eds.), Political Dilemmas of Military Regimes, (Croom Helm, London; 1984).

9   This is a serious weakness in Finer's Man on Horseback.

10 C. Clapham and G. Philip, in Political Dilemmas, discuss these notions in some detail.

11 For example, C. Veliz, The Centralist Tradition in Latin America, (Princeton U.P.; 1980).

12 This account relies heavily on A. Lowenthal, "The Dominican Republic; the politics of chaos", pp. 34-58 in A. Van Lazar and R. R. Kaufman (eds.), Reform and Revolution; Readings in Latin American Politics, (Allyn and Bacon, Boston; 1969).

13 A. Lowenthal, The Dominican Intervention, (Harvard; 1972), and also I. Goff and G. Locker, "The Violence of Domination; US power and the Dominican Republic", in I. L. Horowitz (ed.), Latin American Radicalism; a Documentary Report on Left and Nationalist Movements, (London; 1969).

14 This case is mentioned in T. Draper, The Dominican Revolt, p. 49, (Commentary; 1968).

15 Lowenthal in Reform and Revolution.

16 For a specific study on the military see G. Pope Atkins, Arms and Politics in the Dominican Republic, (Westview Press; 1981).

17 Lowenthal in Reform and Revolution, p. 40.

18 Draper, The Dominican Revolt, p. 49.
19 Lowenthal in Reform and Revolution, p. 41-42.
20 R. H. Immerman, The CIA in Guatemala; The
    Foreign Policy of Intervention, (Univ. of
    Texas; 1982).
21 Pope Atkins, Arms and Politics, p. 52.
22 R. Millett, Guardians of the Dynasty; a
    history of the US created Guardia Nacional de
    Nicaragua and the Somoza family, (Orbis, New
    York; 1977), p. 18.
23 Ibid., p. 21.
24 Ibid., p. 71.
25 Ibid., p. 254.
26 John A. Booth, The End of the Beginning; the
    Nicaraguan Revolution, (Westview; 1982).
27 D. James, "Unions and Politics; the
    Development of the Peronist Trade Unions
    1955-66", (Ph.D., London; 1979).
28 This account is taken from R. Potash, The Army
    and Politics in Argentina; 1945-62, (Athlone,
    1980), pp. 181 et seq.
29 Ibid, p. 187.
30 Ibid, p. 197.
31 L. A. Perez, Army Politics in Cuba 1898-1958,
    (Pittsburgh U. P.; 1976).
32 L. Aguilar, Cuba 1933, (Stanford U. P.;
    1972), p. 150.
33 L. A. Perez, "Army Politics, Diplomacy and the
    Collapse of the Cuban Officer Corps; the
    'sergeants revolt' of 1933", Journal of Latin
    American Studies, Vol. 6, no. 1 (May 1974),
    p. 67
34 Ibid, p. 68.
35 Aguilar, Cuba 1933, p. 166.
36 E. Lieuwen, Mexican Militarism: The Political
    Rise and Fall of the Revolutionary Army
    1910-40, (Albuquerque; 1968) offers a valuable
    history of the period.
37 For a case study see R. Falcon, "The Rise and
    Fall of Military Caciquismo, in Revolutionary
    Mexico; the case of San Luis Potosi 1910-38",
    (D. Phil., Oxford; 1983).
38 L. Meyer et al, Estado y Sociedad con Calles,
    (Colegio de Mexico; 1977), Vol. 11 of Historia
    de la Revolución Mexicana.
39 Ibid.
40 Ibid, p. 66.

41 See Clapham and Philip, <u>Political Dilemmas</u>
    and Perlmutter in <u>World Politics</u>, Vol. 33,
    no. 1.
42 Quoted in O'Donnell, "Modernization and
    Military Coups", in Lowenthal (ed.), <u>Armies</u>
    <u>and Politics</u>, p. 208.
43 Clapham and Philip, <u>op. cit.</u>.

Chapter 4

FROM STATUS TO INSTITUTION; EARLY
PROFESSIONALISATION AND ITS CONSEQUENCES

The collapse of Spanish power in the Americas
left behind no credible central authority in any
country but Chile. In Brazil, however, the
transition from Portuguese rule was far less
traumatic and the monarchy remained until 1889.
One finds two broad patterns, then, in post-
independence South America. In Brazil and Chile
there emerged a relatively stable civilian ruling
class and the military largely kept out of
politics, more as a result of elite control than of
any sense of professionalism. The rest of South
America belongs in a second category. There was
extensive military rule, but of a highly
personalist kind; the military institution did not
begin to cohere until the end of the century. One
might perhaps make a further distinction between
countries in which loosely organised but still
recognisable factions enrolled individual caudillos
(Colombia and Uruguay) - these later evolved into
party systems - and countries where caudillismo
was of a purer type.
Chile stands out clearly from the general
trend. It is a self-contained country which during
most of the nineteenth century could be controlled,
both strategically and economically, by a small
landed elite based in the central valley. This
elite had little to gain by encouraging
caudillismo. Even so, it was unable to avoid a
period of upheaval in the years immediately
following independence in 1817. Between 1817 and
1830 there were thirty changes of government.
After 1830 civilian oligarchs, led by Diego
Portales, began a serious process of de-
militarisation. The measures taken included purges
of officers, mainly Liberals, thought to be out of

sympathy with the government and better organisation of the army which remained. Chilean governments also attended, more carefully than some others, to obvious military grievances. In Nunn's words, "salaries were paid on time".[1] Governments' ability to do this naturally required a moderately well developed bureaucratic structure and some significant sources of income; not all South American governments were as well placed as the Chilean in these crucial respects. The Portales system also involved the creation of a civilian militia - the Guardia Civil - to keep the military in check. Finally, the strategy involved the social (rather than professional) homogenisation of the officer corps. This began with the setting up of a War College in 1832. Its object however was not to expand and professionalise the army, but to restrict and narrow recruitment into it. "The entrance requirements were prohibitive to all but the best educated aspirants to cadet status. Cadets were no longer recruited from the more modest sections of society and this helped to create an extremely homogenous and ingrown cadet and officer corps."[2]

This civilianisation did not occur all at once. Several unsuccessful revolts broke out in the 1830s. Civilianisation was, however, possible because the elite was sufficiently united to adopt status criteria which could be imposed upon the military as well as civil society; it was also sufficiently organised and affluent to maintain a substantial armed presence - in the civil guard as well as the army - which was paid on time. This ability to maintain order was rewarded with the stability which in turn allowed the pursuit of economic development; this further provided the central government with resources. Meanwhile, the military retained a considerable role. It defeated Peru and Bolivia in the war of 1836-8 - a victory which was at that time considered against the odds. Throughout the rest of the country, there were occasional military revolts - none of them successful - and some limited military actions; a Navy skirmish with Spain in 1864, several war scares with Argentina, and in 1879-1883 a comprehensive victory over Peru and Bolivia. There was also a considerable amount of activity against the Arauco Indians on the Southern frontier.

In Brazil there was not even a short caudillo period. The monarchy retained power and the system was used to create and reproduce a Brazilian nobility into which military officers were, on occasion, individually co-opted. The military in Brazil, unlike Chile, were not themselves very much recruited from the elite; more often there was something of a caste element.[3] However, military rank was largely a matter of ascription - of social status rather than bureaucratic performance - and the top military leaders were reconciled to the system by their overriding concern to keep Brazil together as a state rather than allowing this kind of fragmentation which occurred in post-independence Spanish America. The Duque de Caxias, for example, was willing to sacrifice his early republican principles for the higher virtue of national unity.[4] However, the civilian elite remained suspicious of the army throughout the Empire and set up a variety of civil militias as counter-weights to it, or as instruments to guarantee order in localities without the need for military intervention. In Brazil, the vastness of the territory and the system of landownership made this system hard to avoid. However, the army remained in existence as a potential or actual counter-weight to serious rebellions or separatist movements. Perhaps because of the success of civilians in controlling it, the prestige of the military declined up until 1865 and so did the social basis of its recruitment.

In the rest of South America, there was far less stability. Without reviewing the <u>caudillo</u> period in detail[5] some general points can be made. The period has often been seen, very much like the American Wild West, as a heroic or epic one - and for much the same reason as the Wild West, which is that effective central authority was lacking. Contemporaries no doubt hankered for the sheriff but some later novelists and poets romanticised the earlier period (though Conrad[6] decidedly did not). Garcia Marquez's[7]

> Colonel Aureliano Buendía organised thirty-two armed uprisings and he lost them all. He had seventeen male children by seventeen different women and they were exterminated one after the other on a single night before the oldest one had reached the age of thirty-five. He survived fourteen

attempts on his life, seventy-three ambushes, and a firing squad. He lived through a dose of strychnine in his coffee that was enough to kill a horse. He refused the order of merit which the President of the Republic awarded him. He rose to be Commander in Chief of the Revolutionary forces ...

At its extreme, fact did not differ much from fiction. Thus, in Bolivia for example, in 1848 there were no less than fifteen rebellions and "it is somewhat misconceived to refer to the army rather than armies".[8] Armies were small but top-heavy with officers; in 1869 Melgarejo's army consisted of 7 generals, 119 jefes and 345 officers to command 1,996 men.[9] Many of these surplus officers eventually chose the losing side in a "Revolution" and were paid off. Military pensions became a major drain on the state treasury. Nor was this drain restricted to Bolivia. In Venezuela, the first census in Carabobo in 1873 indicates that, of an adult male population of 22,952 there were 3,450 commissioned officers, including 627 colonels and 449 generals.
The economic and military situation of post-independence Spanish America was certainly conducive to caudillismo. Caudillo armies were for the most part based on association of large landowners whose peons would be enrolled for military service. Livestock areas, with their gauchos, could produce rebel armies, militarily competent by the standards of the time, with great regularity. Conversely, bankrupt state authorities could not easily afford to maintain large standing armies - and a large, unpaid standing army was more of a menace than a help. Thus, competing factions of landowners could put armies into the field that would dwarf those of any central authority; in the Venezuelan Federal war of 1859-64, for example, some 40,000 men died at a time when the regular army stood at 3,500.[10] Moreover, caudillismo sometimes fed upon itself, as the successful leader needed to pay off his supporters and perhaps even potential troublemakers from outside his entourage. These pay-offs further impoverished the state, worsened conditions for private capital formation, discouraged international economic contacts and so made it harder for the new government to resist further rebellion. Moreover, caudillismo did not offer a peaceful means of political succession; if

a military leader did find himself able to pacify
his country and ensure a measure of stable
government, his death might unloose more of the
same turmoil which had originally led to his
emergence. At other times, however, caudillismo
could for a time be a stabilising force. Lynch had
portrayed Rosas' Argentina as a Leviathan which
emerged as a direct result of the earlier state of
nature.[11] A few years of peace might, if other
conditions were propitious, encourage a degree of
national prosperity which enabled those who
benefited from it to talk of republican
institutions, stable governments and regular
elections - in short, of political predictability
which might give economic progress a chance.

Overall, then, there were two opposite poles
of political organisation, best reflected by Brazil
and Bolivia. At one end was civilian aristocratic
(or oligarchic) control through internal unity (the
monarchy in Brazil, aristocratic clubs in Chile),
secure property and a distance from civil society.
There was, in other words, a secure status
hierarchy which was attractive to bankers,
investors and settlers and which made possible the
serious beginnings of capitalist development. At
the other end was a less settled but more heroic
pattern in which, to paraphrase Karl Marx, a man
could be a gaucho in the morning, a general in the
afternoon and either a President or a corpse in the
evening. While there was a military, however,
there was no real military structure except in the
comic opera sense; there were several times more
generals in Carabobo in 1873 than there are in the
whole of Venezuela today. The military
institution, in a bureaucratic sense, barely
existed. Military organisation was instead based
closely on the organisation of civil society,
particularly on the hacienda and through the
cacique system of recruitment through personal
influence. The caudillo's objective was the
national treasury as much as political power as
such, and there were few if any serious principles
involved in the various conflicts. The pattern was
not one of unqualified instability, however, and it
did have the effect of gradually centralising
political power; autocracy tempered by bouts of
acute instability tended to replace more
consistently anarchic social organisation.
However, before serious professionalisation of the

military could begin, other changes had to take place.

THE BEGINNINGS OF PROFESSIONALISM

Serious military professionalism got underway at different times in the various South American republics but generally began at sometime between the 1860s and the First World War. "Professionalism" has been a rather over-used word in relation to military studies, and it is worth trying to be clear about the definition. Professionalism can occur only if at least one absolute pre-condition is met. This is the development of a centralised coercive structure which, in Max Weber's words, can successfully claim a monopoly of legitimate authority over the national territory. (Legitimacy, in this sense, has no normative content; it merely means that the authority is obeyed). A military institution cannot be professionalised if it is vulnerable to defeat by irregulars (full scale guerrilla warfare is another matter altogether in that guerrillas are counter-professionals). We have already seen, however, that irregulars did in many cases possess the advantage against the official military in various South American countries during the nineteenth century; as late as the 1890s irregulars were victorious against standing armies in Peru, Colombia and Venezuela. Centralised military authority could only defeat irregulars once the state itself acquired the ability to maintain a standing military, pay salaries on time and purchase up-to-date weaponry. Economic development had a crucial part to play here. World-wide technical change helped as well; in Europe 1848 was the last time that popular rebellion could defeat state power through the use of barricades and other means of popular struggle. By 1871 even the recently defeated French army had acquired the tactics and weaponry to repress a major uprising in the national capital. In even the poorer countries of South America, the military threat posed by irregulars had ceased by 1914.

As for actual definition, professionalism relates to the internal structure of the military. It involves the bureaucratically-determined allocation of command and rank according to defined procedures. There must be a defined base of recruitment, a career structure, a substantial degree of internal autonomy and a set of specifically military values. A higher level of professionalisation is reached as movement occurs toward increasingly bureaucratic norms for promotion (i.e. as formal qualifications and institutional qualities replace status), a higher level of military education and an increasing degree of institutional coherence. This definition contains one possible paradox. It is by no means obvious that, beyond a certain point, further institutional or bureaucratic regularity leads to further improvement in fighting performance. It has indeed been suggested that modern South American militaries have become too bureaucratic to be operationally effective. However, since this discussion is not concerned with fighting capacity as such, professionalism can be defined in terms of progress in an educational and bureaucratic direction. Whether or not this implies progress in any other direction is an empirical and not a definitional question.

Organisational theory suggests a further point, as hypothesis rather than definition; when serious professionalisation begins, it is likely to create forces within the military pressing for its further development; these are likely to create tensions within the organisation as some officers will be threatened by continuing professionalisation. One may expect to find a "generation gap" between older, senior officers and younger ones who have taken advantage of superior education and training facilities. Even more crucially, professionalisation is likely to create tensions between the military and particular civilian authorities and interests, as an extension of military professionalism reduces the discretion which civilians can enjoy over matters which the military comes increasingly to define as lying within its own sphere of influence. This may lead to a direct reversal of the conventional (Huntingtonian) notion that professionalism will reduce the political role of the military. However, the effects of military professionalism upon politics are complex and need further exploration.

As a process, professionalisation can be both gradual and open-ended; and its political implications will be complex and variable. Nevertheless, one crucial and general point can be made; the serious beginning of professionalism marks the point at which it can first be said that the military comes to have interests of its own, notionally separate from those of groups or classes within civil society. Yet in South America at least, the nature and timing of professionalisation, and its political implications, related directly to developments within civil society.

In the Brazilian case, the seminal event was the 1865-70 Brazil war against Paraguay which Brazil ultimately won but only after a great deal of difficulty. The war itself was perhaps the last hurrah of the pre-professional army. Its immediate effect was to increase the size and status of the military and the opportunities for upward mobility which it offered. There were battlefield promotions from the ranks of sergeants and enlisted men and the war also enabled middle ranking officers who fought well to win rapid promotion. Gaps were created both by military expansion, during the war, and by death from disease.

However, when the war ended the size of the army was reduced and, in political terms, the status quo ante was largely restored although slow and limited attempts at reform were made during the 1870s.[12] From the standpoint of the monarchical system, slow and partially aborted reform was the worst of both worlds; disappointed military expectations bred tensions. After 1870 the army's share of the national budget fell from 21% to 10.3%.[13] There were real declines in pay, manpower and military facilities. Even worse for younger officers, there was no clear procedure for the retirement of their seniors; "it might not be an exaggeration to call the post-1870 hierarchy a gerontocracy, for it was not uncommon to find officers still on active duty well into their seventies."[14]

Those officers who reached the top during the Paraguayan War remained staunchly monarchist and conservative. Many of them were well-born. Simmons finds that "of the twenty-six distinguished army and naval officers who served in the period of this study (1853-1889), only nine were listed as of humble origin; of the navy officers, only one could be so classified."[15] Their immediate juniors, however, socially less exclusive and professionally less favoured, began to take a decided interest in professionalism. In 1871 a group of officers set up an unofficial "military institute" but this was soon disbanded after senior officers came to fear that it might factionalise the army. However, pressure continued and "war generation" officers founded the <u>Revista do Exercito Brasileiro</u> in 1882, and also helped set up the Military Club in 1887. This was also the first generation to stress corporate military interests against those of the monarchy; previous military leaders, notably the Duque de Caxias, had served the system before the military - supporting the monarchy on the pragmatic ground that it was a defence against the chaos and fragmentation through which Spanish America was passing. As early as 1865 younger officers tried to take the bold step of setting up a military-political party but their military seniors rejected the idea. It was, however, the generation below, which had not fought in the Paraguayan war at all, that was the most active in the overthrow of the monarchy in 1889 and in the military-politics which followed. These younger officers had benefited from the improvements in military education pressed for by their seniors and were much beter formed professionally than their elders. This younger generation also came more often from urban and middle class backgrounds.

This later period also saw an increase in political activity by sergeants and enlisted men. Although many of these were press ganged and eager to desert, there were avenues of mobility through the ranks. The younger officers, and some NCOs and enlisted men, were also very much influenced by changing political ideas - and particularly positivism and republicanism which were imported from Europe and influential within civil society. At the root of this political activity was a conflict which was superficially similar to that in the United States a generation before; the monarchy was supported by slave-owning northern plantation interests and increasingly opposed by a southern bourgeoisie, centred particularly in Sâo Paulo and on the growing of coffee. The south wanted to attract migrants from Europe and to tie itself to the metropolitan centres of economic power; it found that a hereditary monarchy, a caste nobility and the institution of slavery were major handicaps to its aspirations. Increasingly after 1870, therefore, republican and abolitionist civilian politicians began looking for military support; in some cases they found it. Republican Party leaders deliberately began courting the military, inviting them to join the Republican clubs set up at the time. The government then tried to impose "discipline" on these politicised officers. The rest of the military resented this and closed ranks. A key step here was the formation of the Military Club in 1887. Finally in an atmosphere of growing crisis the monarchy was overthrown in a civil-military coup.

The overthrow of the monarchy in 1889 only briefly moved the military to the centre of the political stage. Officers did, however, achieve one significant victory in the Constituent Assembly which was set up in 1890 and drafted the Constitution of 1891. Military delegates managed to get the following clause inserted into the Constitution.

> The land and sea forces are permanent national institutions destined for the defence of the country without and the maintenance of the laws within. The armed forces are essentially obedient, within the limits of the law, to their superior officers and obliged to support the constitutional institutions.[16]

As Keith points out, there are three key parts to this statement. The stipulation that the forces are permanent institutions, which was explicitly insisted upon by the military delegates, was intended to guard against any possible dissolution of the military and its replacement by the various local militias which (as part of the 1889 settlement) the state governors insisted on setting up. The fear that Brazil might some day be dismembered was still not quite dead. Secondly, the task of "maintenance of the laws within" could give the military the task of controlling internal politics. Finally "obedient within the limits of the law" begged the question of what these limits were and whether the military could intervene if it deemed them breached. Subsequently, it would be the military which would decide what the law was and how it should be enforced.

In immediate political terms the military in 1891 began a retreat from politics. The factor which precipitated military withdrawal was the naval revolt of 1893-4. The navy had previously felt left out of the improvement in military status following the 1889 revolution. In 1893 it joined dissident politicians in Rio Grande do Sul; the rising became a major civil war with around 10,000 dead.[17] When the Federal government finally triumphed, the way was clear for a down-grading of the military and a further strengthening of state militias. These were generally used to keep public order and to settle political scores within states. In the more economically developed states this extended to strike-breaking and other means of class control. Presidents from Sâo Paulo, now the economic heartland of Brazilian capitalism, subsequently came to dominate national politics and up until 1914 at least, could see little role for a professional and central military institution. State militias were generally organised along ascriptive lines, with an overlap between landownership and military command. Nevertheless, the militias of the larger Brazilian states came to enjoy a status which was increasingly denied to the central military institution; in 1906 Sâo Paulo recruited a French military mission to organise its state militia. Significantly, this decision followed a year in which there was intense strike activity and lower class mobilisation - all broken up by the state militia. At the outbreak of the First World War, the <u>forca publica</u> of Sâo Paulo was "better paid, better equipped and better armed" than the central military institution.[18]

Civilian interests which had eagerly recruited the military to do battle with the monarchy and the old social order thus became no less eager to dispense with them once the task had been accomplished. The military-political leaders of the abolition proved unable to resist this pressure because, instead of seeking a defined professional identity, they instead sought to develop their careers in politics in an individualistic and often chaotic way. The period of turbulence and near anarchy which resulted only strengthened the resolve of civilians to keep the military in a backwater.[19]

Having lost power and seen its influence diminished, the military eventually turned once more to "professional" and institutional development. Military manoeuvres in the field, which had been suspended in 1885, were resumed in 1905.[20] In 1906, for the first time, some officers were sent for training abroad - in Germany. By 1910 Prussian-trained officers had returned and began to talk about the need for military reform. In 1913 there appeared the first issue of <u>A Defesa Nacional</u>; its editorial board consisted of 12 lieutenants and 8 captains. This last point further illustrates one of the features of gradual professionalisation - it tends to start from the bottom. Better education, more demanding recruitment and training procedures tend first to increase the quality of young officers. These then come to see their seniors as lacking in military virtues but as nevertheless more favoured than they; this makes for a sense of relative deprivation. Moreover, professionalisation in the sense of better training almost invariably precedes any rationalisation of the system of promotions. Thus older officers remain in place and promotion remains slow - unless accelerated by war or political upheaval. Moreover, at higher levels promotion remains particularist and based on clientelism.

In Brazil many of the purely military tensions to which this process gave rise were expressed in the Tenente movement of the 1920s. By then, the First World War (into which Brazil followed the United States) had shown clearly Brazil's relative military backwardness while once more giving the military an important role for a brief period before the post-war reaction set in. Conscription introduced in 1917 was a further milestone in professional development. However, by 1920 the Brazilian general staff found another matter to concern them; between 1890 and 1920 Brazil had, in general terms, been overtaken by Argentina. (In the nineteenth century Brazil had enjoyed the better of skirmishes with Argentine armies in 1828 and again in 1851-52). This was a serious matter; it was by no means out of the question that the two countries might eventually fight a war. Meanwhile technical training continued to improve slowly, notably after 1919 when a French mission was contracted although this appointment itself proved controversial. Even then progress was uneven and the Brazilian army did not greatly impress outside observers. In his 1921 Annual Report the British Minister noted that "the great failing of the army is in respect of officers, who have no idea of leadership, whose bearing is often undignified and who have but little military skill. Like the men, they are largely negroes or mulattoes."[21]

During this time, national politics was organised at both state and local level through the system of land tenure. State governors built alliances of landlords, who controlled their areas by a mixture of force and favour, and used their state militias to keep control. The state militias were used to doing the "dirty work" of repressing strikes and rebellions and ensuring that election results were satisfactory to the authorities. However, this governorship system in turn depended upon approval by the Federal President. The president frequently used the army to "intervene" various states; however, this intervention brought the federal army directly back into national politics. It was inevitable that army officers should come to feel used when activated in this way and that factional conflicts within the states would in this way have a disturbing effect upon the unity of the Federal army.

Intervention became more frequent after 1918; this may have had something to do with the personalities of the various presidents since then, widely regarded as being inflexible and unbending, but there were some socio-economic influences involved as well. The 1914-18 war had stimulated some import substituting industrialisation, particularly in Rio Grande do Sul, which came to be threatened as the world economy re-opened and the export interests of the coffee growers reasserted themselves. Even in Sâo Paulo, a dissident section of the bourgeoisie grew up after the war which wanted to open the closed and self-perpetuating local political system. Between 1920 and 1930 the Brazilian political system as a whole was in crisis and the young officers' rebellions of 1922, 1924 and 1927 (the Prestes revolt) only emphasised this fact. One young military activist, Juarez Tavora, expressed the views of many when he argued that

> The armed forces do not swear unconditional loyalty to the agents of power, but rather to the Constitution. Their role in the internal mechanism of the Republic is the guarantee of law. It is only within the limits of the law that the army's obedience - indispensable to its own discipline - must be exercised.[22]

In 1930 a revolt finally proved successful and totally changed the context of Brazilian politics.

CHILE

In Chile serious development of military professionalism can be dated fairly precisely to

1886 when Captain Körner, of the German army, arrived in Chile to set up his country's military mission. At this time, the Chilean army was (like the Brazilian in 1870) militarily victorious but increasingly aware of its organisational shortcomings. Chile's defeat of Peru and Bolivia in 1879-1883 was certainly impressive but Argentina, which was increasingly becoming a potential enemy as Argentina's "Indian frontier" was eliminated, would not be so easy. In Chile, however, military professionalisation took place alongside, and in some ways contributed to, an increasing turbulence within civil society as the political control of the large landowners was challenged increasingly by new urban forces. These socio-economic strains were largely created by the rapid economic growth which Chile came to enjoy during the 1880s. As a result, the old aristocracy "lost its cohesiveness ... and this as much as any other late nineteenth century development helped to break the hitherto strong military-aristocracy link."[23] This process of change also led, after 1918, to a prolonged political crisis since the system seemed unable to adapt.

Körner's arrival led to the setting up of the military academy in 1887. This aimed to turn "high flying" lieutenants and captains into senior officers. Körner was assisted in his task by a fairly large German mission; at the turn of the century around thirty German officers were helping to train the Chilean officer corps. Körner was certainly successful in his effort to create a professional consciousness, but - as elsewhere - a side effect of his work was to create tension between the younger "professional" officers and the older "pre-professional" ones. The high-flyers duly emerged, better trained than ever, but had fewer places to which they could fly; the top branches were occupied by older birds who had no intention of moving over or dropping off the perch.

The overthrow of Balmaceda in 1891 was led by pre-professional officers. Above all, it was led by the Navy which was even more aristocratic in its tradition than was the army. Körner, however, supported the rebels out of a desire to maintain the autonomy of his own institution. After the rebel victory, Körner was made Commander in Chief of the Chilean army and professionalisation continued. The social origins of military recruitment broadened and the level of military education improved. However, the 1891 rebellion, like the war of 1879-83, in a sense strengthened the Old Guard. War brings about battlefield promotions, and civil war creates a class of losers who can be removed. The top ranks, therefore, were filled with those who had served with distinction in one or more of these encounters, rather than those who were bureaucratically or educationally qualified. Moreover, those promoted in this way were often young and so able to remain in top positions for many years. The situation was to some extent alleviated in 1900 by the introduction of conscription; this tripled the size of the army, but it was a once-and-for-all measure which created more posts for junior than for senior officers. In 1906 a military reform programme was adopted which reduced the power of the inspector-general of the army and increased that of division commanders. This, however, had precisely the opposite effect to that intended; its object was to strengthen professionalisation by giving Chilean commanders greater control over promotion, but in practice it allowed the partial re-introduction of clientelism which further increased strains and tensions within the army. However, the efforts of successive governments to reform the promotion system further foundered against the inactivity of Congress whose conservative members wanted to maintain a say in military promotions so as to maintain a clientele. Ascription and outside contacts continued to count for more than professional qualifications for promotion to the top military posts.

Meanwhile after 1906 the military was increasingly used by a narrowly-based civilian oligarchy to break strikes and to repress lower class disturbances. Although state militias performed this role in Brazil, it was not uncommon in South America for the military to take such a direct role in social control. This did, however, entail costs for the civilian authorities. Military officers trained to seek glory in the service of their country, were not (then) used to domestic missions of repression; these seemed to reflect, at least prima facie the incompetence of the civilian authorities in not being able to resolve disputes more satisfactorily. It thus encouraged military disrespect for civilian politicians. Moreover, suppression of lower-class unrest might always create a discipline problem within the military; there have been several occasions in which junior officers, NCOs and even enlisted men have compared the disciplinary hierarchy of the military with the class hierarchy of capitalist society and suggested that both "underclasses" had interests in common. Conversely middle ranking officers, whose support was required in order to make repression effective, now found themselves indispensable to the general staff and, above them, to the government. Yet these officers had suffered most from clientelist interference with promotions and with the bureaucratic hierarchy generally.

The frustration of junior Chilean officers soon took on tangible form. A secret military lodge (the Liga Militar) was formed as early as 1907, and an apparently wide-ranging conspiracy against the government failed in 1919. The Liga was committed "to work for the progress of the army"[24] - to improve salaries, rationalise promotions and introduce earlier retirements - but it was also markedly hostile to civilians in general and civilian politicians in particular. However, many of the younger officers pinned their hopes on Alessandri who was elected president in 1920 with an ambitious programme of reform. When hope faded, in 1924, a new secret society (the Junta Militar) was formed which began to meet and discuss military grievances. One of the leaders was Major Ibañez, whose own career reflects some of the frustrations felt by the group. Ibañez was born in 1877. He entered military school in 1896 and graduated in 1898. In 1900 he was made first lieutenant. In 1903 he was sent as part of a military training mission to El Salvador where he served with distinction. He was promoted captain in 1908. Between 1912 and 1914 he attended the war academy, but was not promoted major until 1918 - when he was already forty. He was still a major in 1924. This provides almost a perfect case of a distinguished, but blocked, career of a kind which was typical of the by-now very top heavy Chilean army. The Junta Militar itself was described by the British Minister as being "composed mainly of young officers, not very well paid, weary of the dull routine of their profession, without hope of a war which might satisfy their ambitions and activities, and disgusted with the proceedings of the politicians."[25]

In fact the Junta Militar was not by any means entirely made up of young men. It consisted of one colonel, three lieutenant colonels, nine majors, 6 captains and 4 lieutenants. All were staff officers and war academy graduates, all had command of troops, and many had served abroad. The more senior officers in this group, including Ibañez himself, had twenty-five years of military service and were in their mid-forties. This career profile can be contrasted with that of the military high command whose average age, in 1924, was 54. The high command, which was post aristocratic, contained men who had risen from the rank of private and who had not attended military college; most of them had entered service prior to 1891 and had benefited from the upheaval of that year and from the increase in posts which had followed the introduction of conscription in 1900.

As in the Brazilian case, however, institutional discontents interacted with more general political ones to produce military disaffection. Alessandri's election in 1920 had been accomplished through promises of political and social reform which had greatly raised expectations which could not easily be fulfilled. A further difficulty was that the Chilean economy, which had grown strongly until 1918, then stagnated as a result of falling international demand for nitrate. Civilian conservatives feared that the resulting disappointment might be directed against themselves, particularly against their Congressional representatives who had been active in frustrating reform. Conservative congressmen indeed faced a number of hostile demonstrations in and after 1921. Faced with growing trade union militancy and increasing social mobilisation, they began to place their hope in the army. In 1921 "a distinguished General" told the British Minister that "the one hope for the country in its present state of unrest was the army."[26] Perhaps for this reason, and also because of overall demoralisation, the general staff officers did not actively suppress growing signs of unrest in the middle ranks of the army until it was too late to do so.

As was the case in Brazil, the military moved into power in Chile due to a combination of general social upheaval - in which political systems proved inadequate to cope with new social forces - and specifically military discontents. Both kinds of grievance directed some of the most able junior officers toward political activity and led them to identify their own ills with those of disaffected middle class groups (although only a small minority of officers were actively Revolutionary - men such as Prestes in Brazil and Marmaduke Grove in Chile were conspicuous by their rarity); there was thus a perception of "negative threat" - the idea that the welfare of the military institution was threatened from above rather than below both by general socio-economic mismanagement (and corruption) and by mismanagement which related specifically to the military.[27]

ARGENTINA

The Argentine economy really took off after the fall of Rosas. In 1914 Argentina was one of the six richest countries of the world; it was also 53% urban - more so than France or Germany in that year. Prosperity created a powerful class of landowners protected in the last resort by what was essentially an aristocratic army. Moreover, like most other armies in nineteenth century South America, the Argentine army enjoyed enough activity to permit rapid mobility for successful officers. The permanent conflicts with the Indians, the occasional civil war, and the war with Paraguay between 1865-70, all allowed rapid promotion for men with field achievement. Julio Roca was a colonel at 29 and a general at 40. This situaiton did not change much despite the opening of the War College by Sarmiento in 1869; this college, in any case, started on a very small scale and had no monopoly over entry into the military. The growth of Argentine prosperity, particularly dramatic after 1880, did however allow the political authorities to stimulate the professional development of the military without any of the conflicts and bottlenecks which had created such problems in Brazil and Chile.

The first prerequisite of professionalisation - effective centralisation was achieved by 1880 when Roca defeated a rebellion led by the governor of Buenos Aires. This was the last time that the central army was seriously challenged by irregulars. After 1870 the Argentine army also began to look for foreign models of organisation; the German army, after its victory over France in 1871, was an obvious choice. Under Roca, moreover, the central military authority increasingly replaced state-level militias in the various mundane tasks of social control - intervention in

outlying provinces, putting down political
oppositon and engaging in various forms of
policing.

Matters only began to change during the 1890s
when there was a border incident with a now much-
better-prepared Chile. To meet a possible threat
from Chile, conscription was introduced in 1901 and
the army then underwent considerable expansion. By
this time Argentina had experienced considerable
socio-economic change and was facing large scale
immigration from Southern Europe. The officer
corps, like the landowning elite, had to devote
some attention to the question of national
integration. Thus the military college began to
homogenise the officer corps; it began to move from
status to profession. German influence over the
formation of the officer corps increased further
although there were frustrations and tensions
relating to the German military presence. As
Schiff put it,

> Even the German-inspired Argentine general
> staff found it almost impossible to handle the
> frequently inept, overly large and
> miscellaneous officer corps. Some of its
> members had been trained along traditional
> lines with an adherence to ancient and rigid
> Spanish regulations. Others followed gaucho
> guerrilla tactics. Still others had been
> trained in a number of European countries, in
> each of which they had been taught to believe
> that that country's system was the most
> effective. Many of them, especially political
> appointees, were hardly trained at all.[28]

After considerable political conflict, the
Argentine War Academy was set up in 1900 under
German influence. In 1905 entry into the officer
corps was restricted to graduates of the Colegio
Militar. After 1906 Argentine officers were sent
to train in Germany. German influence reached its
height in the immediate pre-war period, 1908-14,
when German officers serving in Chile were given a
say in Argentine promotions. However, the Germans
in Argentina never achieved the ascendancy managed
by Captain Körner in Chile and there was greater
nationalist opposition to the whole project. Yet,
again unlike Brazil and Chile, the logic of
professionalism was followed throughout the
organisation with the result that promotion

bottlenecks were quickly broken. As Goldwert puts it,

> By 1910 the criterion for promotion had shifted from political or presidential favouritism to mastery of the techniques of modern warfare. Officers of the "Old Army" were being retired in large numbers to enforce the new criterion. A related development was the shift in control of promotions from the presidency to the professional army ... In other words, a peacetime military establishment had become the first institution of state to escape the shadow of presidentialism.[29]

As a result of this better accommodation to the demands of professionalisation, Argentina never experienced a junior officers movement as such or the military-political radicalisation that generally went with it.[30] Instead in Argentina military professionalisation appeared as an apparently successful elite response precisely to the threat of an alliance between the Radicals and a movement of junior officers. Thus in 1890 there was an unsuccessful military rising, in alliance with the Radical Party. There followed a purge of 6 generals, 4 colonels, 5 lieutenant colonels, 12 majors, 19 captains and 60 lieutenants[31], although all were later re-incorporated into the army under an amnesty. There were also military-Radical risings in 1893 and 1905. The last was quite violent and came within an ace of success although, like the others, it involved only a small minority of the officer corps. This time the army really was purged but, at the same time, Conservative fears of a repetition led both to thoroughgoing professionalisation of the military and to the passage of the Saenz Pena law of 1908 which promoted a qualified extension of the franchise and made possible the Radical victory in 1916.

Rouquie provides an excellent picture of the "early professional" army in Argentina.[32] It was formed of Argentine families (an important consideration in a country which was so heavily immigrant), mainly from urban upper-middle and middle class families. Entry into the institution would take place young - a boy was allowed to enter the Military College between 14 and 18; the period of study would last three years. Most officer cadets had attended, though not completed, civilian secondary school before deciding to attend the College.

Promotion for an officer was regular and carried out according to bureaucratic criteria. However, it was also slow and pay for junior officers was low. In 1916-17 a full General would earn eight times more than a Sub-Lieutenant who, in turn, would earn about as much as a skilled worker. A junior officer, therefore, could not easily maintain a middle class life-style (at least not in the cities). Instead, he tended to turn "austerity" into a moral virtue, and associated predominantly with other officers in the same predicament as himself. Even senior officers were not really wealthy. In 1917 the annual subscription to the Jockey Club amounted to three months salary for a Brigadier-General. There were a few officer-members of the Jockey Club but these were men with inherited money. Consequently an aristocratic minority of officers could afford strong ties with civilians, but the middle class majority could not. This aristocratic minority evinced a strong preference, in turn, for the more "aristocratic" sections of the military - notably the cavalry corps which has always played a distinctive part in Argentine military-politics.

In the provinces an officer's salary and prospects counted for far more. Senior officers serving in the provinces were often welcomed into the local aristocracy. Junior officers could also live better and were in some cases able to marry into good local families - frequently allying military status to provincial wealth - but faced the countervailing disadvantage of being more firmly under the eye of their military superiors. This often worked against any weakness junior officers may have shown for excessive civilian contact.

This Argentine army, though hierarchical and exclusive, was by no means wholly reactionary. It welcomed Yrigoyen's election in 1916 and, for a time, was well treated by him. Although the size of the officer corps remained constant during the Radical period - there were 1,394 officers on active service in 1911, 1,304 in 1917, and 1,502 in 1929 - military spending increased and so did the number of enlisted men. There was, however, no major armament programme and Yrigoyen showed no

interest at all in military-led industrialisation.
The military did find itself affected by various
currents affecting civil society. Following some
serious labour unrest during the Semana Tragica,
some soldiers and NCOs tried to form Soviets within
the army, but these were quickly suppressed. The
high command, for its part, was eager to see these
labour agitations suppressed and put pressure on
Yrigoyen to do this[33]; in the event, they had no
reason to complain at Yrigoyen's willingness to
take action. The military also became concerned
when Yrigoyen, in 1921 and 1922, tried to restore
to active service various officers purged for their
Radical stance in 1905 and earlier. In reaction to
this a secret military Lodge (Logia San Martin)
was set up in 1922 calling for the maintenance of a
professional army, but this was dissolved a few
years later after it had succeeded in its main aim
of persuading Alvear (President 1922-28) to
nominate General Justo as War Minister.

The Argentine military moved into politics in
1930 for reasons which had more to do with the
weakness of the civilian government than with the
strength of the conspiracy to overthrow it.
Yrigoyen (re-elected in 1928) had run out of
constructive ideas and preferred instead to
encourage the Radical Party to engage in
increasingly intense conflicts with the opposition
minorities which related more to issues of position
than policy.[34] Regarding the military, Yrigoyen
became increasingly willing to overrule
professional criteria by making appointments on the
basis of assumed personal loyalty. Many
conservative civilians, meanwhile, had become
influenced by Prima de Rivera in Spain and
Mussolini in Italy rather than democratic models
and did not need very much provocation to call for
an end to civilian rule. Above all, however,
Yrigoyen had become virtually senile but was
irreplaceable by his own party, and the government
simply lost its grip.

The 1930 coup was led by a military minority
and would almost certainly have failed if the
government had been better organised. Many loyal
officers waited for orders which never came.
Although the coup leaders were counting on (and
indeed received) conservative civilian support,
civilians were not at the centre of the conspiracy.
The War Academy and the younger officers there were
particularly golpista (and the jeunesse dorée

of Buenos Aires was particularly warm toward the coup[35]) largely because authoritarian government seemed the wave of the future. However, no particular sector of the military determined the success or failure of the conspiracy. There is no simple relationship between social origins, or German training, and the coup. As Potash notes, "Argentine officers were acting out of a variety of motives and not as members of a military caste."[36] Nevertheless the coup of 1930 had major and far-reaching significance for the evolution of Argentine politics - both military and civilian.

BOLIVIA

A much weaker process of professionalisation took place in a much less developed South American state - Bolivia after its devastating defeat in the War of the Pacific. There were some limited beginnings of professionalism after 1880; some officers were sent abroad for training and the military college was set up in 1891. The main obstacle to professionalisation during this period was budgetary; there were too many retired officers on pensions and not enough money in the public treasury.[37]

More serious efforts to professionalise the army followed the "Federalist Revolution" of 1900. This allowed a major purge of the old army; 317 men were retired after 1901 and further purges followed unsuccessful rebellions of 1902 and 1903. In 1907 conscription was introduced; although this was by no means widely enforced, it did increase the size of the army. The Bolivian army, however, faced one problem which its Argentine and Chilean counterparts did not. Not only was there an ethnic division of Bolivian society, but there was also a linguistic one; officers were mainly white and spoke Spanish and enlisted men were Indians who spoke Quechua. This distinction gave Quechua-speaking NCOs disproportionate importance within the army and it was difficult to refuse them commissions even though this tended to work against institutional cohesion. Thus in 1901 an NCO school was set up; it accepted men who were literate, who had four years military service (including two as NCOs) and who were of 1 metre 60 cm. in height; this last provision was subtly racist - few pure-blooded Indians would reach the necessary measurement.

The period after 1900 saw an increase in military pay and a gradual improvement in military discipline. This became increasingly necessary as the military was used to put down challenges to central authority; harassment of Indian villages was almost routine and after 1923 the military was increasingly used against the tin miners. Discipline was further strengthened by the attachment of a German military mission of a dozen officers, under Colonel Kundt, in 1911. However, Kundt and his mission had to return to Europe in 1914 but were allowed back into Bolivia in 1921. By this time the military had become distrusted by the government since the high command was believed to be hostile to the Bolivian politician Saavedra who took power at the head of a military faction in 1920. Saavedra set up a Republican Guard which briefly became a match for the military. Although the Republican Guard was later de-mobilised, there was little further progress in strengthening the Bolivian army. This remained in a state of unpreparedness until its disastrous defeat at the hands of Paraguay in the Chaco War after 1932.

VENEZUELA

Professionalisation in Venezuela took place far later than in the Cono Sur. The hesitant pace at which it took place, however, and the consequences in the shape of a young officers movement, bear certain similarities to the situation in Chile and Brazil. Centralisation began seriously under General Cipriano Castro who in 1899 led the last successful provincial revolt against Caracas. A further provincial revolt, in 1902, narrowly failed. Castro set up a General Staff early in the century entrusted with regularising criteria for promotion. Under Gomez, who replaced Castro, the military academy began functioning in 1910 and Chilean officers, hired as advisers, began working in 1913.

However, Venezuela was unusual in the degree to which President Gomez (1908-35) was able to achieve an ascendancy over the country. His very personalist form of rule set back the professional development of the Venezuelan army until the late 1930s (the Navy and Airforce, which were not perceived as political threats, were relatively freer to organise professionally). Under Gomez, the army officer corps was heavily drawn from the Andean states of the country, and particularly from Tachira which was the dictator's own state; Burggraaff estimates that between 75% and 90% of army officers during this period were Andean.[38] It was combat proven, but only against the various local insurrections which continued to threaten from time to time; promotions related to military performance in these encounters. "Anyone who exhibited valor on the battlefield could become a general without the slightest acquaintance with the rudimentary principles of military science."[39] Gomez would also promote his own favourites, who rose rapidly though the ranks at the expense of the better-trained but worse-connected academy graduates. "It was possible for an Academy graduate to remain a lieutenant until near retirement age."[40] Moreover, these junior officers were often assigned to non-military roles, such as service on Gomez' own haciendas. This proved generally unpopular. These professional discontents played an important part in a rising of young officers in 1928, in which a section of the army allied itself with student rebels such as Betancourt, Leoni and Villalba. This rising was led by an army captain, Rafael Alvarado, and three lieutenants and it enjoyed heavy support from the cadets. Its failure led to an even greater emphasis on personal loyalty within the military and a further setting back of professional development.

After the death of Gomez, serious professionalisation finally began. The military academy was re-organised and promotion procedures were regularised. However, López Contreras (Minister of War during the early 1930s and President 1936-41) had to be careful not to disturb the old Gomecista generals who continued to monopolise the senior ranks. Thus promotion was slow for the younger professionals, and the pay of junior officers remained low. Over the next dozen years, the generation gap within the military rather than diminishing, continued to intensify.

In mid-1942 a group of junior officers in the Caracas garrison began to communicate their discontents. They were soon joined by three slightly more senior officers, Major Julio César, Captain Mario Vargas and Captain Pérez Jiménez who had returned from training at Chorrillos in

Peru where, as we shall see, a junior officers movement was also developing at around this time. The group only turned themselves into a formal organisation, the UPM, in mid-1945 but by this time they were ready to act.

Outside the military, the conflict between the gomecista old guard and newer groups created by oil-based development was no less obvious than was the same conflict within the military. As with the military, the democratic civilian opposition felt that the reforms offered by the post-Gomez governments were too little too late. López Contreras did allow some degree of political organisation although he ended by deporting a number of opposition leaders. Medina Angarita, López' designated successor as President, also moved slowly to open the system and in 1945 sought the agreement of the opposition parties to a compromise presidential nominee. However, the agreement failed when the chosen successor suffered a medical breakdown and Medina chose another candidate regarded by the opposition as quite unsuitable. Meanwhile, the rapid growth of Caracas, of public and urban employment generally, and of trade union organisation had left behind the old clients of Gomez and his personalist political system. By 1945 the regime, despite the undoubted fact that it had moved some way from the old dictatorship, came to be regarded by its civilian opponents, no less than by junior officers, as a frustrating legacy from the past.

SOME COMMON FEATURES

The beginnings of military professionalisation had somewhat different consequences in each of the five countries reviewed here. There were, however, certain underlying similarities.

Serious capitalist development in South America began in the second half of the nineteenth century. Its most spectacular manifestation was the opening of the Argentine pampa and the very rapid economic development of that country, particularly after 1880. By 1930 Argentina was generally regarded as a developed country, perhaps the fifth wealthiest in the world. The Uruguayan interior also benefited immensely from new transportation techniques - particularly the refrigerated steamship. In Brazil, the coffee boom in São Paulo led to a shift in economic power from North to South and an interest in republican capitalism as against the old monarchical and slave-owning society. Chile benefited, after the War in the Pacific, from its nitrate conquests. Countries to the North, however, did not benefit to anything like the same extent; capitalist development was much weaker in Bolivia, Peru and Ecuador and, until their respective oil and coffee booms, Venezuela and Colombia.

Capitalist development in nineteenth century Latin America required foreign lending, a measure of direct foreign investment and was also facilitated by a good deal of European migration. All of these, in turn, depended upon political stability and a measure of reform. European immigrants would not want to compete with slave labour in Brazil, nor would foreign investors feel confident in a country dominated by <u>caudillos</u> and afflicted by civil war. Economic and social progress, therefore, lay in the direction of civilian government, regular elections, an impersonal judiciary etc. All of these were possible in an age before mass politics threatened and before the October Revolution led propertied interests to fear the Communist menace. Elections could be held, but literacy qualifications, nationality restrictions, the control of rural voters, or at times straightforward ballot rigging, might enable civilian elites to avoid the danger of popular power.

In the Southern Cone during this period, progress, civilian government and military professionalism appeared to go together. Economic progress enabled professionalism to take place; war colleges could be opened, regular salaries paid to conscripts, and a professional officer corps could be paid enough to make the career attractive. Moreover, the apparent stability of republican institutions and the reality, in some countries at least, of economic progress seemed to confirm the advantages of civilian rule. Propertied interests had no wish to return to the age of anarchy or arbitrary personal tyranny; the world of Thomas Hobbes had given way to that of John Locke.

Developments in weaponry made easier the maintenance of a central civilian authority. In Europe, 1848 was the last time that standing armies could be defeated by armed populations; around fifty years later, the last <u>caudillos</u> were overthrowing regular armies in South America. Railways, repeating rifles and artillery made the task progressively more difficult to accomplish unless at least a section of the regular army could be induced to defect. Military science spread with arms salesmen (who were naturally more interested in governments which could pay than those which could not) and, subsequently, with foreign missions which also improved the quality of military organisation.

External threat was another important factor in stimulating military professionalisation. There were two major wars during the nineteenth century - the War of the Triple Alliance and the War of the Pacific. There were also a number of war scares, involving Chile and Argentina and, as the twentieth century arrived, Argentina and Brazil as well as Peru, Bolivia and Chile. Brazil also played an admittedly very limited belligerent role in the First World War. Undoubtedly the possibility of major wars within South America played an important part in military preparation and thinking throughout this period.

Finally there is the more ambiguous relationship between military professionalisation and internal coercion. Here the record is varied. The Brazilian military was deliberately kept out of an internal coercive role, entrusted instead to the state militias, precisely because of fears that this would bring the military into domestic political conflict. In other countries, however, the military was often used routinely to break strikes, suppress demonstrations and - where this was a problem - defeat peasant movements or land invasions. In some cases (notably Chile) this seems to have contributed toward problems of discipline, in other cases not. It certainly emphasised the point that discipline within the militay institution needed to be tight; it would certainly be dangerous if mutinous troops or NCOs were to make common cause with striking workers or (after 1917) civilian Communists. As we shall see, such cases did occur during the 1930s.

Tight discipline was obviously an essential feature of a serious professional structure. In order to enforce it, the military needed to acquire the characteristics of a self-contained organisation; this, in turn, led to resentment at those ties to dominant civilian groups which were allowed to remain. In practical terms, professionalisation developed from the military academy. This excluded both the lower classes and also, in most cases, the sons of the very wealthy (although in Argentina, where the civilian elite remained on better terms with the military than in most other countries, there was a small but influential minority of aristocratic officers); opportunities of promotion through the ranks were consequently curtailed although this proved far more difficult to stop in Bolivia and Peru (because of the language barrier between officers and men) than in other countries. At the training college, military <u>mores</u> were inculcated, including a healthy scepticism of all things civilian and a conviction that an officer was a man apart from, and largely superior to, civil society. Moving on from the military academy, the better education, harder lifestyle and more demanding career structure imposed upon military officers further encouraged this sense of separateness and superiority.

This new pattern meant that civilian elites largely lost control over the structure and outlook of the professional military institution which they had done so much to bring into being. This development was, of course, potentially dangerous - as became clear in Brazil in the aftermath of the overthrow of the monarchy and in Argentina following military participation in Radical rebellions in 1890 and 1905. Except in Argentina, where the elite's reaction was more considered, the civilian elite sought to maintain its position by a continuing politics of clientelism - by co-opting and fostering the careers of selected military officers - in a way which the more professional but less successful soldiers could not help but resent. This resentment took the form of junior officers movements in Brazil and Chile and also (as we shall see) in Peru and Venezuela.

These junior officers movements became serious, however, only when they connected successfully with dissident groups within civil society - themselves usually opposed, in the same way but for different reasons, to the old oligarchic political systems. This alliance, specific in terms of time and place, has often but erroneously been seen as evidence of "middle class" military behaviour in a universal sense. In Brazil, military rebellions became fused with a broader-based movement against the government in

1930; in Chile the general political chaos created by demands for social reforms, and attempts to block them, allowed a junior officers movement to take control of the state after 1924; in Venezuela an alliance between junior officers and Acción Democrática led to the armed overthrow of the government in 1945. These movements are the subject of the next chapter.

NOTES

1   F. Nunn, The Military in Chilean History; essays on civil-military relations 1810-1973, (U. of New Mexico; 1976).
2   Ibid, p. 42.
3   J. Murilho de Carvalho, "Elite and State-Building in Imperial Brazil", (Ph.D., Standford; 1975).
4   R. A. Hayes, "The Formation of the Brazilian Army and the Military Class Mystique 1500-1853", 1-27 in H. Keith and R. A. Hayes, Perspectives on Armed Politics in Brazil, (U. of Arizona; 1976), p. 22.
5   See, for example, J. Lynch, Argentine Dictator; Juan Manuel de Rosas 1829-52, (Clarendon Press; 1981), R. Gilmore Caudillism and Militarism in Venezuela 1810-1910, (Ohio U.P.; 1964) and J. Dunkerley, "Reassessing Caudillismo in Bolivia 1825-79" in Bulletin of Latin American Research, Vol. 1, No. 1, October 1981.
6   J. Conrad, Nostromo.
7   G. Garcia Marquez, A Hundred Years of Solitude, (Penguin; 1972), p. 100.
8   Dunkerley in Bulletin of Latin American Research, p. 15.
9   Ibid, p. 16.
10 J. Dunkerley, "The Politics of the Bolivian Army; Institutional Development 1879-1935", (D.Phil., Oxford; 1979).
11 Lynch, Argentine Dictator.
12 W. S. Dudley, "Professionalization and Politicization as Motivational Factors in the Brazilian Army Coup of 15 November 1889", Journal of Latin American Studies, Vol. 8, No. 1, (May 1976), 101-125, and Campos Coelho, Em Busca de Identidade.

[13] Campos Coelho, *Ibid*, and W. S. Dudley, "Institutional Sources of Discontent in the Brazilian Army 1870-1889", Hispanic American Historical Review, Vol. 55, No. 1.

[14] Dudley, *Ibid*, p. 41.

[15] C. Simmons, "Military Leaders in National Politics 1853-1889", 27-51, in Keith and Hayes Eds., Perspectives on Armed Politics in Brazil, p. 37.

[16] Quoted in H. Keith, "Armed Federal Interventions in the States during the Old Republic", in Keith and Hayes Eds., Perspectives on Armed Politics in Brazil, p. 53.

[17] C. Cortes, "Armed Politics in Rio Grande do Sul", in Keith and Hayes, Ibid.

[18] F. Nunn, Yesterday's Soldiers; European Military Professionalism in South America 1890-1940, (Univ. of Nebraska; 1983), p. 22.

[19] Campos Coelho, Em Busca de Identidade, Ch. 3.

[20] F. Nunn, "Military Professionalism and Professional Militarism in Brazil 1870-1970; Historical Perspectives and Political Implications", Journal of Latin American Studies, Vol. 4, No. 1, 29-54 (May 1972).

[21] FCO 371 A1857/1857/6.

[22] Quoted in Keith, "Armed Federal Interventions" in Keith and Hayes, Perspectives on Armed Politics.

[23] F. Nunn, The Military in Chilean History, p. 71.

[24] Quoted in F. Nunn, Chilean Politics 1920-31; The Honourable Mission of the Armed Forces, (U. of New Mexico; 1970).

[25] Hohler to Chamberlain 22 January 1925 (A982/193/9).

[26] Vaughan to Curzon 23 July 1921 (A6488/851/9).

[27] For the notion of negative threat see C. Clapham and G. Philip Eds., Political Dilemmas of Military Regimes, (Croom Helm; 1984).

[28] W. Schiff, "The Influence of the German Armed Forces and the War Industry of Argentina; German Co-operation with the Argentine military", in Hispanic American Historical Review, Vol. 52, No. 3 (August 1972), 436-456.

[29] M. Goldwert, "The Rise of Modern Militarism in Argentina", extract in B. Loveman and T. Davies, The Politics of Antipolitics, (U. of Nebraska; 1978).

[30] D. Canton, La Politica de los Militares Argentinos 1900-1971, (Buenos Aires; 1971).

31 A Rouquie, Pouvoir Militaire et Societe Politique en Republique Argentine, (Paris; 1976).
32 Ibid.
33 D. Rock, Politics in Argentina 1890-1930; the Rise and Fall of Radicalism, (Cambridge U.P.; 1975).
34 P. Smith, Argentina and the Failure of Democracy; conflict among political elites 1904-55, (U. of Wisconsin; 1974).
35 Rouquie, op. cit., p. 185.
36 R. Potash, The Army and Politics in Argentina 1928-45; Yrigoyen to Peron, (Stanford; 1969), p. 54.
37 Dunkerley, "Institutional Development".
38 W. J. Burggraaff, The Venezuelan Armed Forces in Politics 1935-59, (Colombia; 1972), p. 15.
39 Ibid, p. 18.
40 Ibid, p. 22.

Chapter 5

THE MILITARY INSTITUTION IN POLITICS; THE FIRST
WAVE

At the end of 1930, Chile, Argentina,
Venezuela, Peru and Brazil were all either under
military rule or military-backed civilian regimes.
In 1920 only Venezuela and perhaps Peru belonged in
this category. In Argentina and Chile military
rule occurred despite the fact that civil society
(or as some would say the political culture) had
already achieved a considerable degree of
sophistication; a number of writers, modernisation
theorists before their time, openly predicted prior
to the September 1930 coup in Argentina that such
an event could not possibly occur in so urbanised
and developed a country. In Peru and Venezuela,
more backward despite Venezuela's phenomenal oil
boom, the revolt against clientelism and
dictatorship (led, in both countries as elsewhere
in South America, by junior officers) had yet to
reach maturity. Meanwhile, in all cases there
remained the question of how military rule was to
be organised; in no country did the military have a
political mission as such. Instead a leader, or
group of leaders, either emerged from the military
or (if civilian or retired) acquired a personal
following within it. Political success required
that this be maintained; this, in turn, required
something of a juggling act between the various
forces involved in politics at that time.
One necessary condition for future stability
following a military coup was that the revolted
officers kick away the ladder which they had
mounted. Otherwise there was the danger that one
successful military revolt would open the
floodgates and lead to anarchy within military
ranks. One possible technique of stabilising the
situation was a process of distancing, according to

which the military-political leader would present
himself as an ordinary President (come to power by
unorthodox means) dealing at arms length with the
rest of the military. However, after junior
officers movements had been successful, it was
necessary to pay more attention to the military
constituency; if it was to be pacified, it had to
be offered something in return. Although the
military institution did not always keep control of
the presidents which it had made, it benefited from
the apparent threat which it now posed to political
authorities of all kinds. Yet if military
presidents sometimes ruled, the military
institution ruled only indirectly. In this guise,
the military could act as a court of last resort to
which opposition forces, as well as those within
the government, might occasionally appeal. A
military-backed president, therefore, at the
minimum had to ask (and accept) military advice on
issues of military concern and to avoid doing
anything which might bring the military into
disrepute. In practice (during the period in
question) this involved retaining at least modest
popularity (not necessarily majority support)
within civil society; this, in turn, involved
maintaining a real social base.

These latter conditions bear directly upon the
military relationship with civil society. The
dilemmas facing military rulers of this type have
been extremely well explained by Huntington.[1]
The context, it should be remembered, is one of
continuing economic growth and developing social
organisation. Military rulers, Huntington argued,
could try to retain power and restrict
participation; the Argentine military tried to do
this after 1930. The problem here, however, is
that governments which sought support only from
traditional classes risked isolation from new
groups which were constantly in the process of
formation. Such isolation made gradual transition
from conservative rule difficult; there was the
danger of a violent lurch when the traditional
mechanisms for maintaining control broke down.
Alternatively these rulers could try to retain
power and expand participation - as Vargas and
Perón were to do. However, a military leader who
turned himself into a "populist" - a leader, in
other words, who sought to use his official
position to win popular support from below by
taking an (at least) rhetorically radical stand

against other established interests, risked losing his military base. Alternatively the military could seek to resolve its dilemma by handing back power to civilians. This happened in Chile in 1932 and it is possible that the Argentine military made a serious mistake in refusing to allow Alvear's moderate Radical party to win open elections during the 1930s. However, in most cases, returning power meant allowing back precisely those forces against whom military action was taken in the first place - the old guard in Brazil, APRA in Peru, Alessandri and the Conservatives in Chile or the Radical Party in Argentina. For reasons which were personal and institutional as much as socio-economic, this tactic was adopted only by the unpopular and rapidly fragmenting Chilean military. In other cases, military-backed regimes which held power in 1930 remained recognisably the same until the end of the Second World War.

The restoration of military quiescence after the political upheavals of the period was by no means an easy task. In most cases it required that the degree of professionalism be considerably extended. It is generally true that South American military institutions frequently seek to become "more professional" after a period of political turbulence but there were, as we shall see, good reasons for the transformations of the 1930s.

BRAZIL

A case in point is that of Brazil. Here only a minority of officers had supported Vargas in his overthrow of the "Old Republic"; the revolt was made by a lieutenant colonel and did not have the support of a single general on active duty.[2] The immediate effect of this was to increase further the turbulence in military ranks, already considerable after the failed revolts of 1922 and 1924. Senior officers, particularly those who had not taken part in the 1930 movement (and these were the majority), felt threatened that the junior officers might continue their political activities and even radicalise. The politically active junior officers themselves were unwilling to be cheated of the fruits of their victory by the rules of military seniority. The military as a whole was worried that the amnesty offered in November 1930 to officers expelled or cashiered after the revolts of 1922 and 1924, would further complicate promotion prospects. Immediately after the 1930 coup, therefore, "almost all of the leading generals of the era" were conspiring in one form or another.[3]

The senior and/or conservative officers set up the Uniâo de Classe Militar movement in 1931 while the reformers set up a club, the 3 de Octubro, in the same year. This club had 200 original members; a recent study of 88 of these, on whom information is available, found that 27 were civilians. Of the 61 military men, seven were generals, another seven were colonels or majors, nineteen were captains and twenty four were lieutenants. The identity of four other military men is unknown.[4] The club definitely aligned itself on the "Left" of the political spectrum; it supported Vargas strongly against the regionalist politicians of the "Old Republic". Gradually, however, merely reformist officers began to reveal a difference of approach from the more radical ones. In 1932 some influential reformist officers, notably Goes Monteiro and Oswaldo Aranha, withdrew from the club and this then went into a decline. After 1932 the situation changed again after the defeat of the Sâo Paulo rising. After this revolt 10% of the officer corps was expelled; these were later amnestied but still forbidden to return to active duty. Thus, the tenentes, led by Goes Monteiro and the politically orthodox younger officers led by Dutra (who was a lieutenant on the wrong side in 1930 but won his way back into favour after helping to put down the Sâo Paulo revolt of 1932) found it easier to come to some sort of arrangement.

NCOs were also important in the 1930 revolt. Many NCOs were more radical than their officers and more politically active. NCO revolts failed in 1931 and 1932 and, an even larger NCO revolt, modelled on that of Batista in Cuba, failed in 1933. The manifesto of the NCOs who rose in 1933 was signed by 412 sergeants; it stressed the low social origins of its members and made a number of demands including the right of NCOs to enrol in military academies and to become officers. The 1933 revolt was put down harshly. Three leaders were shot and many others were tortured. As the Brazilian army was structured in 1930, NCOs played a particularly important role. The possibility of commissions for petty officers remained open (it was not ended until 1937); battlefield promotions were commonly awarded, officially on a temporary basis but there was a tendency for these to become permanent. In 1932 there were 1,459 sergeants commissioned in this way and only 324 academy trained second lieutenants. The inevitable conflict between NCOs and junior, academy-trained officers which stemmed from this situation was after 1933 resolved in favour of the junior officers.

The dangers of fragmentation or revolution inherent in this situation was quickly apparent to moderate officers on both sides of the political divide. Goes Montiero, a former tenente, expressed the fear that "politics would continue to be practiced inside the army preventing the implementation of the politics of the army".[5] Carvalho outlines three different "role models" as they existed in the early 1960s and a fourth which came to command acceptance as a synthesis of the earlier ones.

1 Traditionalist model. This stressed the external role of the military and wanted to keep out of politics. It was expressed in the União de Classe Militar.

2 Reformist/Interventionist - i.e. Tenente. This expressed the view that "the army is the vanguard of the people" and lay behind the Clube 3 Octubro.

3 Radical/Communist. This was influenced by Prestes, the military hero and tenente of the 1920s later turned Communist. This wanted a complete restructuring of the military to turn it into a radical political force.

The third view was politically unrealistic. Military radicals had little chance of building bridges with the generally anti-military civilian Left. Within the military, NCOs were still a career class with men continuously re-enlisting and hoping for promotion to officer. They had few links remaining with civil society. Enlisted men, despite the formal existence of conscription, still came from "lumpen" sectors rather than the working class as a whole and were unpromising material for Revolutionaries. However, the NCOs revolt of 1933 and the full-scale Communist rising of 1935 led both to a closing of ranks and to a greater sense among the "traditional" officers that internal politics could not be divorced entirely from external security. The result was a synthesis of outlook among non-radical officers, which was given full expression in 1937 with the imposition of the Estado Novo, and marked

> an alliance of the military reformists and those in the armed forces who considered themselves professionals. The latter accepted interventionism, provided it was done under the control of the hierarchy; the former accepted hierarchical control, provided the hierarchy agreed to intervention.[6]

The late 1930s also saw a series of reforms within the Brazilian military aimed at imposing tighter hierarchical control. The system of conscription was tightened up so as to allow a higher turnover of soldiers. Conditions of work for NCOs improved. Efforts were also made to eliminate the rank of sergeant as a career grade. In 1939 it was decreed that nobody would be allowed to remain a sergeant for more than nine years. The size of the officer corps was increased - it more than doubled between 1930 and 1944, from 4,185 to 10,087. The military academy was reformed and given a monopoly on entry into the officer corps. These reforms aimed to put more emphasis on ideological indoctrination of cadets. Entry restrictions were also imposed in order to homogenise intake into the officer corps - or, more crudely to keep out "Jews, Blacks, sons of immigrants or of unmarried parents, and candidates whose parents were suspected of having undesirable political views".[7] In 1937 the military was also dis-enfranchised in order to prevent the possibly disruptive effect of political competition.

During the 1930s the military also increasingly achieved ascendancy in Brazilian politics. Liberal opponents of the military were weakened by their divisions and the defeat of the São Paulo revolt of 1932. Later in the decade, the military seemed to many to be a lesser evil than the Communists or the Fascists, who revolted unsuccessfully in 1938. Many leading civilians, threatened by these various developments, were willing to concede on the political question in return for assurances on the social question. The imposition of the openly dictatorial <u>Estado Novo</u> by Vargas in 1937 was widely accepted by the Brazilian elite.

The late 1930s also saw the beginning of an important new development. This was the creation of an embryonic military-industrial complex. It was true since 1930 that military officers had served freely in non-military positions. Between 1930 and 1938, 40 military officers were appointed <u>interventors</u> in Brazilian states compared with 47 civilians. However, only from 1937 can it be said that "a civilian-military technocracy began to emerge".[8] In 1938 the CNP, the state oil company, was set up with direct military backing and involvement.[9] The military also moved directly into the development of the steel industry and were invited to participate with the first motor engine development in Brazil. Already the military had purchased many of its requirements locally and after 1939 the connections between the military and its suppliers became increasingly close; it was always military policy to "buy Brazilian" where this was feasible.[10] During the war the War Ministry set up a "Department of Manufacturing" in order to liaise directly with civilian-run companies.

A stronger, more ordered and more powerful military institution also had important implications for national politics. Vargas' triumph in 1930 was already, in a sense, the triumph of the centre against the regions - notably against the powerful states of São Paulo and Minas Gerias. This centralising perspective was strengthened further after the defeat of the São Paulo rising in 1932. Following this defeat, the São Paulo state militia began a decline. Later in the decade Brazilian followers of rival European totalitarianisms began to mobilise dangerously - with failed revolts from both Communists and Fascists. The Integralista movement was the more dangerous of the two because it was undoubtedly a mass organisation and also had an appeal within the military, particularly within the Navy.[11]

By 1937, however, the junior officers of 1930 - Goes Monteiro, Juarez Tavora and (on the other side) Gaspar Dutra - had now reached senior positions in a much better organised military institution. They were able to deliver the support of the army to Vargas so that the latter could declare his <u>Estado Novo</u> dictatorship. The Integralistas were declared illegal (along with all other parties) in 1938. Connections with civil society, between 1937 and 1945, were "top-down" rather than representative. Patronage and clientelism were undoubtedly important but this period was also the nearest Brazil has ever come to a full corporate state. There can be no doubt that the tenente leadership was fully behind this new development.

It is only superficially a paradox that the radical tenentes of the 1920s supported the dictatorial rule of the Estado Novo. The Estado Novo was not less authoritarian than the Old Republic but it was different in three main ways. It was more centralist, more efficient, and more concerned to promote industrialisation. In retrospect, then, what had offended the junior officers was not private property itself - despite the radicalism of many tenente pronouncements - but rather the political system and distribution of power with which it was associated. The landowning and commercial bourgoisie of Sâo Paulo and Minas Gerias, as controller of the political system, had to be fought; and it was fought and defeated in 1930 and again in 1932. The "new" industrial bourgeoisie, from the same states, subordinated to military-led plans of national development and industrialisation, was treated as a valuable ally and supporter. The military hierarchy had, during this decade, climbed into membership of the top elite (and individual officers whose causes had prospered booked their own places within the elite). The relative stability which these new arrangements produced is well documented by Carvalho in a table which is reproduced below.

Table 5.1 Military "incidents" in Brazil 1930-45.

Major Actors	1930-4	1935-9	1940-5	Total
Generals	9	6	2	17
Other Officers	15	12	2	29
NCOs	20	13	1	34
Enlisted Men	6	7	1	14
Total	50	38	6	94

Carvalho (1982), p. 195.

The imposition of the Estado Novo also suggests another important factor in the attitude of the new military leadership - its pro-Axis sympathies. There was a considerable mutual courtship between Brazil and Germany between 1938 and 1940. However, ultimately the United States was able to win a kind of support from the Brazilian government - it could, after all, bid higher. A US army mission was sent to Brazil in 1940 and began to train its rapidly increasing army (50,000 strong in 1939; 200,000 strong in 1942). The United States also provided important assistance for the Volta Redonda steel works, which was a major step in Brazilian industrialisation. In August 1942 Brazil declared war on Germany and in 1943 a Brazilian expeditionary force - the FEB - was brought into existence to fight on the European continent.

The FEB was of far more importance to the future of Brazil than to the outcome of the war. It greatly strengthened Brazilian links with the USA and also brought to the forefront a group of Brazilian officers who had seen armed combat alongside US troops and officers. These included Castello Branco and Amaury Kruel (then lieutenant colonels), Cordeiro de Farias and General Zenobio da Costa. These officers apparently fell out during the war with Lott and Dutra, both pro-Estado Novo officers very close to Vargas, whose support for the Brazil-US alliance was by no means secure.[12] After 1945 the rivalry between these pro-US officers (later to be called the Sorbonne group) and the pro-Vargas nationalists (with their own authoritarian sympathies) was to be one of the dominating factors behind Brazilian military-politics.

ARGENTINA

The military government which immediately followed the overthrow of Yrigoyen in Argentina was led by Uriburu and substantially composed of civilians, almost all of whom were Conservatives. Three retired officers were appointed state governors, but none of these had been involved in the original conspiracy.[13] The main military influence on the government came through Uriburu's asesores. Uriburu, himself a retired officer by 1930, still retained a strong military following. It was this, rather than his formal command of positions, which led to the success of his conspiracy.

Uriburu himself, however, did not remain in power for long. In September 1930 the full effect of the Depression had not been felt in Argentina; it did make itself felt soon after and effectively put an end to any chance of Uriburu winning full popular support. Elections for the Buenos Aires province went ahead as scheduled in April 1931; the Radical Party, now led by Alvear, won convincingly. Uriburu could not easily allow them to regain power but had insufficient support to continue himself. He resolved his dilemma, after the failure of a pro-Radical military revolt in July 1931, by agreeing to hold elections in November 1931 but banning the Radicals from participating. These were then "won" by General Justo - a military officer from an aristocratic background with support from civilian conservatives and from within the military. Subsequently, between 1931 and 1943 Argentina was ruled by military-backed regimes, fraudulently elected but supported by civilian conservatives, in which the President was either a retired officer or a civilian under indirect military influence.

The military high command used this position, as it had in Brazil, to step up the level of military professionalism and increase its command over resources. Again, as in Brazil, the threat and then the fact of world war were propitious for an expansion of military influence within the political system. In military-political terms this meant, as also in Brazil, that there was some form of accommodation within the military (although not within the political system as a whole) between those who had won and lost in 1930. Some officers were indeed purged after 1930 but promotions in and after 1932 did not discriminate overtly against Radical officers; these were instead encouraged to identify themselves as officers first and Radicals a poor second. An increasing number of military officers came to feel that the Radical Party was now a threat to military discipline - particularly since pro-Radical revolts led by General(r) Toranzo in 1931 and General(r) Lascano in 1932 were both actively supported by NCOs. A failed Yrigoyenista rising in 1933 attracted hardly any military support. Meanwhile the Justo government, and those which followed, were careful to balance the various forces within the system - conservative liberals, moderate Alvearists and outright Fascists.

The size of the military institution and the military budget rose rapidly after having fallen away during the Depression. In 1936 24% of the national budget was taken up with military spending - an unprecedented figure for Argentina. In the late 1930s there was another major reorganisation of the military and a considerable expansion of military education. "By 1940, approximately one quarter of all officers in the ranks of lieutenant through major were thus attending classes; and for the first time colonels were to be enrolled in a special course offered by a newly created institute known as the Centro de Altos Estudios".[14] During the period a German military mission remained in Argentina where the pro-Axis sympathies of the military were never seriously concealed until almost the very end of the Second World War.

With the outbreak of war in 1939 the Argentine military further strengthened its institutional position within the country. In 1941 General Savio received permission from the government to set up a Dirección General de Fabricaciones Militares. This was allowed to undertake joint ventures with civilian-run companies and soon began to make its presence felt. It was also helped by close connections with the German Embassy and by the end of the War had become a major factor on the Argentine industrial scene.

During the war, pro-German officers made strong efforts to influence national policy. A pro-Nazi coup attempt in 1940 failed but in October 1941 a group of "nationalist" army officers presented President Castillo with a list of demands which amounted to the imposition of semi-open dictatorship and the removal of influential pro-Allied figures (of whom the most influential was now General Justo) from positions of influence. Castillo gradually began to comply with some of these demands. He also, after 1941, began a further military build-up with the army increasing in size from 50,000 in 1941 to 120,000 in 1944.

Pro-Axis feeling had something to do with an ideological and cultural affinity, not so much with Germany, as with Fascist Italy and Franquista Spain. It also had much to do with anti-Americanism particularly after Brazil ceased its courtship of Germany and entered firmly into alliance with the United States. The United States responded with a generous series of loans and military aid to Brazil (which, as we have seen, did much to help develop the military-industrial complex in that country) and also extended help to Chile which was also staunchly pro-US. Argentina thus felt embattled and the hegemonic position which it had enjoyed during the 1930s in the buffer states of Bolivia, Paraguay and Uruguay seemed threatened. Moreover during the 1930s Argentina had seen itself, with more than a touch of wishful thinking, as a competitor of the United States for preponderancy within South America. Another undoubted factor in Argentine thinking was that the Axis countries, while they controlled continental Europe, were undoubtedly a better market for Argentine food exports than the United States or Britain (with its Commonwealth allies) could hope to be.

As the military tide turned against the Axis, the Argentine military was presented with both a crisis and an opportunity. The crisis lay in the prospect of irresistible US hegemony over South America, in the collapse of Argentine markets in Europe, and in the enhanced prestige of the "democratic" forces within Argentina. The latter included the civilian Left (and of course the Communist Party), the Radical Party - which many observers felt was still the natural majority party in Argentina though it had undoubtedly declined since 1930 - and some Anglophile members of the traditional upper class (although the British community in Argentina was strangely neutralist during the war). The fear, then, was that the military-conservative coalition might be unable to avoid open elections in the democratic post-war climate and that they would be heavily defeated by some form of Popular Front regime which, under the circumstances (and one must remember that the Cold War had not yet begun), might also have received strong support from the United States.

The opportunity, however, probably only dimly glimpsed at the time, even by a political genius like Perón, was to combine support from the military, from industry and from mass mobilisation in order to open the political system on terms acceptable to those already within it. As a neutral and comparatively wealthy country, which could take over the considerable Axis interests left in Argentina toward the end of the war, there were the necessary resources to do this.

In discussing strategies, however, one must abstract considerably from the rapidly changing and confusing pattern of events between 1943 and 1946 which largely determined the pattern of post-war Argentina. The emergence of Perónism has been very extensively discussed elsewhere[15] and will only be dealt with here in barest outline.

The GOU was formed on 10 March 1943. It was a secret military organisation, probably put together on the initiative of Colonel Perón.[16] It was fundamentally pro-Axis and opposed Argentine involvement in the Second World War; there was, by this time, some pressure from within the government for a belated and symbolic entry into the war to improve Argentina's later relationship with the United States and the United Nations. The GOU was, like so many organisations of its type, predominantly made up of middle ranking staff officers - there were 3 colonels, 13 lieutenant colonels, 3 majors and a captain.[17] There were, as we shall see, career reasons for the activism of middle rank officers of this type. The GOU officers were particularly opposed to the selection of the traditionalist conservative Patron Costas as President in 1943 to succeed Castillo. The GOU appear to have talked to a number of civilians, as well as other officers, with the same viewpoint. The Radical Party was apparently willing to accept General Ramirez, the War Minister, as President in preference to Patron Costas. Castillo, belatedly aware that plotting was afoot, sacked Ramirez on 3 June and was overthrown on 4 June, before the military conspiracy had time to take its full shape. The coup was, in Potash's words, "a hasty improvisation".[18]

Immediately before the coup the GOU also approached General Rawson, who was planning a coup of his own, as was General Anaya. The resulting movement involved a military coalition involving some pro-Allied and neutralist officers as well as the GOU. Indeed, of the fourteen officers who met to plan the coup on 3 June, only two were from the GOU. Perón began his rise only in the post-coup manoeuvring. First Rawson became president but did not remain long in office; Ramirez quickly outmanoeuvred him and Perón became deputy war minister under General Farrell. Perón used this position to put GOU officers into strategic places.

Subsequently Farrell took over the government and Perón further strengthened his influence, serving for a time as War Minister and - far more famously - as Minister of Labour.

The political rise of Perón has been discussed in detail elsewhere. What is of interest here is the very considerable development of the military institution between 1943 and 1945. We have already seen that the Argentine career structure had been thoroughly reformed after 1905 and that this was probably responsible for the non-emergence of a junior officers movement in Argentina on the lines of Brazil and Chile. The GOU could hardly be considered as such since it played only a small part in the 1943 coup and was disbanded not long after; it seems, rather, to have been little more than a personal machine for Perón. It is worth noting, however, that promotion in Argentina was slow and that this was a fact making for some resentment - particularly after the political activity and excitement of 1930-32 had given way to a more sedate form of national politics. Moreover, middle ranking officers had particular reason to feel threatened as the war drew to a close and the prospect of military cutbacks loomed; the generals could enjoy their pensions and depart in peace, but the majors and lieutenant colonels had nowhere else to go.

As the system stood prior to 1944, a brilliant officer could become a senior general after 31 years service.[19] Rouquié found that of a sample of 21 officers promoted general in 1944 or earlier, who had entered the military college between 1875 and 1900, the average age was 53. This was not out of line with European practice. However, the system then introduced made for more selective but more rapid promotion. The central idea was to introduce a "two track" system; the inside track was for high flyers, namely officers destined for combat duty. An officer so designated could, if he passed through the system in minimum time, become a brigadier general at 44. The outside track was for officers designated for garrison duty only; these would be promoted more slowly. The aim of this change was to remove the frustration felt by talented officers forced to remain overlong in comparatively junior ranks and who were therefore tempted to turn to politics in order to speed the process. The younger officers of 1943, however, solved their problem in a more emphatic way. The

military-political musical chairs which took place
between the June 1943 coup and the election of
Perón in February 1946 brought about the forced
retirement of many officers and the accelerated
promotion of those immediately below them. We have
already seen that the war years as a whole were
ones of very considerable military expansion.
There were thus created senior positions into which
Perónist officers could quickly be moved.

The 1943 coup also speeded up even further the
development of military-industrial links. This was
partly the result of accelerated government
spending. In 1945 over 40% of the Argentine
budget, some 6% of Argentine GNP, was devoted to
the military - a wartime figure in a country only
nominally at war. There was also a good deal of
war propaganda, directed mainly by implication at
Brazil and Uruguay. It is possible that some
Argentine officers believed that, with the defeat
of Fascism in Europe now imminent, the pro-US
countries in South America might be encouraged to
turn on Argentina. There was certainly no doubt of
the real hostility with which Washington reacted to
the June 1943 coup in Argentina.[20] Most
officers, however, may just have felt that the good
times (for the military) might soon be over and
that it was important to undertake the reorganis-
ations, make the contacts and buy the weapons that
would assure the future of the military institution
even if it temporarily lost control of politics.
It also helped that there were Axis interests in
Argentina which could be bought at the end of the
war for a song.

In any case, Fabricaciones Militares
(interestingly enough headed by a personal opponent
of Perón[21]) was extremely active during this
time. It bought SEMA, an industrial company owned
by an Austrian citizen, although it kept on the old
personnel.[22] It also established connections
with four Sociedades Mixtas so as to extend its
range throughout heavy industry in Argentina. From
then on, it became increasingly common for personal
as well as institutional contacts to be established
between military officers and Argentine industrial
companies.[23]

When Perón was elected in February 1946 (an
election in whose outcome the military did not
significantly interfere), the Argentine military
had entrenched itself at the centre of the socio-
economic, as well as the political, system. As

Canton put it, the military had become the "other oligarchy".[24] It had acquired political and commercial interests, as well as its own bureaucratic ones, and used these to assert itself as one of the key power-centres of Argentine society.

CHILE

The Chilean case, in contrast to that of Brazil and Argentina, is one in which the military completely failed to install itself at the centre of the economy and political system. It is interesting to see why this should be so.

The military movement which began in September 1924 was always a more complex and ambiguous affair than the Brazilian or Argentine coups of 1930. The movement began when fifty junior officers attended the visitors gallery of the Chilean Senate and heckled a debate on military matters. Immediately afterwards Major Ibañez formed a Junta - no more than a military society - in order to put pressure on the government. Senior officers, expressing sympathy with the movement, soon set about co-opting and trying to control it. However, President Alessandri, rather than fighting until the end, resigned precipitately and left the country. An Admiral took over as front man, and Chile found itself unexpectedly under military rule. Interestingly enough, this military move was supported both by the Chilean Communist Party and by the parties of the far-Right[25]; it had been directed mainly against the parties of the centre.

The new government found itself under immediate pressure from Ibañez' Junta. It agreed to a request to retire one hundred senior officers, thus making space available for the promotion of Ibañez's supporters. Ibañez also called for various social reforms. These were not enacted in full but the government did push through most of the social reform legislation previously proposed by Alessandri and held up in Congress. There followed a period of confusion until January 1925 when a new secret society was set up by Ibañez and Grove, now lieutenant colonels, and included twenty more junior officers. This society, unlike the earlier Junta Militar, was not a pressure group but rather a military conspiracy which organised a coup later that month. This time the Right did oppose Ibañez, and so did many Naval officers but junior naval officers and crewmen took the side of the conspirators and so prevented the navy taking effective preventative action.

The opposition to Ibañez was, however, stronger than he had expected and, rather than risk a civil war, he accepted a compromise. He agreed to become War Minister only and to allow Alessandri to return as President. Ibañez then intended to carry through a complete military reorganisation. He had, however, not gone very far in this direction when, in late January, he faced an abortive coup attempt involving several officers (including the father of General Augusto Pinochet) and NCOs of the Valdivia regiment, supported by the civilian Right and by many of the officers who had been retired or purged in the preceding year. Ibañez also had to face an abortive naval revolt in September. Nor did relations with Alessandri run smoothly; in September Ibañez again forced Alessandri to resign and Figueroa took over as figure-head president. From then on Ibañez was clearly in control and took power formally in 1927.

Ibañez did, at first, have considerable civilian support. His former allies, both the Communists and the Right, now opposed him but much of the political centre - including much of the Radical Party - which had originally been pro-Alessandri had now switched over. So had the newspaper El Mercurio and the Church. Public opinion as a whole, moreover, was clearly in his favour. Like the Brazilian tenentes, Ibañez' politics owed much to Southern European models; his was perhaps a benign, very Chilean form of Fascism - plebiscitary, moralistic and superficially radical.

Like many other military men who came to power, however, he did not encourage others to follow his example. The armed forces were not involved directly in his administration although individual officers did participate in the bureaucracy and there were five military cabinet ministers. Ibañez and his war minister Blanche, however, continued with the task of developing military professionalism despite (or perhaps because of) a number of civil-military conspiracies during this very turbulent period.

The Ibañez regime was, however, caught by the Depression which hit Chile harder than any other Latin American country. It found the Chilean military unwilling to maintain Ibañez against

growing popular unrest and at the same time unable
to find an alternative political strategy. Ibañez
resigned in July 1931 under pressure from War
Minister Blanche. After a brief interregnum,
Montero, an old politician, took over and later,
while elections were being prepared, he gave way to
Trucco. Trucco began a purge of Ibanistas which
was interrupted by a serious, though abortive,
naval mutiny in September 1931.

The roots of the Navy rebellion lay in the
fact that naval commanders were out of step with
the Ibanistas in the army, whose success encouraged
radicalisation among more junior ranks of the navy.
Problems were exacerbated in 1930 when the
government, under the impact of the recession, cut
the pay of the navy. A group of enlisted men
approached the Navy Minister Latorre who refused to
help.[26] On 31 August 1931 the mutiny began with
the enlisted men demanding wage increases. The
following day, the men successfully seized the
Santiago-based navy and set up a committee to run
it. This committee made a number of political
demands on the government. These became
increasingly specific and detailed as time went on.
The revolt was supported by the Chilean Communist
Party and quickly spread. It won some support from
NCOs and men in the Air Force. However, the air
force officers stayed loyal and obeyed government
instructions to attack the Navy on 5 September.
This counter-attack proved successful and the
rebels surrendered shortly after.

The treatment of these rebels then became a
political issue. At first court martials were set
up and some death sentences were passed. However,
in the increasingly open political climate, these
became a focal point for Left-wing political
mobilisation and were quickly commuted. There
followed a period of indecision until, after the
prisoners launched a hunger strike, the Alessandri
government finally amnestied them.

The naval revolt, and the publicity
surrounding the subsequent treatment of the rebels,
accelerated the decline in military discipline
which followed the downfall of Ibañez and
aggravated the political confusion which followed.
Another aggravating factor was the purging of the
army by anti-Ibanistas now restored to power. In
October 1931 elections were held and won by
Montero. However, on 4 June 1932 there was another
military coup, this time from the far-Left. It was

headed by Davila, Matti and Puga. For twelve days Chile became a Socialist Republic. On June 16 Davila emerged as the strongest figure in the new government which now moderated its tone slightly but remained on the Left.

The June coup, however, was something of a last straw for the civilian establishment which had been alienated by the earlier period of military rule and then by the upheavals of 1931. Chile then, unlike Argentina or Brazil, experienced a strong anti-military reaction which brought about the resignation of Davila in September. Elections scheduled for October resulted in victory for Alessandri who this time managed to serve out his presidential term.

Alessandri's victory led to the removal of almost all the higher echelon of politically active officers. As Nunn points out, "all generals and all but three colonels listed in the army roll in 1931 were retired by the end of 1932."[27] A civilian militia was set up to check the power of the military although this was dissolved in 1936. Subsequently the civilian elite became united in their determination to keep the military out of politics in Chile.

The result of successful civilian control of the military was a reduction in the latter's status, and a big cut in the army budget after the Second World War. The military, and particularly the army, became as a result a far more tightly sealed unit than military institutions in other parts of South America. The army's main social contact was with the provincial landowners, themselves a downwardly mobile class during the post-war period; there was little social interaction between army officers and members of the Santiago haute bourgeoisie. The army's relative loss of status was marked by a lowering of the social origins of army recruits.[28] Notwithstanding some grumbling, however, - and failed minor conspiracies in 1939, 1946, 1948, 1951 and 1955, (and a protest at pay and conditions in 1969) - the military was unable to check the decline in its influence until it was encouraged to take power by the crisis of 1970-73.

The junior officers movement in Chile, then, did not firmly entrench the military within the political system. One reason for this is that Chile was too small to harbour hopes of continental power, so that the military did not develop a strong early interest in leading a project of industrialisation (although the state did take a limited role in oil exploration under Ibañez). Another factor was that Alessandri in 1933 finally succeeded in putting together a strong civilian conservative party. Much of the explanation for Chile's later political development lay in the specifically political events which followed the Depression. Ibañez in 1931, unlike some later military rulers of Chile, was too scrupulous to engage in major repression when he became widely unpopular; at the same time, he departed without having prepared a line of retreat. In consequence both military discipline and civilian politics fell into a state of confusion which finally triggered a strong civilista reaction. It is doubtful that a Chilean military regime will again make the same mistake.

BOLIVIA

The countries considered so far - Brazil, Argentina and Chile - had benefited considerably from economic growth from the second half of the nineteenth century. By 1920 Chile and Argentina were relatively advanced countries (despite obvious and severe social problems) and Brazil, although more backward overall, had a powerful and relatively highly developed South East. All three countries also enjoyed a considerable amount of institutional continuity in the first century after independence. It is not entirely surprising, therefore, that some combination of professional military development and reformist politics should have been possible within the overall context of a relatively stable socio-economic system.

The economically weaker and socially more fragmented Andean Republics - notably Bolivia and Peru - could not easily afford such a combination. Bolivia and Peru nevertheless confronted both reformist movements and what might be called "professional" unrest within the military. The results, however, were very different. In Peru a tightly-knit landed oligarchy emerged triumphant; in Bolivia, however, the consequence was Revolution and the overthrow of both the old army and the old system.

A further factor was also present in the Bolivian case - namely military defeat. The Chaco War both had the effect of mobilising a significant proportion of the Bolivian population under arms for the first time and, in defeat, in creating radical disaffection with a whole generation of political leaders. The immediate political result was the emergence of a kind of military radicalism, called military socialism by its supporters, under Presidents Toro and Busch. The local Standard Oil subsidiary was nationalised, but the country's tin mines and system of land tenure were left untouched.

There is insufficient space here to chronicle the vicissitudes of Bolivian politics between 1938 and 1952.[29] The main developments, however, are clear enough. One of these was the emergence of the MNR, a broad nationalist movement with a reformist orientation not dissimilar in type perhaps to Acción Democrática in Venezuela or Apra in Peru. Its urban middle class leadership tended to be pushed Left by the party's willingness to enrol the radical (and heavily repressed) tin miners and, on the other hand, by the repression which it suffered from the conservative governments of 1946-52. The MNR also had its supporters within the military. The Bolivian military had its own secret lodge, Radepa, which began to emerge publicly under the Villaroel government in 1943. As in other cases, "membership was almost exclusively made up of middle-rank veteran officers at the major and colonel level."[30] The level of factionalisation and purging in the Bolivian case was however unusually heavy; the defeat of a major pro-MNR revolt in 1949 appeared at the time to mark the final demise of the military nationalists but what has become clear in retrospect is how weak the army had been left by its repeated factional conflicts.

Elections held in 1951 resulted in overwhelming victory for the MNR, a victory which was unacceptable both to civilian conservatives and army commanders. A coup therefore followed, but the result was to disunite former supporters of the government. The MNR again found allies, this time among senior officers for various reasons disaffected with the military regime, for another coup attempt of its own. This faced discovery and was therefore brought forward to April 1952 and again appeared at first to have been aborted. The coup's military allies accepted defeat and sought their personal safety. The MNR, however, distributed weapons and called on the active help

of the tin miners. These proved too much for what
was left of Bolivia's demoralised and badly-
equipped conscript army and, after two days of
fighting, the rebels emerged triumphant. The
Bolivian Revolution had begun.

PERU

Peru, like Bolivia, failed to undergo a
serious process of capitalist development during
the nineteenth century. It had experienced a brief
guano boom in mid-century but little else. Peru,
again like Bolivia, also lost two wars with Chile
during this century; the second defeat was
shattering. After around 1890 serious economic
growth did begin, but the economy had become
heavily foreign-dominated and there was little real
development.[31]
In 1895 the Peruvian army was defeated, for
the last time, by an army of irregulars; this
defeat ushered in a period of civilian rule which
lasted - with interruptions - until 1919. The
serious beginnings of professionalisation also
began after 1895; a French mission began to train
the Peruvian army in 1897 and a military academy
was set up at Chorrillos. The first students
graduated in 1901. Yet the process of
professionalisation was largely aborted by the
vicissitudes of national politics. It was also
made more difficult by the language gap between
Spanish-speaking officers and Quechua-speaking men;
this gave particular importance to the role of NCOs
who could not easily be excluded from the
opportunity to become officers. Sergeants were
promoted freely into the officer corps until the
1930s.
General Sánchez Cerro seized power in 1930
and, after a period of unprecedented political
confusion, was elected president in 1931.[32] His
main opponent was Haya de la Torre, leader of the
Apra party. Apra had been formed a few years
previously as a reformist-nationalist party with a
pronounced base in the north of the country. Haya
refused to accept his electoral defeat in 1931,
alleging fraud, and organised a number of
rebellions. One plan went disastrously wrong in
1932 when Apra rose in revolt, captured the
military garrison at Trujillo and massacred its
occupants. The military recaptured and counter-
massacred, even more ferociously, and a section of

the military became anti-Apra for the next
generation. In 1933 an Aprista succeeded in
assassinating Sánchez Cerro, who was succeeded by
General Oscar Benavides; Benavides, a prominent
general with a record of bravery and good contacts
with the landed elite, remained in power until
1939.

It was under Benavides that serious
professionalism began to develop within the
Peruvian military. An increasing proportion of the
officer corps was made up of Chorrillos graduates -
80% by 1939 - and military education and discipline
improved. As in other countries, however, these
improvements began among junior officers and led to
tensions between these and their worse-trained and
often politically-appointed superiors. It was
perhaps not surprising that Apra sympathies
continued to be common among the junior officers.

Indeed Apra, all the more after the violent
repression of 1932, continued to conspire against
successive governments. Between 1930 and 1939,
according to Villanueva, "there were 37 civil-
military rebellions of which 30 included Aprista
participation and 36 had a clear military
character."[33] Despite the intense antipathy
toward Apra felt by much of the traditional upper
class and many members of the military, Aprista
support in the military was not completely dead.

Apra was in fact willing to deal with almost
any figure who appeared willing to improve its own
organisational position. It supported Manuel
Prado, a prominent member of the Peruvian economic
elite, for President in 1939 after Benavides had
been persuaded by the February revolt that it was
necessary to hold elections. Prado, who promised
to legalise the Apra party, was duly elected with
Aprista votes. Something of a political detente
between a section of the civilian establishment and
Apra appeared possible after the outbreak of the
Second World War, and particularly after the
Japanese attack on Pearl Harbour, since Prado, Apra
and the Communist Party all took strong pro-Allied
positions; a section of the economic elite, notably
the owners of El Comercio, retained some Fascist
sympathies but this preference became markedly less
popular after 1941.

In 1941 the Peruvian military also fought a
brief but successful war against Ecuador.
Subsequently, all of those who had played any part
in the campaign were heavily promoted. It seems to

have been this which finally turned the discontents
of passed-over junior officers into action. A
secret military lodge, the CROE, was set up in 1944
composed of around 100 officers below the rank of
colonel; Major Villanueva was one of the main
organisers and felt, with the others, that his was
the highest "career" post in the military. Further
promotion depended on patronage.[34] CROE's
manifesto, circulated in 1945, was an almost
perfect model for junior officers movements
everywhere in South America;

> A few generals and chiefs who had benefited
> from the government are not the army; not even
> a part of it. They are a few individuals,
> nothing more. They do not have the weight of
> opinion of the officer corps behind them
> because they lack professional prestige, lost
> through their dedication to national politics.
> The modern officer has a higher concept of
> discipline than his superiors.[35]

As in other cases, this young officers
movement coincided with a period of political
realignment outside the military. The economic
elite was split by the war while Apra, now keenly
supported by the US Embassy, appeared in a strong
position to influence post-war developments.
However, Haya de la Torre was damagingly unable to
make up his mind whether he wanted political
respectability and acceptance from the elite or
whether he wanted a democratic rupture with the
pre-1945 order. Unlike Betancourt in Venezuela at
the same time, he ultimately chose respectability
but did so in such a way that he gained virtually
no credit; there had already been too much Aprista
violence and Haya's hesitations now seemed to his
enemies to smack more of irresolution than of
pronounced willingness to adopt a strategy of
moderation.

In any case, before elections were held in
1945, a group of radical officers (including
Villanueva) planned a wide-ranging insurrection but
Apra - which had originally encouraged the officers
- later withdrew its support and the revolt failed.
However, this failure did not lead to repression.
Elections went ahead as scheduled although Haya,
rather than stand himself, supported the election
of Bustamante who granted a general amnesty for all

officers, including those involved in the rebellion earlier in the year.

Bustamante and Apra continued to seek a clientele within the army even after electoral victory. Congress used its power to control promotions and in 1946 Apra introduced into Congress a bill to lower the retirement age in the army and to increase the pay of junior officers. This bill did not become law, but it earned Apra further enmity from the high command. In 1947 Bustamante broke with Apra and there then followed a decisive period for the future evolution of Peruvian politics.

Here the best inside account is provided by Villanueva. He records that in 1948 there were two parallel Apra-military conspiracies. One was between Haya and some senior officers including the very enigmatic General Marin. The other involved more junior members of Apra and also of the military. By this time there were already in the Navy and Air Force a career class of sub-officers with no opportunity of promotion into the officer corps proper. The army, however, had not yet developed along these lines, and there was no career structure for NCOs. These tended to remain in office for long periods through a continual process of re-enlistment. Many hoped to become officers, either by attending the third year at Chorrillos or through direct promotion, with the patronage of a friendly senior officer or (as in some cases in 1941) on the battlefield. These NCOs, in all services, suffered many career discontents and were wide open to political penetration from outsiders.

In the event, Apra's attempts at penetration were too successful. On 3 October rebellion broke out among the navy - in one case under a naval commander, in others under enlisted sailors.[36] At first things went well for the rebels, but the senior officers who were sympathetic to Apra panicked at the prospect of being part of a movement which they could not themselves control. Haya panicked also and begged his army contacts to assume leadership of the movement. When this failed, Haya disowned the rebels and the rebellion collapsed. This tactic did Haya little good for, less than a month later, a Right-wing and strongly anti-Apra coup, led by General Odría and (at civilian level) Pedro Beltrán, successfully took power in Peru. This marked the final end of

Aprista attempts to take power through subverting the military.

Like Benavides in the 1930s, Odría (who was also a war hero, in his case from the 1941 conflict with Ecuador) was strongly supported by the economic elite. His coup was a major defeat for Apra and it led to a major purge of officers and men implicated in the earlier revolt although, for various reasons, this was much less severe than had been expected. Apart from those whose careers were lost, the junior officers did win a victory of a kind. Their attempts to play a role in national politics had certainly been aborted, but Odría decided to undertake a far more thorough programme of professional development than any previous military government. Within a generation, the Peruvian military achieved a level of bureaucratic and political sophistication almost as impressive as that reached in Brazil.

VENEZUELA

Although chronologically out of alignment, the experience of the Venezuelan military in politics from 1945 to 1958 is interesting as a source of comparison. We have already seen that the early 1940s saw the beginning of a young officers movement in Venezuela. It seized its opportunity in 1945 when, because of a disputed succession to President Medina, the previous near-consensus surrounding Venezuelan politics fell apart. The junior officers movement then approached Acción Democrática, the largest political party in Venezuela now becoming increasingly frustrated at being kept out of power by political manoeuvring. The junior officers proposed that they should launch a coup which would put AD in power; all the officers asked in return was the right to control the military.[37] AD, after some initial reluctance, agreed. The coup was hurried forward after the authorities discovered the plot and arrested Pérez Jiménez, one of its leaders; consequently the coup turned out to be violent - there were hundreds of deaths - but ultimately successful.

The junior officers initially kept their word and handed over national power to AD - which then enjoyed landslide electoral victories in 1946 and 1947. Meanwhile the junior officers consolidated their control over the military institution. All generals appointed before October 1945 were summarily dismissed; Pérez Jiménez and the other junior officers did not promote themselves generals. Pérez Jiménez, although one of the most senior officers in the army, was only a lieutenant colonel when he launched his second coup in November 1948. He did, however, set up a new state security body - the Seguridad Militar - in 1946.

Acción Democrática meanwhile began to rule in an aggressively populist manner. It had already developed an impressive clientele and was now able to reinforce its position through the use of state resources. Booming oil markets and AD's successful renegotiation of terms with the oil companies gave AD unprecedented resources for political use. Meanwhile opposition forces became increasingly threatened and came to believe that AD's electoral machine would give the party an ascendancy for a generation. Disturbed in this way, the opposition again looked to the military for intervention.

Thus the military coup against AD in 1948, also led by Pérez Jiménez, was supported by practically all of the opposition forces within the country - the Church, the upper classes and the opposition parties. It seemed at first as though another "moderating" coup was planned and that power would soon be handed back to civilian moderates or conservatives. In fact, however, Pérez Jiménez manoeuvred his way into a personalist dictatorship having taken advantage of the assassination of a military rival (Diego Chalbaud) in 1950 and annulled elections in 1952 when it became clear that he was about to lose.

By the late 1950s it had become clear that nothing remained of the Venezuelan junior officers movement except for the personal ambitions of Pérez Jiménez. He did, it is true, begin promoting officers (starting with himself) to the rank of general in 1955 after a ten year hiatus, and he did something to expand military education. However, his treatment of the military was very personalist and did nothing to professionalise the system of recruitment or promotions. On the contrary he surrounded himself with a clique and the two key figures in his repressive apparatus were in fact civilians. Generals and admirals (notably Larrazábal) who Pérez Jiménez believed might be a threat were sidelined. Finally, it had become apparent by the end of 1957 that Pérez Jiménez intended to remain in power indefinitely.

SOME COMPARISONS

Taking these countries together, then, three sets of contrasts emerge. In Brazil and Argentina the military was extremely successful at installing itself at the centre of the economic and political system and in professionalising its own institution. One obvious reason for this success was the second world war. Although South America was only peripherally involved, its importance to the international outlook of the larger South American countries should not be underestimated. Informal alliance with Argentina was an important way for Germany to try to undermine US influence over the hemisphere.[38] Similarly the close Brazilian-US alliance had important political implications for the post-War period. The general staffs of both Brazil and Argentina had to take into consideration the possibility of war with the other; the fact that this did not happen by no means demonstrates its implausibility. Indeed, although actual war involving South American countries has been comparatively rare, war preparations have been considerably more frequent.

One should also point out that the economic conditions conducive to the creation of a military-industrial complex were present in far greater measure in Brazil and Argentina than elsewhere. These are physically and demographically the largest countries in South America and both had enjoyed considerable industrial development. In 1935, for example, oil consumption in Argentina was 52,260 b/d, in Brazil 17,085 b/d, but in Venezuela only 2,211 b/d and in Peru 8,219 b/d (1935-39 average).[39]

Internal political reasons were also involved in the military ascendancy. Both military institutions had launched coups in 1930 and both then had to confront a period of internal turbulence. The turbulence was greater in Brazil where abortive NCO and Communist revolts did much to solidify the command hierarchy; in Argentina the tension with respect to the military hierarchy was considerably less. In both cases, however, the military avoided direct contact with the day-to-day business of governing. The Brazilians supported Vargas, a civilian politician of considerable popularity, uncanny political skill and a support base of his own. The Argentines generally supported the local oligarchy and the conservative party. Both bases of support were ultimately too restrictive (in the case of Brazil particularly after 1937) and both institutions had to accommodate themselves to a far more open style of politics after 1945. Nevertheless both institutions benefited from the fact that their fortunes were not tied exclusively to a particular individual or particular style of politics; the Brazilian military was to demonstrate the fact with its coup against Vargas in 1945. The professional consolidations which followed the coups of 1930 meant that presidents acceptable to the military needed to have a political base <u>on</u> the military rather than a political base <u>within</u> it.

In contrast to Brazil and Argentina, Chile in the late 1920s and Venezuela in the 1945-58 period provide examples of military intervention which was ultimately to be decisively reversed. The impetus to military involvement was similar in both cases, and not unlike the impetus in Brazil; junior officers movements in both countries owed much to professional frustration at the incomplete organisational development of the military. Professionalism had reached the lower ranks of the officer corps but not yet the top. Junior officers blamed both their seniors and the political system for their frustrations and set up military movements in order to change both system and army. Both movements found national politics surprisingly easy to penetrate in view of the frustration felt by reformists at the rigidity of the established order. Moreover, once the leaders of the two military movements achieved initial success, they remained in active politics and eventually took over the running of the government. Personal ambition played an important part here (particularly in the Venezuelan case) but for whatever reason the junior officers' original objective of professionalising the military became subordinated to more general political involvements. Thus, instead of uniting the institution, they ultimately divided it on the basis of civil-military cliques - around or opposed to Ibañez in Chile and Pérez Jiménez in Venezuela. Ibañez' shorter stay in office was undoubtedly due to the fact that he was overtaken by the Depression while Pérez Jiménez was able to

take advantage of the Venezuelan oil boom. Chile
had also enjoyed a strong civilist tradition at the
time of the military involvement while in Venezuela
Pérez Jiménez could scarcely be said to have
overthrown a democratic tradition; indeed his
downfall owed much to character weaknesses.

Ultimately the failure of both of these
movements (if they can indeed be considered
failures) was due to the fact that their leaders
clearly "crossed over" into politics rather than
remaining with the military and strengthening its
role within the political system; this had happened
in Brazil after 1889 but did not happen after 1930.
It is possible that a stronger institutional
consciousness could not easily be created in
Venezuela and Chile because these countries lacked
an obvious international role (internal security
had not yet become a paramount official concern of
the military). However there did remain military
institutionalists. These, themselves in some cases
former allies of the military-political leaders
(Blanche in Chile, Larrazábal in Venezuela)
eventually distanced themselves from the
personalist regimes headed by Ibañez and Pérez
Jiménez once these had become generally unpopular.
In general terms, a political base within the
military of the kind enjoyed by Ibañez and Pérez
Jiménez is only sufficient in combination with a
good deal of civilian support; without it the
military-politician is vunerable to counter-cliques
within the military encouraged by their own contact
with civilians.

When these military-politicians fell, the
military had nothing with which to resist the
restoration of civilian politicians. There was
instead a period of intense confusion in Chile
which itself strengthened *civilista* desire to
assert proper control over the military. In
Venezuela there were (as we shall see below) a
series of military revolts after 1958 but these all
failed and it is not at all clear that, had one
succeeded, the officer involved would have been
able to form an effective government. However, the
restored civilian politicians were careful to
remove some of the professional discontents which
had originally triggered the junior officers'
protest. In Venezuela, as we shall see, the degree
of military professionalism was considerably
extended under civilian rule.

Finally we come to Peru and Bolivia where a similarity of background fails to explain a complete disparity in outcome. In Peru there was during this period no clear historical break of the type occuring in the other countries. The Peruvian military was in 1948, as it had been in 1919, a political battleground to be fought over by rival caudillos. Benavides, Leguía, and Sánchez Cerro had all used the army to come to power and promptly downgraded it. Yet it seems by no means implausible to suggest that opportunities for a political break did exist in Peru during the 1940s - either along the Venezuelan pattern (reformist party plus young officers) or the Bolivian (reformist party forced to adopt what was effectively a revolutionary position). The decisive factor here appears to have been a failure of leadership; Haya de la Torre enjoyed most of the characteristics of a successful political leader except for the ability to deliver a final blow. Instead, he hesitated and was lost.

In the longer term, the political turbulence of the 1940s convinced the military elite after 1948 (against some resistance from civilians) that the professional development of the military needed to be extended. As we shall see, there was a rapid acceleration in the level and quality of military training after 1948, coupled with a general improvement in the Peruvian economy. The moment for an alliance between junior officers and civilian reformists had now been definitively lost.

In Bolivia, however, the same combination of a blocked reformist party and a frustrated cadre of junior officers led, not to reaction, but to Revolution. The civilian elite in Bolivia was too weak to co-opt its challengers and could not readily accept even the mild reformism of Villaroel (1943-46). For its part the MNR, given the stakes involved in the conflict, was in 1952 willing to radicalise decisively rather than accept defeat. The result of its radicalisation was the virtual destruction of the Bolivian army and a serious attempt - unhappily abortive - to create a stable and popular form of government.

NOTES

[1] S. P. Huntington <u>Political Order in Changing Societies</u>, Ch. 4.

[2] J. Murilho de Carvalho, "Armed Forces and Politics in Brazil", <u>Hispanic American Historical Review</u>, Vol. 62, No. 2 (May 1982), p. 207.

[3] <u>Ibid.</u>, p. 195.

[4] M. Conniff, "The Tenentes in Power; a new perspective on the Brazilian Revolution of 1930", <u>Journal of Latin American Studies</u>, Vol. 10, no. 1 (May 1978).

[5] Carvalho in <u>HAHR</u>, pp. 213-214.

[6] <u>Ibid.</u>, p. 200.

[7] <u>Ibid.</u>, p. 205.

[8] <u>Ibid.</u>, p. 221.

[9] Philip, <u>Oil and Politics</u>.

[10] S. Hilton, "Armed Forces and Industrialists in Modern Brazil; the drive for military autonomy 1889-1954", <u>HAHR</u>, Vol. 62, No. 4 (Nov. 1982), pp. 729-674.

[11] P. Flynn, <u>Brazil; a Political Analysis</u>, (Benn; 1978).

[12] L. Tambs, "Five Times Against the System; Brazilian Foreign Military Expeditions and their Effect on National Politics", pp. 177-207, in Keith and Hayes, eds, <u>Perspectives on Armed Politics in Brazil</u>.

[13] A. Rouquie, <u>Pouvoir et Societe Politique</u>, and R. Potash, <u>The Army and Politics in Argentina 1928-45</u>.

[14] Potash, <u>Ibid.</u>, p. 109.

[15] For example, M. Murmis and J. Portantiero, eds, <u>Estudios Sobre las Origines del Peronismo</u>, (Siglo XXI; 1971), R. Potash, <u>The Army and Politics in Argentina</u>, W. Little, "The Popular Origins of Peronism" in D. Rock, ed, <u>Argentina in the Twentieth Century</u>, (Duckworth; 1975), J. C. Torre, "Sobre as Origens do Peronismo", <u>Estudios CEBRAP</u>, No. 16 (April-June 1976) and T. Di Tella, "Working Class Organizations and Politics in Argentina", <u>Latin American Research Review</u>, Vol. 16, No. 2 (1981).

[16] Potash, <u>ibid.</u>.

[17] <u>Ibid.</u>, p. 168.

[18] <u>Ibid.</u>, p. 192.

[19] Rouquie, <u>Pouvoir et Societe Politique</u>.

[20] R. B. Woods, "Hull and Argentina; Wilsonian Diplomacy in the Age of Roosvelt", in Journal of Inter-American Studies and World Affairs, Vol. 16, No. 3 (August 1974), pp. 350-371.

[21] Potash, Army and Politics, p. 9.

[22] "The Militarization of Argentina on Fascist-Totalitarian Lines", (US State Department; 1946) is an informative, if very biased, document.

[23] Rouquie, Pouvoir et Societe Politique.

[24] Canton, Politica de Los Militares Argentinos.

[25] Nunn, Chilean Politics 1920-31.

[26] W. F. Slater, "The Abortive Kronstadt; the Chilean Naval Mutiny of 1931", HAHR, Vol. 60, No. 2 (May 1980), pp. 239-268.

[27] Nunn, Chilean Politics, p. 175.

[28] R. A. Hansen, "Military Culture and Organizational Decline; a study of the Chilean army", (PhD, UCLA; 1967).

[29] For a detailed account see H. Klein, Parties and Political Change in Bolivia 1880-1952, (Cambridge U.P.; 1969).

[30] Ibid., p. 370.

[31] R. Thorp and G. Bertram, Peru 1890-1977; Growth and Policy in aι. Export Economy, (McMillan; 1978).

[32] For this period in general see V. Villanueva, Ejercito Peruano; del caudillaje anarquico al militarismo reformista, (Lima; 1973) and, more specifically on Sanchez Cerro, S. Stein, Populism in Peru; the emergence of the masses and the politics of social control, (U. of Wisconsin; 1980).

[33] V. Villanueva, Apra y el Ejercito (1940-50), (Lima; 1976), p. 21.

[34] D. W. Masterson, "The Peruvian Armed Forces in Transition 1939-63; the impact of national politics and changing political perspectives", (Ph.D., Michigan State; 1976).

[35] Ibid., p. 104.

[36] Villanueva, Apra y el Ejercito.

[37] W. Burggraaff, The Venezuelan Armed Forces.

[38] F. Gellman, Good Neighbour Diplomacy; United States Policies in Latin American 1933-45, (Johns Hopkins; 1979).

[39] Philip, Oil and Politics, p. 80.

Chapter 6

MILITARY POLITICS IN THE POST-WAR DECADES

BRAZIL

The post-war period in Brazil really began
with a coup against Vargas in October 1945. As the
war drew to a close Vargas was facing much the same
problem as the Argentine military. Although never
as pro-Axis as the Argentines, Vargas was himself
under pressure from a now much stronger' liberal
pro-US group within the military - whose most overt
manifestation was the FEB in Italy. Vargas, like
Perón, responded to this pressure by preparing the
ground for a political opening. He sought to play
two cards at once. One card was the patronage
machine which had been set up throughout Brazil
under the Estado Novo. The other was the
increasing importance of the urban vote, and within
it, of organised labour which Vargas hoped to co-
opt by using the plainly corporatist labour law of
1943.[1] Vargas did, however, make a concession to
his critics by promising to step down and place his
personal machine at the disposal of General Dutra,
the War Minister. However, amid suspicions that
Vargas was plotting to continue in power, his
enemies combined to overthrow him.
Elections went ahead at the end of 1945 and
Dutra was in fact elected. His main opponent
Eduardo Gomes - a Brigadier General - represented
the UDN. This began a political division in Brazil
which would recur with increasing intensity until
1964. The UDN was strongly anti-Vargas and anti-
populist, economically liberal and relatively pro-
US. It had close connections with the military
officers who had served in Italy. This experience
was no less important in forming the outlook of a
section of the military than the tenente movement

149

had been a generation earlier. Yet the tenentes and the Italian-campaign officers now tended to find themselves on different sides. The tenentes had been sympathetic to centralisation and state control, and leant toward the Axis powers until 1942 after which they tended to become nationalists ("third worldists" before the term came into existence). The Italian campaign officers were staunchly pro-US, economic liberals (at least in theory) and (again for the most part in theory only) democrats. Their difficulty was that Vargas had created two parallel political machines - the old patronage network and the new working class organisation - which together were electorally almost impossible to beat. Of the four national elections held between 1945 and 1964 the UDN won only one, and even then under highly unusual circumstances. For most of this period, then, the FEB officers found themselves in the political wilderness and concentrated instead on restructuring the army.

For the military as a whole, the post-1945 restoration of democracy raised the problem of adaptation. At first the difficulty was more apparent than real, since the military played a crucial behind-the-scenes role during the Dutra period, but if the political system really expanded to incorporate new urban groups, the influence already enjoyed by the military might be threatened. This problem led to two different responses, which could be seen in the Petrobrás campaign (mainly led by the military nationalists) and the creation of the ESG (by the FEB officers).

Interesting light is cast on the Brazilian military institution in 1948 by a CIA report of the period. This stressed the important political role which the army (in particular) was continuing to play. "The effectiveness of the army as a pressure group results from (a) the close social and family relationships of the officer class, (b) the high degree of group spirit throughout the army generally, and (c) the practice of having army officers holding important government posts."[2] Apart from the War Ministry, the national security council was important in the policymaking of the Dutra government; the army was important, for example, in the decision taken in 1947 to make the Communist Party illegal. Within the institution itself, conscription was not really enforced; each year 35,000 youths were conscripted out of an

eligible maximum of 500,000. The relatively small
size of the army - 170,000 in a country of around
40 million people - meant that it impinged little
on civil society. Internally the military was
fairly professional, though less so than the
Argentine army after 1944. Promotion was in theory
determined by military seniority and the order in
which an officer graduated from the military
academy; in practice, however, politics, evident
merit and other factors were taken into
consideration.

It was within this, still relatively small
although highly influential, institution that the
military liberals and nationalists battled for
supremacy. The military nationalists, were mainly
interested in asserting state control over the
economy - a control which would of course extend
opportunities for military officers. The
nationalists used the Military Club for their
purposes.[3] Membership more than doubled between
1946 and 1948 and the nationalists won the Club
elections. Subsequently, the military nationalists
became the moving force behind the Petrobrás
campaign - which aimed to ensure that Brazil
retained a state oil monopoly.[4] In this
campaign, military nationalists attracted
considerable civilian support - from the vast
majority of the civilian middle class - but also
picked up some strange bed-fellows, including the
Brazilian Communist Party (quite powerful despite
its enforced clandestinity) which, for reasons of
its own, was interested in the issue of oil
nationalism. In the short run, the campaign was a
success but in the longer run it exposed
nationalist officers to the accusation that they
were pro-Communist. Anti-Communist scares in the
early 1950s (during the Korean War) and the early
1960s (following the Cuban Revolution) were major
setbacks to the cause of the nationalists.

Open political agitation also made the
nationalists vulnerable to the accusation that they
were undermining military discipline,
factionalising the army and generally weakening its
unity. Concerns of this kind, above all, led to
the formation of the ESG in 1949. The ESG was a
military staff college which was set up directly by
the authoritarian liberals - notably General César
Obino and Lieutenant Colonel Cordeiro de Farias -
with the help and advice of the US military
mission. US instructors served with the ESG until

1960. The ESG was made directly responsible to the armed forces general staff and given its own intelligence services although it was not given any direct command role. Those who set it up instead turned it into a doctrinal centre. Italian campaign veterans were given jobs as instructors and sought to use the school to spread their own views. The ESG was concerned to attract, not only rising military officers (normally in their pre-colonel year) but also influentials from within civil society. By 1966, 599 ESG graduates were military officers, 224 were from private industry and commerce, 97 worked for decentralised government agencies, 39 were Congressmen, 23 were judges and 197 were professionals of various kinds.[5]

The actual teaching at ESG increasingly reflected a concern for internal subversion rather than external territorial warfare. This concern was strengthened by the various international developments of the post-war period - Dien Bien Phu, Algeria, and subsequently the US experience in Vietnam. The teaching reflected a "total" concept of society in cases such as this. As Stepan explains,

> The ESG doctrine strongly emphasised that modern warfare, whether conventional as in World War Two, or revolutionary, as in Indochina, involved the will, unity and productive capacity of the entire nation. ... National security for the ESG was seen to a great extent as a function of rationally maximising the output of the economy and minimising all sources of cleavage and disunity within the country.[6]

This doctrine was sometimes expressed in a way which seemed alarmingly totalitarian. General Golbery do Couta e Silva, for example, once wrote that, "The military war is substituted by a total war ...; it becomes a global war, as well as an indivisible one and, - why ignore it? - a permanent war."[7] However, the basic orientation of the ESG rather reflected a kind of authoritarian liberalism. Liberals everywhere face the basic dilemmas that economic liberalism and political liberalism (civil liberties, freedom of association, the right to vote) may only be contingently related and that political liberty, under certain circumstances, may be self-destructive. ESG-linked officers had no doubt of the answer and revealed themselves as authoritarians first and liberals only subsequently. They believed that democracy and civil liberties were only acceptable if they led to an acceptable result; Kubitshek and a tame Goulart were perhaps tolerable - Vargas or a radical Goulart were certainly not. The Brazilian people, if necessary, had to be "forced to be free". What the ESG-officers came to regard as electoral failures could be rationalised, in their eyes, by the view that political error was a symptom of underdevelopment. This line could be, as it eventually became, a justification for a fairly long period of military rule which aimed at accelerating economic development while holding down political mobilisation. Moreover, the anti-subversive element in ESG doctrine could be held to give almost unlimited power to the internal repressive and intelligence agencies of the state for as long as any threat of "subversion" could be said to exist. The opportunity to put this doctrine into practice came after the Cuban Revolution.

The direct influence of the ESG over Brazilian politics increased gradually and predominated by 1964. In 1955 nearly half of all Brazilian generals had graduated from the ESG and by 1962 the proportion reached 80 per cent. As we have seen, the ESG influence over civilians was also considerable and many civilians served as instructors on a variety of matters which went far beyond the purely military. One observer has written that "the ESG worked out a policy for the country which included the military dimension, and not a military doctrine which encompassed politics."[8]

The ESG was not alone in seeking to push the Brazilian officer corps toward authoritarian liberalism. From 1950 the United States began the systematic training of Latin American military officers in Panama, and Brazilians were well represented among the various cohorts. Moreover, following an agreement signed in 1952, direct military co-operation between the two countries continued at a high level. Between 1950 and 1960, 3,998 Brazilian officers were trained in the United States and US military aid increased considerably after 1961.

A further strengthening of the nexus between the US, the ESG group and Brazilian capitalism took place gradually from the 1950s. Previous Brazilian development had occurred first through agriculture and later through a combination of heavy industrial development (in which the military played a key role) and light consumer goods industries in which local capital played a key part. From around 1955, however, the development of capital goods and more sophisticated consumer durables (notably vehicles) came to play an increasingly important economic role. With this development came a notable increase in investment by multinational, mainly US-owned, corporations. It is not surprising that a close tie developed between this new business class and the ESG. Dreifuss, after detailed examination, concludes that "it is important to note that already in the mid-1950s and even more so in the early 1960s military participation in private business was a fact, although not as widespread a phenomenon as their participation in techno-bureaucratic agencies or as their presence in the boards of directors of multinational and associated corporations after 1964."[9] Dreifuss perhaps goes too far in allocating primary responsibility for the 1964 coup to IPES (a kind of Right-wing think tank set up in 1961 and including the prominent ESG-officer General Golbery do Couta e Silva) and the entrepreneurial group IBAD. Nevertheless, there can be no doubt that the authoritarian liberals behind the 1964 coup represented a far-reaching civil-military coalition which the ESG had done much to create.

The creation of the ESG and later tightening up of military education (particularly the strengthening of ECEME after 1961) also strengthened the purely professional character of the Brazilian military. As Stepan put it,

> To be eligible for promotion to the rank of general, an army line officer was required to graduate from the Military Academy, the Junior Officer's School and the three-year General Staff School (ECEME), whose written entrance examination is passed by less than a quarter of the applicants.[10]

The situation had changed markedly from 1948 when, as we have seen, graduation from the military academy, together with seniority, fundamentally determined promotion. Instead, as in Argentina after 1944, the system was both tightened and streamlined to permit high flyers a rapid ascent. Consequently, the rank structure became bottom heavy and the rat race for top positions became fierce. Patron-client relationships within the military were further reduced in importance. This system made junior officers easier to control than had once been the case.

Ranged against the ESG-officers was a rival group who might be designated populist-nationalists. These were pro-Vargas and, though some were quite Left-wing, were on the whole centrist in Brazilian electoral terms. They generally favoured an extension of state control over the economy (and were particularly active in the Petrobrás campaign). They took a relaxed view of deficit spending and preferred economic dirigisme to any very great reliance on the free market. They tended to be paternalist rather than exclusionary in their attitude to public opinion. They were also, on the whole, more in favour of an independent foreign policy as against the rigidly pro-US line demanded by the authoritarian liberals.

There is not much space here for a full account of the vicissitudes of Brazilian politics between 1945 and 1964.[11] It is perhaps worth just mentioning that the military (and civilian) populists won most of the tactical battles until the early 1960s. At the end of Dutra's term of office (during which time the Petrobrás campaign was a clear victory for the populists), Vargas was re-elected President. He was, however, overthrown by authoritarian liberal officers (with civilian encouragement) in 1954. These, however, were unable to consolidate their victory and in 1955 the PSD candidate, Kubitschek, defeated the UDN in presidential elections. In 1960 Janio Quadros was elected president for the UDN, although he was something of a maverick figure and not particularly close to the UDN's military supporters. Quadros resigned in 1961 for reasons which have still not been fully explained and was succeeded by the radical vice-president Goulart. Far-Right officers attempted a pre-emptive coup against Goulart (who was visiting China at the time of Quadros' resignation) which failed badly.

During Goulart's presidency (1961-64), however, the political balance within Brazil changed decisively. For one thing, the Brazilian

economy went steeply into recession. At the time
many economists believed that this was due to
fundamental weaknesses in its development strategy,
and in particular the so-called "exhaustion" of
import-substituting industrialisation.[12] Subsequent economic analysis has rather tended to cast
doubt on this view, and stressed rather some
neglected problems of cyclical adjustment and also
the economic consequences of the growing political
upheaval. Nevertheless the spectre of stagnation
after years of rapid growth (the Brazilian economy
had been particularly dynamic from 1945 to 1960)
tended to break up the broad concensus which had
hitherto existed (at least within the populist
camp) on economic policy-making. Some felt that
the solution lay in the adoption of radical reforms
which would alter the Brazilian pattern of income
distribution, while others believed it necessary
merely to adopt "structuralist" economic
stabilisation measures; Goulart at first leaned
toward the latter view but, as he became more aware
of the political cost of deflation in democratic
Brazil, he switched toward the former and became
generally more radical. Not a few Brazilians found
this thoroughly alarming.

The second major factor in the growing
polarisation was the success of the Cuban
Revolution and of attempts to spread this
throughout Latin America. The Brazilian Communist
Party did not in fact adopt an armed strategy but
it did agitate with increasing aggressiveness and
increasing visibility. The result was to destabilise the management of certain state
companies (notably Petrobrás), and to aggravate
Brazil's economic difficulties. The Cuban
Revolution also increased the importance of
Brazilian foreign policy. Quadros and later
Goulart tried to avoid being too openly anti-Cuban
- a standpoint which was bitterly resented by pro-
US officers. Finally, for various partly technical
reasons, the techniques of labour control which
populist governments had adopted since 1945 began
to break down at the end of the 1950s. Without
these essentially manipulative techniques, the
government was faced with the need to bid very much
higher for labour and urban support - for which it
faced competition from a variety of other
sources.[13] The result was not so much open class
conflict as an increasingly unmanageable and

chaotic situation which created fears on all sides
that extreme solutions were in prospect.
 The immediate background to the 1964 coup will
be discussed in chapter 8. It is however clear
that Goulart's own sharp move to the Left in early
1964, admittedly under very strong pressure from
men as well as events, precipitated his overthrow.
He seemed to connive at the undermining of military
discipline when he rejected moves to punish a group
of sergeants who staged a demonstration in late
1963 following a Supreme Court decision barring
them from electoral politics, and' even more
damagingly undermined the efforts of his own Navy
Minister to discipline enlisted sailors after an
abortive mutiny early in 1964. It is evident that
neither of these events amounted to a serious
threat to the military institution but they did
alienate Goulart's few remaining military
supporters and made them resolve to act before the
situation got worse. When the coup came, its
leaders were surprised by their own success.
Goulart's unpredictability and growing radicalism
had diminished the ranks of the military populists
to almost nothing.

ARGENTINA

 Following his election in 1946, Perón
appointed General Sosa Molina as War Minister.
Although a loyal Peronist, Sosa Molina was also a
confirmed "institutionalist" whose main task, as he
saw it, was to calm the military down after the
frenetic political activity of the 1943-46 period.
Just as after 1930, a period of intense political
activity was to be followed by a period of
consolidation and professional development.[14]
Promotions were by no means limited to pro-Peronist
officers; there was some political bias in their
favour but this was limited. As Potash notes, "A
competent officer who devoted himself exclusively
to the profession could look forward to a normal
career; at least before 1949 it was not essential
to make an overt show of political faith."[15]
Those who had manoeuvred against Perón in October
1945 were, however, removed.
 After Perón's election, Washington decided to
make peace with Buenos Aires and subsequently
helped Argentina to undertake a major programme of
rearmament (earlier efforts in this direction
having been blocked by US refusal of export

licences). Meanwhile <u>Fabricaciones Militares</u> played an active role in Perón's industrialisation plans. In 1947 General Savio won government approval for the setting up of a mixed company under military control in order to develop the steel industry and also to set up an arms industry within Argentina.

The structure of the Argentine military did not greatly change during the Peronist period. The opposition Radical Party pressed to have the Military Academy's monopoly over officer recruitment ended and to make ascent through the ranks possible. In 1953 provision was made for such ascent but this change in the regulations remained a dead letter.[16] The Radical Party also pressed, unsuccessfully, to facilitate the entry of lower class youths into military-run secondary schools; again the regulations were changed but the change was not enforced.

From around the end of 1949, however, Perón seems to have tried to tighten his personal control of the army. The War Minister was changed and a far more uncritical loyalist was appointed. Perón also insisted on an oath of allegiance from military officers; not many refused to sign but many of those who did resented the perjury which they were being required to commit. At the same time Perón increased financial benefits to military officers. In 1950 a further step was taken in accelerating the promotion structures for middle ranking officers and during the 1950s the posts available at the level of colonel and general increased while those at more junior levels slightly declined. These various remunerations helped sweeten for military officers the increasingly apparent truth that after 1949 the Argentine economy had run into serious trouble and that any major rearmament programmes were now out of the question for the forseeable future.

Perón's efforts to de-professionalise the Argentine military (i.e. to partially replace bureaucratic norms with political and patronage ones) took another step forward in 1950 when the law was changed to enable military officers on active service to accept party political nominations for any elective post without damage to their careers. In the past officers could accept such nomination, but time spent in elective office did not count toward promotion. Now, provided that an officer received permission from his superiors, he could hold elective office while continuing to pile up seniority for subsequent promotion. Perón also enacted various minor reforms aimed at improving the status of NCOs.

Under the circumstances it is perhaps not surprising that, within the officer corps on active service, opposition to Perón began to develop strongly among the staffs of military and naval colleges in the Buenos Aires area and, above all, in the War Academy.[17] Those involved in preliminary discussions of a plot included Generals Lonardi and Aramburu. By 1951 two military conspiracies were afoot, one led by Lonardi and the other by retired General Benjamin Menéndez, an inveterate conspirator. Both leaders approached civilians; Lonardi received promises of support from the Radical and Socialist leaders. Lonardi's plot was partially discovered although Lonardi himself escaped detection. Moreover almost at the same time Perón, apparently fearful of military reaction, dropped an earlier plan to make Evita Perón his vice-presidential nominee when he stood for re-election in 1951. This removed one major source of military discontent.

Lonardi then held back his move but Menéndez did launch a rebellion in September 1951. This failed badly in military terms but did have important political consequences. Perón became increasingly dictatorial while also purging the military extensively; around 200 officers lost their positions of whom 111 were gaoled and 66 fled the country.[18] In the short run, this purge did enable Perón to put his supporters in positions of influence. In the long run, however, his success was less clear. Those who were not clearly for him were now at least potentially against him.

Although Perón was re-elected in November 1951 with a large majority, military plotting thereafter never really ceased. As plots were discovered and suppressed, so the factionalism of the Argentine military increased. Perón also sought to protect his position by arming the CGT. Ironically after economic difficulties began to mount around 1950, and even more so after his wife's death in 1952, Perón moved in policy terms toward the centre if not toward the Right. Yet the level of political tension continued to mount. Moreover, Perón's efforts to turn the military into a personal machine continued. Indeed, his drive to destroy all sources of independent influence, first in the unions, then in the military and finally in the Church, was perhaps the key to his whole period in power. In any case, promotions in 1954 for the first time blatantly reflected Perón's preference for verbally loyal supporters as against competent military officers.

Perón remained too strong to be overthrown by a rival military faction until his political position with the nation at large began to weaken in and after late 1954. The main reason for this weakening was his conflict with the Catholic Church. The steps leading up to his actual overthrow were discussed in chapter 3; at the end, conspirators were virtually queueing up to try to overthrow him. One consequence of this was that the factionalisation of the military encouraged by Perón after 1950 (in the misguided hope that he could turn it into a personal political base) continued after 1955. Inevitably officers too closely identified with Perón were dropped after his overthrow. Within the army 63 of the 86 generals serving under Perón were removed. Potash notes that

> Reliable totals are not available, but it is clear that as of early 1956 hundreds of officers were affected and possibly over 1,000 were forced into retirement. Noncommissioned officers, whose loyalty to Perón had been demonstrated in the past, were also forced out of the service in a wholesale manner.[19]

To the change brought about by these removals was added the reincorporation of those who had been dismissed following the abortive coups of 1951 and 1955. Around 170 were so re-incorporated. These soon found themselves resented by those who had remained within the institution.

After both the 1930 and 1943-5 upheavals, deliberate efforts were made by the new authorities to calm political agitation in the military. This did not happen after 1955 and factionalism, if anything, worsened in the following years. It did not help that the "victors" of 1955 found it difficult to agree on a coherent political strategy over and above keeping Perón and the Peronists out of power. A Peronist rebellion led by General Valle in June 1956 was brutally put down (see also the discussion in chapter 7). However, there were major internal conflicts in November 1955 (leading

to the resignation of Lonardi) and November 1956.
This process of factionalisation culminated in
armed conflict in 1963 between the two main
military factions, the azules and colorados.[20]
    The azules and colorados to some extent
reflected natural tendencies within any South
American military institution - representing
nationalists and liberals respectively. The
azules were on the whole Catholic nationalists
whose opposition to Peronism was by no means root
and branch but rather reflected a sense that Perón
had damaged the military institution largely for
reasons of personality. As this may suggest, the
azules were above all devoted to the restoration
of military professionalism which, they felt, could
only be accomplished during a period of civilian
rule. The azules later showed a good deal of
interest in the idea of establishing a kind of
Peronism without Perón; Onganía at one point
seems to have considered running in presidential
elections after striking a bargain for Perón's
support. The colorados, however, tended to be
economical liberals - strongly anti-dirigiste and
anti-trade union. They were also less reluctant
than the azules to countenance an indefinite
period of military dictatorship, particularly after
the overthrow of Frondizi in 1962. They were also
less committed to the virtues of military
discipline and more willing to use their factional
position in the military to advantage; many of them
had been restored to rank after the failed
rebellion of 1951 and some (like retired General
Benjamin Menéndez) were inveterate conspirators.
    After a number of setbacks during 1962, the
colorados in april 1963 staged a last rising
against the azul military establishment and were
put down decisively. The colorados were now
extensively purged. The military leadership which
emerged from the confrontation felt that the level
of factionalism in the Argentine military was
becoming dangerous and that it was time to put a
stop to it. Elections were held on schedule in
1963, ironically leading to the victory of the UCRP
who had been the main civilian supporters of the
colorados.
    Between 1963 and 1966 the azules, now
convincingly led by Onganía, carried out a re-
professionalisation of the military. Much more
emphasis was put on hierarchical authority than in
the past; military training was increased and made

more rigorous; military contact with civilian politicians came to be frowned upon although the military continued to deal with civilians of other kinds.[21] Military contact with civilians "tended to be concentrated on technocrats and 'apolitical' civilians in large organisations (above all private) ... the civilian contacts during the 'legalist' period tended to be defined within the framework of a subordinate relationship in which the armed forces ... received 'technical' information over a wide range of social problems."[22]

The Brazilian influence is quite perceptible on Onganía and the azules. They even imported the ESG Doctrine of National Security with its emphasis on the internal situation. They also signed a "programme of military assistance" with the United States and received a number of US advisory missions. In carrying out these organisational changes, the military acquired a sense of mission which was, if anything, even more exalted than before. It was the role of the military, wrote Onganía, to "preserve the moral and spiritual values of Western and Christian civilization, to maintain public order and domestic peace, to promote the general welfare, to sustain the enforcement of the Constitution" etc.[23] What Onganía appears to have had in mind was not less military intervention in politics (despite the "legalist" label attached to him) but rather military intervention of a better quality.

Indeed, one factor moving the military to return to active politics was a concern to keep active politics out of the military. As O'Donnell put it, "Many officers believed that their corporate interest in maintaining professionalism and cohesion would be seriously endangered if they persisted in their decision to suspend direct political participation."[24] Their fears that a return to Peronism would re-introduce factionalism into the military were almost certainly well founded.

During the 1946-63 period as a whole the Argentine military lost many of the political advantages which it had enjoyed immediately prior to 1945 and which it had seemed to maintain with the election of Perón in 1946. Its own political factionalisation perhaps reflected the decline of the Argentine economy and the fragmentation and lack of political consensus within the country as a

whole. It is true that the picture was (from a
military point of view) not wholly grim.
Fabricaciones Militares continued to expand its
activities and links between military officers and
private business tightened even further. The
military remained a lucrative profession even if
not a particularly secure one. However, its
factional in-fighting had cost it a great deal in
terms of public reputation and also gravely damaged
the quality of policymaking throughout the period
but particularly after 1955. By 1963 it was also
becoming clear that the values of military
hierarchy and discipline really were being
threatened by continuing factionalisation. Had
this not been effectively checked thereafter there
might have been a real possibility of junior
officers or NCOs becoming politicised. In 1962-63,
however, a decisive part of the military felt that
the time had come to re-professionalise; this
changed the nature, but not the fact, of
subsequent military intervention in politics.

PERU

The development of CAEM in Peru had an effect
on the officer corps which is at any rate
comparable with that of the ESG in Brazil. CAEM
was set up in 1950 by officers whom Odría
had "kicked sideways" because of his distrust for
their Aprista sympathies. Like the ESG it taught
economics and sociology as well as purely strategic
matters. It thus developed an all-inclusive
doctrine of counter-insurgency involving the need
for development and reform as well as the need to
combat subversion per se. This changed
orientation is very clear from an analysis of
military journals after 1954 (when the General
Staff founded the Revista de la Escuela Superior
de Guerra).[25] Like the ESG, moreover, CAEM had
an influence throughout military ranks by tying
educational achievement even more tightly to
promotion prospects. One of the leading figures in
setting up the new institution attached a great
degree of importance to improving military
education which he felt was crucial to an
improvement in its professional self-regard.
Einaudi quotes him as saying that before the Second
World War "when a general met an ambassador, he
turned red in the face and trembled".[26] By 1968
the officer corps was probably, on average, the

best educated of any professional group in Peru. As well as CAEM one should also mention here the importance of CIMP which, set up in 1948, centralised the military education system under a single command.

This expansion in military education contributed toward other changes in the structure of the military. Until the late 1940s, an officer's promotion prospects (as in Brazil) depended on his graduation number from the military academy; this tended to penalise late developers or those who were intellectually talented but lacked discipline. Such men were now able to make up lost ground if they performed well in the later education system while those who had done well early had to continue to prove themselves. The overall result was to make it easier for high-flyers to get to the top without the help of civilians or other clientelist relationships.

CAEMista doctrine was markedly different from that taught at the ESG. Central to it was a notion of "negative threat" - a feeling, in other words, that the real danger to Peru came from above as much as below. The Peruvian elite, or so the military came to be taught, was a danger because it blocked reforms which alone could turn the masses away from insurgency. An important catalyst to this kind of military thinking came from the, in military terms quite unsuccessful, Castroist guerrilla movement in Peru in 1965. The Peruvian military felt that, although the rebels had been defeated, violence might well recur unless the government made a determined effort to improve social conditions in rural Peru. In a formal analysis General Mercado Jarrín (who later played an important role in the Velasco government) talked of a

'latent stage of subversion' ... defined as the presence of Communist activity exploiting national weaknesses. This Communist activity, which took a variety of forms, was containable for the present. But the existence of national weakness continually threatened to point the balance against the forces of progress and order.[27]

CAEM never produced a detailed programme of needed reforms. Nor was it as radical as certain key colonels in the intelligence services, who had

conducted research into the nature of Peru's
dominant civilian classes and were disgusted by
what they found.[28] It was, however, the most
politically influential centre for the diffusion of
broad reformist nationalist values (with the
possible exception of El Comercio which moved
notably to the Left after 1960) in opposition both
to the dominant laissez-faire position of most of
the civilian elite and to the ideological influence
of US training in Panama. It has been suggested
that there was also a certain rivalry between CAEM
and Panama-trained officers over the respective
levels of prestige of the two institutions[29]; by
the late 1960s CAEM was clearly the winner.

CAEM's growing importance related to the
increase in the size of the Peruvian officer corps,
which doubled in and after the 1941 conflict with
Ecuador. Before 1940 the very best officers were
sent to France for two years or more but this
system was too expensive for more than a tiny
minority; after 1950 US training partially filled
the gap but was relatively basic and general.
Thus, whereas in 1940 all of Peru's generals had
some foreign training, by the 1960s this was true
of only around one half.[30] The demand for good
officer training schools within Peru expanded with
the supply.

CAEM was generally hostile to civilian
politicians whom it tended to regard as incapable
of serious action. Many Peruvian officers
supported Belaúnde in 1963 but soon became
disillusioned with him. As early as 1963 a CAEM
document circulated which stated that "the sad and
desparate truth is that in Peru, the real powers
are not the Executive, the Legislative, the
Judicial or the Electoral, but the latifundistas,
the exporters, the bankers and the American
investors." Moreover, unlike the ESG, CAEM did not
at first invite civilians to attend its courses
although this policy changed in the later 1960s
(too late for much effect to be felt on the post-
1968 military government). There were some
civilian instructors - by no means all of whom were
associated with the civilian Left - but there was
no real attempt to use CAEM to put together a
civil-military constituency on the ESG model.
Instead there was something of an anti-civilian
bias. Villanueva points out that "CAEM rationalised the old antagonism felt by the military man
towards the civilian."[31] In doing this, it

increased the self-confidence of the military and
its willingness to rule directly in its own right
rather than merely holding the ring for civilians.
Eventually, General Velasco would say, "Our role as
governors is inseparable from our role as military
officers."[32]

The relationship between the military
hierarchy and dominant interests in civil society
was very different in Peru from Brazil or
Argentina. There was (at any rate until 1968) no
military-industrial complex and very little state
enterprise; nor were military officers prominent on
the boards of private sector companies. On the
contrary, Einaudi observed of the pre-1968 period
that,

> there is almost a complete lack of contact
> between the military and the social and
> financial elite of Peru. Of the 630 men who
> in 1963 belonged to the boards of directors
> and top management of the 86 largest business
> enterprises in Peru, only 4 were military men,
> and in fact the only ones, as far as can be
> determined, ever to have served in the
> military. Of these four, one retired general
> and one retired colonel were presidential
> appointees on the boards of semi-public
> corporations; another was an active-duty
> colonel serving as an adviser to the board of
> an explosives manufacturing company. ...
> None of the 51 members of the board of the
> National Agrarian Society in 1963 was a
> military man, although one had a brother who
> was an army officer. Similarly, fewer than
> one per cent of the members of the exclusive
> Club Nacional are military officers.[33]

Without a military base, as such, in the
Peruvian economy, it was relatively easier for
members of the Peruvian elite to co-opt officers on
an individual basis. This co-optation was widely
recognised, both by those who practised it and
those who opposed it, as an important factor
predisposing senior officers to take a conservative
political line. However, the increase in the size
of the officer corps after 1940 and its increasing
level of professionalism made the strategy of co-
optation more difficult. Even so, cases can be
found where rising young officers found civilian
"Godfathers". One well-known case involved the

relationship of Velasco and the Prado family which will be referred to in the next chapter.

The Peruvian military did however take an institutional interest in a number of quasi-political fields even when the country was being ruled by civilians. These institutional interests tended to expand in the years before 1968. One of these was the status of frontier areas; in 1958 CAEM published a proposal for the development of the Central Selva. This was sidelined by the government of the day but was a sign of things to come. In 1962 the military took advantage of a brief period of rule to set up Peru's national planning institute. A number of military officers also served at Cabinet level downward during periods of civilian rule. Two important figures in the post-1968 military government - Ernesto Montagne and Fransisco Morales Bermúdez - had previously served in Belaúnde's cabinet.

In political terms the Peruvian military evolved a great deal after 1948. Odría's coup was the last time that it acted to support the civilian oligarchy and even then Odría soon broke politically with these civilian allies and began to seek a political base of his own. He adopted a paternalist policy toward the Lima lower classes somewhat reminiscent of Sanchez Cerro (or even Perón but on a much less impressive scale), based largely upon the ample provision of public works for Lima.³⁴ By 1956, however, Odría had become alienated from his former military comrades and was also unacceptable to the civilian elite. When his formal term of office expired, he was forced to resign. Elections were held and the military formally returned to barracks.

The military launched another coup in 1962 following inconclusive election results and a period of party political manoeuvring. This was strikingly different in form to earlier moves. No individual figure was allowed to emerge (when Perez Godoy seemed about to do so, he was forced to resign by the rest of the military); instead, the military as a whole took over the government. Limited social reforms were enacted; some officers wished to go further but were prevented by their colleagues.³⁵ The <u>Junta</u> promised that new elections would be held in 1963 and they were. The candidate preferred by most of the military, Fernando Belaúnde, was duly elected. The military's early enthusiasm for Belaúnde, however,

soon turned to disappointment (although it is only
fair to point out that Belaúnde faced real
problems, particularly with an opposition-
controlled Congress, and the early expectations
which he aroused were not entirely realistic). By
1968 many officers had come to believe that there
was no alternative to a long period of military
government.

In the twenty years leading up to 1968 the
Peruvian military had professionalised more rapidly
and completely than any other in South America with
the possible exception of the Brazilian. At the
same time, Peru did not develop a military-
industrial complex along the lines of Brazil or
Argentina nor was there a concerted attempt to
civilianise the political process as occurred in
Chile and (as we shall see) Venezuela and Colombia.
The military remained at the political centre of
Peru, but increasingly discontented at the way in
which Peruvian politics was developing; in
socio-economic terms it remained on the outside
looking in. Finally, as we shall see in more
detail in chapter 9, the Peruvian military's
relations with the United States deteriorated
markedly during the 1960s. For all of these
reasons, a sharp change in its political alignment
might reasonably have been expected towards the end
of the 1960s.

CIVILIANISATION: COLOMBIA AND VENEZUELA

In Brazil, Argentina and Peru the post-war
years saw changes in the pattern of military
organisation which led to a different type of
military rule from the mid-1960s (rule which will
be considered in detail in subsequent chapters).
In Colombia and Venezuela, however, the pattern of
politics was quite different; here there occurred
apparently successful processes of democratisation
after 1958 despite an increase in the professional
sophistication of the military.

In Colombia, military rule had never been as
pervasive a feature of political life as in the
rest of South America. During the nineteenth
century the two political parties, Liberal and
Conservative, "were the central, inescapable basis
of political life".[36] These party groupings
sometimes collaborated and sometimes fought, but
had no interest in developing a strong professional
army. The army was kept weak throughout the

nineteenth century, and was defeated by semi-irregulars as late as 1899. Some military professionalisation took place under Reyes early in the twentieth century, but only in 1943 did a graduate of the Escuela Militar reach the rank of full-general.[37]

Colombian parties were above all, multi-class patronage institutions in which patronage was shared out between the parties according to various understandings. However, the system came under increasing strain during the 1940s due to what might be called a "crisis of modernisation" - the patronage system could not easily cope with expanding metropoli, greater social organisation, militant trade union activity etc. These social changes led to the parties becoming increasingly ideological and less clientelistic - the Liberals in order to capture this new urban support, the Conservatives in order to react against it. The political parties were gradually pulled apart from below, despite the attempts of the party leaders to reach some form of accommodation. The more intense political conflict led the parties to try to capture partisan control of the military, and officers were increasingly brought in to such normally civilian positions as mayoralties and governorships. In 1949/50 democracy came close to breakdown; in 1950 the Liberals abstained from the national elections which were won by Gomez, a paticularly militant Conservative, who was in his turn overthrown by a military coup in 1953.

The Rojas Pinilla military government then set about trying to organise a clientelist following of its own, but this led the existing parties to regain some form of unity and to press successfully for a return to civilian rule. The traditional parties continued to rely on factions within the military in order to offset Rojas Pinilla's attempts to create a faction of his own. Rojas Pinilla, trying to rule on a personalist basis but lacking political sureness of touch, fell from office in 1957 and electoral politics returned. However, the parties had meanwhile agreed on a specific form of consociationalism. For the first sixteen years of civilian rule, power alternated between the major parties; from 1974 direct elections were introduced. Politics remained client-based, largely consensual and of positive appeal to only a minority of the population. Electoral turnover has been regular and no important social group has been decisively alienated since 1958.

Since 1958 the military has undergone both expansion and considerable further professional development.[38] It has continued to play an active role on the margins of the political system. It has considerable freedom of action to deal with Colombia's various <u>guerrilla</u> movements and has also been actively policing (or enjoying the benefits of) the narcotics trade. It has, however, largely confined its attentions to a broadly-defined understanding of its professional concerns (in which the right to impose military justice on suspected subversives is presently its strongest professional claim). Nevertheless, military rule remains an available option should civilian rule for any reason totally break down.

The transition to democracy in Venezuela is in a sense more surprising since, until 1958, that country had only three years' experience of democratic government. By 1958, however, Venezuela was a rich country as a result of its oil boom, and oil wealth gave the Venezuelan elite an unrivalled ability to use its financial power for the purposes of co-optation. This meant that, providing a consensus could be established within the elite, there was less danger of stability being undermined by class conflict. In a positive-sum environment, a wide variety of groups could be satisfactorily paid off. At a more tactical level, moreover, the almost universal unpopularity of the Pérez Jiménez regime created an initial political "space" into which democratic institutions could move.

Given the fact that Pérez Jiménez himself was very much a factional ruler, it was almost inevitable that his overthrow would initially increase factionalism within the military, as political involvement of various kinds overlaid the formal hierarchy. Unlike post-1955 Argentina, however, civilian politicians and business figures showed an impressive degree of unity. When, in July 1958, Defence Minister (Air Force) General Castro Léon first tried to win the support of conservative civilians for continuing military rule and subsequently offered the presidency to Eugenio Mendoza, a prominent businessman, he was met with total refusal. There were, in fact, a number of attempted coups from both the Left and Right between 1958 and 1962, but none of them enjoyed serious civilian support (except from the far-Left which was probably on balance a liability in terms of securing military unity) and none came close to success. The detailed story of the de-factionalisation of the Venezuelan military after 1958 has yet to be told. However, most writers agree on the explanation for the successful transition to civilian rule; a high degree of consensus among the various sectors of the political elite (including the political parties) coupled with an effective system of co-optation to head off serious class conflict or polarisation from below.[39] At first there was an explicit consociationalism, with the 1958-63 government being made up of a multiparty coalition, and single-party rule emerging only in 1966. The decision of the Marxist parties to adopt guerrilla warfare against the government during the early 1960s if anything strengthened the democratic order. Civilian governments were willing to allow the military free rein in order to stamp out the "subversives", and were in return strongly backed by the United States. The Caracas economic elite was reassured by the defection and revolt of Acción Democrática's Left wing and saw no advantage from a return to factional military rule. Gradually the situation stabilised; the political parties abandoned their plans for radical reform while the conservative elite came to accept the democratic system.

Despite the continuing existence of civilian rule, however, the military has continued to play an important role. The 1960s saw a continuing tightening of professional standards within the Venezuelan military which culminated with the setting up of a staff college - Ia den - in 1970. The Venezuelan military can now be described as an academic bureaucracy. The military has also benefited, like many civilian interests, from lavish budgetary treatment; the Venezuelan military budget is secret but it is clear that military pay is generous and - for senior ranks - probably higher than in the United States.[40] Venezuelan generals are rich men.

The areas of military corporate concern - again broadly defined - are well respected by civilians. Military justice is still applied to "subversives", as well as within the ranks of the military itself. At the same time there is an undoubted "anticipated reactions" effect within civilian politics, of steps which civilian

governments fear to take due to possible military
response - high up on the list of such steps is a
settlement of the outstanding border disputes with
Guyana and Colombia. Nevertheless, civilian
presidents have not hesitated to assert their
authority over the military, and minor "incidents"
in 1969 and 1978 ended with the emphatic assertion
of civilian ascendancy.

One of the main difficulties now facing
military officers who want to play a political role
is the speed of promotion and the earliness of
retirement. A military career is an undoubted
rat-race until an officer reaches the rank of
colonel, and then he has only a few more years
before retirement. Retired officers are often
frustrated but find that they have lost their
contacts in the barracks (where the newly promoted
are jealous of their privileges) and retain few in
civil society. In Arroyo's words, retired officers
are "truly generals without soldiers".[41] A
number of retired officers do work in the private
sector, but recruitment here tends to be diffuse;
there is no military-industrial complex as such,
and retired officers cannot therefore act as a
bridge (as they do, for example, in Brazil) between
the military and industrial society.

IN CONCLUSION

One important theme of this discussion
concerns the variety of civil-military permutations
in South American politics, and the importance of
these in the professional development of the
military institution. Nevertheless, the main
development in the post-war decades, the
introduction of what might be called political
professionalism (which Stepan, with slightly
different emphasis calls "new professionalism"[42])
had a clear impact throughout the region. The
Brazilian military was in the vanguard of this new
creation, followed by the Peruvian. The Argentine
military was at first too heavily factionalised by
Perón and then by his opponents to develop so
strong an institutional perspective but began to do
so in the early 1960s. In Chile, Colombia and
Venezuela, where factional military rulers had at
various times been replaced by a secure civilian
ascendancy, the military was unable to develop in
the same way. The military was, of course, brought
back into Chile in 1973 after a period of intense

social conflict but it could then draw on the experience of military rule in Argentina and Brazil. In any case, as we shall see, military rule in Chile has been far more personalist than in the other cases. It fell to Brazil, Peru and Argentina to pioneer types of "institutional" military government during the 1960s. The role of stable civilian politics in keeping the military out of power will be considered again in the concluding sector; for now, discussion will focus on cases in which the military has taken over the government.

The political professionalism already mentioned in some sense marks the completion of the cycle which began when South American military institutions first began serious professional development. It marks the point at which professionalism reached the high command and so ended the tension previously existing between well-trained, but frustrated, junior officers and their politically-appointed superiors. Junior officers movements became a thing of the past, with the resulting reduction of the impact of factional political influence on the military. (Of course professionalisation as a process never really ends - there are always new technologies and political lessons to assimilate - but it does, after a time, become institutionalised.)

This "closing" of the military finally turned the military high command into an elite in its own right. The political-professional military developed an autonomous organisational basis, a distinctive political outlook (based on the doctrine of "internal security") and means of liaising with outside sources of power and wealth on terms acceptable to itself. Since the basis of its power was the obedience of subordinates, the military elite had to give due weight to the interests of its own institution; anything which was a threat to military discipline was a threat to itself. This did not necessarily make generals interventionist and reactionary - there remained a certain range of political viewpoints within the military - but it did introduce influences which, taken as a whole, were decidedly conservative.

There is, of course, a substantial overlap between what - in the popular imagination - is the "typical" outlook of a military officer and the outlook of a political-professional military. Attributes include a dislike of civilian politicians ("demogogues"), "corruption" and entrenched political cliques ("oligarchs"). It is, however, still worth stressing the way in which such viewpoints related to the new organisational rationality; officer corps had not always been opposed to populist leaders (for example, Perón), and Ibañez himself was no mean demogogue. Factional military leaders had often in the past been only too happy to intrigue with civilians - consider Pérez Jiménez or the Argentine colorados. Popular mobilisation and factional military involvement were not opposed for purely aesthetic reasons but because they threatened the power of the military high command. Civilian technocrats, asesores and other allies were welcomed because they could assist the military in achieving its goals.

As an elite in itself, the political-professional high command was naturally interested in developing relationships with other elites. Where, as in Brazil, the aspirations of the military ran in common with those of the US and the local capitalist class, they became firm allies; in Peru where interests appeared to conflict, the post-1968 military regime became just radical enough to break down barriers to its own institutional advancement but not so radical as to support open-ended popular mobilisation. In some kind of general sense one might indeed, as the "structuralists" assert, expect to find a broad correspondence between the interests of the military elite and the domestic (and international) capitalist class - the one maintaining the system and the other attempting to produce economic growth. Elites naturally do share some kind of common interest in maintaining a system which gives them their power. In particular cases, however, conflicting organisational interests - or the logic of particular political situations - have led to quite different outcomes. Before turning to particular cases, however, it is worth turning for one final look at the military institution - this time from the perspective of those within it.

NOTES

1 P. Schmitter, Interest Conflict and Political Change in Brazil, (Stanford U.P.; 1971).
2 "The Military in Brazil" (1948) reproduced on microfilm by University Publications of America (1979).
3 R. A. Hayes, "The Military Club and National Politics in Brazil", in Keith and Hayes, Armed Politics in Brazil.
4 Philip, Oil and Politics, Ch. 11.
5 p. 250, A. Stepan, "The New Professionalism of Internal Warfare and Military Role Expansion", in A. Lowenthal, ed, Armies and Politics.
6 Stepan, The Military in Politics, p. 128.
7 Quoted in R. Castro de Andrade, "Brazil; the military in politics", in SLAS Bulletin, No. 26, March 1977.
8 Ibid., p. 69.
9 R. Dreifuss, "The Brazilian Military Coup of 1964", (Ph.D., Glasgow; 1980).
10 Stepan, The Military in Politics, p. 249.
11 A very good account is provided by T. Skidmore, Politics in Brazil 1930-64, (Univ. of Wisconsin; 1967).
12 See the discussion in Ch. 2 above.
13 K. P. Erickson, The Brazilian Corporative State and Working Class Politics, (UCLA; 1978).
14 Potash, The Army and Politics in Argentina 1945-62, p. 55 et. seq.
15 Ibid., p. 56.
16 Ibid., p. 86.
17 Ibid., p. 123.
18 Ibid., p. 135.
19 Ibid., p. 215.
20 See Ibid. for a detailed discussion of the azul vs. colorado divide up until 1962. Also worth consulting on this is Rouquie, Pouvoir Politique.
21 G. O'Donnell in Lowenthal, Armies and Politics.
22 Ibid., pp. 234-35.
23 Quoted in Ibid., p. 207.
24 Ibid.
25 A. Stepan, The State and Society; Peru in Comparative Perspective, (Princeton; 1978).
26 L. Einaudi, "Peru", in A. Stepan and L. Einaudi, Latin American Institutional Development: changing military perspectives in Peru and Brazil, (Rand Corp; 1971), p. 17.

[27] <u>Ibid.</u>, p. 28.
[28] See Stepan, <u>The State and Society</u> and Philip, <u>The Rise and Fall of the Peruvian Military Radicals 1968-76</u>, (Athlone; 1978).
[29] Interview with General Jose Graham, Lima, September 1981.
[30] Einaudi, <u>op. cit.</u>, p. 58.
[31] V. Villanueva, <u>El CAEM y la Revolucion de la Fuerza Armada</u>, (Lima; 1972), upon which much of this paragraph relies.
[32] Quoted in <u>Nueva Cronica</u>, 22 December 1971.
[33] Einaudi in Stepan and Einaudi, <u>Latin American Institutional Development</u>, pp. 42-43.
[34] D. Collier, <u>Squatters and Oligarchs; Authoritarian Rule and Policy Change in Peru</u>, (Baltimore; 1977).
[35] V. Villanueva, <u>Un Año Bajo el Sable</u>, (Lima; 1963).
[36] A. Wilde, "Conversations among Gentlemen" in Linz and Stepan, <u>The Breakdown of Democratic Regimes</u>, p. 35.
[37] <u>Ibid.</u> On this period, see also D. Premo, "The Colombian Armed Forces in Search of a Mission", in R. Wesson, ed, <u>New Military Politics in Latin America</u>, (Stanford U.P.; 1982).
[38] See also J. M. Ruhl, "Civil Military Relations in Colombia; a societal explanation", in <u>Journal of InterAmerican Studies</u>, Vol. 23, No. 2, (May 1981), pp. 123-147.
[39] See E. Aroyo, "Elections and Negotiation; Democracy in Venezuela", (Ph.D., London; 1983), T. Karl, <u>Petroleum and Political Pacts in Venezuela</u>, (Woodrow Wilson Paper; 1981) and D. Levine, "Venezuela since 1958; the consolidation of democratic politics" in Linz and Stepan, <u>Breakdown of Democratic Rule</u>.
[40] <u>Ibid.</u>
[41] <u>Ibid.</u>, p. 392.
[42] A. Stepan, "The New Professionalism of Internal Warfare and Military Role Expansion", in A. Lowenthal, <u>Armies and Politics</u>.

Chapter 7

SOUTH AMERICAN MILITARY INSTITUTIONS; A VIEW INSIDE

Despite the power and wealth which senior officers enjoy, there is surprisingly little pressure on places at officer training school. In Argentina, for example, 7,874 candidates applied for admission to the military college between 1960 and 1970, of whom 3,859 were accepted.[1] In Brazil "from 1950 to 1965 for every academy slot there were fewer than two applicants many of whom could not qualify for physical or health reasons, so the number actually able to sit for a military career was lower still."[2] In 1965 the entering class was almost 50% short of a full quota - while the civilian engineering college at Rio was besieged with demand.

The military colleges as such tend to accept candidates in their late teens. However, the military does run a system of boarding schools for sons of officers and NCOs which also accepts outsiders. Many boys, therefore, join the military system very young. Stepan noted that "probably up to 90% of the present post-war generation of army officers in Brazil entered the military academic system around the age of twelve."[3] McCann's data confirms this; he finds that "in the 1962-66 period, only 7.6% of the cadet corps had attended civilian high schools, while sons of military men comprised more than 40% of the entering cadets."[4] A Peruvian military-run school was the subject of Vargas Llosa's savage fictional portrait in La Cuidad y los Perros. Whether the initiating brutalities portrayed in this book were exaggerated or not, the youth - in some cases extreme youth - of entrants into the military system might certainly be expected to increase a sense of military separateness from civil society. Moreover, there is quite a strong caste element in

177

officer recruitment and there is some evidence that
this has been increasing. In Brazil the figure has
increased from around 20% in the early 1940s to
over one third in the early 1960s. In Argentina,
between 1967 and 1970 of a total of 1,544
candidates admitted to the military academy, 436
(28.2%) were the sons of officers and a further 211
(13.2%) the sons of NCOs. Rather more than half of
the intake, therefore, came from the rest of civil
society. In Ecuador Fitch finds that just over 16%
of the cadet intake is made up of sons of officers,
but also that the proportion of sons of corporals
and sergeants has been increasing; the intake of
sons of officers remained almost constant between
the late 1930s and the early 1960s, but the size of
the officer corps as a whole increased considerably
during this time.[5] In Chile, where information
is less readily available, a survey of 37 generals
retired between 1952 and 1964 found that 26% were
sons of military officers.[6]

A course of study at the military college
normally lasts three years and the graduate becomes
a sub-lieutenant. Although academic qualities are
important at the college, a great deal of emphasis
is placed on "character formation" and there is an
effort to indoctrinate these recruits with military
values.[7] This intense discipline remains in
place for junior officers. A former US military
attache has described the life of a junior officer
as follows,

> Discipline is rigid within the officer
> complement; the colonel's whim is absolute
> law, and in isolated areas the society
> approaches that of a 'total institution'.
> Near the cities life is less confining, but
> the colonel will still take an interest in the
> subtenente's social life and overall
> behaviour and he must have the permission of a
> higher authority to marry.[8]

This discipline is reinforced by the knowledge
that, even among graduates of the military college,
many are called to the higher ranks of the army but
few are chosen. Unlike their nineteenth century
counterparts, modern South American armies are not
top heavy, indeed quite the contrary. In Argentina
in 1950, for example, only 4.7% of the army officer
corps was in the ranks of general or colonel
(compared with 10.2% in the case of the US) while

fully 54.8% were first lieutenants or below
(compared with 22.7% in the US).[9] This very
constricting rank structure is in operation
elsewhere in South America; in Brazil Stepan finds
that 39.5% of the officer corps in 1964 was made up
of lieutenants compared with only 33.5% within the
US army of that year.[10] This bottom-heavy
structure means that real power is vested in those
with control over promotion. This control is
fairly arbitrary and there is little or no right of
appeal.

The intensity of the rat-race indicated here
is even more apparent if one considers another
important feature of South American armies - the
speed of promotion and earliness of retirement.
Retirement is rigidly set to take effect thirty
years after the beginning of active service; in
most cases an officer will retire in his early
fifties. In Argentina, for example, Onganía was a
brigadier-general at 45 and a full general at 49.
Lanusse was a general at 44.[11] This accelerated
promotion structure means that officers will remain
at a particular rank for only around three years -
and an officer who is passed over for promotion is
normally expected to retire.

Beyond the junior ranks, academic attainment
becomes increasingly important. Given the relative
absence of combat experience, educational
qualifications become the main criteria for
promotion. There are a series of further
examinations for an officer to pass as he rises
through the hierarchy toward the rank of major.
At this point, a military officer is likely to see
himself (with reason) as better educated than most
civilians and may also regard military life as
superior to that of civilian. As Corbett puts it,
officers' "training and the high degree of
institutional socialisation involved cause them to
look upon the military officer as a superior being.
In the officer's view, his calling and its high
purpose set him aside from other men and lend to
his actions an unselfish aura that is
uncharacteristic of his environment, where
opportunism is the norm among politicians, lawyers,
businessmen and other professionals."[12] Needless
to say, this attitude is heavily reinforced through
the content of military training and instruction
where it is generally a latent and occasionally a
manifest objective to emphasise the superiority of
the military life.

In order to become a really senior officer, it is now generally necessary for a major to pass through a staff college, usually in the year immediately prior to promotion to colonel. At this point life becomes easier, and civilians are brought in sometimes to attend the courses and at other times as instructors. Questions of politics and sociology are introduced, and the civil-military contacts made may later have a political as well as a merely educational significance.

The main staff colleges, notably the ESG and CAEM, also introduced a military ideology of national security which was accepted, with few modifications, by military institutions elsewhere in South America. Since this ideology was discussed, in outline, in the previous chapter there is no need to tackle it again here. It is worth making the point, however, that a specifically military ideology can, under certain circumstances, act as a temporary substitute for approval from civil society. South American military governments are not, for the most part, messianic regimes but there are always fanatics in uniform (just as there are in civilian clothes) and variants of military ideology did appear to some officers during the 1970s to provide a necessary and sufficient justification of prolonged and extreme forms of military rule.

CIVILIAN CONTACT AND THE MILITARY

Thus far, we have focussed on the distinctive, institutional characteristics of South American officers. These, perhaps not surprisingly, are most emphasised in the military college and in junior military ranks. Senior officers, however, do deal with civilians and both influence, and are influenced, by them. At the level of colonel and above, where the political role of the military is likely to be at its greatest, it ceases to be true that "the world becomes the barracks". On the contrary, perspectives widen sharply. It is therefore useful to outline some of the main forms of civil-military contact in South America.

To begin with, there is the press. Officers undoubtedly read newspapers and are influenced by them. Stepan[13] specifically relates the degree of success or failure of coup attempts in Brazil between 1945 and 1964 to the attitude of the major newspapers. In Peru, El Comercio for many years enjoyed a special relationship with the military and, as we shall see, the press played a major part in the politics of the post-1968 military government. In Ecuador, Fitch[14] finds that the press is an important medium, although not the only one, through which officers come to acquire a sense of public opinion; this, in turn, as perceived by the military, plays an important although by no means wholly dominating role in its political behaviour.

The influence of the press extends much further than promoting or resisting a change of government. In Brazil after 1974, for example, a major press attack on the "statisation" of the economy had a considerable impact on national economic policy. In Chile after 1973 the owner of the main daily newspaper, El Mercurio was one of the inner-circle around Pinochet. In 1977 his newspapers launched a major "expose" of the activities of the internal security organ (the DINA). This was part of a concerted campaign which succeeded in its main aim of reducing the political power of the DINA and destroying the career of its head, General Contreras.[15]

The press enjoys this influence because it is, depending on the particular circumstance, often sympathetic to military rule. It is certainly not unconditionally democratic. Thus the military coups in Brazil (1964), Argentina (1976), and Chile (1973) were supported by much of the press as were both post-War Peruvian coups - 1948 and 1968. Booth concludes of the Peruvian newspapers that "as a group they were not consistent defenders either of political democracy or of civil rights other than their own right to publish. Both La Prensa and El Comercio reserved their strongest editorial venom for their elected political opponents and treated military governments and military institutions with respect bordering on servility."[16] In the event, this did not do the newspaper proprietors much good, for they were expropriated by the military regime in 1974. Even after that, however, civilian journalists and editors continued to have an important influence in the evolution of the military regime as officers sought to enrol them in their various inter-bureaucratic battles.[17]

Taken as a whole, the press in South America does not have a mass readership as the term would be understood in Europe or the US. Nor is there a tradition of investigative journalism or editorial independence. The press is, therefore, more clearly designed as an instrument of influence within the political elite. Some proprietors, owners of businesses in a number of sectors, use their newspapers to promote group or family interests. More often, however, a newspaper becomes the mouthpiece of a particular viewpoint or interest - in whose defence it can be highly polemical when the need arises. The press is in civil society, therefore, but not necessarily of it; it is, in an important sense, a half-open institution ideally adapted to playing a role in what are in some ways half-open civil-military political systems.

A second civilian influence on the military is the role of the <u>asesor</u> or personal adviser. It is common throughout Latin America for anyone in a position of political authority to have a team of advisers (on the United States rather than the British pattern) some of whom will be little more than young office boys but others will be serious advisers and confidantes. In some cases officers will rely mostly upon other military men, but civilians often do find their way into an inner military circle. It is, of course, not unknown for such civilians to complain later that their advice was not heeded but there can be no doubt of the influence of civilian advisers in at least some major areas of policymaking under military governments. To give three examples, civilians played a major part in persuading the Peruvian military government in 1969 to launch a radical programme of agrarian reform - against the advice of the military agriculture minister who then resigned.[18] Civilian advisers also played an important part in engineering the expropriation of Gulf Oil in Bolivia and in advising the radical Ecuadorian oil minister, Captain Jarrín, in 1972-74.[19]

It is of course true that these civilian advisers are co-opted from civil society and are not necessarily representative of it; this point was well made in Cardoso's theory of bureaucratic rings (see chapter 2). These advisers will have political views of their own but are unlikely to have strong party connections; such connections would in most instances represent a handicap to their selection. Nevertheless advisers will have had experience of the civilian world and are likely to be more receptive to new ideas and argument than is perhaps the average South American military officer.

Another group of importance are the economic technocrats. One can include here both those who work primarily for the private sector and key public sector economists in the Central Bank, the big nationalised industries, the planning ministry etc. There is, in fact, a good deal of turnover among South American economists between the university, the Central Bank, the IMF and other international agencies, and the big private sector companies (many of which will be foreign controlled). A number of them will, at different times in their careers, have worked in all of these different places. Indeed in most South American countries it is accepted and understood that there exists a class of "technocrats", often with advanced degrees from American universities, who are entrusted (particularly but not exclusively during periods of military government) with the main tasks of economic management; technocrats themselves tend to come together in groups and to compete with rival technocrats on the basis of ostensibly technical but in fact political differences (monetarists vs. structuralists; Friedmanites vs. Keynesians etc.). It is common for the military when in government to select an individual or group and to give him/them wide powers over the running of the domestic economy. In post-1964 Brazil, Roberto Campos was the first to be given this role; a few years later he gave way to Delfim Netto; there were the Chicago boys in Chile; Vegh Villegas was twice made super-minister in Uruguay; in Argentina military rulers since 1966 have given similar powers to Krieger Vasena, Dagnino Pastore, Martínez de Hoz and Roberto Aleman. During the 1930s the famous economist Raul Prebisch served conservative military-backed governments in Argentina. Technocrats of this type are rarely associated with Right-wing political parties (most of the Chilean Chicago boys were originally Christian Democrats, not members of the Right-wing National Party) but they have shown little reluctance to serve military governments and have often advocated a hard line against labour or other obstacles to technocratic efficiency. One might also mention the fact that the larger and more sophisticated South American countries have a civilian foreign policy establishment which also serves, willingly enough, under military as well as civilian rulers. Pérez de Cuellar, currently Secretary General of the UN, played a major part in shaping the foreign policy of the Velasco regime in Peru. Similarly Costa Mendez played a key part in influencing Argentine policy toward the Falklands.

Relations between civilian technocrats and military officers are not always easy. There are many cases of highly able technocrats being forced out of government because of opposition from relatively ignorant military officers. There have also been cases where civilians holding formal government positions have had their plans frustrated by military men in formally more junior positions. A well known case occurred in Brazil in 1970 when General Geisel, at the head of Petrobrás, blocked the attempt of the civilian oil minister to allow foreign oil companies to explore for oil in Brazil. Nevertheless there can be no doubt that civilian technocrats do play a genuinely powerful role in South American military governments.

It has often happened also that military officers, conscious of the likelihood that they would later be involved in government, have deliberately sought various forms of preparation from civilians. This preparation has most often taken the form of staff college lecturing. The management of the American-owned International Petroleum Company in Peru had no doubt of the importance of this preparation. They believed that a civilian nationalist who habitually lectured at CAEM had successfully turned officer opinion against them; they were right, the company was expropriated by the military in early 1969. In Chile, prior to the 1973 coup, a detailed economic plan, drawn up by the Chicago boys, was leaked to military officers known to be sympathetic to the opposition so as to reassure them that an incoming military government would know what to do about the economy.[20]

The influence of interest groups proper is harder to assess in general terms although the topic does warrant serious consideration.[21] It is certainly true that what may superficially seem to be interest groups may upon investigation turn out to be paper organisations subject to various forms of official manipulation. It is also true that even quite well established economic interest groups can be swept aside by military governments determined not to listen to them; the Velasco government in Peru destroyed the National Agrarian Society and Pinochet's Chicago boys paid little attention to the complaints of industrialists' groups when engaged in their economic restructuring. Indeed, given the centralist outlook of many military officers, they may see something almost illegitimate in groups ostensibly representing only sectional interests.[22] Nevertheless the military in government will eventually need to cope with particular interests within civil society; as we shall see, these cannot always be ignored or suppressed and the experience of governing can itself be a broadening process.

Of more importance in terms of the military institution is the influence of the Church. Most officers are Catholic, and when the Church does speak out on social issues its voice cannot easily be ignored. It is very rare for a Church hierarchy to mount an open challenge to a South American government (the case of Perón in 1955 was highly unusual), but the Church is likely to voice grievances, help certain forms of popular organisation and take a defined line on a variety of social issues. Again, this topic deserves more attention than it can be given here.

Finally there is the US Embassy. US influence in the politics of most South American countries is very much less than its influence in Central America and the Caribbean. Its role in military training is considerably less, and the US itself has consistently seen South American politics as less critical to its own interests than Caribbean/ Central American politics; the fact that South American militaries have generally been able to prevent civil war and revolution has been a further limiting factor in US involvement. It is certainly not the case that Washington can provoke a military coup, or return to barracks at will; Nixon's efforts to persuade the Chilean military to launch a coup in 1970 have been well documented, but did not prove successful.[23] On the other hand, the fact that US influence on South American militaries has at times been exaggerated does not prove it to be negligible. The Pentagon, like the Church and the press, has the opportunity, unlike almost all other outside influences, to enter the barracks on a day-to-day basis. This must be a factor of some importance.

One should also consider the direct impact of
the military's role in politics and the economy.
For the military, access to government is lucrative; officers seconded to administrative duties
generally enjoy double salaries even before
anything else is taken into account. Even when the
military is not actually in government, civilian
rulers generally find it expedient to place
military men in public sector agencies. In Brazil,
the military played an important part in
stimulating domestic manufacturing during the
Second World War, particularly of military-related
materials. It was the policy of the services to
"buy Brazilian" if possible and the Ministry of War
actually set up a department of manufacturing.[24]
This military involvement in state companies
continued subsequently. In 1960 the Brazilian
press was complaining that the military had taken
the oil nationalist slogan "the oil is ours" rather
too literally; over one hundred positions in the
state oil company were then being held by military
men. The position has not changed much overall
since then. Now the Brazilian air force controls
Embraer, the state aviation industry; the navy
dominates nuclear research and is directly involved
in the nuclear power industry; the army runs a
whole series of industries and is also involved in
a large arms manufacturing industry, both for
domestic consumption and for export. Even Brazil's
biggest pension fund is controlled by the army.[25]
In Argentina, there is a direct military role in
the economy through the conglomerate Fabricaciones
Militares set up in 1941 under the impact of war.
This company was, by the 1960s, producing capital
goods for the state oil company and other public
sector agencies and also produced considerable
amounts of chemicals for direct sale. The military
also played an important role in developing the
Argentine car industry.[26] It even set up a
metallurgical training centre - CITEFA - which has
trained civilian mining engineers. Fabricaciones
Militares has the right to join private sector
companies in joint ventures; this is how it began
its involvement in the chemical industry and also
helped develop the Argentine steel industry in
which it continues to play a major role. In Peru
the great extension of the state's role in the
economy after 1968 greatly increased the number of
jobs held by military officers, to such an extent
that there was a civilian reaction against it.[27]

In this case, and in general, the direct relationship between the military and much of the productive structure - particularly in metals and heavy industry - goes a long way to explain the appeal of economic nationalism.

Apart from this direct connection, it is also true that retired officers often go to appointments in the private sector. As we have seen, South American officers retire comparatively early and generally look for a second career. Many employers, particularly those which rely on orders or supplies from the military-controlled section of the economy, will want the access that comes from employing a retired officer. Moreover, not all of these associated officers would yet have retired - quite frequently officers will ask to be placed in the reserve for the few years immediately before retirement so that they can seek, or pursue, outside employment in preparation for retirement itself. (This practice of employing former military men has at times led to some surprises; the manager of a foreign company with a Peruvian subsidiary told me of a time when he recruited a retired Colonel and found him forcing his subordinates - middle-aged managers - to go through an hour of rigorous physical exercise before the factory opened: the officer was quickly transferred before any of the managers collapsed.) Moreover, this process by which personnel, contracts and orders are routinely exchanged between the civilian and military sections of the economy opens the way for mutual cultivation of officers and businessmen. In Brazil, for example, some businessmen were invited to attend courses at the ESG while, in the early 1960s, a private sector interest group energetically used its military contacts to encourage a coup against President Goulart.[28] In Peru the Prado family, which owned the Banco Popular (as well as a newspaper) brought their cultivation of military officers to a fine art - although this did not prevent their eventual destruction by the radical military government after 1968.[29]

In the larger countries of South America, there is ample scope for military involvement in the domestic manufacturing sector. In the smaller countries, officers' remuneration often takes more openly illicit forms. In the case of Paraguay, for example, as Painter points out, "the division of the smuggling operations and whole sectors of the economy between military officers is well documented, and points to the key factor behind the military's loyalty to Stroessner. This contraband was and is, as Stroessner himself has candidly remarked, 'the price of peace'."[30] The involvement of Bolivian generals in the cocaine trade is even more blatant although this is unusual in that it is a divisive factor in politics - not least because of public opposition from the United States. Military participation in industrial ventures, however, can often reinforce corporate cohesion. Even so, it would be unwise to ignore the fact that military officers have also enjoyed a good deal of illicit enrichment in the larger countries of South America. Even where civilians are in power, they will rarely wish to confront the military over questions of this kind - they will have problems enough as things stand. Thus successive civilian governments in Venezuela have made sure that the military is exceptionally well paid and they positively encourage the employment of retired officers in civilian concerns. They do not wish the military to conclude that a coup would be to its financial advantage.[31] Moreover, in neither Venezuela nor Colombia have allegations of smuggling by military officers been pursued with particular vigour.

Retired officers may also seek employment in more directly political roles. In Argentina, Astiz found that 14% of those in his sample of army officers were elected to "important public offices" after their retirement and a further 7% were appointed ambassadors.[32] Where they remain politically interested, retired officers can play an important mediating role between civilians and military men. They will have contacts on both sides of the fence and will be able to convey information in both directions. Some retired officers, with a high level of prestige, may also harbour political ambitions directly. Retired general, and ex-president Aramburu in Argentina certainly hoped to be invited back into the presidency in 1970 before his murder which sparked off a major political crisis.

MILITARY INTELLIGENCE AND SOCIAL CONTROL

Even within the internal security forces, the military does not act alone without contact with civilians. For example, the principal element in

General Pinochet's repression in Chile, the DINA, recruited directly from Right-wing extremist groups (notably Patria y Libertad) which had been operating before the coup with at least tacit support from much of the civilian Right (which, it is worth remembering, polled over one third of the total vote in 1970). By mid-1974 DINA had some 600 full time professional agents of whom some 20% were civilians - these were generally selected from the most "sensitive" jobs such as the murder abroad of Chilean opponents of the regime. DINA continued to expand until 1977 and it relied heavily on both paid and volunteer informants - many of them civilian.[33] Similarly the counter-terrorist campaign of the post-1976 military in Argentina had connections, via the triple-A (AAA) alliance, with sections of the Peronist Right. In Venezuela, the Pérez Jiménez dictatorship deliberately gave responsibility for the worst of the repression to two civilians in charge of the Seguridad Nacional; Pérez Jiménez apparently did not want to give these jobs to military officers for fear it would give them a bad name.[34]

Another, perhaps equally sinister, connection between the military and society has grown up recently in the form of strong internal intelligence agencies. The DINA, in Chile, was created at the end of 1973, superseding a number of mutually competitive and organisationally weak agencies. The SNI in Brazil was set up after the 1964 coup by General Golbery do Couta e Silva (a leading ESG intellectual) and took on such powers that Golbery himself later confessed, "I have created a monster". According to a later report[35], the SNI by 1980 had 60,000 retired officers working at various points within the Federal Government, 35,000 of these within state companies. The SNI also had connections with private, civilian run, businesses and even undertook business adventures of its own. A considerable number of civilians were also on the SNI payroll (which was a generous one). In Peru, the military intelligence services were developed greatly after the peasant movement in La Convención in 1962-3, and the failed Castroist insurgency in 1965. Officers linked to the intelligence corps played a major role in the 1968 military coup and the subsequent military government. Only in Argentina was this centralising tendency successfully resisted by regional military commanders; this lack of centralisation, however, was one reason for the comprehensive failure of the 1976-83 military regime.

MILITARY STRUCTURE AND BEHAVIOUR

Taken as a whole, therefore, military relations with civil society correspond neither to a pattern of complete isolation ("the barracks becomes the world") nor to the alternative pattern sketched out by the "middle class military" school ("the military is part of civil society and must therefore respond to it"). The early socialisation of the military is indeed isolating, with both heavy indoctrination and a rigorous selection procedure employed to weed out unsuitable material and mould accepted officers. Given the youth at which officer training begins, one would expect the impact of character formation to be considerable. Later, however, military interaction with civilians increases markedly. Colonels, generals and retired officers play a major part both within the military institution and within civil society. At this level (which is the level at which political involvement takes place), it is necessary to talk about a civil-military system. The nature of this system itself has major implications for politics.

The existence of this military institutional structure, and its pattern of interaction with civil society, can only be maintained if certain rules of behaviour are observed by the top military elite (the colonels and generals). The benefits from keeping to these rules are considerable, and there is good evidence that the implicit code of behaviour involved is - as in all tightly structured institutions - fairly well understood.

MILITARY DISCIPLINE AND POLITICS

The first point to be made is that South American military hierarchies attach a very high priority to the maintenance of military discipline, for it is this which gives the military its role as power centre. It might be objected that this point is trivial in that military hierarchies everywhere concern themselves with discipline; in other parts of the world, however, the military has either sought to maintain its discipline by disclaiming a political role or else political intervention has tended to bring about the fragmentation of discipline (as in various Afro-Asian cases). Some writers have treated the polarity - intervention vs. discipline - as an invariable contradiction. This, however, is too simple and affords too much explanatory importance to the concept of legitimacy. What matters, in countries where military intervention does take place, is how power is organised rather than how it is legitimised. Undoubtedly, as we have seen, military rebellions and coups, and military involvement in factional politics, have had destabilising effects on South American militaries; one only needs to consider Argentina from 1951 to 1963 and Venezuela from 1945 to 1962. Nevertheless, the potential conflict between discipline and involvement has, for the most part, been managed successfully - at first through alternating periods of intervention and professional development (as in both Argentina and Brazil after 1930) and subsequently through the evolution of a specifically military rationale and pattern of involvement, carefully selected so that discipline is not undermined. This latter condition has been related to the development of staff colleges and doctrines of counter-insurgency. This need to manage the discipline/involvement question generates certain constraints on military political behaviour and certain tensions in the military political outlook which are worth systematic exploration.

The first and most fundamental constraint is that control over the hierarchy must be vested in senior officers, in practice this means those with the rank of colonel and above. This control must be defended against two possible enemies, civilian outsiders and military juniors. As far as the first category is concerned, we have seen in preceding chapters how "professional" military demands for autonomy from civilian influence were a powerful motive for political intervention in a number of cases, most notably in Chile in 1924/5. Moreover, once fully established, the military high command in all South American countries has shown a pronounced antipathy toward individual civilian politicians perceived as threatening to military discipline. Examples include Goulart in Brazil (whose failure to deal properly with NCO and enlisted sailor unrest was a major factor in his overthrow[36]), Haya de la Torre in Peru (for many years after the Trujillo massacre and, even more so, after the failed 1948 risings), and Perón in Argentina for many years after 1955. The military hierarchy has also shown a total antipathy to those whom it has labelled "subversives", who aim at destroying the established order and, within it, the role of the military hierarchy. This mentality makes it lamentably easy for atrocities to be committed against those labelled in such a way.

Maintaining discipline within the ranks can be facilitated by the careful structuring of the military hierarchy. The highly academic/bureaucratic nature of the South American professional army, with its boyhood recruitment and early retirement, makes little sense from an operational military perspective. It does, however, make a great deal of sense from a military/political perspective. Conscription over a short period is the most effective way of filling the ranks with non-political soldiers; career soldiers more easily acquire career grievances and may seek a means of expressing them.

The NCO rank is a difficult one to handle. If mobility were allowed into the officer corps from NCOs, the educational criteria for promotion would be jeopardised and bad feeling would be created (as it was in many South American armies early in the century) between those with good formal qualifications and those risen through the ranks. Efforts, made in Brazil under the Estado Novo, to de-professionalise the NCO rank by putting a limit on length of service ultimately failed because of the increasing complexity of the work done by NCOs and the need to accept it as a career service. Thus in Brazil (as elsewhere) the military hierarchy remained extremely sensitive to the threat of NCO rebellion (reacting sharply in 1963 and again in October 1964), while the Left identified the NCO rank as a weak link through which the military could be penetrated. If the CIA is to be believed[37], the Soviet Union in late 1963 discounted the likelihood of a coup in Brazil because it believed that NCOs and enlisted men could be relied upon to prevent one. However, while NCOs do have direct influence over their own troops, the complex co-ordination necessary to launch an NCOs revolt against senior officers would be extremely difficult to achieve and would almost certainly be fairly easy for military intelligence to penetrate. There is recent evidence, indeed, that the Brazilian sergeants

192

revolt of 1963 was thoroughly penetrated by
military intelligence. NCO movements are more
likely to occur under conditions of general
political turbulence (Brazil, and of course Cuba,
in 1933; Peru in 1948; Argentina in 1956; Brazil
again in 1963; Bolivia - as we shall see - in 1971
and possibly, the military feared, Chile in 1973)
when the high command's normal political defences
are down and when a spontaneous upheaval might be
expected to spread. Indeed, one of the reasons why
military high commands in South America often feel
threatened by mobilisation politics and civilian
"indiscipline" is because they fear that disorder
might spread into the ranks of the military itself.
The hierarchy does however seek to keep politics
out of NCO barracks by, in most cases, forbidding
sergeants or enlisted men from voting or being
candidates in national elections. In a less
political way, NCO loyalty is generally secured
through various minor privileges, of which the most
important is probably access to military education
facilities for their children; many sons of NCOs
themselves become officers.

Moreover, when NCOs do participate in revolts,
particularly if they are in alliance with
civilians, penalties can be drastic; a measure of
tolerance, in contrast, is generally afforded to
rebellions which involve only senior officers. By
way of comparison, the Valle coup attempt in
Argentina in 1956, which was pro-Peronist and
involved senior officers, NCOs and civilians, was
punished with a number of executions (18 military
figures and 9 civilians were shot); in comparison,
a failed coup in 1979 led by General Menendez and
involving almost nobody else was punished by 60
days of house arrest. Although some of those
executed after the 1956 rebellion were in fact
senior officers, they were heavily punished not so
much for rebelling, but for rebelling in
conjunction with NCOs and civilians. The point was
made quite explicitly by General Aramburu,
president of Argentina in 1956, that exemplary
sentencing occurred because the Valle rising
threatened the rank structure of the military.[38]
The conclusion is inescapable; a revolt against the
government may be a venal sin - but a revolt
against the rank structure of the military is a
cardinal one. In some cases NCO and enlisted men's
rebellions have been treated relatively more
leniently (in Chile after 1931, in Peru after 1948)

but this has usually been where political conditions have made drastic measures inopportune. Such rebellions have always been treated far more seriously than risings by commissioned officers.

The characteristic of "discipline" also involves an arms-length relationship between the military and all civilians. As we have seen, there are many elements in the life-experience of military officers which tend to create a psychological military sense of distance from civilians. These include early recruitment (often from military families), intense training, frequent postings to often remote parts of the country, the content of military training and indoctrination, the intensely meritocratic nature of military promotions and above all the discipline itself. Einaudi points out in the case of Peru that "because discipline is a virtue restricted to the military, officers who have frequent and continuing contact with civilians run the risk of contamination, or losing their discipline, and of no longer being sufficiently military in the eyes of their colleagues."[39] A more hostile critic has described the Argentine military's world as a "closed, hermetic structure. Most of the officers' wives are the sisters or daughters of men in the military. Nearly all are related, and whenever there's a military regime, the civilians who participate are mostly relatives of the military or individuals who have frequented military circles in precise anticipation of that moment when the military will take power."[40] As we have seen, senior military offiers do interact with civil society in a number of ways, but many - perhaps most - do so with a certain reserve. Any alliance with civilians is rarely more than arms-length and conditional.

Much the same can be said about any relationship between the military hierarchy and any government, military or civilian. Political authority is respected up to a point, but never afforded unconditional allegiance; this remains true even if the political authority happens to be military. Military governments suffer from internal coups just as civilian governments face overthrow by the military. The mere transformation of a general into a president distances him to some extent from the military hierarchy; any differences may well be settled quietly by pressure and negotiation, but when a military government is discredited and an acceptable alternative looms into view, it becomes vulnerable to overthrow. The military institution will not want to become trapped into a fixed political allegiance for ever for fear of losing its own independence. Thus although political circumstances may on occasion leave no other choice, a South American military hierarchy will rarely want to put all of its eggs into one basket. For this reason, conditions which help protect the institutional structure of the military may also make for a certain instability within national politics or at least a reasonably rapid turnover of government - a moderate degree of political turnover underlines the indispensability of the high command and increases its bargaining power. Too much instability makes for factionalisation and weakness, but an excessively entrenched authority may enable a ruler to turn the military into a personal machine. It is worth remembering that the only South American dictators this century to have held power for more than a decade are Gomez in Venezuela, Stroessner in Paraguay, Pinochet in Chile, Leguía in Peru and Vargas in Brazil; this is quite a short list when one considers the many periods of military or military-backed rule and the military's own authoritarian characteristics. Only one of these has ruled as dictator in a major South American country since 1945.

It follows from this that the officer corps, despite its discipline, is by no means politically homogeneous. Junior ranks are expected to be largely apolitical, but senior officers may embrace a limited range of political views. In most cases[41], the situation seems to be that most officers are relatively unpolitical most of the time. Military-political activity will be undertaken by competing minorities of officers, usually coming disproportionately from certain elite groups within the military (cavalry officers in Argentina, intelligence officers in Peru and, after 1964, in Brazil). The outcome of this political competition will be settled at certain key movements (at the takeover of power, or during subsequent crises) by the active involvement or passive disposition of the silent military majority. This silent majority will be concerned, above all, with the unity and welfare of the military institution and will therefore rein in policies or figures seen as excessively radical, reactionary or simply factional. Once these initial or crises conflicts are settled, the victorious military-political minority will continue to rule according to its own programme until another crisis emerges and a further change of strategy is demanded. The pattern during periods of military (as well as civilian) government, then, is of long periods of uneventful rule, punctuated by short periods of crisis.

Broadly speaking, the political views of military-political minorities in South America can be located across a spectrum ranging from authoritarian liberal at one extreme to populist-nationalist at the other. The authoritarian liberals are above all concerned with neoclassical economic principles and with capitalist development; they are likely to be pro-US, unless (as in the case of Pinochet for example) their advances to Washington are spurned. Liberal officers will be highly suspicious of popular mobilisation and radically hostile to "subversion". They may support the idea of democracy in principle, but will in many cases be unwilling to abide by the results. Examples of authoritarian liberals include the ESG group in Brazil, the Colorados in Argentina, Pinochet in Chile and the Peruvian navy under Velasco. Such men often have, and can usually expect to acquire, contacts with the civilian elite in general and, on occasion, with multinational and other private sector employers in particular. At the other extreme, the populist-nationalists are strong supporters of state enterprise, particularly those which the military itself controls, and of domestic industry generally. They have relatively little interest in formal democratic institutions but may well seek a form of paternalist popularity. They have no interest at all in unpopular austerity measures or with the principles of comparative advantage; within military governments (notably in Argentina) they have often been bitter enemies of successive economics ministers. The more radical populist-nationalists (such as the pro-Velasco officers in Peru and Perón's military allies in Argentina) are willing to contemplate measures redistributing income and property and stimulating popular participation, provided that the military does not lose its grip on the situation. Uncontrolled popular mobilisation will generally meet united military opposition.

The character and outlook of the military institution is only a part, although an essential part, of the explanation of military behaviour in politics. The other essential part is the character of national politics itself, in the various cases and circumstances in which the military finds itself. Once a military regime takes power, it comes to behave as a government facing many of the characteristic problems of economic management, international relations and others which are far from specifically military. The behaviour and fate of some recent military governments in South America will be the subject of the next section.

NOTES

1 Rouquie, Pouvoir Militaire, p. 640.
2 F. McCann, "The Brazilian Army and the Problem of Mission 1939-64", Journal of Latin American Studies, Vol. 12, No. 1 (May 1980), 107-26, p. 122.
3 Stepan, The Military in Politics, p. 40.
4 McCann, op. cit., p. 123.
5 Fitch, The Military Coup d'Etat, pp. 26-27.
6 R. A. Hanson, "Military Culture and Organizational Decline; a study of the Chilean army", (Ph.D., U.C.L.A.; 1967).
7 C. Corbett, The Latin American Military as a Socio-Political Force; case studies of Bolivia and Argentina, (U. of Miami; 1972).
8 Ibid., p. 18.
9 Rouquie, Pouvoir Militaire, p. 626.
10 Stepan, The Military in Politics, p. 50.
11 Rouquie, op. cit..
12 Corbett, The Latin American Military, p. 19.
13 The Military in Politics.
14 The Military Coup d'Etat, pp. 115-6.
15 J. Dinges and S. Landau, Assassination on Embassy Row, (New York; 1980).
16 D. Booth, "The Reform of the Press; myths and realities", pp. 141-185; D. Booth and B. Sorj, eds., Military Reformism and Social Classes; the Peruvian Experience 1968-80, (McMillan; 1983), pp. 150-151.
17 For an insider's account of this period, see G. Thorndike, No. Mi General, (Lima; 1977).

[18] P. Cleaves and M. Scurrah, Agriculture, Bureaucracy and Military Government in Peru, (Cornell; 1980), Ch. 2.

[19] Philip, Oil and Politics.

[20] On the Chilean case, see P. O'Brien, J. Roddick et al, Chile; the Pinochet Decade, (La Bureau; 1983). On IPC in Peru see A. J. Pinelo, The International Petroleum Company in Peru, (Praeger; 1973).

[21] For an interesting study of a particular case, see A. Ferner, "The Industrial Bourgeoisie and the Peruvian Development Model", (D.Phil., Sussex; 1977).

[22] This point emerges clearly in the Brazilian context. See P. Schmitter, Interest, Conflict and Political Change in Brazil, and N. Leff, Economic Policy-making and Development in Brazil 1947-64, (New York; 1968).

[23] S. Hersh, "The Price of Power; Kissinger, Nixon and Chile", Atlantic Monthly, December 1982, pp. 31-58.

[24] S. E. Hilton, "Armed Forces and Industrialists in Modern Brazil; the drive for military autonomy 1889-1954", Hispanic American Historical Review, Vol. 62, No. 4 (Nov. 1982), pp. 629-674.

[25] M. Walker, in The Guardian, 11 August 1983.

[26] Rouquie, Pouvoir Militaire.

[27] D. Becker, The New Bourgoisie and the Limits of Dependency; mining, class and power in "revolutionary" Peru, (Princeton; 1983), p. 211.

[28] R. Dreifuss, "The Brazilian military coup of 1964", (Ph.D., U. of Glasgow; 1980).

[29] D. Gilbert, "The Oligarchy and the Old Regime in Peru", (Ph.D., Cornell; 1977).

[30] J. Painter, Paraguay in the 1970s; continuity and change in the political process, (Institute of Latin American Studies, Working Paper No. 9; 1983).

[31] E. Arroyo, "Elections and Negotiation", (Ph.D., London; 1983).

[32] C. Astiz, "The Argentine Armed Forces", Western Political Quarterly, Vol. 5, No. 2 (Dec. 1969). Dinges and Landau, Assassination in Embassy Row, p. 132.

[33] W. Burggraaff, The Venezuelan Armed Forces in Politics 1935-58, (U. of Missouri; 1972).

[34] Latin American Regional Report, 6; Brazil, July 1984.

35 The Military in Politics.
36 C.I.A. Report on Brazil, 28 September 1963, declassified 14A, (1976), (Carrollton Press, Washington).
37 Interview with Armaburu quoted in Rouquie, Pouvoir Militaire.
38 Einaudi in Stepan and Einaudi, Latin American Institutional Development, p. 18.
39 J. Timerman, Prisoner without a name; cell without a number, (Penguin; 1982), p. 94.
40 This picture emerges from Potash, The Army and Politics, (both volumes) and Lisa North, "Ideological Orientations of Peru's Military Rulers", pp. 245-275, in C. McClintock and A. Lowenthal, The Peruvian Experiment Reconsidered, (Princeton; 1983).

Chapter 8

DILEMMAS OF MILITARY REGIMES

"The basic problem about military regimes is not how they can gain power, but what they can do with it."[1] There are, in fact, only a limited number of ways in which military governments can be organised. The ability of military rulers to organise themselves in one of these ways will be considered by the nature of the military institution, the state of civil society and the abilities and preferences of the military-political elite. Military rule occurs in environments where, by definition, illegitimacy is not a crucial constraint upon military action. Nor, again by definition, does the absence of positively expressed popular support make military rule impossible. What is crucial, however, is the fact of political organisation and the need to reconcile it with military command.

Most South American military institutions are, as we have seen, quite highly developed organisationally. Hierarchy is established and discipline normally maintained. Moreover, although there are many points of linkage with civil society, officers are rarely ambivalent as to their military identity. This is both a strength and a weakness in political terms. It means that presidents cannot succeed in the long term by relying only on the support of one faction within the military, or by pursuing a policy of divide and rule within the institution. This is not to deny that there are sometimes factions within the military which can be turned to the advantage of a ruler, but there is always (or almost always) a "professional" cadre of officers whose primary loyalty is to the military itself rather than to any particular ruler. The relationship between these officers (not always the most senior) and any political leadership (whether military or not) will be one at arms-length. Under these circumstances, there are only a limited number of feasible patterns of military rule, or patterns of military-political involvement. It might be useful to discuss these in turn.

Before doing this one further point should be noted. There is a dynamic in military rule which cannot be captured completely through static categories. However, it is important to distinguish at a minimum between the nature of a military coup, the post-coup regime and the political evolution of this regime. What is interesting is the attempt to specify the nature of some of the most common transitions while discussing what they reveal about the general problems of military rule.

THE MODERATOR PATTERN

In the moderator pattern (guardianship in Huntington's terminology[2]), the military holds power directly only for short periods but has some form of arbitrating relationship with civilian politics. It will remove presidents who fail in some important way or those who "breach the constitution" (i.e. act in a way in which influential groups within civil society deem unacceptable). On the whole, however, the military will hold the ring and will permit a variety of civilian parties and interests to compete more-or-less openly. The best Latin American case of this pattern is that of Brazil 1945-64; the military played an important behind-the-scenes role throughout the period and removed two presidents (Vargas and Goulart) for their apparent excesses. A non-Latin American example would be Turkey between 1960 and 1980.

For a stable moderator pattern to work, however, there must be no marked conflict between military and electoral preferences. Yet the fact and anticipation of military involvement are both likely to create such a conflict. Those "moderated against" may become increasingly unwilling to accept military terms of political reference, while those who hope to gain from military involvement may have no incentive to increase the workability of government or their own electoral appeal. They may instead have every incentive to play a spoiler role in the hope of bringing about a state of crisis so as to encourage military intervention. The system also requires that those military officers who wish to take a more direct role in politics do not succeed. In almost every case in South America, military governments which have quickly handed back power to civilians have done so only after the defeat of officers who wanted a longer-term dictatorship. This is true of Peru in 1962-3 (Perez Godoy and Bossio were removed), Brazil in 1954-55 (where a coup within a coup occurred before power was handed back) and even Argentina 1962-3 (with the azul vs. colorado conflict). Conversely in Argentina after 1930 (when the coup appeared ex ante to be of the moderator type) and (as we shall see) in Brazil after 1964 the military did not wish to hand back power even to moderate former presidents (Alvear and Kubitschek respectively) who had earlier served full terms with no serious problems with the military.

Thus, moderating military involvement tends to move inexorably if slowly toward direct military rule; something of this transformation can be seen in Argentina between 1963 and 1966, Brazil between 1961 and 1966, Peru between 1962 and 1968 and Ecuador between 1966 to 1972. This is not only a Latin American sequence of events; something of the same abandonment of "moderator" principles has recently occurred in Turkey and Nigeria. In this next section, therefore, there will be relatively little reference to the politics of moderating military rule; the focus, instead, will be on the long-term military regimes to have governed the main South American countries since the mid-1960s.

VETO COUPS AND AUTHORITARIAN RULE

Another common type of military coup is the veto. Veto coups (for example Chile 1973, Argentina 1976) are directed, not merely against the government of the day, but against civilian politics in a far more profound sense. They are commonly, though not invariably, reactions against mass mobilisation and the resulting threats, feared by the military, to order and discipline. The corrollary tends to be that veto coups are likely to give way to long periods of military rule. But how is this to be organised?

One possibility might be "pure" military authoritarianism, tending at its extreme to

something approaching military totalitarianism.
One might define a military-totalitarian regime as
one in which the internal security forces are
active and unchecked, in which the decisions of
government are purely arbitrary and in which the
government claims to be legitimised by its own
ideology (in these cases a combination of
developmentalism and national security doctrine).
"Classic" totalitarianism is usually defined more
in terms of ideology, subordinate mobilisation and
the abolition of the citizen's private life than
the definition offered here. Yet there are two
crucial common characteristics - arbitrary and
extreme state violence in which many people are
tortured and killed (the unmarked car, the midnight
knock at the door), and the replacement by ideology
of direct links between the state and society. The
repressive forces responsible for state violence
will, over time, tend to create their own "threats"
and expand their own level of activity
indefinitely. The metaphor used in all such cases
is one relating to internal warfare against
"subversives", "the class enemy" or the "anti-
nation" as the case may be. The absence of any
accepted relationship between state and society
means that there is no way in which the state may
be held accountable to civil society.

However, even within the most repressive
military regimes, there are important factors
working against the development of a sustained form
of totalitarianism (though not necessarily against
short-term reigns of terror). One of the most
important will be the desire of the military as a
whole to keep the internal security forces in
check. Repression may be accepted as necessary,
but it is usually directed against a finite enemy
over a finite period - which is not to deny that
security forces have at times committed outrages or
used their power for private advantage. While it
remains a conceivable possibility, there is no case
so far in South America of the internal security
forces successfully challenging the command
structure of the officer corps (the nearest case
was perhaps under Pérez Jiménez in Venezuela) in
a serious way over a period of time (isolated cases
have of course occurred). Where there have been
conflicts between advocates of continuing state
terror and comparative moderates within the
military regime (under Geisel in Brazil and
Pinochet in Chile) the extreme hard liners have

usually lost out. Moreover, as and when the large scale practice of state terror comes to be checked, it becomes impossible for a military regime to discount entirely representations made by important groups within civil society - the Church, sections of the press, some trade unions, employers organisations etc. The regime then comes to need at least a limited political base within civil society and deliberately seeks to cultivate it.

Recent South American experience has therefore shown that military governments have been capable of adopting policies of ideological control and state terrorism for short periods. They have not so far, however, been able to operate indefinitely without a political base within civil society and without some at least semi-formal procedures by which demands can be articulated and some government accountability assured. A reign of terror is possible, therefore; sustained military totalitarianism, on the basis of existing evidence, mercifully is not.

Neither is it possible for a "pure" authoritarian regime to operate indefinitely without either extreme repression or a recognisable basis of civilian support. Onganía attempted to rule Argentina in such a manner, but without success (as we shall see in chapter 10 below). A non-repressive military regime has no means of preventing organised groups from within civil society (trade unions, the press, the Church etc.) from putting pressure upon it; nor ex hypothesi can such a regime mobilise support of its own without changing its character decisively. A 'pure' authoritarian regime may on occasion - as in Argentina in 1969-72 - respond to popular pressure by seeking an accommodation with its opponents or - as in Brazil in 1968 - may respond by moving in a harder-line direction.

MILITARY CLIENTELISM

If a military regime cannot easily survive without some form of organised popular support, an obvious alternative is to try and find civilian allies. Ideally for the regime, these allies should cost little in policy terms. As Clapham and Philip suggest, "the essential element in the transaction is the military's capacity to attract subordinates who are on the one hand sufficiently influential to make their support worth having, and on the other insufficiently strong and independent to threaten the military itself."[3] Patterns of social stratification in South America tend to facilitate this kind of clientelism. Most countries still have substantial rural populations, with landlord-peasant land tenure systems which make clientelist relations easy to establish; the ability of the post-1964 Brazilian government to develop a rural clientele is a case in point.[4] Moreover, the provision of services to poor urban areas can also be organised in a way which facilitates clientele relations.[5] Crucially, however, it requires resources to distribute; clientelism can be practised effectively enough during periods of economic prosperity but may look a little threadbare in the midst of a slump.

Military clientelism is a very characteristic pattern of military rule in South america. It can work in quite highly developed societies (e.g. Pinochet's Chile) as well as in much poorer ones (Stroessner's Paraguay). It is normally associated with a general conservatism on socio-economic questions which makes the regimes acceptable to dominant groups which the regime need not co-opt directly. Some observers might therefore see these regimes as pro-capitalist first and clientelist only second. However, given the dependent character of South American economies, and their vulnerability to cyclical fluctuations, there is always an uncertain relationship between economic policy and economic success and the most successful military clientelist regimes are not always the most (or the least) orthodox in terms of economic policy. There can, however, be little doubt that military-clientelist regimes are unusually vulnerable to severe economic setback; conversely, however, economic success is unlikely to be enough to support a military regime unless this is used deliberately to create a social constituency.

The classic way of making popular support effective is through plebiscite or election (Brazil since 1964 and Chile since 1973 offer contrasting types). Sometimes, however, this can be bungled leading either to unexpected defeat (Uruguay 1980) or to the discrediting of the regime through blatant ballot rigging (Pérez Jiménez 1957).

Another problem which faces institutional military rulers more than personalist ones is that of making suport available to the regimes as a whole rather than military-political figures.

There are many examples of personalist military rulers achieving a degree of success in winning popular support but, often in doing so, becoming unacceptable to the rest of the military institution (Rojas Pinilla, Odría). It is true that Pinochet in Chile was for a time able to combine the confidence of the military with a significant degree of popular support, but Pinochet has been allowed more leeway by the Chilean military than his Brazilian, Argentinian or Uruguayan counterparts. In these latter cases, the difficulty of attracting popular support is more obvious, although the post-1964 Brazilian regime attempted, with some success, to channel support by taking over and subordinating the pre-1964 party system.

Military clientelism can be a highly durable form of rule. Franco and Salazar were particularly effective exponents, and their success has led to work seeking to identify a specific "type" of authoritarian politics. Linz' famous criteria of authoritarianism, mentally rather than ideologically, limited pluralism and limited police power, have been much discussed[6], but there is a concensus - shared by Linz himself[7] - that South American military regimes have rarely approached the stability of their Iberian counterparts. Much of the reason was that Franco and Salazar were able to rely to some degree on traditional institutions (the Church and, in Spain, the monarchy) and on traditional nationalism of a kind not readily available to rulers in South America. Also important is the fact that South America has suffered from more virulent trade cycles than post-war Spain or Portugal. Several consecutive years of negative economic growth can have a powerfully undermining effect on any regime. Perhaps the key factor, however, has been the greater independent weight and independence of outlook of the military itself within South American military regimes as compared with Franco and Salazar. The relatively lesser independent strength of the Chilean military under Pinochet (for reasons to be explored below) may tend to indicate support for this hypothesis.

BREAKTHROUGH COUPS AND MILITARY POPULISM

The third in Huntington's coup classification is the "breakthrough" coup. Some breakthrough coups in other parts of the world have indeed been comprehensively system-transforming; examples include Egypt, Iraq and Ethiopia. South American breakthrough coups, however, have been a good deal less radical, perhaps because the system of military hierarchy and discipline has enabled senior officers to prevent such radicalisation. However, there have been military coups in South America which have been radical in terms of their effect on popular participation and on property reform. Some radical coups have either aborted quickly (as with Grove in Chile in 1932) or have tapered off into indecisive regimes (as in Ecuador after 1972), but there have occasionally been serious military-led reform movements. These can perhaps be labelled as military-populist. It is the essence of a populist movement or government (as understood here) that it is supported by influential formally conservative groups (including military officers) who, as a result of frustration or crisis, broke with the conservative political establishment and sought to expand the scope of effective political involvement - to bring in a new political world to redress the balance of the old. Cases include Ibañez in Chile (in 1925-27), the early years of Argentine Peronism and of the Velasco regime in Peru.

The term "populism" is itself potentially ambiguous and should be defined with some care. Populism is defined here as a policy by which a government seeks to build or maintain a cross-class base of social support by high spending policies on social welfare and industrialisation. Such a policy is mobilising but not seriously revolutionary. Typically this policy involves alienating export interests (who will favour a free market) and suppressing (or at best competing with) class-based parties who seek mass support (particularly Marxist parties). Because a populist policy will almost certainly make influential enemies, it is important that it prove popular enough to win friends; otherwise it will surely fail.

The difficulties attached to policies of this kind are considerable.[8] For one thing, mobilisation is easier to start than to stop. Populist policies arouse expectations which they cannot generally satisfy (although in a dynamic economy it may be several years before this becomes fully apparent). There then arises a more intense conflict between those who want to radicalise further and those increasingly hostile to such radicalisation. In specifically economic terms, populism typically involves deficit spending and (almost invariably) discrimination against exports. This will eventually lead to a balance of payments crisis and the need for retrenchment. Popular support is then alienated or, alternatively, the adjustment is postponed until the problem reaches horrendous proportions. When this happens, there may be a military reaction.

A difficulty attaching more specifically to military-populism is that populist policies are often accompanied by the demagogic appeal of a particular leader. Popularity attaching to such a leader may be destabilising if it creates resentments among the military; if an attempt is made (for example by Perón, although he was by then no longer a military ruler) to factionalise the military, then a reaction is likely even if the socio-economic situation is by no means critical. Conversely, a populist policy without a personalist leader may prove inefficient at winning sufficient popular support; General Velasco in Peru provides a good example of a comparatively unpopular populist. Under these circumstances, bureaucratic structures directed towards mobilising support for the regime may constitute an actual liability.

Military populism, therefore, has never been a durable and successful form of rule in South America. It has led either to withdrawal from power or to a form of factionalism. Nevertheless, despite their ultimate political failure, such governments have had a major impact on South American history.

FACTIONAL COUPS AND FACTIONAL RULE

Factional coups are far more likely outside South America than inside it. They are particularly likely when a tribal or ethnic loyalty overrides, in the minds of most military officers, loyalty to the military institution as a whole. Where loyalty to the military institution constitutes the decisive political allegiance, as is generally the case in South America, this will be a strong factor working against the success of factional coups and against the durability of factional regimes. Caudillos of the past century were perhaps factional rulers, but twentieth century Latin American examples are largely confined to non-South American countries (Somoza and Batista are obvious examples of factional rulers). South American military rulers factionalise the officer corps at their peril; the Venezuelan coup of 1948 was a veto coup, and when Pérez Jiménez became too much like a factional ruler he was overthrown.

Extreme factionalism outside South America, as some of these examples have indicated, is often a prelude to major political transformation. If the primary loyalty of military commanders is not to the military institution itself, then this becomes something to be captured rather than a power centre in its own right. In the former case, the transformation of the political system and the reorganisation of the military can go together - post-1974 Ethiopia and Revolutionary Mexico may serve as examples. As these cases indicate, this transformation of the military may permit a reorganisation of state power in a way which creates a new political settlement. In South America, however, the power of a political leader (even if he is himself a military officer) vis-a-vis the officer corps is strictly limited. If he attempts to "meddle" with it (as, for example, did Perón), he is likely to be overthrown. Thus the military institution becomes the permanent feature in any political equation; the form of government is, in contrast, only temporary.

CONCLUSION

This broad typology may cover the main types of military rule in South America (and many military governments will in practice have some hybrid characteristics, or will be composed of members pursuing different objectives). The most interesting question, however, is whether one can plot a series of dynamics with any degree of confidence. The following chapters will be concerned, above all, with the political evolution of the most important military governments in South America since the mid-1960s. It should soon become clear that there is a high degree of uncertainty in the political evolution of military regimes. It is, however, possible to indicate some common paths which, as a matter ot historical record, a number of military regimes have followed and some typical consequences that have resulted.

It appears a general truth that successful military coups require a broader degree of support than is necessary to sustain a military government. To put the matter differently, the aftermath of every military coup will disappoint some of its original supporters and surprise many outside observers. Many examples can be presented of this general point; few contemporary observers at the time of the respective coups expected the post-1964 Brazilian military to last a generation, Pinochet to last over a decade, or the Velasco regime to carry out a sweeping land reform. The immediate post-coup period (like the immediate pre-coup period) will normally be a time of extreme tension and uncertainty. After a time, however, the military will either elect for a short stay (and "moderate") or for a long stay in which case it will either seek a clientele or try to do without one.

Military regimes which try to do without some kind of civilian clientele either come unstuck or find themselves having to evolve towards a fairly harsh form of dictatorship. Such a dictatorship will itself, however, be sustainable for only a few years. At some point, then, a regime which may initially seek to govern "above society" and alone must either find some more-or-less organised civilian support or (as with two recent Argentine military experiences) lose the political initiative to the opposition in a way which presages a disorderly retreat from power. This therefore leaves two possible patterns of long-term military rule - populist/nationalist and authoritarian/ clientelist. Both of these types of rule have prospered for long periods and might in theory continue indefinitely (although succession conflicts and inherent conflicts of interest within the ruling coalition might create growing strains and tensions under certain circumstances). The factor which has most commonly served to undermine both types of regime has been a shortage of resources; populist/nationalist governments often overspend and suffer the consequences, while governments of both types can fall victim to externally-generated ecomomic crisis.

Even without a shortage of resources, there are a number of mechanisms may serve to undermine a military government. What is crucial is that there should appear divisions among the original supporters of the military regime; the less solid this support, the more easily such divisions may appear. A country with divisions within the economic elite will be more difficult for the military to rule than a country in which there is a basic homogeneity (this point will be considered again in the conclusion); moreover, a country suffering from intense class conflict - or, put differently, "threat from below" - will be easier for the military to rule than one where this is lacking. What does seem to be generally true is that when military regimes become discredited, they can lose their grip very rapidly. The logic behind this discrediting is that of collective action[9]; it will pay supporters of military regimes to remain loyal only for as long as they expect others to do so. Coalitions which support these regimes are, above all, alliances of convenience which will not long survive severe setback (unless of course the consequences of abandoning ship are perceived as highly dangerous). When a military regime does become discredited in this way, it will seek to hand back power to civilians in some kind of controlled return to democracy. Under these circumstances, however, the position of the military is surprisingly weak. It faces the classic problem of the obsolescing bargain; as the political process opens, so the military loses the capacity to shape events. For civilian politicians, what may look like an acceptable accommodation with the military at the beginning of such a process may come to seem a shameless sell-out by the end. For the military, what may seem to be a clearly defined strategy of returning to barracks may subsequently become seriously unstuck as the favourites of the military are repudiated by the voters. The key to this transformation lies with civilian politicians. If they allow themselves to be played off against each other (which may be unavoidable if they are separated by irreconcilable differences of principle), then the regime may emerge strengthened and should be able, at least, to manage a satisfactory transition. If civilians, and particularly the civilian parties, manage to retain a united front then the military regime will have little choice but to return power unconditionally. The return of power, however, like the initial post-coup period, will be a time of high uncertainty.

NOTES

1 Clapham and Philip, "Political Dilemmas of Military Regimes" in Political Dilemmas, p. 1.
2 Political Order, Ch. 4.
3 Op. cit., p. 13.
4 P. Cammack, "Clientelism and Military Government in Brazil", in C. Clapham, ed., Private Patronage and Public Power; political clientelism in the modern state, (Francis Pinter; 1982).
5 On the Peruvian case see A. Stepan, The State and Society; Peru in Comparative Perspective, (Princeton; 1978) and D. Collier, Squatters and Oligarchs; authoritarian rule and policy change in Peru, (Johns Hopkins; 1976).
6 J. Linz, "An Authoritarian Regime; Spain", in E. Allardt and S. Rokkan, Mass Politics in Political Sociology, (New York, Committee on Political Sociology; 1970), pp. 251-283. See also G. Philip, "Military Authoritarianism in South America: Brazil, Chile, Uruguay and Argentina", in Political Studies, (1984), Vol. 23, No. 1.
7 J. Linz, "The Future of an Authoritarian Situation of the Institutionalisation of an Authoritarian Regime: the case of Brazil" in A. Stepan, ed., Authoritarian Brazil; origins, policies and future, (Yale U. P.; 1973).
8 See D. Gilbert in Studies in Comparative International Development, 1978.
9 See A. Przeworski, Some Problems in the Study of the Transition to Democracy, (Woodrow Wilson paper No. 61; 1982).

Chapter 9

THE BRAZILIAN REGIMES SINCE 1964

Many political observers, including the US
Ambassador, at first believed that the Brazilian
coup of March 1964 would be of a "moderator" type,
in which the military would play an active part in
deciding who would govern but stop well short of
establishing a long-term dictatorship. Lincoln
Gordon, on 4 March 1964, cabled the State
Department that "if reaction to Left-wing coup
attempt led to temporary military takeover, they
would be quick to restore constitutional
institutions and restore power to civilian
hands."[1] It was certainly the expressed
intention of those who assumed formal government
positions after the coup, notably Castello Branco
the first president, to return power to an elected
civilian government. Those key civilian
politicians who supported the coup - notably Carlos
Lacerda, governor of Guanabara state (i.e. Rio de
Janeiro), Magalhâes Pinto (governor of Minas
Gerias) and Adhemar de Barros (governor of Sâo
Paulo) - were also looking for a short interregnum
which would enable one of their number to become
president in the elections scheduled for 1965. A
key military component of the 1964 coup was the
Sorbonne group, whose past history had included the
Italian campaign and the ESG (for more detail, see
chapter 6). Apart from Castello Branco himself and
his close military advisers (Ernesto Geisel and
Golbery do Couta e Silva), crucial support for the
coup came from a number of other officers who had
fought in the Italian campaign. Those tenentes
who had come to oppose Getulio Vargas after 1945,
notably Juarez Tavora and Cordeiro de Farias, were
also solidly behind the coup. For some of these
officers, the coup could be seen as the settling of
old scores. Those officers who had successfully

removed Vargas in 1945 and 1954 and later been defeated at the ballot box had now won decisively and were in a position to impose their will. Yet this group, for all its frustrations with Brazilian populism, was by no means fanatically Right-wing. It looked for a democracy without populists but not a democracy without electors. Lincoln Gordon's assessment, quoted above, reflected the assumption that this coalition, which was close to and fully supported by the US Embassy, would prevail.

Also involved in the coup, however, was a group of military hard-liners who were anti-civilian in general and anti-Left in particular. Perhaps typical was General Mourao Filho, one of the earliest and most determined conspirators against Goulart. In April 1963, when General Mourao was already conspiring, the CIA described his views as follows.[2] He wanted "to get rid of extreme Leftists and Communists", to introduce a determinedly pro-US foreign policy, to clamp down hard on organised labour, "to do away with professional politicians", "to restrict the military from entering politics" and "to promote social justice" by means of an agrarian reform. While neither Mourao Filho nor the other hard-liners enjoyed great intellectual gifts or a pronounced coherence of view, the hard-liners differed decisively with the Sorbonne group (and civilian supporters of the 1964 coup) in their diagnosis of whom the coup was directed against or (to put the matter differently) where the main threat to the country came from. The Sorbonne group and the politicians sought to overthrow Goulart for what they regarded as his abuses of power and his unwillingness to manage the economy decisively or to curb the Marxist Left. For the hard-liners, however, these objections did not go to the root of the matter. This root lay in the whole pattern of post-war politics in Brazil with its populism, "demogoguery" and occasional mass mobilisation. Many hard-liners drew their ideological inspiration not from democracy at all but from Fascism. This is not to say that they were fully-fledged Fascists (whatever such a term may have meant in post-1964 Brazil) but it is notable that Fransisco Campos and Carlos Medeiros de Silva, who had played an important part in drawing up the Estado Novo Constitution, were quickly brought in to draw up the first Institutional Act of the new government. Unlike

the Sorbonne group, moreover, the hard-liners had
few strong views about economic management; the
Sorbonnistas were economic liberals in a country,
and a military institution, in which nationalist
views were much more pronounced. The hard-liners
were never prisoners of any particular economic
doctrine.

In order to understand the appeal enjoyed by
hard-line officers, it is necessary to look in
slightly more detail at politics immediately prior
to 1964. We have already seen that factionalism
had been re-introduced into the Brazilian military
after the return to democracy in 1945; it had
played its part in the Petrobrás campaign and led
to the setting up of the ESG in reaction. During
the 1950s political conflicts created some
difficulties for the military institution but
nothing unmanageable happened. The position
deteriorated in 1961 when an abortive coup was
attempted following the resignation of Quadros,
which aimed to prevent the accession to power of
(then) Vice President Goulart. The military Right
was seriously discredited by this episode which
General Golbery later described as "a disaster for
the army".[3] When Goulart did take office, he was
able to take some revenge on those who had moved
against him by moving known opponents, or men of
suspect loyalty, away from command positions.
Goulart after 1961, like Perón after 1951, may
have had good reason to promote his friends and
remove his enemies but it seems that this
increasing factionalisation worked against him in
the long-run as the more "professional" officers
joined inveterate Right-wing conspirators in
seeking his overthrow.[4] This factionalisation
undoubtedly had its impact after 1964 for those who
felt that their careers had suffered under Goulart
had few scruples about purging those who had
prospered. As Stepan points out[5], the purge of
the military after 1964 was conducted on a scale
which was unprecedented for post-war Brazil. Up
until then, those who had lost out as a result of
political change may have suffered some limited
career damage but they almost always remained
within the military. After 1964 this ceased to be
the case. On 11 April, less than a fortnight after
the coup, 122 officers were formally expelled from
the military; many others were pressured into
resigning. Thus, of the 29 officers promoted
general by President Goulart, only five remained

generals on active duty in 1968. It is also worth noting that the purge did not extend only to active Goulart supporters. Men who had taken an active part in the 1964 coup, but who were judged to be unsound, or whose face did not fit, were also eased out; sometimes participants had over-optimistic ideas about the posts they would fill after the success of the coup and turned against the regime when their ambitions were disappointed.

In post-1964 Brazil, as in other cases elsewhere, the existence of "purged men's shoes" had a markedly hardening effect on those who remained within the institution. The last thing which these rapidly-promoted officers wanted was an amnesty for those whom they had removed. Any return of civilian politicians would raise this danger; fear of such a development added to support from within the military for the hard-liners.

Hard-line officers were also very much concerned with problems of internal security. One reason for their pronounced dislike of populist politics was its apparent threat to military discipline. These fears were given particular force by the sergeants movement of 1963 which was briefly discussed in the last chapter.

Many officers certainly felt that the 1964 coup was not necessarily the end of the NCO threat. An abortive sergeants plot was in fact discovered in October 1964 featuring at least twenty conspirators.[6] In general, there was a feeling within the military that an early return to open politics might make discipline harder to maintain. The military hard-liners in Brazil were not the first or last in Latin America to perceive a conflict between full democracy and the order and discipline of the military institution.

It would, however, be misleading to identify hard-line pressures as coming from the military alone. Another important series of pressures came from Right-wing politicians who feared electoral defeat at the hands of the Left or of "corrupt" (i.e. populist or machine based) politicians; such people preferred the administrative elimination of their opponents to the requirements of electoral competition. Subsequently, hard-line civilians looked for the removal even of those opponents who had originally supported the 1964 coup. Thus Magalhaes Pinto, the UDN governor of Minas Gerais, was one of the earliest to put pressure on the incoming military government to extend its range of purges.[7] Similarly, the largely patrimonial conservative politicians of the North-East demanded the removal of their radical challengers. In Sâo Paulo, a hard-line grouping (including Ruy Mesquita, the owner of the Estado de Sâo Paulo) successfully asked the regime in 1966 to set aside the popularity and patronage network of the outgoing governor, Adhemar de Barros (an early supporter of the 1964 coup), so that they could themselves impose a new governor backed by federal power.[8] Politicians who could not win and economic interests who feared the consequences of opposition victories were by no means unwilling to call on hard-line military support. Only in retrospect did the military hard-liners appear friendless.

POST-COUP POLITICS

Political conflict between the leaders of the 1964 coup began almost immediately after the coup itself. Some kind of alliance seems to have been formed between Magalhaes Pinto, the civilian leader of the coup, Adhemar de Barros and General Costa e Silva who was the most senior general on active service at the time of the coup. Costa e Silva immediately proposed that the post-coup president should be a civilian (as had been the case following the military coups of 1930, 1945 and 1954). This suggestion was violently opposed by Carlos Lacerda whose own choice for president, Castello Branco, was supported by other coup leaders; Lacerda's proposal implied a short military interregnum followed by the return to an elected civilian president in 1965. Both Lacerda and Castello Branco assumed that Lacerda himself would be the leading candidate for this position. After a series of meetings and a major row between Lacerda and Costa e Silva, Castello Branco was indeed selected interim president.[9] Costa and Lacerda had however become enemies and Costa set out to turn Castello Branco against Lacerda; as Lacerda became increasingly critical of the government, Costa e Silva's task became easier.

The second significant battle was fought out in June 1964. By this time the military had begun to set up an internal repressive apparatus. Soon after the coup IPMs (military-police investigations) were set up across the country to eliminate "subversion" and, incidentally, to settle old scores. The central government, in trying to control these organisations, found itself forced to move further in the direction of repression.[10] Moreover, Costa e Silva, who was now Minister of War, hoped to use the hard-line in order to prevent Castello Branco from handing back power to a civilian politician. In June 1964 Costa e Silva was telling Lincoln Gordon that many officers blamed Kubitschek as well as Goulart for the "mess" of the pre-coup period. Kubitschek, after a hostile press campaign, was on 8 June banned from standing for public office for a period of ten years. Kubitschek himself, a moderate nationalist who largely maintained his personal appeal when, as president of Brazil 1956-60, he ruled over a booming economy, was unacceptable to civilian supporters of the coup largely because he was popular and therefore a threat to their own presidential aspirations. For the hard-liners, he was merely a civilian politician and therefore suspect. His quick political elimination should have served as a warning to others, but did not.

By the end of 1964 there were signs that Castello Branco, although personally secure, was beginning to lose the political initiative. Costa e Silva, though loyal to the government, was by no means committed to the ESG "project" of economic liberalisation, political reform and eventual democratisation; nor was this project universally popular within the military. Moreover Castello Branco, while retaining friends and colleagues, was now largely without heavyweight political allies. Lacerda's increasingly erratic behaviour had made him impossible to work with and, of the other leading civilian politicians, neither Adhemar de Barros nor Magalhaes Pinto was generally sympathetic to the <u>Sorbonne</u> line. Faced with the unrewarding need to take orthodox counter-inflationary measures and attempting liberal economic reforms which went against the grain of past Brazilian development strategies Castello found his government becoming unpopular and his allies fractious. He did not respond with any serious effort to carve out a political base of his own, either within the military or among his civilian allies; most crucially, he did not attempt to prepare a military successor. His friends later came to regard this as a bad mistake because it meant that they lacked a focal point from which to organise their opposition to Costa e Silva - a bitter enemy of some **Sorbonnistas** and a man with few scruples about attracting hard-line support. Lacerda's own apparent strategy, of seeking to use the military hard-line against Castello Branco, was even more clearly nonsensical since the hard-liners had no desire to hand power to any civilian. Costa e Silva was a far more credible candidate for hard-line military support than Lacerda could ever be. The Castello Branco/Lacerda conflict generally weakened both men and strengthened the hard-line.

Another series of conflicts surrounded the making of economic policy. Castello Branco had largely handed over the Economics Ministry to Roberto Campos, a close civilian ally of the Sorbonne group, who (with the exception of one or two ingenious fiscal innovations) found it necessary to apply a broadly orthodox IMF stabilisation policy to Brazil in order to counter a rate of inflation rising toward 100% p.a. Although the ensuing recession was not particularly severe by later standards, it did not form a propitious climate for early elections. Moreover, the climate of recession re-opened the perennial conflict between liberals and nationalists in Brazil. The liberals wanted a dismantling of the centralist state which had grown up during and after the Estado Novo, while the nationalists wanted to keep a strong state presence.

The Sorbonne group, in addition to having an intellectual preference for democracy and for close alignment with the United States, were also strongly in favour of a market economy which included fiscal orthodoxy and acceptance of foreign investment. Economic liberalism and monetarist economics were, however, unpopular within society as a whole and particularly with the nationalist Left. This unpopularity created an inconsistency. If the government was to pursue a determinedly liberal (in economic terms) programme, it could not easily liberalise politically for fear of having its policies challenged and reversed. The tactic actually adopted was to gamble on a quick success which did not materialise; Brazil remained in relative recession until the end of 1967. This apparent economic failure - or, perhaps more accurately absence of alignment between political and economic strategy - strengthened the position of harder line officers who tended to be nationalist rather than liberal. Like their Estado Novo predecessors they sought to find in

an assertive domestic and foreign policy a cause
which would justify repression and also a source of
popularity which could act as a substitute for
formal democratic procedures. They were not
interested in carrying out repression for a cause
which they did not support, and objected strongly
to the prospect of returning power to civilians as
soon as the economy improved.

THE TRANSITION TO LONG-TERM RULE

        Castello Branco lost control of politics
during 1965. The year began well enough. Mayoral
elections were held in March in Sâo Paulo and were
won by a regime supporter. Thus encouraged,
Castello Branco ordered that direct elections for
state governor be held, again on schedule, in
October 1965. Presidential elections were,
however, postponed for a year. Most of the
governorship elections in fact passed off without
major incident but one result had far-reaching
implications. In Guanabara Lacerda's chosen
successor for governor was defeated by a Kubitschek
supporter. This result was by no means unwelcome
to Castello Branco; indeed, the latter appears to
have promoted it by disqualifying a far-Left
candidate and so increasing the credibility of the
moderate opposition. What was significant is that
the election brought about the definitive breach
between Lacerda and Castello Branco. Tensions
between the two had already increased in August
1965 as a consequence of the reform of political
parties undertaken by the government. Politicians
supporting the regime (mainly from the PSD and UDN)
were ordered to form ARENA and those opposing it
(mainly from the PTB) to form the MDB. In Sâo
Paulo, however, there were tensions between
Lacerda's supporters in the UDN and the PSD which
did not support Lacerda; Castello Branco prevailed
upon the Paulista UDN to enter ARENA over Lacerda's
objections.[11] Lacerda had earlier flirted with
the idea of setting up a political party of his
own. After the election defeat Lacerda's allies
in Congress - a substantial minority within the
purged institution - began to attack the
government. In Minas Gerais also, the moderate
opposition candidate defeated the representative of
the "Revolution".
        The military hard liners felt threatened by
this return to factional politics and feared that

an unacceptable civilian would win the elections
which were still scheduled for the following year.
Thus, as the CIA commented on the election results,
"the eventual winners were political moderates
individually acceptable to the government. But
the election results were not acceptable to the
revolution in the eyes of its military
guarantors."[12] The elections also increased the
political temperature; Kubitschek returned from
exile and Lacerda was becoming increasingly
polemical. On 5 October, various hard-line
officers led by General Albuquerque Lima and some
colonels based at the Vila Militar in Rio de
Janeiro began moves to overthrow Castello Branco.
Costa e Silva negotiated their quiescence, promising a tightening of authoritarian control in
return. Castello Branco then went to Congress and
asked for some limited repressive measures in order
to "strengthen the revolution". He found, however,
that his ability to control Congress had ended;
indeed Castello Branco's "largely informal
parliamentary bloc disintegrated, as former PSD and
UDN supporters polarised around the standards of
Kubitschek and Lacerda."[13] He thus had little
option but to introduce Institutional Act No. 2
which decreed that the elections for president due
in 1966 would be indirect (i.e. pushed through a
rubber stamp Congress); the Act also abolished the
existing political parties in Brazil pending reorganisation to be decided upon by the military.

The ending of plans to hold open elections in
1966 really marked the end of the "moderator"
project. It led to the resignation or withdrawal
of many civilian supporters of the 1964 coup and to
a considerable decline in military popularity. It
was, however, not yet clear what was to come. The
hard-line was still predominantly a reactive force
rather than a positively organised one. Its
emergence even appears to have taken the CIA by
surprise. At the end of 1965 this reported that
"until recently it (the hard-line) represented an
unorganised small minority of both active and
retired officers. During the past several weeks,
however, there has been evidence that shortly
before the gubernatorial elections a loose
organisation had begun to develop among middle-
grade officers, some of whom reportedly had begun
plotting."[14] They were, in fact, particularly
strong in the repressive agencies where officers
feared a political opening which would call them to

account. They also had some evidence that
pro-Goulart officers were continuing to plot.
Indeed, the CIA reported that in late September
1964 a Brazilian general and two colonels went to
Montevideo to talk to Goulart and Brizola, and that
Brizola and the PCB had also been discussing the
possibility of a rising. In order to cope with
threats of this kind Castello Branco set. up an
overall military intelligence network, the SNI,
under the direction of General Golbery. When,
after Costa e Silva became president in March 1967,
General Medici took over the SNI this became
another centre of hard-line pressures.

In 1966 Costa e Silva achieved his ambition of
using the hard-liners to promote .his own
presidential candidacy. As Stepan put it, "Costa e
Silva emerged as a leader because he was felt to be
sympathetic to the somewhat inarticulate but
nonetheless powerful sentiments for a more
militant, authoritarian government and a less pro-
American and more nationalist stance."[15] By then
the moderating strategy had clearly failed. The
Second Institutional Act, in addition to ending
direct elections, was followed by the undermining
of the position of pro-regime politicians. Quadros
had his political rights suspended. for ten years,
Adhemar de Barros was forced out by hard-liners
following political reorganisation in Sâo Paulo,
and Lacerda moved quite sharply to the Left and out
of serious contention. Magalhaes Pinto alone
remained close to the centre of power. Between
1966 and the early 1970s Brazil moved rather
unsteadily in the direction of military
totalitarianism.

When Costa e Silva took office in March 1967,
he sharply increased military representation in his
Cabinet. One key appointment was General
Albuquerque Lima as Interior Minister. Albuquerque
Lima was the most prominent hard-line officer and a
possible candidate to succeed Costa e Silva.
Another key appointment (though it did not seem so
important at the time) was that of Delfim Netto as
Finance Minister. Two other key appointments
promoted men with hard-line sympathies, General
Jayme Portella to be head of the military
household, and General Medici to be head of an
increasingly powerful SNI. Both were conditionally
loyal to Costa; neither was a doctrinaire hard-
liner, but both (like Costa himself) were
opportunists willing to rely on hard-line support

when it suited them. The hard line had not yet won
its last victory however. The last of the old
politicians, Magalhaes Pinto, was made Foreign
Minister and a number of Sorbonne officers, notably
the Geisel brothers, retained strong positions in
the army. However, the Sorbonne group as a whole
suffered a sharp loss of influence. Castello
Branco was killed in a plane crash in 1967 and
General Golbery, who had made his hostility to
Costa e Silva too apparent, found himself in the
political wilderness.

Costa himself, however, proved incapable of
giving a political lead. Delfim continued for a
time with the orthodox deflationary policies of his
predecessor amid their growing unpopularity while
Costa himself continued to be vague about the re-
shaping of the political system. He began by
promising to "humanise" the regime but no action
followed. Meanwhile, various opposition groups -
beginning to recover confidence after their defeat
in 1964 - began to challenge the regime. A part of
the problem was that, within the Brazilian
military, only the Sorbonne group had been able to
articulate clearly what kind of system it wanted.
The Sorbonnistas would have preferred a democracy
in which their opponents lost, but were willing to
settle for some form of co-existence with
acceptable politicians within some kind of
electoral framework. The fact that such co-
existence could occur only in the context of some
active political management by the military-
political elite was a point largely overlooked by
the Sorbonnistas during the 1960s although they
would not again make the same mistake when their
chance came a decade later. The rest ·of the
military was more nationalist, less interested in
preserving democratic forms, not interested at all
in political institution building but concerned
instead with the actual performance of the military
regime measured in terms of its success in
combatting "subversion" and in managing the
economy.

Although the actual course of events between
March 1967 and August 1969 is complex[16], their
effect was to resolve the uncertainties which were
perhaps the most prominent feature of the Costa e
Silva administration. In the end, the hard-liners
achieved most of what they wanted in terms of
internal security while the business supporters of
the regime, particularly the Sâo Paulo

bourgeoisie, got an expansionary policy to suit
them. To cover the main events very briefly, late
1967 and much of 1968 saw opponents of the military
government take to the streets - students were
particularly active in their hostility to the
regime and were joined by some sectors of the
Church hierarchy. Organised labour was also
becoming increasingly restive due to the deflation
and quite sharp fall in real wages as well as for
more clearly political reasons. These popular
attacks on the regime only made the hard-liners
more determined. When a Congressional Deputy
attacked the military in fairly sharp terms in
October 1968, the government demanded that Congress
should lift his immunity so that he could be tried
in the courts. When Congress refused, it was
briefly dissolved and the regime passed
Institutional Act No. 5 which centralised power in
the presidency to an unprecedented degree. In mid-
1969 a section of the Left began armed attacks on
the government which responded by the free use of
arbitrary arrest and torture (although not on the
scale adopted by the Southern Cone regimes in the
subsequent decade). Finally in August 1969 Costa e
Silva was taken ill. Subsequently, normal
constitutional procedures were again suspended and
the military hierarchy alone set about choosing a
new president. The procedure adopted was that
every general on active duty (118 from the army, 6
from the navy and 61 from the air force) was to
sound out his subordinates and then inform the
senior generals of their findings. Two serious
candidates emerged, General Medici and General
Albuquerque Lima. Eventually General Medici
received the nomination.

Medici was something of a compromise choice
within the context of the military as a whole. He
was preferred to Albuquerque Lima by most of the
military establishment as well as by the São Paulo
business community, which disliked Albuquerque's
brand of military nationalism, and by the United
States. Medici was in political terms something of
an unknown quantity, whose career had been spent in
military positions and more recently as head of the
SNI. He was an accommodationist rather than a
hard-line officer and, while relying on Delfim
Netto to carry out his economic policy, he allowed
some Sorbonnista officers back into the inner
councils of the state. The most important of these
appointments was Orlando Geisel who was made

Minister of War; from the beginning, Orlando's brother, Ernesto Geisel, was regarded as a strong candidate to become Medici's successor but he was given the less immediately sensitive position of President of Petrobrás.[17]

The Medici regime, while certainly not fully totalitarian, approached the police state form of government in two key respects. There was very little contact with forces within civil society (although some fairly meaningless Congressional elections were held in 1970) and the government placed emphasis instead on its outputs - its economic performance and its effectiveness against subversion. More important, it gave unchangeable power to the various internal repressive agencies that operated during the period. As Flynn points out, "it is not possible fully to understand the nature of Brazilian politics and the control exercised by the regime, especially from 1969 onwards, without appreciating the terrorizing impact of the widespread and systematic use of torture for political purposes."[18] It appears that there were in fact three different sets of internal repressive agencies. The most centralised and powerful was the SNI which, though moderately hard line, was neither politically extremist nor the most brutally repressive agency. It was, however, a formidable bureaucratic agency at the centre of the regime. There was an SNI nucleus in every ministry, formally subordinate to the minister and entrusted with screening ministry recruits, but in practice often concerned with policy and in all cases far more influential than its formal role might suggest. The SNI nucleus was also present in each state governor's office and in every municipality. In 1971 the SNI set up its own training school - an important step in protecting its own institutional identity in the qualification-conscious military establishment and also an opportunity to establish direct links with civilians. As Schmitter put it, this led to "the creation of a vast information-gathering network, using both the most modern techniques of data processing and retrieval and the most medieval methods of 'data extraction', that penetrates all private institutions and levels of government."[19] A second set of repressive agencies were the DOPS, organised by the military commanders of each state. Thirdly there was OBAN which worked partly independently of the military institution; it drew much of its financial support from business interests, happy to use it as a form of labour control. Torture and murder of union activists, particularly in Sâo Paulo, was a marked feature of the police state phase of the military regime. Finally, there were various organisations, including death squads, probably operating independently of the military and the government but satisfied that they could act with impunity in the climate of the times.

In organisational terms, the Medici government was highly decentralised, and Brazil was largely run by two different hierarchies which reported to the presidency. Economic policy was in the hands of Delfim Netto who acted as "superminister" for the economic side. Military and security affairs were conducted from within the military itself; the key figures here were the army minister (Orlando Geisel) and, more important, the SNI.

The armed Left began its long awaited offensive in September 1969 capturing the US Ambassador and securing the release of a number of political prisoners. This further stimulated the activities of the repressive apparatus. The armed Left, never in a position to mount a serious challenge to the regime, was largely stamped out by the end of 1971 but the repression continued largely unchecked.

The other side of the Medici period was the so-called Brazilian miracle; this involved several years of extremely rapid economic growth which followed Delfim Netto's abandonment of austerity in late 1967 and subsequent pump-priming activities. The growth rates achieved were fairly impressive - around or even above 10% for seven successive years to the end of 1974 - although not out of line with the figures achieved during previous Brazilian booms.[26] There were also some genuine policy innovations, notably the extensive use of indexation to limit the distributional conflicts caused by Brazil's continuing high inflation rate. This was also the period in which Brazil first became a serious exporter of manufactures and in which Brazilian agriculture began to diversify its exports decisively away from coffee and sugar. Other aspects of economic policy were less constructive, however. The miracle involved a liberal degree of borrowing from abroad, an acknowledged worsening of income distribution (particularly as consumer credit, a major engine of

growth, was allocated disproportionately to the
middle class) and increasing dependence on imported
energy (notably oil). To the extent that the model
"required" a worsening in the relative position of
unskilled labour (a "requirement" which both
policymakers and their critics accepted as a fact
although economic theory is far from unambiguous on
this), it seemed to justify a policy of tight
labour control. This also involved manipulating
(on occasion downright falsifying) the official
figures on prices and growth. Another, in this
case reasonably popular, aspect of the Medici
period was the development of various "mega
projects" by state agencies; there was a vast road-
building programme, a very ambitious public housing
programme and even a serious literacy programme.
Needless to say, military spending was not
neglected either during the period. The public
sector in general terms, and the big state
companies in particular, became more important than
ever before.

As Medici's term was drawing to an end in
1973, some high ranking members of the military and
the government were beginning to feel uneasy at
both the inegalitarian and the repressive aspects
of the regime. Although 1973 was a spectacularly
successful year in terms of economic growth, it was
becoming clear that the Brazilian economy was
reaching the limits of its capacity and that a
slower growth process would be necessary in
subsequent years; by this time, moreover, the
worsening distribution of income was becoming a
matter of concern to a number of elite figures,
even including Medici himself. Moreover, with the
insurgent threat defeated, some key figures became
concerned at the extent to which the regime had
become isolated from civil society and dependent on
its own repressive forces. An important indicator
of this change appeared in September 1972 when
O Estado de Sâo Paulo protested against new
regulations governing press censorship by sending a
telegram to the Justice Minister accusing the
government of reducing Brazil "to the condition of
a banana republic". The Church also gradually
became more outspoken against government repression
during this period (although the Brazilian Church
is on the whole less influential than its Spanish-
American counterparts).

The selection of General Ernesto Geisel to
succeed Medici at the beginning of 1974 was an

indication that a limited move in the direction of economic nationalism and political liberalisation was in prospect. Geisel was a Sorbonnista but one whose relations with the Medici group remained cordial; he was greatly helped by the fact that his brother was Army Minister when the selection process was undertaken. During this period he retained his friendship with General Golbery who, in 1974, was recalled from the political wilderness and given a key advisory role in the new regime. It has been suggested that, had Medici been fully aware of this friendship, he would not have accepted Geisel's candidacy.[21] Geisel had, as head of Petrobrás, acquired something of the reputation, unusual among Sorbonnistas, of an economic nationalist. His original aim was to carry through an economic strategy which would have strengthened the industrialisation process (in particular developing a capital goods industry which had been rather neglected in earlier years) and possibly improved the distribution of income. After Geisel's selection, however, but before he took office there was a sharp increase in the international oil price which presented Brazil with immediate and severe balance of payments difficulties. Although the fact did not become apparent immediately, Brazil faced a far more adverse international economic climate in the years after 1974 than it had in the preceding decade.

THE BEGINNING OF LIBERALISATION

Nevertheless, Geisel's first cabinet did indicate a possible shift in the direction of economic policy. The new planning minister, Severo Gomes, was - like Geisel himself - something of a nationalist and eager to reduce the prominence of the rapidly growing multinationals in the Brazilian economy. He also favoured a greater degree of protectionism after the partial opening of the Brazilian economy to imports in the late 1960s. Gomes did, however, have to share control over economic policy with Mario Simonsen, a more traditional representative of São Paulo's business interests, who was Finance Minister. In retrospect, it is easy to exaggerate the extent of this "nationalist" departure in economic policy-making; Simonsen defeated Severo Gomes in an important bureaucratic battle in May 1977 and the Planning Minister later resigned. In October 1975, moreover, Petrobrás' monopoly of domestic oil exploration - a very sensitive nationalist issue in Brazil - was broken by the introduction of foreign companies although in the event this step has so far proved of little practical importance. However, there was a continuation of one trend from the Medici period - a rapid expansion of public investment, particularly in big showcase projects. Some of these were strongly supported by the military itself - particularly the roads programme (under Medici) and the nuclear power programme, which became increasingly important after an agreement with West Germany in 1974. Brazil also rapidly developed a major arms industry during this period and by the end of the 1970s was a significant exporter of weapons.

Geisel's government was certainly different from Medici's in one key respect. Although Medici was certainly an authoritarian figure, he ran a fairly decentralised government. After the two hard-line rebellions of October 1965 and November 1968, Medici had no desire to challenge the army. Geisel, though in some respects more liberal, was far more directly in control of events than his predecessor. His inner-circle - made up of Generals Golbery, Figueiredo and Hugo Abreu and the civilian Reis Velloso - was made up of confidantes rather than executives.²² This centralisation, as well as the lukewarm economic nationalism and the sometimes courageous political liberalisation, were the main hallmarks of the Geisel period.

Although the Geisel government was seriously interested in political liberalisation, its actual policies were limited by its reactions to three key events. The first of these was the sharp worsening of Brazil's terms of trade resulting from the increase in world oil prices. A popularity-boosting tactic of growth with redistribution was now largely out of the question although efforts were made to bring about modest reductions in income inequality. However, despite the increase in Brazil's import bill, the economy continued to grow at a respectable rate for the rest of the decade, aided by a further increase in foreign borrowing. The miracle was over, but the recession had not yet begun.

The second key event was the Congressional election due in November 1974. Congressional elections had in fact gone ahead in November 1970 at the height of the repression but were regarded by most political observers, and much of the electorate, as a meaningless exercise. The November 1974 elections were far more serious. They were an attempt to test the water before the regime considered a full democratisation. Geisel and Golbery hoped that the "miracle" years had created a constituency for a moderate conservative government which might now restore direct elections for president in the serious expectation of winning. The campaign was open and the opposition MDB, which had been widely considered as no more than a paper organisation during the Medici years, took on a serious identity.

The 1974 elections resulted in a convincing moral victory for the MDB. The government party, ARENA, did manage to retain a majority but only by running up victories in the largely rural north east and interior of the country where traditional clientelist political machinery could still be relied upon to deliver a vote for the government. In the cities the government lost badly, both in working class areas and among middle class voters.[23] Ironically, therefore, those who had benefited most from the Brazilian miracle (the urban middle classes) were unwilling to support the government while those who had benefited least from it could still be whipped into line through traditional clientelist methods.

The third key event involved the politics of São Paulo state, which need to be considered in a little more detail. São Paulo is economically by far the most powerful state in Brazil. Ever since the defeat of the 1932 rebellion, however, it has been under-represented in political life but at the same time allowed a degree of autonomy in conducting its own affairs. Between 1948 and 1964 a crucial buffer role was played by Adhemar de Barros. Under Medici the most powerful paulista in Brazilian politics was Delfim Netto who, when Finance Minister, maintained contact with leading figures in the São Paulo business community. Delfim expected to become governor of São Paulo after Medici left office and hoped to use this position as a political base from which to launch a presidential candidacy. However, Delfim reckoned without Geisel who strongly disliked him for reasons which were partly personal and partly political. Delfim's efforts to become governor of São Paulo were blocked and he was instead made Ambassador in France; Geisel gave the São Paulo governorship to Egydio Martins, a personal loyalist without a strong political following within the state. This decision immediately split the governing party in São Paulo and contributed to its fairly comprehensive defeat in the elections of November 1974. It also left important sections of the São Paulo business community increasingly free to criticise government policy; under Medici the policy-making system was theoretically centralised and inflexible but much of the paulista bourgeoisie retained personal access to Delfim. This was no longer possible and Delfim's replacement, Severo Gomes, was something of an economic nationalist whose preferences were certainly not universally shared by the economic elite. Lacking access to the state apparatus, then, sections of the paulista bourgeoisie began to use the press in order to criticise what they saw as excessive state control over the economy. They also increasingly came to feel that it was important to recapture control over the governorship of São Paulo in order to secure access to the , policy-making apparatus; this required a degree of democratisation if subsequent governors were not also to be imposed by fiat.[24]

While some of the paulistas responded to the Geisel regime by calling for more openness and more democracy, however, others put their faith in reaction. We have already seen that the São Paulo military commander and some members of the paulista economic elite were in control of significant repressive agencies. Geisel sought to check the power of these by sending a personal loyalist, General D'Avila Melo, to command the army of São Paulo. D'Avila, however, soon proved to be a man unworthy of the trust which Geisel had placed in him. As early as April 1975 it was being reported that D'Avila "made his peace with the coalition of policemen, bankers and industrialists who have ruled São Paulo for many years"[25] and that his own defection was weakening the position of Geisel and Golbery, not only in São Paulo, but in Brasilia where other officers were waiting for the president to stumble or to show weakness. By October 1975 a hard-line conspiracy against Geisel was well advanced.

At this point, some hard-liners within the São Paulo security agencies (whether acting alone or in concert with others is not clear) sought to increase the pressure on the Geisel regime. The tactic was to extract a confession under torture from a well-known Jewish journalist in Sâo Paulo that would have tied him to General Golbery in some form of corrupt "Zionist" conspiracy; this could then be used in the media to discredit Golbery and damage Geisel. The plot failed completely, however, when the journalist died under torture; his death provoked a popular outcry which showed that much of the Sâo Paulo middle class had had enough of repressive agencies, death squads and the like; it also created anxiety among prominent generals who feared the implications of using arbitrary arrest and torture in intra-elite disputes. Following a further death-under-torture three months later, this time of a trade union militant, Geisel was strong enough to dismiss D'Avila and arrange a more loyal replacement.

This incident was important, first, in that it gave Geisel the first decisive victory over hard-line officers won by any Brazilian president since 1964. Secondly, following the dismissal of D'Avila, various centres of internal repression and torture were dismantled; the SNI remained powerful - perhaps more powerful than ever - but it was not a centre of the extreme hard-line. Indeed, Geisel's appointed head of the SNI, General Figueiredo, was a personal friend and ally who already knew that he was to be Geisel's chosen successor.[26]

This transformation meant that the regime had to exercise forms of social control other than through brute force and terror. Although this did not immediately lead to an outburst of popular mobilisation, it did mean that strikes (virtually non-existent between 1968 and 1974), press criticism of the government and the occasional demonstration once again began to occur. It also meant that the government needed civilian allies more than was the case earlier. Indeed, the dismantling of the most repressive aspects of the authoritarian state meant that differences within the broad coalition of regime supporters needed to be handled with tact and flexibility if the coalition itself was not to fall apart. This would prove a difficult undertaking since, as McDonough has painstakingly documented[27], the Brazilian elite is not characterised by a unity of outlook; moreover, its viewpoints are diffuse rather than factionalised.

The Geisel regime responded to these various challenges by returning to some very traditional techniques of political control; clientelism and machine politics in the rural areas, compromise and bargaining in the urban centres. In São Paulo, for example, D'Avila's successor - General Dilermando Monteiro - began working discreetly alongside Egydio to re-establish government control.[28] He established a working relationship with the progressive wing of the Church, put pressure on the opposition to moderate their demands for further measures of political liberalisation, and maintained friendly contact (but at a distance) with those members of the paulista elite closely associated with D'Avila. These, in turn, dropped their hard-line stance and (once it became clear that there would be no recriminations) cautiously began to accept the idea of a political opening. Yet both Egydio and Dilermando ultimately remained representatives of Brasilia and, as liberalisation continued, it became clear that São Paulo would have to be given an authentic voice of its own in high places. This gradual liberalisation, moreover, did not occur only in São Paulo; the same gradual process took place across the whole of social and political life within Brazil.

Soon after the sacking of D'Avila, attention began to turn to the succession to Geisel, due to be announced in 1978. We now know that Geisel had already decided to impose General Figueiredo, head of the SNI, as his successor but contemporaries did not. Most assumed that the selection would be made through a sounding process from within the military (as had happened in 1969 and again in 1973), while some hoped that it might herald a more complete opening of politics.

The "political openers" received a rude shock in April 1977 when Geisel closed Congress briefly in order to announce a package of measures which made it effectively impossible for opposition parties to win a majority in the electoral college where the presidency was decided. The presidential term was also extended by one year, from five to six. Geisel's main rival, however, came from the hard-line right. War minister Frota attempted to build a civil-military constituency of a hard-line character in order to pressure Geisel to support his own candidacy - as the hard-liners had supported Costa e Silva in 1965. In October 1977

Generals Figueiredo, Golbery and Abreu held the army in line while Frota was summarily sacked.[29] This left the way clear for Figueiredo. Following Figueiredo's nomination, rival candidates were put forward both by the opposition MDB (Bentes Monteiro) and, more significant in the longer term, from a dissident wing of ARENA (the indefatigable Magalhaes Pinto). Neither of these, however, could seriously dent Figueiredo's majority. At the very end of 1978 Geisel took a final liberalising measure by repealing the 5th Institutional Act.

THE UNRAVELLING OF MILITARY RULE

The electoral setback for the government in November 1974 and the dismissals of D'Avila and Frota largely defined the parameters of the military regime during its process of liberalisation. Broadly speaking, three main forces needed to be taken into account. One was the military institution. This was to be disciplined and kept away from the day-to-day concerns of politics. Geisel and Golbery were strongly hostile to military factionalism and to unchecked military repression. On the other hand, the military was still needed to defend the authoritarian state. Figueiredo attempted successfully to still its anxieties in 1979 by offering an amnesty which among other things covered all illegal acts committed by members of the security forces during the worst years of the repression. Both Geisel and (at the beginning) Figueiredo also catered to the military's material interest by encouraging the expansion of state companies under direct military control - notably in the arms and nuclear industries - and expanding the role of the SNI itself. Overall, it can be said that the regime after 1974 did suceed in reducing and finally largely eliminating the factional political involvement of the military.
The second major force was the opposition. After the 1974 elections it became clear that the opposition did have the potential to win open presidential elections. Such an outcome was, however, unacceptable to the regime. Yet, if the regime was to successfully rein back the security forces, it needed to offer the opposition enough to "keep it in the game" so that it could be relied upon to discourage most drastic forms of popular

disaffection. What the regime did offer was
progressive liberalisation - with the threat of
repression if the opposition became excessively
assertive - and the promise of eventual democracy;
the regime was in fact slowly travelling toward
democracy but in the hope of never having to
arrive. When direct elections for state governor
were held in 1982, however, the regime's ability to
control the process went into a rapid decline.

Liberalisation short of democracy also had the
effect of making various Brazilian interest groups
far more assertive. The radical wing of the
Church, increasingly active in Brazil and courted
by the Geisel government, became involved in trade
union affairs. In May 1978 there occurred the
first major strike in Brazil for a decade as car
workers walked out in Sâo Paulo. This was
followed by a whole series of further strikes and
the emergence of a new unofficial trade union
leadership with connections to the Church; in 1979
"Lula" (Luis Ignacio de Silva) became a household
name. There were also student demonstrations in
1977 and demands began to be made for a more rapid
opening up of the democratic process. Meanwhile
sections of the press, headed by <u>O Estado de Sâo
Paulo</u> began to attack the government's economic
policies and, in particular, the excessive
"statisation" of the economy. Gradually, moreover,
the press began to refer openly to the torture and
murder carried out by the security forces under the
Medici regime and the image of the military was
therefore damaged.

The third major force after 1974 was the most
difficult to handle. This was made up of pro-
regime politicians. The party reforms of 1965 and
the practice of indirect elections gave the regime
a strong advantage over the opposition.
Nevertheless, the requirements of electoral
politics could not, be dismissed entirely and the
regime became to some extent dependent on its
civilian political allies - particularly those who
controlled the big political machines in rural
areas and in the North-East of the country. As the
political system liberalised, so the government's
dependence on these politicians - and their own
dependence on the popular vote - steadily
increased.[30] ARENA politicians now had the
formal power to make and unmake governments and it
would soon be their turn to resent "holding the cow
while others received the cream".

Geisel's own treatment of ARENA politicians, as well as of the military, bordered on the autocratic. In 1978 he simply imposed Figueiredo and demanded ARENA support for his candidate. Indeed, in the late 1970s there was some discussion of the possible "Mexicanisation" of the Brazilian system (the creation of a six-year presidential term in 1977 was perhaps a pointer to official thinking). This would involve a strong presidential system, reproduced over time by nomination of candidates from above, held in place by a dominant party with the opposition and the military being confined to peripheral roles. However, the Brazilian government - unlike the Mexican - suffered the disadvantage of not being able to manufacture electoral victories at will and had a far more fractious government party to control. Powerful economic interests were also becoming unhappy at the prospect of indefinite military rule; in June 1978 a group of eight business leaders mostly, though not exclusively, from São Paulo, publicly called on the government to speed its return to democracy. With the repeal of the 5th Institutional Act in 1978, the regime gave up a key instrument for maintaining the loyalty of its own supporters. As politics became more open, government supporters had more cause to fear electoral defeat; this had the effect of reducing their loyalty and increasing their flexibility.

General Figueiredo, therefore, inherited a system that was already showing signs of strain. However, he continued with Geisel's policy of liberalisation and sought to strengthen his position in two further ways. Unlike Geisel, who was a somewhat austere figure, he began to seek a degree of popular appeal, appearing in public in "ordinary" settings and generally appearing more human than the military stereotype; he even on one occasion attacked a heckler with his fists. Moreover, unlike Geisel, he had no personal animosity toward figures in the Medici government - as became clear in July 1979 when he appointed Delfim Netto to a key economics portfolio.

At the same time, however, he retained General Golbery as his adviser; Golbery was unquestionably the shrewdest military-political tactician of the entire period and he continued with his work of periodically re-designing the party system in the interests of the government. In November 1979 the

two party system suddenly became four, as the
opposition was divided into three by <u>fiat</u>.
Instead of a polarity, the government looked for a
spectrum of parties which would enable the
"moderate" opposition party (the PP) to be co-opted
into the system since it was led by figures with
whom the regime could work. Government control
over resources, and its increasingly open use of
patronage mechanisms, were intended to make such
co-optation rewarding. It was then confirmed that
direct elections for state governor would be held
in 1982 with the regime confident that, even where
it lost, it could use state resources to co-opt
winning governors into the government fold.
Meanwhile, or so it appears, Figueiredo and Golbery
had provisionally decided that the new head of SNI
- General Octavio Medeiros - would be nominated for
the presidency in 1985 with a full return to
universal suffrage by 1991 - by which time all
opposition politicians who had been prominent
before 1964 would be too old to stand.

This carefully designed plan came seriously
unstuck in 1981. For one thing the Brazilian
economy - badly hit by the second oil shock as also
by the first - was now clearly going into recession
(from which it only began to emerge at the end of
1984). Electoral and popular repercussions were
inevitable, although nobody could yet say what
these would be. Perhaps relating to this, some
senior military figures began to have second
thoughts about the political opening. A major
scandal occurred early in 1981 when two army
officers, carrying bombs to be set off in order to
stimulate Left-wing terror, blew themselves up in
transit. Although the incident was desperately
hushed up, it had major implications for elite
politics. Golbery wanted a full enquiry and purge;
Medieros, Golbery's former protege, blocked him.
Golbery responded by withdrawing support from
Medieros and, after a short interval, resigning
from the government. This deprived the government
of its most effective political operator and also
turned Medieros into a figure who was now
unacceptable to moderate supporters of the
government and added to the uncertainty about the
succession. At the same time, the high command
made clear their own unwillingness to return to a
politics of repression.

The government's second major setback occurred
soon after when Figueiredo became seriously ill and

left Brazil for treatment in the USA. His illness, from which he never fully recovered, further undermined the possibility of decisive political leadership from the centre - essential if the Geisel/Golbery system was to be maintained. Moreover, in Figueiredo's absence his civilian Vice-President Aureliano Chaves briefly took over and used the time to promote his own candidacy within the governing party (now called the PDS) to succeed Figueiredo; this had never been part of the latter's plans and the two men broke openly. By 1984 it was public knowledge that they were not even on speaking terms. Aureliano was believed to be both conversant with and unforgiving of growing corruption within the government. Moreover, he did not prevent the opposition using Figueiredo's absence to defeat another electoral strategem proposed by the government.[31] This would have allowed each party to run rival candidates for particular posts under the same label; such a strategem would have allowed competition within the governing party which could still return its candidate if its candidates together received more votes than those of the opposition. With the defeat of this project, the PDS found it increasingly difficult to maintain unity.

In November 1981 the government appeared to have reversed its defeat when it persuaded Congress to adopt a counter-measure which forced all parties to put up candidates for all elected offices in 1982. This forced the main opposition parties to compete with each other at all levels; since elections were decided on the basis of "first past the post", the government expected to benefit from the resulting split. However, this measure had one unintended consequence which was to work strongly against the government. The new electoral rules gave no role to the PP - the small, moderate party created by Golbery in 1979 in order to provide a half-way house for the regime to use; the PP did not have the resources to put up candidates for all posts. Instead its leading members went back to the largest opposition party, the PMDB, which then began to acquire real political weight and to look seriously like an alternative government. The regime had thus undermined its own strategy; it had regained its majority but lost its touch.

The elections of 1982 went badly for the government. It retained its support in the North East (in some places against expectations) but lost control of the crucial states of Sâo Paulo, Minas Gerais and Rio de Janeiro. Brizola's victory in Rio triggered alarm within the military, but the vote was respected and opposition governors were installed. However, the result was not without its consolations for the regime; it retained a blocking minority in the Chamber of Deputies and a majority in the electoral college to decide on Figueiredo's successor. A stronger opposition could, perhaps, be accommodated. Moreover, with the exception of Brizola, the main opposition governors were political moderates who had no intention of taking radical measures or otherwise upsetting the political applecart.

The man who finally did upset the applecart was Paulo Salim Maluf. Maluf was a businessman of Lebanese extraction, fabulously wealthy and aggressively capitalist but by no means a political insider. However, during the Medici period he began his ascent through the politics of Sâo Paulo becoming Mayor of the city in 1973. After 1974 he became loosely identified with the hard-line business opponents of Geisel but never took his opposition too far. When the nomination for the governorship of Sâo Paulo led to serious conflict between a Geisel loyalist and a clear opponent, Maluf emerged as a compromise candidate and became governor in 1978. Maluf used this period to extend what was already an impressive personal machine throughout the state; in 1982 he was elected to Congress and the following year made it clear that he was himself a candidate for the PDS nomination for president.

By 1983, therefore, there were three candidates for the succession. Aureliano had become progressively more radical after 1981, supporting a move to scrap the electoral college and return to election by universal suffrage. He attracted support from a number of well-placed PDS members who could not stand the prospect of another military term but these were by no means enough to compete with the payroll vote which the government could mobilise. Nevertheless, Figueiredo manoeuvred throughout 1983 to head off support for Aureliano; he made a number of concessions including the explicit promise that the next nominated presidential term would be the last. He also offered to cut the length of the term from six years to four. However, this was not enough and Aureliano maintained his candidacy.

239

Maluf was a far more serious candidate. His appeal was largely personal and highly effective in a constituency which had, in the past, been regarded merely as election fodder. In the Geisel/ Golbery system, the party was to be controlled from the top, and its individual members were to follow instructions. Maluf could offer far more than this to neglected minor politicians who, as a group, were electorally formidable. He was charming, he offered personal favours and, in at least some cases, bribes. The regime, faced with Figueiredo's illness and the recession, had neither the energy nor the means to combat these blandishments. When General Andreazza - once Minister of Transport under Medici - was finally presented as the official candidate for the succession, his own machine was already trailing badly.

Maluf, however, made enemies as well as friends. The old political bosses - who now formed the backbone of the government party - resented Maluf as an upstart without a decent respect for traditional methods. To paraphrase Marx, in place of the old disguised forms of control exerted by paternalist political authorities, Maluf offered the cash nexus. Moreover, the old politicians were becoming alarmed at the government's growing unpopularity - largely the result of recession; they began to fear that if they were forced to seek re-election in 1986 under the old system, they risked being heavily defeated. Many of them, in 1983 and even more in 1984, began looking discreetly for ways to desert what was beginning to look like a sinking ship.

The opposition, meanwhile, began to consider its short-term prospects with renewed optimism. The moderate opponents who, following the 1982 elections, had effectively captured the PMDB moved to take advantage of these divisions within the PDS. The PMDB nominated Tancredo Neves - an elderly, reassuring figure who had served both in the Vargas (1951-54) and Goulart governments - as their candidate. He was a man with broad popular appeal who would have the further advantage of being acceptable to the bulk of the military. He was, in fact, so moderate that the more radical opposition parties at first refused to support him. Tancredo, like Aureliano, was from Minas Gerais, and the two men soon put together a deal. Consequently, Aureliano abandoned his doomed PDS candidacy and swung his support behind Tancredo;

with the PDS vote split, Tancredo had a real
chance of victory in the electoral college. Under
these circumstances, the PMDB quickly dropped its
support for direct elections and concentrated on
winning according to the existing rules. Their
position became far stronger in July 1984 when the
PDS nominated Maluf. A substantial section of the
PDS - including both the northern governors and
much of the São Paulo business elite - immediately
switched its support to Tancredo.

By late 1984 Tancredo was the overwhelming
favourite to become president. He had the support
of the bulk of public opinion; opinion polls showed
overwhelming majorities in his favour and Maluf
could scarcely venture into the open for fear of
hostile demonstrations. Maluf had by then become
something of a scapegoat for the unpopularity of
the government; he was an easier and more
accessible target than the military high command.
Since the vote in the electoral college was public,
no Brazilian politician who wanted an electoral
future could readily vote for Maluf; memories would
not have faded by 1986. Tancredo also enjoyed
support from the two key bases of Brazilian
politics, the traditional landed/political interest
of the North East (largely motivated by self-
preservation) and the business elites of the
Centre-South; only a few businessmen connected
with foreign companies supported Maluf's aggressive
economic liberalism. Tancredo also had the
reluctant acquiescence of the military, whose
senior members disliked Maluf as an interloper and
wanted to avoid the serious public order problems
that threatened should Maluf be elected.[32]
Tancredo Neves also promised quietly that, if he
were elected, he would not permit recriminations
against the outgoing government, or against
military figures. Maluf's own base of real
support was his personal machine and the minor
politicians who had by then become attached to it.

Whichever candidate won, however, 1984 was the
year in which military government in Brazil
effectively ended. Andreazza's defeat by Maluf
ensured that (barring coups) the next president
would be a civilian who had run a successful
campaign against the government machine. A return
to universal suffrage by the end of the decade also
seemed assured. Military government ended not with
a bang but with a whimper.

PATTERNS OF MILITARY RULE IN BRAZIL

The military remained in power in Brazil for
two full decades but at no time succeeded in
finding a secure political centre of gravity. At
the beginning, the government was in the hands of a
civil-military coalition which had organised and
launched the March 1964 coup. Although Castello
Branco became the first president, civilian
politicians played a highly influential political
role for at least a year after the coup. This
civil-military coalition eventually fell apart due
to its internal conflicts; the rivalry between
Lacerda and Castello Branco was particularly
important. This rivalry, however, cannot be seen
in simple civilian vs. military terms; in April
1964 General Costa e Silva wanted a civilian
president, and Governor Carlos Lacerda had
objected.

These internal conflicts, and the danger which
they seemed to pose to the durability of the
regime, stimulated a hard-line military reaction.
Although the hard line at first included civilians
as well as officers, its effect was to reduce the
influence of civilians over the government both in
October 1965 and, even more decisively, in October
1968. There followed a period in which government
was almost entirely in the hands of military
officers and technocrats - a form of government
which might be described as military-totalitarian.

After no more than a few years, however, the
military high command showed signs of disgust and
threat at this direct military role. It
factionalised the military, tended to isolate it
from former allies, and created an atmosphere of
repression which ultimately threatened to undermine
the authority of the government itself. Under
Geisel, therefore, the military was slowly but
determinedly withdrawn from direct political
involvement and the political climate liberalised.

Geisel and Golbery originally hoped that past
economic success would have been enough to allow
the government to develop an authentic popular
base. The 1974 elections were disillusioning,
however, and the regime set out to create an
authoritarian system (the Geisel/Golbery system)
which depended on machine politics, a degree of
electoral manipulation and a process of bargaining
with the electoral opposition.

For several years this system seemed to work, but ultimately under Figueiredo the regime failed to control its own nominal supporters sufficiently to guarantee the succession for a candidate of its own choice. Since the system was in fact little more than a series of devices for controlling the succession, it was finally destroyed in 1984 when Andreazza was defeated in his attempt to become president. This ultimate defeat can be attributed to several causes - the world recession, Figueiredo's own illness and political abstractedness, and the sheer momentum of progressive democratisation. Eventually, if the process of slow democratisation continued, the regime's politicians were bound to hear voices from below more loudly than those from above; once this happened, the military regime was bound to end.

NOTES

[1] Lincoln Gordon to Thomas Mann, 4 March 1964, (Declassified 84E, 1975).

[2] CIA Station Report 30 April 1963, (Declassified 12D; 1976).

[3] Stepan, The Military in Politics, p. 112.

[4] Ibid., pp. 165-168.

[5] Ibid., pp. 222-223.

[6] CIA Station Report 8 October 1964 (Declassified 14D; 1976).

[7] Magalhaes Pinto to Castello Branco 13 May 1965 (in Castello Branco archive, Getulio Vargas Foundation, Rio). See also Luis Viana, O Governo Castelo Branco, (Rio; 1975), p. 64.

[8] The story is told in a lengthy memo, Abreu Sodre to Luiz Viana, 28 September 1971 (in the Castello Branco archive).

[9] Again, for details, see the Castello Branco archive, particularly the memo from Costa Cavalcanti (22 October 1976).

[10] P. Flynn, Brazil; a political analysis, (Benn; 1978), p. 332.

[11] Abreu Sodre memo, Castello Branco archive.

[12] Station Report 29 November 1965 (Declassified 14E, 1976).

[13] Ibid.

[14] Station Report 28 December 1965 (Declassified 14F; 1976).

[15] The Military in Politics, p. 251.

[16] See Flynn, <u>Brazil</u>, and R. M. Schneider, <u>The Political System of Brazil; Emergence of a "modernizing" Authoritarian Regime 1964-70</u>, (Columbia U. P.; 1970).

[17] On his performance in Petrobrás see Philip, <u>Oil and Politics</u>, Ch. 18.

[18] <u>Brazil</u>, p. 435.

[19] P. Schmitter, "The Portugalisation of Brazil?", in A. Stepan, ed., <u>Authoritarian Brazil</u>, p. 224.

[20] J. Serra, "Three Mistaken Theses Regarding the Connection between Industrialisation and Authoritarian Regimes", in D. Collier, ed., <u>The New Authoritarianism in Latin America</u>.

[21] A. Stumpf and M. Pereira Filho, <u>A Segunda Guerra; sucessao de Geisel</u>, (São Paulo; 1979).

[22] W. de Goes, <u>O Brasil de General Geisel</u>, (Nova Frontera, Rio; 1978).

[23] See B. Lamounier's article in <u>Government and Opposition</u>, Spring 1984, and Maria D'Avila Kinzo, "The MDB in São Paulo", <u>Bulletin of Latin American Research</u>, Vol. 3, No. 2, (July 1984). On elections in general see M. J. Sarles, "Maintaining Political Control through Parties; the Brazilian Strategy", <u>Comparative Politics</u>, Vol. 15, No. 1 (Oct. 1982).

[24] A de Medieros, "Politics and Intergovernmental Relations in Brazil 1964-82", (Ph.D., London; 1983), p. 390.

[25] <u>Latin American Newsletters</u>, 11 April 1975.

[26] Stumpf and Pereira, <u>A Segunda Guerra</u>.

[27] P. McDonough, <u>Power and Ideology in Brazil</u>, (Princeton U.P.; 1981).

[28] De Medieros, "Politics and Intergovernmental Relations".

[29] De Goes, <u>O Brasil de General Geisel</u>. See also the Brazil chapters in H. Handelman and T. Sanders, <u>Military Government and the Movement toward Democracy in South America</u>, (AUFS, Bloomington; 1980).

[30] For a good account of this transformation in São Paulo and Espirito Santo, see A. De Medieros, "Politics and Intergovernmental Relations".

[31] A good account of these electoral developments appears in B. Lamounier and A. Moura, <u>Political Economica e Abertura Politica no Braxil 1973-83</u>, (IDESP, Texto 4, São Paulo; 1984).

[32] A. de Barros, in "Back to Barracks; an option for the Brazilian Military", (mimeo, IUPERGE, Rio; 1984) suggests that the Falklands war led to a renewed military concern with international conflict as opposed to internal security and thus facilitated a return to barracks.

Chapter 10

MILITARY   GOVERNMENTS   AND   MILITARY   FAILURES   IN
ARGENTINA

The   Argentine   military   coup   of   June   1966
scarcely   came   as   a   surprise   even   to   the   overthrown
government.   It   had   been   plotted,   semi-publicly,
for   nearly   a   year.   In   retrospect,   however,   1966
marks   a   clear   turning   point   in   Argentine   history.
It was the   beginning   of   a   deliberate attempt to
impose   a   new pattern of   politics   by   dictat.   If
there was a   "model"   of   political organisation in
the minds of   the general, it   was   that of Franco's
Spain.   Thus   the   coup   was neither a   "moderating"
attempt to   shuffle the political pack, nor was it a
response to a major   social   breakdown   and   crisis.
This   is   not   to   say,   however,   that   those   who
participated   in   the   coup all had a clear idea of
how   the   military   government   would   eventually
evolve.

The psychological ingredients of the coup were
of   two   main kinds.   There   was   a   "politics   of
frustration"   as Argentina's   relative decline since
the Second World War was becoming apparent; in 1950
Argentina was still a   richer   country than France.
By 1966 it was officially regarded   as a developing
country.   It   had   appeared to most observers that
the Argentine economy had   emerged   from the Second
World   War   in a particularly strong and   promising
position, but   things   had evidently gone very sour
since   then.   It was   for   this,   rather   than   any
specific mismanagement   under the Illia government,
that the military   sought   an authoritarian remedy.
Secondly there remained the fact   of Peronism.   The
military,   like   the   Peronist   movement,   was
authoritarian,   hierarchical and nationalist.   Some
senior officers,   more   in   the   air force and army
rather than the navy, found something   to admire in
Peronism   although   this   admiration   stopped   well

short of tolerating Perón's return to power. Nevertheless, there was a certain ambivalence toward Peronism in part of the officer corps rather than an uncomplicated hostility.

The coup was led by Ongania and the azul wing of the military - notably Generals Pascual, Alsogaray and Lanusse. Its leaders were unhappy with the Illia government's preference for the Colorado faction of the army and unwilling to entertain a Peronist victory in elections scheduled for March 1967. However, what united them more was a conviction that party politics in Argentina had been played out. This was a matter on which the generals could expect a great deal of agreement from the majors and lieutenant colonels in the army. In his near contemporary account, Corbett reported that "there is a broad middle level of officers who have little faith in democratic, representative systems. To them politics is an opprobrious term."[1]

There had, of course, been a great deal to give encouragement to this viewpoint since 1955. Above all, the anti-Peronist parties had not succeeded in dealing with the continued support for Peronism. Both Frondizi and Illia had failed to prevent the electoral re-emergence of Peronism despite its proscription in the 1958 and 1963 elections. The azul officers' objections to Peronism were less to its pro-trade union and statist policies than to Perón's scandalous personal behaviour and factionalisation of the military. In May 1966 General Alsogaray was reported by the CIA as saying that the military, though determined to prevent a Peronist victory in the March 1967 elections, were nevertheless not anti- Peronist as such.[2] They had been in touch both with the leading Peronist trade union officials and with Perón; Perón had agreed to support the coup under certain conditions. (One may suggest in passing here that Perón himself may well have been playing a tactical game, but there is no doubt that the CGT did want to bargain with the military government.[3]) Alsogaray also reported that the coup would be pro-US in its foreign orientation (Illia had caused a good deal of irritation to the azules by refusing to support the US intervention in the Dominican Republic in 1965). The coup leaders set as their main objective, however, the development of the economy. One may note in passing that the Illia

247

government's management of the economy had by no means been wholly unsuccessful - Illia was the last Argentine president up until the present day to have left office with the economy stronger than he found it. The point was, however, that desarrollismo had become an ideological underpinning of the Azules. Its objectives were technocratic and anti- political; its claim to support rested on its supposed managerial competence.

In this underpinning, however, there were difficulties. In other Latin American countries, desarrollismo tends to denote a state-led, vaguely progressive pattern of growth with a particular concern for industrialisation. The Argentine economy, however, had developed well beyond the stage where this kind of policy could make any sense. Argentina had an export agriculture upon which an extensive and inefficient manufacturing sector had already been constructed. The "easy" early stage of industrialisation had been accomplished (although very inefficiently) under Perón; what Argentina now faced were serious inflationary and balance of payments bottlenecks.[4] The economic liberal response, which was to attempt to adjust internal Argentine prices to world market prices, would make it more attractive to export and so break the foreign exchange bottleneck, but would also destroy a good deal of inefficient local industry (through tariff reform) and depress urban wages. An attempt to promote industrial growth without performing such an adjustment would lead to even more severe balance-of-payments and financing problems.

An alternative strategy with superficial appeal was that of capital-deepening - that is to say, encouraging the development of capital and heavy intermediate goods industries. Yet capital-intensive industry of this kind would consume investment resources heavily and would only benefit a minority of the population and it would not avoid the familiar inflation and balance of payments bottlenecks; Frondizi had tried such a strategy and it had failed. There was also a further drawback; capital-goods industries were largely dominated by foreign patents and sources of supply and would therefore impose additional costs on an already difficult balance of payments; attempts to relieve this problem by attracting direct foreign investment could lead to political problems -

especially if, as it appeared, foreign dominated
sectors of the economy were developing ahead of
those controlled by local capital. Thus, whereas
desarrollismo in the context of other countries
with either more internationally efficient or less
resource-consuming manufacturing sectors could be a
consensual programme which might appear a plausible
substitute for open politics (as perhaps in Brazil
between 1932 and 1945), the Argentine variant was
certain to be bitterly divisive no matter what
detailed policies were chosen. In putting
desarrollismo forward as a substitute for
politics, Onganía and his supporters were courting
difficulty - a "nationalist" strategy could not
work while a "liberal" one risked isolating the
government from everyone except a few exporting
interests and, perhaps, multinational corporations.

This economic difficulty had an unusually
direct political corrolary which is that the
government had to make an early choice as to which
constituency it wanted to cultivate; as O'Donnell
has pointed out[5], the popular Argentine
perception of politics was that it was largely a
zero-sum activity, and this gave the military
little scope for coalition building. The June 1966
coup was, however, supported by the CGT which hoped
to gain access to the Ministry of Labour and, at
best, to move toward a nationalist-syndicalist
state - Peronism, in a word, without Perón. Yet
the military also attracted support from economic
liberals who wanted a coup directed not only
against politicians but also against organised
labour. There had been major strike waves in 1959
and 1964 and the CGT had made use of relatively
open political conditions to show some undoubted
muscle. The economic liberals wanted a return to
policies of capitalist growth in which politicians
and trade unions played little or no part.

A second level of political ambiguity related
to the implications of government without politics.
Argentina in 1966 did not face a threat from the
armed left and it was not clear even to most anti-
Peronists that authoritarian military government
was the only solution to radical Peronism. Thus,
while there was little public opposition to the
June 1966 coup (the political public having become
quite used to cynical political manoeuvres of one
kind or another), there was certainly no strong
feeling of threat within the dominant classes of
civil society - no need (as there would be in 1976,

or as there had been in Brazil in 1964) to close
ranks behind a military government without
question. Yet the military regime was considerably
more repressive than its predecessors, often in
foolish and unnecessary ways. Mini-skirts were
banned, as well as all political parties; theatres
were censored as well as opposition periodicals; in
late 1966 there were major clashes between police
and student demonstrators in Buenos Aires as a
result of a half-baked attempt at university
reform. Many intellectuals went into exile, and
Buenos Aires university has not yet fully
recovered. Overall, the Onganía government got
the worst of both worlds; it was repressive enough
to alienate much of the middle class and to
antagonise opponents of the regime, but not so
repressive as to be able to deal with its real
hard-line enemies - some trade union officials and,
from 1969 onwards, urban insurgents. The regime
was, in fact, an unusually direct exponent of
barrack-room paternalism; civilians and politicians
were neither treated respectfully at arms-length
(as in the moderator pattern) nor regarded as the
enemy (as in the police-state pattern). Rather
they were treated as unruly recruits who needed a
dose of discipline - moral standards were to be
improved (and skirt-lengths increased), student
politics banned and the work ethic emphasised.

If at one level the post-1966 period was one
in which this conflict, between de-mobilising
politics and divisive economic policymaking, was
played out, it was at another level the field in
which a personal duel was fought out between Perón
and Onganía (and later Perón and Lanusse). Few
military regimes in South America have had to face
an opponent of Perón's skill and unscrupulousness.
The military did not help its own position by
banning all political parties immediately after the
coup. The military's earlier strategy of
encouraging anti-Peronist political parties was now
at an end and these too moved over into opposition.
They had not been strong enough earlier to compete
with Peronism, but their strength when combined
with Peronism was sufficient to add to the
military's difficulties.

Moreover, the politico-military duel was
personal in both directions. Although the June
1966 coup was institutional (i.e. it was led by the
top army commanders), Onganía quickly established
his personal ascendancy over the incoming

government which soon ceased to have any direct connection with the top military commanders. In November 1966 Onganía dismissed General Pistriani as army minister following the latter's complaints that the military as a whole was not given sufficient influence over policymaking. (In August 1968 he dismissed General Alsogaray as army minister following similar complaints.) At first, moreover, Onganía's cabinet reflected his own brand of Catholic nationalism. This was, in Argentine military terms, comparatively moderate.[6] These Catholic nationalists admired Franco and were strongly pro-clerical (in 1966 there was little, if any, radical Catholicism in Argentina). They admired technocracy, but were not uncritically pro-capitalist. They had vague corporatist aspirations and hoped for national unity; they little understood the fundamental depth of socio-economic conflicts in Argentina (this was, at a subjective level, one of the main reasons for their failure). This strand of military thinking lay somewhere between two extremes; one of these was more aggressively nationalist and mobilising (and was seen more directly in Argentine foreign policy in 1976-82) and the other was "liberal" according to the local political idiom, but more precisely hard-line capitalist. The "liberals" were more aware and hard-nosed "developmentalists" than Onganía and less interested in any form of social paternalism.

The "political Catholics" in Onganía's cabinet quickly made themselves unpopular with the Buenos Aires middle class by their enforced morality and subsequently went into a relative decline. Gradually the political balance within the Onganía government began shifting in favour of the economic liberals. The Argentine economy began to run into difficulty in late 1966 and the liberals were better able than the nationalists to offer coherent solutions. In December 1966 the Cabinet was reshuffled, and Krieger Vasena - a leading economic liberal who had earlier served under Aramburu - was made economic "super-minister" with control over the labour as well as the economics ministry. At this point the CGT, which at first found a good deal of sympathy in Onganía's Labour Ministry, withdrew its sympathy from the government and, sharply overestimating its own bargaining power, began to launch attacks upon it. A major strike initiative launched in February

1967 flopped badly. Following this victory over
the CGT, Krieger Vasena, in March 1967, began
imposing his orthodox-liberal policies in earnest.
The peso was devalued and controls on capital
movements were ended. The effect of this was to
leave the peso undervalued and transfer income (and
incentives) to the export sector. The incentives
were reduced by new export taxes which reduced the
fiscal deficit. Meanwhile government spending was
cut sharply in real terms and both wage levels and
union activities were held down. In 1967 prices
rose 27%, largely as a result of government
measures, but the balance of payments moved
strongly into surplus. At the same time, the
government made a major effort to attract foreign
investment which did increase considerably up until
the end of 1969. Argentina also became a minor
exporter of manufacturing exports. This policy led
to a sharp worsening in income distribution
although not to stagnation; indeed, GNP growth was
considerable in and after 1968.

Effective opposition to the government was at
first slow to form. The CGT had been badly wrong-
footed by the turn of events and now divided into
hard and soft-liners. The soft-liners tended to be
concentrated in more modern sections of Argentine
industry which had something to gain by a modified
desarrollista policy while the hard-liners were
in the inherently more vulnerable sections. Perón
was at first willing to support both strategies,
hoping to use the soft-liners to weaken Onganía
within the military while the hard-liners prepared
an offensive against the government but at the same
time suffered comparatively heavy repression. In
March 1968 this split was formalised with the CGT
Azopardo, led by Vandor, representing the majority
soft-line and the CGT Colon, led by Ongaro, the
hard.

At the end of the 1960s another political
force emerged into Argentine politics which needed
to be reckoned with. This was the violent
opposition. There were two main armed groups. The
ERP, the less important, was avowedly Trotskyist
(perhaps Castroist would be a better word) and
aimed to overthrow the state through a guerrilla
campaign centred in the north of the country, and
notably around Tucuman. The second armed group,
the Montoneros, were of much greater
significance.[7] The Montoneros were, at least in
aspiration, Left Peronists; their ideology was

somewhat confused (with Fascist as well as Marxist elements) but their organisation ruthlessly centralist and hierarchical. Their historical formation is complex, but one should mention both the general closing up of politics due to the rigidity of the main political organisations (Peronism, the Radical party and the military) and the resulting generation gap between the old guard and younger men anxious to enter politics. The Montoneros' relationship with Perón is more complex than has sometimes been portrayed, but until 1972 it seems safe to say that each sought to use the other and that they did indeed have a mutually strengthening effect. The Montoneros did not begin their campaign in earnest until 1970, but the preparations were underway from around 1969; the first important assassination, that of Vandor, took place in May 1969.

THE FALL OF ONGANÍA

In May 1969 violence erupted in Cordoba, the second city of Argentina and one where disaffection from central authority was by no means new. It began with student protests at an increase in canteen food prices and quickly spread to strikes and riots. The impact of this outbreak was not so much that it proved the strength of the civilian opposition to the government (although it is true that the protest was supported by urban middle class and even small business groups who were traditionally anti-Peronist rather than anti-military) but that it showed the government's weakness. The slowness and hesitancy of the government's response made public what was already clear to those with privileged information; the military hierarchy was not an uncritical admirer of the government's economic policies or even of Onganía himself. The military nationalists had in many cases felt betrayed already by Onganía's own attachment to his liberal economists; they were not yet strong enough to take over the government but were certainly able to establish themselves as a force to be reckoned with. The old azules (particularly including Lanusse[8]) felt that Onganía had over-personalised his rule, and had done so in order to impose a corporatist nationalism which they felt to be alien; they also felt that Onganía had neglected the military hierarchy excessively and dismissed its most articulate representatives; Lanusse, in particular, felt that Onganía should now listen more closely to the army command. His first demand was for the dismissal of Krieger Vasena. The hard-line Right was also upset by the Cordobazo and drew from it the conclusion that the government should tighten its control over the trade unions, forget completely about an eventual alliance with them (an option which Onganía had not finally ruled out), and should attempt to impose a full-scale corporatism. They also concluded, however, particularly after Onganía removed Krieger Vasena and began to move in a "nationalist" direction, that it might be better to find an alternative president, a transitional figure such as perhaps Aramburu, who could continue with the economic policy while buying time through the promise of eventual elections.

Onganía himself, therefore, was in a greatly weakened position; he could repress to some degree but he could not simply repress; instead he was forced to try to conciliate from a position of weakness. His government, in other words, was on the run and his opponents were quick to seize the advantage. Onganía's attempts to negotiate with the CGT Azopardo were set back when Vandor was assassinated by the Left and efforts to find some basis of understanding with the trade unions did not prosper. When the regime sought conciliation, the conciliationists faded like the Cheshire cat - leaving behind only Perón's mocking smile - and Onganía remained exposed. The regime, which did become somewhat more repressive toward labour hard-liners after the Cordobazo, was blamed by most of public opinion for the resulting conflicts. Yet, the regime had by this time abandoned its liberal economic strategy (the resignation of Krieger Vasena was accepted in June 1969) and lost the very limited approval which it had earlier enjoyed from those who had supported it.

By the end of 1969, therefore, the situation had reached impasse. Were it not for what was to follow, one might have attributed this to an attempt to impose military rule on a society which was already too sophisticated, urbanised and pluralist to accept it. (One might note in passing that, with the Brazilian military government also in some disarray by the end of 1969, this was a plausible time to generalise about the limitations of authoritarian rule in South America). Onganía

had succeeded neither in winning popular consent
for his strategy nor in terrorising public
opposition into quiescence. He had too readily
adopted the typical military perspective that
ruling was largely a matter of administration (at a
purely technical level, indeed, public sector
management did improve considerably in 1967 and
1968) and had failed to understand that this was
not enough in as well developed and politically
sophisticated a country as Argentina. Yet this
failure largely reflected the deep splits within
the Argentine elite itself. Onganía began (in
1962-3) as a military nationalist; after 1967 he
became an authoritarian liberal. But he did not
carry his constituency; he merely sought to
marginalise it from influence by selectively
dismissing key military officers. General Julio
Alsogaray, following his dismissal as army
commander in 1968, remarked that "Onganía adopted
a <u>Franquista</u> model in his treatment of civilians,
but he behaved like a president of Switzerland in
his treatment of the military."[9] In the end,
Onganía needed his officers in order to counter
the trade union militancy which his own policies
had done so much to create. By then, however, they
no longer needed him.

Onganía was overthrown in June 1970, after
refusing demands by General Lanusse to announce
plans for a return to civilian rule. Instead, he
continued with public expositions of his
corporatist ideas. In response to dissatisfaction
among army officers, who feared renewed national
unrest if moves toward democratisation were not
made soon, Onganía tried to remove Lanusse but was
himself removed instead. The final precipitating
factors in his overthrow were a repetition of riots
and demonstrations in Cordoba in May (the
anniversary of the original <u>Cordobazo</u>) and the
murder of ex-president Aramburu shortly afterwards.
Aramburu had increasingly been spoken of as a
possible transitional president between Onganía
and some form of elections. His murder was blamed
on the government although it was in fact committed
by the Montoneros. In one of its first operations,
the Montoneros had the double satisfaction of
removing a possible obstacle to the return of
Peronism and further discrediting the Onganía
government. This murder marked a sinister portent
of what was to come.

The June 1970 coup was, like that of June 1966, supported by a variety of different groups. The most immediately dominating figure, however, was the army commander Alejandro Lanusse who, like Onganía, had been a prominent azul but who had become worried by the government's growing isolation from civil society and wanted to open some kind of dialogue with non-Peronist civilian politicians. However, General Levingston, a relatively junior general to whom the task of government was directly entrusted, had different ideas and began to move in a more nationalist direction. After June 1970 the military government offered more conciliatory policies but without any effort at democratisation; instead, it offered a form of clientelism in return for more "nationalist" and expansionary economic policies. Thus although the peso was devalued soon after Levingston took office, there was no mention of a wage freeze as there had been in 1967. On the contrary, the government found itself committed to a broad tactic of expansion. Moreover, Krieger Vasena's years of authoritarian liberalism, although unsuccessful in their own terms, gave subsequent governments more room to pursue expansionary policies than had earlier been the case. The world economic boom between 1970 and 1973 also helped here.

What the Levingston government attempted was a policy of "Peronism without Perón". Economic policy moved some way back in a nationalist direction and became rather more expansionary; in October 1970 it was placed under control of a capable nationalist technocrat, Aldo Ferrer. The military itself was brought in from the wings to which it had been confined by Onganía and was given a direct place in the bureaucratic structure (the mere fact that Levingston was not a considerable military figure and did not have an important personal base in the military played an important part in persuading other officers of his acceptability; he had only limited control over the composition of his own first cabinet[18]). A Peronist civilian was made Minister of Labour and efforts were made to negotiate a deal with the CGT leaders. However, Perón himself, the Radical Party (which would have been left without a role had the Levingston plan succeeded) and the increasingly active armed Left, all worked against an alliance between the military nationalists and the trade union <u>blandos</u>. In November 1970 the government's strategy was severely damaged when the Peronists and Radicals together formed an association called <u>Hora del Pueblo</u> which called for the early holding of elections which, the government hoped, could be postponed for four or five years.

By this time, faced with mounting waves of strikes (a particularly serious one occurred at the Fiat works in Cordoba in January 1971) and escalating political violence, the military reiterated its demand for some kind of political normalisation. Levingston was by this time widely suspected of trying to prepare for a personalist-nationalist dictatorship which was unacceptable both to economic liberals and to trade union radicals whose active militancy made many officers long for a withdrawal from politics. In March 1971 Levingston was removed by Lanusse (who had retained the grip over the army which he had established at the time of Onganía's removal) who quickly announced a firm intention to call early elections. A prominent member of the Radical Party was made Minister of the Interior and entrusted with their órganisation.

THE RETURN TO DEMOCRACY

Lanusse was a semi-aristocrat as well as a military man. He had strongly supported the June 1966 coup. By early 1971, however, he had come to realise that the game was up. He later wrote[11] that the Cordobazo convinced the top military command that government without politics was insufficient to create a national consensus and that the military needed to engage in some positive institution building. Between 1969 and early 1971, moreover, it had become clear that the armed Left was becoming a serious threat to public order. Lanusse believed, along with some but not all later writers[12], that the Montoneros and other terrorists were using the name of Perón in order to maximise support for what was essentially a strategy of their own; Lanusse was convinced that if Perón returned he would disown them and make it easier for the security forces to deal with them. Otherwise, as Lanusse put it in his later book, Perón could remain as "terrorist commander-in-chief" in exile in Madrid without running any personal risk. At the same time, in 1971 Perón -

showing signs of age and talking about semi-retirement - did not look very formidable electorally. The chance could, perhaps, be taken. Thus the Lanusse government immediately began a dialogue with civilian politicians. In January 1972 political parties were legalised but the regime declared that candidates who wished to present themselves for the forthcoming elections had to be in the country by August 1972 - this was a clear effort to exclude Perón; in July the election date was fixed for March 1973. The military's tactic was to build up the anti-Peronist electoral alternative (it should not be forgotten that the Interior Minister was an active Radical) and to hope that - with elections organised on a run-off basis - the Peronists, without Perón as candidate, would fail to reach 50% on either the first or second vote. This strategy was damaged, however, when it became clear that Ricardo Balbin - an uninspiring politician of the old school - would be the Radical candidate.

The military on a whole supported Lanusse's strategy although not universally so. There was some pressure for a continuation in power - this came both from "Brazilianists" who wanted an orthodox military dictatorship and "Peruvianists" who wanted a more radical form of military regime. A small rising of "Brazilianists" occurred in May 1971, but this failed completely. Later in that year there was also a minor rising, this time by "Peruvianists" at least tacitly backed by Levingston. Neither the "Peruvianists" nor the "Brazilianists" in fact appealed very much to the military as a whole. The military could not plausibly compete with the Peronists for popularity (despite the fact that a small number of Right-wing unions did tacitly indicate a preference for continuing military rule), but nor could they return to a hard-line dictatorship without isolating themselves utterly from civil society and running the risk of having to face "subversion" without any popular support. There seemed no real alternative to a tactical withdrawal from government on the best terms available.

These terms, however, were less good than they had hoped. Perón did commit himself to elections as the military had hoped; however, when returning briefly to Buenos Aires in November 1972, he refused any kind of alliance with Lanusse but instead managed to extend his political support by

including various small parties in a broad
electoral front. He subsequently selected a
"loyalist" member of his own entourage to run in
his place. Campora was duly elected in March 1973
when he received very close to 50% on the first
ballot; the military cancelled the second round so
that it would not turn into a triumphal procession
with a foregone conclusion - and instead accepted
Campora's victory. The candidate widely perceived
to be closest to the military received just 0.02%
of the vote.

It was not long, however, before· democracy
appeared to break down. For one thing, political
violence increased rather than declined. Moreover,
the increasingly active operations of counter-
terrorists and a number of individuals out for
personal revenge added to the violence. By
mid-1975, the wave of Left-wing assassinations (and
kidnappings) had come to include trade union
leaders (Jose Rucci was killed in 1973), moderate
politicians, businessmen and above all members of
the security forces, although surprisingly the
Montoneros at first devoted most of their attention
to the police rather than the army.

Some of the most notorious figures involved in
counter-terrorism at this stage were Right-wing
Peronists anxious to ensure that Left-wing violence
did not bring the military back into power. They
hoped that they themselves would be able to
eliminate the "subversives" before the military
officially moved in to do so. The notorious
Triple-A (AAA) organisation operated from the
Ministry of Social Welfare, run by Jose López
Rega, sometime astrologer and now adviser to Isabel
Perón (who succeeded her husband as President upon
the latter's death in July 1974). Last, but by no
means least, were plain clothes units from the
regular army itself; these units were created for
counter-insurgency purposes and allowed to arrest,
torture and murder with complete freedom, promoted
and shielded by very senior officers who would deny
publicly that anything of this nature was taking
place.

Another serious problem for the government was
the deteriorating economy. The Lanusse
government's economic strategy was subordinated to
electoral considerations. Ferrer resigned and in
April 1972 Lanusse decreed the first of a series of
generous wage increases unmatched by any
improvements in productivity; as in Allende's

Chile, there was an immediate boost to the economy, as the rate of capacity utilisation increased, but inflation became a severe and increasing problem. By late 1972 it was 60% p.a. and rising. After March 1973, efforts to deal with the economy took the form of wage and price controls. There is some dispute over whether such a policy could ever have been adequate to the problem, but there can be no doubt whatever that it failed completely during this period. During 1972 and 1973 Argentina benefited from a considerable improvement in its terms of trade which allowed some real increase in domestic purchasing power. From 1974, however, serious problems developed in the external sector (due, not least, to an EEC ban on beef imports) and internal purchasing power had to be checked. However, the political situation then appeared too delicate to permit deflation; controls at this stage merely suppressed the symptoms of inflation which subsequently really took off. By March 1976 it had reached 700% p.a. and was rising fast.

Finally, one should briefly mention developments within the Peronist movement. Campora was quickly regarded as too Left-wing by the Peronist Right; trade union leaders bitterly resented his amnesty and soft-line on terrorism, particularly since prominent union leaders continued to be the target of assassination from the Left. Perón apparently instructed him to resign and was himself elected president in October 1973. He chose as his vice-president his wife Isabel - more to keep other contenders out than through any positive qualities of her own. This tactic created a difficult situation in July 1974 when Perón died and the inexperienced and (as it turned out) incompetent Isabel took over. By this time there were a number of extremely strange and sinister characters in positions of political influence, and Isabel's autocratic and Right-wing sympathies eventually succeeded in alienating not only the Peronist Left (by now in a state of armed conflict) but also much of the trade union bureaucracy. In November 1975 Isabel apparently asked the military to step in, but they refused; in March 1976, however, they finally relented and did so.

The Peronist experience of 1973-76 persuaded many officers who had, in 1971-72, reluctantly come to accept a return to democratic rule that democracy could not work well in Argentina. There was probably even more support within the officer corps for a long period of military rule in 1976 than there had been a decade earlier. Within civil society as a whole, the coup was greeted with some relief as well as enjoying the active support of the business and commercial Right which longed to see some effective government and some competent economic management.

MILITARY RULE FROM VIDELA TO VIOLA

The post-1976 government was the first serious attempt in Argentina at rule by all three of the armed forces. This represented a major improvement in the position of the Navy, skilfully negotiated by Admiral Massera, from which the Air Force also benefited. The army was also keen, after its experiences under . Onganía, that no strong individual figure emerged and that a collegiate style of rule was therefore retained. In economic terms, the Navy was a powerful voice in favour of economic liberalism mainly because it has not acquired the degree of economic power enjoyed by the army (and, to a lesser extent, the air force). The other forces, however, had interests of their own which did not fit easily with the economic policies to which the regime was ostensibly committed.

Following the coup, the Argentine generals made two strategic choices, both of them implicit in what had already happened, but both of them very damaging to the long-term prospects of the government. The first was to continue the "dirty war" against the "subversives" rather than pursuing them through quasi-judicial means. It was already, of course, rather late for the Argentine military to pull out of its alliance with right-wing terror groups of other kinds. The counter-insurgency battle had been fought by dirty means at least since July 1974 and the military had already soiled its hands fairly thoroughly. Precise details of relationships between the triple-A and the military command are, of course, not readily available but, despite military dislike of some of the triple-A leaders (notably Lopez Rega), it would appear that there were always close connections between the two; after the coup in March 1976, the military in any case took over the basic structure of the triple-A.[13] Moreover, the military took over a direct and overall counter-insurgency role in

November 1975 following Montonero attacks on several military garrisons.[14] It was also true that confidence in the judicial process had been badly shaken by Campora's 1973 amnesty. A secret decree in 1975 did provide for the imposition of the death penalty by military courts for terrorist offences but open executions would have highlighted the repressive measures already being taken which the authorities were anxious to shield from world attention. Further, it would have been hard for the leaders of a Catholic country to refuse a Papal request for clemency on behalf of any captured guerrillas. Instead, the counter-terrorists in practice pursued their quarry with little or no legal support or sanction.

It must be admitted that this type of repression was very effective in destroying the Montoneros and ERP. Once the conflict between the state and these organisations was fought out in purely military terms, the advantage inevitably lay with the state which had superior fire-power and command over resources. The climate of terror contributed to the isolation of the rebels; many people who might have taken a <u>political</u> stand against the dictatorship were cowed into silence. However, in political terms the Argentine military sowed serious trouble for the future.

Some Argentine conservatives (notably the <u>Buenos Aires Herald</u>) did advocate a "judicial" approach to the terrorists but the idea was quickly rejected (if, indeed, it had ever been seriously considered). Instead the military went for the more sinister alternative of death or kidnap squads operating from unmarked cars aiming to capture, interrogate (under torture) and often kill those whom they suspected of terrorism. The military also set up concentration camps where their victims could be isolated and slowly destroyed at the whim of their captors; pregnant women were in some cases kept alive just long enough to give birth. They were then killed and their children "adopted".

The military leadership also showed a remarkable naivete as to how this kind of activity (or such parts of it which became public) would look to the outside world. The psychological impact of "disappearances" on friends and relatives was even greater than death might have been, and it was not long before the mothers of disappeared people began to mount their vigil outside government offices in the <u>Plaza de Mayo</u>. In 1979 the Argentine government even allowed the Inter-American Commission on Human Rights to visit Argentina (a visit which coincided with a rash of car stickers asserting that <u>Argentinos son justos y humanos</u>), despite the inevitability of a strongly negative verdict (which duly materialised).

Repression was also organised in a very decentralised way. Decentralisation was inevitable given the deep conflicts both within and between the military services in Argentina; it was also a mechanism by which as many officers as possible were directly involved in the repression so (the military hoped) as to reduce the chances of a "Nuremburg-style" calling to account of the worst military torturers. Under these circumstances, such comparatively moderate officers as Videla and Viola, despite their formal positions of authority, did not enjoy complete control over what was happening. Hard-line army officers, and the even harder-line Navy, operated with almost complete independence, torturing and murdering as they saw fit. Indeed, hard-liners within the military also used the power given them through their control over terror to put political pressure on other sectors. The comparative moderates, Videla and Viola, soon found themselves under pressure from the extreme hard-liners - Camps, Rivieros, Suarez Mason and Menendez, not to mention Admiral Massera. Timerman recounts the case of one family tortured in order to secure a confession which could be used against a political ally of General Viola, in order to damage the political credibility of the latter.[15]

The second fateful decision taken by the incoming Videla government was to avoid sustained "Chicago school" measures in dealing with Argentina's inflation problem. There was considerable austerity at the beginning, but this was not sustained. The economy did go into recession in 1977-78 - rising exports ensured a positive GDP growth in 1977 but consumption fell; in 1978 GDP as a whole fell. The reduction in real wages which triggered this recession did have some positive effect on inflation, which fell from 160% in 1977 to just over 100% in 1978 and around 90% in 1979. Argentina's external position, for a short time, improved substantially.

At some time in 1978, however, this politics of austerity was abandoned. One of the main

reasons for this was military opposition to further
spending cuts. The military officers who already
controlled much of the public sector and who had
"intervened" many other state companies became as
anxious as any civilian manager to protect their
own budget share, and the de-centralised structure
of the military made it difficult for the
government (and particularly for the civilian
economics minister, Martinez de Hoz) to over-rule
his formal subordinates. Moreover, in January 1978
Argentina and Chile came close to war over the
Beagle Channel dispute; Argentina responded to this
war scare by beginning a major arms build-up. This
was still not complete in April 1982. It had also
been decided, much earlier, to hold the World Cup
in Argentina in 1978; the military now saw in this
a chance for public relations success and no
expense was spared to ensure the success of the
tournament.

Apart from these purely military reasons for
increased spending, it was also true that the
military was concerned not to alienate the trade
unions excessively. They feared that the
"subversives" who had been successfully isolated
(or who had effectively isolated themselves) from
the rest of civil society could be given at least
moral support by the working class if the latter
was pressed too hard by austerity measures.
Although organised labour was not formally
recognised, the government undoubtedly carried out
quiet soundings in the unions and interestingly
allowed Peronist leadership to continue to control
at least some of their former strongholds.

As an alternative to the painful, but usually
efficacious, measures recommended by orthodox
monetarists, the government became attracted by the
recommendations of a rival monetarist school. This
suggested that inflation could be reduced by
pegging the external rate of exchange; this, so it
was argued, would force down prices in the
"tradeable" sector of the economy (particularly if
tariffs were also lowered) and would have a
depressing effect on prices in the rest of the
economy. Although this line of policy proved (in
all countries which attempted it) to be an
expensive error, it did have a limited
"technocratic" respectability. Moreover, in the
very short-term it seemed to have some success;
there was a marked recovery in the real economy in
1979 and the rate of price inflation continued to

fall slowly. Problems did not really build up until 1981.

One of the main shortcomings of the "exchange rate stability" programme was that it placed a heavy burden of adjustment on private capital movements when, as invariably happened, the trade account swung heavily into deficit. This did not seem much of a problem at a time when the international banks were at their irresponsible wildest. Many private Argentine citizens, however, noted the growing cheapness of the dollar and the country's growing trade gap and were happy to export their savings; the government, covering unintentionally for this private capital outflow, heavily increased the national debt. Meanwhile Buenos Aires became one of the most expensive capitals in the world.

The eventual failure of this economic strategy was quite remarkably complete. The high exchange rate had only a limited effect on inflation (which never fell below 80% p.a. in any year after 1976) but savaged domestic industry as effectively as the worst monetary squeeze. (Import liberalisation, which was another aspect of policy, had a compounding effect on domestic industry.) Industrial production fell by a quarter between 1976 and 1980. In 1981 the policy was destroyed by a speculative panic. Billions of dollars left the country (representing a permanent loss to the economy, and involving not a few corruption scandals) and the peso had to be devalued heavily. Inflation began to increase, from a "low" of 80% p.a. to over 400% by the end of 1983, and living standards were really squeezed. By the end of 1981, therefore, economic policy had achieved none of its objectives. Inflation was over 100% and rising; unemployment was increasing and living standards for those in work were falling; industrial production had fallen disastrously and, if this were not enough, Argentina had also greatly increased the size of its foreign debt to finance little more than speculation. Austerity measures, which might have been forgiven in the immediate aftermath of a military coup, now had to be applied to a restive and resentful populace.

The magnitude of this failure was even more apparent since, as all Argentines know, Argentina is potentially a rich country. (There is a popular saying in Argentina that a Japanese works 358 days in the year to live for just one week like an

Argentine.) Unlike Chile and Brazil, it is largely
self-sufficient in energy and was thus not greatly
concerned by the oil shock of 1979-80. Since
Argentina's exports are mainly agricultural, they
were less vulnerable to world slump than are (say)
those of Chile. Moreover, Argentine exports
received a particular boost in 1980 when President
Carter considerately imposed his grain embargo on
the USSR. Indeed, Argentina's export performance
was, in general, less unsuccessful than other
economic aspects; the failure, above all, was one
of economic management.

The man who was caught in possession by this
economic disaster was not General Videla but rather
Viola. Upon taking power in 1976, the military had
given the provisional presidency to Videla. In
1978 the <u>Junta</u> moved to consolidate its position;
the presidency was to be rotated on a three-year
basis and Videla was allowed to serve until March
1981. Real power, however, was vested in the
<u>Junta</u> which was made up of the three service
commands plus the president. Thus, the government
was essentially subordinated to the military and,
in practice, had very little freedom of action over
military commanders (regarding the dirty war) or
over the military budget. Heir apparent to Videla
was the <u>Junta</u>'s other army member, the former
army commander Roberto Viola. He took over in
March 1981 allowing Galtieri to become the new army
commander. Viola had originally intended to follow
up the "success" of the military against the
insurgent Left by instituting some form of
political liberalisation, possibly along the
Brazilian (or Mexican) pattern. This would
strengthen the presidency and the visible
government, at the expense of the military
hierarchy, and would give civilian politicians a
subordinate role to play within the system.
Whatever chance of success such a programme might
have had, and it would never have been very great,
it was completely destroyed by the failure of
economic management described above. Viola
resigned (ostensibly on health grounds) in
December 1981 and was replaced by Galtieri - who
this time retained his army command alongside the
presidency.

DISASTER AND RETURN TO BARRACKS

By the end of 1981 it had become clear that the military regime in Argentina had failed economically and, although succeeding in the physical destruction of "subversion", had created major political problems for themselves in the manner of their doing so. One way out remained, however. The Argentine military had begun to consider adopting an unprecedently belligerent foreign policy after their "dirty war" victory.[16] Military adventure offered the possibility of a political victory and might have made feasible the military's main objective - re-entry into civil society on its own terms - despite the economic failures and the "dirty war".

When General Galtieri removed Viola as president in December 1981, the Argentine military had (we now know) already decided upon a policy of increased international belligerence. It was, however, a matter largely of chance that the Falklands proved to be the first target. By the end of March 1982 Argentina had already taken a belligerent line with Chile over the long-lasting Beagle Channel dispute, semi-officially laid claim to half of Paraguay (leading to a sharp diplomatic protest from the latter) and publicly provided proxy troops to help the United States in Central America. Galtieri thought that a strong pro-United States line on other matters would be enough to protect him from the reaction to the Falklands seizure that eventually occurred. He later told a journalist that he had considered himself "the spoilt child of the Americans".

There is no need here to discuss the Falklands conflict in any detail. Plainly it did not go well for Argentina, where the shock of military defeat was accentuated by the mendacity of earlier official accounts of the fighting. As Rouquie put it, "the manipulation of opinion was conducted in a masterly way; from 2 April to 13 June, helped on by nationalist fervour, the Argentine armed forces were supposed to go from triumph to triumph. On 14 June General Menéndez surrendered at Port Stanley."[17] Following military defeat, then, the military government was as discredited as it is possible for any government to be. Subsequently the military did in fact move with some political sophistication; it was able to restore discipline within the ranks, which had at one stage seemed to be threatened, and its departure from power was comparatively well managed, but the damage, perhaps irreversible, to the reputation of the military had already been done.

The first step in the military retreat from power was the removal of Galtieri. The army also refused to accept the Air Force Commander, Llami Dozo, as the new president - fearing, no doubt, that the latter might seek to maintain himself in power. Instead, the army chief of staff deliberately chose as president a retired general, Bignone, who had no military-political base of his own to preside over a retreat from power. (The air force was so upset at this turn of events that it left the ruling Junta for several months.) Elections were promised for January 1984 and then brought forward to October 1983, long enough - as the military hoped - to restore some measure of credibility to its own institution. Hard-line rumblings from within the army were just strong enough to deter any inflammatory civilian criticism of the military but not strong enough to bring the holding of elections into serious question. Thus, after a time, civilian political parties - which had retained an impressive unity while demanding elections - began to switch their attention to fighting the campaign. Meanwhile the military began a period of institutional convalescence; new arms were bought, a measure of internal discipline restored and internal enquiries found a manageably short list of officers to take the blame for everything that had gone wrong. Courts-martial were recommended for Generals Menéndez, Galtieri and a few other army officers and also for Admiral Anaya and Llami Dozo. Thus the military was able to pre-empt civilian demands for vengeance to some degree while also hoping to improve its own credibility and morale as an institution. It was, however, a good deal less successful at heading off growing pressures on the human rights issue. In April 1983 a military statement that the desapareceidos should be considered dead was greeted with outrage and contempt; in September, just before the elections, the Junta passed an amnesty law seeking to absolve members of the security forces from all responsibility for their earlier behaviour. Leading civilian candidates for election, however, promised that this law would be repealed. Meanwhile, as in 1972-73, the outgoing military entirely abdicated its responsibilities for economic management and instead took the line of least political resistance; attempts at austerity during late 1982, insisted upon by the IMF, led to considerable strike activity and were then abandoned. By October 1983 the rate of inflation was 400% and rising.

One interesting feature of the last year of military rule was a major split between the military and the financial elite, each of whom blamed the other for Argentina's increasingly pressing economic problems. Martinez de Hoz found himself in official disgrace; the other neo-liberal economist Alemann, who served for a time under Videla and again for a few months under Galtieri, became strongly critical of the military. This split found its most dramatic expression in October 1983 when the head of Argentina's Central Bank found himself briefly under arrest for agreeing to a re-scheduling of the country's foreign debt on terms which the Air Force, in particular, found objectionable. Under these circumstances (and also because foreign policy tilted 'Left' under Bignone) the last constituency of the military - financial and business interests - openly deserted it.

Raul Alfonsin was elected president in October 1983 with a surprisingly decisive majority. The Peronists lost a great deal of support because of a perception that some key Peronists had been too closely associated with the "dirty war" and other discreditable aspects of military government. During the election campaign Alfonsin alleged that there was a secret "labour-military pact" which plotted to ensure the continuation of a broadly military corporatist pattern of politics even after the elections. This kind of campaign worked extremely well; Alfonsin's success was due to the electorate's perception that he was the candidate most likely to ensure a clean break with the failures and defeats of the past.

Although it is much too early to pass judgement, the Alfonsin presidency will be a fascinating test of the extent to which a seriously disgraced military institution can be held accountable and reduced in its influence by an incoming civilian government. It is already clear that the military has been able to retain its discipline under a set of circumstances which in other parts of the world might well have led to advanced factionalisation and decay. Moreover, although military influence will be somewhat reduced, there is no doubt that it will retain many of its privileges.

It is worth pointing out that, at the end of 1983, the military's control of economic resources was greater than ever. Fabricaciones Militares, according to one estimate[18], had an annual turnover of $2,200m, around 2.5% of GNP. It had significant shareholdings in twenty two companies, nine of which were involved in making military equipment. The military as a whole controlled a whole range of activities within the Argentine economy; it even directed the national ballet. Although less important than this indirect military expenditure, the actual military budget amounted to 37% of public spending during 1983. Early indications suggest that Alfonsin's government will enforce substantial cuts in military expenditure and some reduction in overall military influence in the economy, but that both will remain at what, by any other standards, must be considered very significant levels.

Even more significant was the very thorny question of military justice. When taking office, Alfonsin came under extreme pressure from human rights groups, and relatives of the desaparecidos, to allow the investigation of matters relating to the dirty war in civilian courts. This, however, was seen as dangerously excessive and, as a compromise, military courts were allowed to investigate these matters subject to review by civilian courts. Alfonsin also directly began proceedings against the nine officers who had comprised the three military Juntas in power between 1976 and 1983. A small number of other officers, particularly notorious murderers and torturers, were also the subject of legal proceedings. Meanwhile, and perhaps more important in the long run, full publicity was at last given within Argentina to the various horror cases of abduction, torture and murder which were kept secret (with the collusion of much of public opinion) during the dictatorship.

THE FAILURE OF MILITARY RULE

In 1966 military rule was widely seen as some kind of political solution in Argentina. By 1983 it had come to be regarded as the country's most serious political problem. By then, military governments had brought the country military humiliation, domestic torture and bloodshed and economic failure on a scale which utterly dwarfed the failures of the much-despised earlier regimes of Frondizi and Illia.

There are many reasons why a stable Franquista authoritarianism could not have worked in Argentina. One of these is that Argentina, already in 1966 mainly urban, substantially middle class and politically highly sophisticated, had few potential sources of support for sustained authoritarianism. Classic authoritarian rulers such as Louis Napoleon in France and Franco in Spain, together with present day cases such as the Brazilian military and the Mexican PRI, have drawn much of their support from the countryside. In Argentina the landowning class has happily supported authoritarian governments but its weight has been diminished by the lack of a rural clientele. The strength of Peronist trade unions and general working class self-identification has also worked against any strategy of urban co-optation; survey evidence also suggests that the subjective attitudes of most Argentines, well-informed and cynical about politics, makes them unavailable for co-optation by an authoritarian regime.

Another "structural" factor (which has presented severe difficulties for civilian as well as military governments) stems from the complexities of the Argentine economy with its export-generating agriculture and its relatively inefficient import-consuming industry; this structure makes it impossible for any government to secure broad agreement among the dominant classes for a general policy of developmentalism. Any economic strategy will inflict severe pain among at least some producing sectors. What is worse, Argentina has suffered from an increasingly severe inflation from the early 1970s. A succession of bungled anti-inflationary policies over the last decade have not only failed to solve the problem but have also had severe side effects such as substantial de-industrialisation and the acquisition of a fairly large foreign debt.

These factors would be damaging to civilian as well as military regimes, but the military suffered crucially from three further handicaps. For one thing, the military institution has been extending its role in the socio-economic system over the past

271

fifty years. There is a military presence - during periods of military rule - in most nationalised industries and, through <u>Fabricaciones Militares</u>, there has also been considerable military influence in the private sector of the economy. Direct military spending also increased sharply, particularly - it appears - after 1976 although official statistics are inevitably obscure on this point. Now, a key justification for the neo-realist argument (considered in chapter 1) that military rule could be more efficient than that of civilians is that the military is somehow "above society" and therefore capable of enforcing a transfer of resources from consumption to investment and of protecting the capitalist sector from the insatiable demands of interest groups. Once the military becomes a substantial consumer of resources, this whole argument collapses. The effect of military rule, or the threat of it, will then be to increase military consumption (arms purchases, inefficient military-run state enterprises, straightforward corruption). The more the military does rule, the more military consumption is likely to rise and the less the effectiveness of economic stabilisation measures or of efforts to promote investment undertaken by military governments. In Argentina after 1976 this ceased to be a peripheral problem and became a central one.

Another specifically military problem was the utter insensitivity of military governments to those sections of civil society not entrenched in heavy bureaucratic organisations. The Onganía regime treated the CGT with some sophistication and it could, perhaps, scarcely be blamed for its failure to cope with Perón - but its wanton alienation of a whole section of middle class youth (following the repression of student demonstrations in Buenos Aires in 1966) and its unconditional hostility to the main non-Peronist parties were both expensive blunders which played completely into the hands of the Peronist Left. It also created the conditions for the emergence of serious urban terrorism in 1969-71. If this was farce, the behaviour of the post-1976 regime was tragedy. Undoubtedly there had developed a major challenge to the social order by 1975-76 and any government would have needed to react with some energy. Nevertheless, the casual and cynical brutality of the military after 1976 - and its utter obliviousness to how its actions would subsequently appear - had much to do with the mentality of the military itself. The combination of threat, moral self-righteousness and non-accountability is often a precondition for the emergence of genuine evil - and it is far more likely to emerge in authoritarian institutions in threatening settings than under other circumstances.

The third problem specific to the military in Argentina, more so than in some other South American cases, was a chronic level of factional disunity. This was sufficiently severe to threaten the stability of military rule, though not severe enough to threaten the nature of the military institution itself. When the institution did seem to come under threat - in 1962 and, more seriously, in 1982 - its high command agreed upon a retreat from power. There can be no doubt, however, that this level of disunity seriously hampered the ability of military governments to perform specific tasks whether of economic management responding to militant trade union activity after the Cordobazo or negotiating a compromise peace after the Falklands invasion.

Yet such was the entrenchment of the military in Argentine political society that it took humiliating defeat by a foreign power to break decisively its internal political grip. This defeat followed a classic foreign adventure by a government facing domestic unpopularity, anxious to secure its survival and to protect the interests and reputations of those within the system. Even after such a defeat, the military has retained its institutional identity, its command over a significant share of national resources, and its capacity to undertake political action at some point in the future. As has been the case with other South American countries, it has been easier to bring the military into the political system than to induce it to leave.

NOTES

[1] C. C. Corbett, The Latin American Military as a Socio-Political Force; case studies of Bolivia and Argentina, (Centre of Advanced International Studies, U. of Miami; 1972).

2 "Increased tension in relation to a possible coup attempt by the Argentine military", CIA Station report dated May 1966, reproduced in microfilm collection by University Publications of America 1979.

3 See D. James, "Unions and Politics; the development of Peronist trade unions 1955-66", (Ph.D., London; 1979).

4 For a general account of the post-war Argentine economy see A. Ferrer, Crisis y Alternatives de la Politica Economica Argentina, (Buenos Aires; 1977).

5 G. O'Donnell, "Permanent Crisis and the Failure to create a Democratic Regime; Argentina 1955-66", in J. Linz and A. Stepan, The Breakdown of Democratic Regimes, (Johns Hopkins, Baltimore; 1978).

6 For general accounts of Onganía and his period see R. W. Perina, Onganía, Levingston, Lanusse; Los Militares en la Politica Argentina, (Belgrano, Buenos Aires; 1983) and G. O'Donnell, Argentina 1966-73; el estado bureaucratico-autoritario, (Belgrano, Buenos Aires; 1982).

7 On the Montoneros, see R. Gillespie, Soldiers of Perón; Argentina's Montoneros, (Oxford Univ. Press; 1983).

8 See Lanusse's later account, Mi Testimonio, (Buenos Aires; 1977).

9 Lanusse, Ibid., p. 6.

10 Lanusse, Ibid., and O'Donnell, Argentina 1966-73.

11 Lanusse, Ibid.

12 Gillespie, op. cit., but also see the remarks in C. Szusterman's review in Journal of Latin American Studies, May 1984.

13 J. Timerman, Prisoner without a Name; cell without a number, (Penguin; 1982).

14 Gillespie, Ibid., p. 204.

15 Timerman, Prisoner without a Name.

16 See G. Philip, "Argentine Politics and the Falklands Issue", in Brassey's Defence Yearbook 1984.

17 A. Rouquie, "Argentina; the departure of the military", pp. 575-87 of International Affairs 59 (4), Autumn 1983.

18 "Argentina", in Latin American and Caribbean Yearbook, 1984.

Chapter 11

MILITARY RADICALISM AND AFTER IN PERU

The coup of 1968 involved a far broader coalition of forces than was realised at the time. One important element was the old neo-liberal Right. This had opposed Belaúnde for his public spending policies, his (very limited) economic nationalism and for the tax reforms imposed in mid-1968. In retrospect, it is hard to see why such exception should have been taken to so limited a set of measures but there can be no doubt that some key members of the old oligarchy wanted Belaúnde removed. Gilbert states that

> members of several oligarchic families who attended a dinner shortly after the coup were 'ecstatic' at the turn of political events; according to one of the participants, 'they thought they had a second Odría'.[1]

One of the leading oligarchic families, the Prados, strongly supported the coup according to Gilbert,

> The Prados, according to several sources ... gave the military a considerable sum of money to help finance the coup ... (in early 1969) the Prados were on particularly good terms with the government and had easy access to the president ... In April 1969, when the government was apparently in the midst of an effort to gain investor confidence, Mariano Prado led a group of bankers which publicly declared its support for the regime.[2]

The main factor behind this support was the expectation that a military government headed by General Velasco would be sympathetic to the interests of the Prado group, even if not necessarily the class to which the Prados belonged. In 1968 the Prado financial empire, which centred on the Banco Popular, was in serious trouble; the main reason for this was that it had been managed as a political bank and (partly) as a source of personal resources rather than as a serious business enterprise. Gall found that at the time of its eventual bankruptcy in 1970, the bank was involved in

> something approaching a Mafia-style operation of systematically using depositors' money for loans to politicians and businesses and to the head of the clan's homosexual partners. These unpaid loans were kept on the books as assets, and dividends on non-existent profits were distributed among stockholders.[3]

The Banco Popular was, however, an attractive purchase for a US bank eager to secure a foothold in the growing Peruvian market for credit; according to the plan, a US bank would quietly "clean up" the bad and political debts and the purchase price, reflecting the bank's value to a foreign purchaser, would guarantee the Prados survival. The 1960s did in fact see a considerable inflow of US banking capital into Peru and the whole credit system became increasingly connected with multinationals.[4] However, the Belaúnde government - under pressure from nationalists - blocked the Prado sale.

The Prados had reason to hope for better things from General Velasco. Velasco came from a moderately poor provincial family in Piura; he was able to finish secondary school but joined the army briefly as a private in order to save money to buy a uniform and enter the military academy in Chorillos. He was too identified with the military to suffer from the fact that he was the son-in-law of a prominent Aprista; his first important post in the army was as director of the Chorillos academy from 1950 to 1953 under the strongly anti-Aprista General Odría. Velasco was subsequently cultivated by the Prado family which, as we have seen, was always eager to co-opt any promising young military officer. Gilbert notes that,

> when Manuel (Prado) was still in office, Mariano had intervened on Velasco's behalf to save his career from a hostile minister of war ... Some members of the Prado family had maintained personal ties to Velasco; Max Pena Prado, for instance, had been an usher at his wedding.[5]

The Prados were perhaps the most influential, but by no means the only, early oligarchic supporters of the Velasco regime. Others included former friends and allies of Odría. Odría himself was still alive and politically active in October 1968, and supported the coup warmly. So did <u>La Prensa</u> and its proprieter Pedro Beltrán, and so did various elite figures linked with the Atlas Security Company.[6] The Ayulo family, which held shares in the Banco de Credito, apparently supported the coup in the hope of reducing the influence of the Prados on the incoming military government.[7]

The civilian neo-liberals had contacts with other officers besides Velasco. There was General Jose Benavides, a relative of Marshal Oscar Benavides (President in 1914 and again 1933-39) and a man whose conservative sympathies were beyond question. Although he was not in the coup conspiracy - his military posting, in Iquitos, was too far away - Benavides had from an early age nursed poltical ambitions. He was quickly made Minister of Agriculture and this reassured conservative interests that there would be no serious agrarian reform. General Valdivia, a friend of various Odrístas and a firm believer in neo-liberal economics, became Finance Minister. General Maldonado Yanez, who became Development Minister, had close military connections with the Pentagon, dating back to the counter-guerrilla of 1965. Finally, the Navy remained strongly conservative although its political influence was limited by the involvement of senior naval officers in a corruption scandal which had broken, and been quickly hushed up, earlier in 1968.[8]

The neo-liberal Right, however, were by no means the only supporters of the coup. On the other side there were younger officers, mainly from the Intelligence Services, who were among the initiators of the military conspiracy. Their influence could be seen clearly in the coup manifesto which was issued on the day after the takeover of power,

> Powerful economic forces, both national and foreigners supported by Peruvians, being motivated by overwhelming greed, retain political and economic power and frustrate the popular desire for basic structural reforms.

The most obvious strand in the thinking of these officers was economic nationalism of a mildly dependentista variety, very much in keeping with the teaching of CAEM (chapter 6). It was an undoubted fact that the Peruvian economy in 1968 was very heavily penetrated by direct investment from abroad, overwhelmingly from the US, and this tendency was continuing. Fitzgerald[9] has calculated that around one half of the "modern" sector of the economy was foreign-owned. One large foreign concern, the US-owned International Petroleum Company (a subsidiary of Jersey Standard), had been in dispute with successive Peruvian governments over its legal title; even those who were far from ultra-nationalists, were by no means happy with the IPC's very insensitive handling of the question.[10] This unhappiness culminated when an agreement with the Belaúnde government in August 1968, intended to be definitive, instead proved highly controversial and triggered allegations of corruption. Velasco, already plotting a coup, attended a meeting of Peruvian generals which discussed the matter in September and reported the outcome as being "twenty-nine against the agreement and seven traitors".[11] Apart from anti-IPC feeling, upon which the radical nationalists would later capitalise, the Peruvian military was also becoming increasingly anti-American. Einaudi later summarised the change.

> Until the 1960s, ... given the fact of US power and the profits of being associated with it, most Peruvian officers considered their relationship to the United States, while unsatisfactory, still about the best attainable under the circumstances. Although verbally they often supported nationalist claims against certain US interests ... the

military as a whole did so rather mechanically, more in defence of ultimate ideals than in hopes of their immediate realisation ... Since the mid-1960s, however, (events) have led most officers, particularly in the army, to downgrade the importance of relations with the outside world, including the United States, in favour of tightened nationalist efforts at military directed self-help.[12]

The main events which had brought about this transformation were, first, open US hostility to the military coup of 1962 and apparent pro-Apra partisanship; second, some conflicts between the Pentagon and Peruvian military commanders over the best way to handle the 1965 insurgency; and, finally, the US suspension of aid to Peru following the Peruvian decision in 1967 to buy supersonic Mirage jets. This last decision was something of a last straw for Peruvian-American relations, after other setbacks involving the IPC dispute, and was universally condemned in the Peruvian Congress.

Apart from this nationalism, the radical military officers were anxious to extend and increase the efficiency of Peru's often inefficient and corrupt laissez-faire state. This perhaps reflected a typical military desire to extend the role of the state into areas which it could directly control, and it also resulted from an at least partially justified contempt for the leading Peruvian capitalists - not least the Prado family. Finally, the military radicals were anxious to carry out social reforms in order to incorporate the majority of Peruvians into political society. Their diagnosis of Peru was that it was a country where formal democracy was a farce, where the rich had no sense of social responsibility and where revolution was threatened from below unless it was first carried out from above; this diagnosis was undoubtedly over-simple but no less undoubtedly sincere. The civilian current nearest to this approach was radical Christian democracy; according to this way of thinking, social conflict was illegitimate but so was extreme inequality, and it was the task of rulers to reduce the latter so as to eliminate the former. A number of Left-wing civilians holding much the same perspective played a major part in devising and drawing up key elements in the government's programme. These

civilians lacked a power base of their own and were
in many cases only too happy to co-operate with the
military authorities.

The relationship between the military radicals
and CAEM has been a subject of some dispute.[13]
There was, in fact, little direct CAEMista
influence on the actual programme of the military
radicals since CAEM was not a policymaking body.
Nor were the main military radicals (with the
exception of General Graham) associated directly
with CAEM; some of the most radical colonels had
never graduated from the Centre. Nevertheless, it
is fair to say that CAEM's own broadly nationalist
perspective helped create a climate of opinion
within the military which directly facilitated the
more detailed and thoroughgoing radical nationalism
of the Velasco government.[14]

The radical nationalists were considerably
aided by one of the most conservative institutions
in Peru - the newspaper El Comercio. El Comercio
was owned by the Miró Quesada family; this was not
technically a member of the "oligarchy" because the
family had no significant economic interests beyond
the newspaper itself. However, the Miró Quesada
family was one of the oldest and best-connected in
Peru, and also one of the most conservative. The
newspaper itself was the oldest, most read and
most influential in the country and had particular
attractions for military officers. Editorial
policy reflected a hatred of APRA which grew after
the murder of the then-proprietor by an Aprista in
1935 and, partly for this reason, expressed
considerable sympathy for the Fascist countries
prior to 1944. One of its other hatreds, however,
was the International Petroleum Company and this
hostility gradually reached consuming proportions.
After 1956, Apra moved into alliance with the
government of Manuel Prado, and El Comercio
played a major part in the nationalist anti-IPC
campaign of 1959-61. This appeared to be a
radicalising experience for the ageing proprietor,
Don Luis Miró Quesada, particularly after the IPC
began discouraging US companies from advertising in
El Comercio. A younger Miró Quesada, Alejandro,
had particularly good military contacts - and had
indeed lectured at CAEM during 1959; he was
sympathetic to the nationalist (though not radical)
aspirations of many officers.

The editor of El Comercio, Augusto
Zimmerman, later became one of the leading civilian

figures in the Velasco government. He became a close personal friend of Velasco, and later served as his asesor, while for a time retaining the confidence of the Miró Quesada family. As would become evident later, however, Zimmerman's own sympathy with radical reform went considerably further than that of his proprietor. In the early months of the government, he served as a crucial ally in Velasco's efforts to present himself as the leading Peruvian nationalist. In doing so, he was able to swing El Comercio itself behind Velasco.[15]

Apart from the neo-liberals and the radical nationalists, there was a large number of officers who were happy to support - or at any rate to accept - the coup but who did not have any very strong ideological inclination or position. North's study of the political identity of officers who served in the military government between 1969 and 1976, while perhaps relying too much on officers' overt pronouncements, is convincing in assigning a clear majority of officers to the Centre or Centre/Right.[16] Like the ESG group and the hardliners in Brazil, the Peruvian neo-liberals and radical nationalists were competing minorities struggling for the decisive allegiance of a larger number of politically less-committed or more moderate officers. Among those who were influential early on was General Montagne, son of Odría's electoral opponent in 1950 whom the dictator had imprisoned and also brother-in-law of the reformist cardinal bishop Landázuri - both reasons for his leaning toward the reformists. Another was General Artola, son of an officer who was Cabinet Minister under Odría, unscrupulous in his personal habits and willing to relate to Velasco largely on a basis of personal friendship (at least until his dismissal from the government by Velasco in 1971). There was also General Mercado Jarrín, who had been influential in CAEM and had at least a limited sympathy with the radicals although he was not really a radical himself. It was this, largely uncommitted, group that the radicals had to win over.

The crucial mistake made by the neo-liberals in the ensuing power struggle was to count on the support of General Velasco who subsequently became one of the most determined of the radicals. Velasco's enemies have quoted his willingness to marry the daughter of an Aprista, serve under

Odría and ally himself to the Prado family as
evidence that he was no more than an opportunist,
perhaps motivated also by petty social resentments.
This, however, is probably to underestimate him.
The most important point is that Velasco was an
army officer first and foremost. His scale of
values, and mode of behaviour, was military rather
than civil-oligarchic; such values made it
permissible to lie to civilians but imperative to
protect what he saw as the interests of the
military. This, in 1968, made him (as it made
other officers) a strong nationalist with more than
a touch of anti-Americanism. Moreover, like many
Peruvian officers, he was genuinely concerned with
the plight of the poor; this was partly the result
of paternalism and partly of fear. Undoubtedly
there was a certain opportunism in his rise to
power, but it would be wrong to characterise him as
a man without settled conviction; it was more that
he lacked articulateness. McClintock gives an
interesting sketch of his character as follows,

> He was never described an an intellectual or
> even as particularly bright. ... he owed his
> professional achievement to good, solid
> military behaviour and a fine feel for
> people's strengths, weaknesses and
> sensitivities. ... Velasco was further
> described as daring and impetuous, but
> possessed of a strong moral fiber and
> characterised by good intentions.[17]

After the coup of 3 October, the radical-
nationalists were able to achieve momentum by their
successful challenge to IPC. Velasco managed,
first, to tie his own personal fortunes to the
anti-IPC battle and, second, to use his success in
this encounter to advance the cause of the
radicals. At no time did Velasco's opponents make
a concerted attempt to stop him, partly because
individual ambitions stood against the emergence of
a common front and partly because it was very hard
for Velasco's opponents to appeal to offers against
an apparently successful military nationalist.

The military government moved quickly to stage
a confrontation over the IPC. The Talara refinery
and installations were seized by the government on
9 October; the decision was taken by the group of
radical colonels who had masterminded the coup and
who were now close personal allies of Velasco. It

met little resistance, either from Peruvians or from the US government (the US was at that time in the middle of a presidential election campaign). Late in October, the government gave Ruíz Eldredge the task of preparing the official legal case against the company; the case would amount to a claim for damages against IPC in excess of the total value of that company - thus amounting to its total confiscation. Ruíz Eldredge was the senior lawyer on the Lima bar, but he was also a long-standing nationalist on the IPC issue and a man who had expounded his views at CAEM for several years, to some considerable effect.[18]

It was in this increasingly nationalist atmosphere that the question of Velasco's continuation in office was settled in January 1969. His opponents pointed to the fact that his retirement date was arriving and suggested that a retired officer should not serve in a military government. If they had succeeded in removing him, it is likely that presidential elections - due in mid-1969 - would have gone ahead on ·schedule. However, in the event, the only concerted opposition which Velasco faced was from the old Odríista section of the military and from two officers - Valdivia and Maldonado - very closely linked to the United States. Indeed, it is not difficult to see why the alternative presented to Velasco - a soft-line on IPC, a broad pro-US position and a fairly early withdrawal from power - was not particularly attractive to the Peruvian army (naval support for such a line might have been greater but the navy was neutralised politically by evidence of earlier corruption); it is more difficult to see why a more conciliatory figure did not lead the opposition to Velasco but the reasons here appear to be largly personal. One crucial factor in Velasco's survival, however, was the outspoken support which he received from El Comercio - support which Velasco's asesor Zimmerman was instrumental in securing. Thus, Velasco's future was submitted to a sounding process within the army and the feeling was that he should continue as president and that his retirement date should be postponed indefinitely.

Early in February the Peruvian government carried out the final expropriation of IPC's assets. It launched an intense diplomatic effort to prevent the US from invoking the "Hickenlooper Amendment" which would have formally cut aid to

Peru and it also stepped up pressure on the United
States in a number of other ways, arresting fishing
boats and, in May, refusing to receive the
Rockefeller Mission. In the event, the US
administration decided not to impose the
Hickenlooper Amendment and, although aid was in
fact quietly cut, this decision appeared to be a
major political victory for the Velasco government.
After securing his position in January,
Velasco moved quickly to consolidate his power. A
crucial first step had already been taken at the
end of 1969 when the radical colonels who had
supported him were all promoted general; they thus
became eligible to command troops and also to serve
in the government. A second step occurred with the
removal of Valdivia and Maldonado from the
government early in 1969; in addition to replacing
them, Velasco carried out an "administrative
reform" which increased the number of posts in the
government. Although careful to promote a few non-
radicals (Morales Bermúdez came into the Cabinet
at this time), this enabled Velasco to place
radical nationalists in a number of the new
ministries; it is worth noting also that Velasco's
Cabinets, unusual even for military regimes, were
all-military. Finally, Velasco set up a personal
staff agency, COAP, which was given the task of
vetting proposed legislation before it came to
Cabinet. This organisation, headed by General
Graham, became the real power-centre of the radical
nationalists as would become clear in the following
months.

THE REFORMS BEGIN

COAP was heavily involved in the preparation
of the next major step by the Velasco government -
the radical agrarian reform announced in June 1969.
We have already seen that Velasco's first minister
of agriculture, General Benavides, was a
conservative officer whose commitment to agrarian
reform was suspect. However, it was quickly
decided to move ahead with some kind of agrarian
reform so Benavides duly set up a policy-making
commission in his ministry intending to produce a
law which would be extremely restricted in its
scope. This commission was largely made up of
personal civilian allies of the minister.[19]
However, two civilian technocrats, unhappy with the
lack of radicalism in the draft legislation, took

their complaints to the then-Colonel Rodríguez Figueroa, a radical officer and a close ally of Velasco. Rodríguez brought in General Graham, the head of COAP, and both officers agreed that the proposed new law had to be made more radical. Accordingly when Benavides' draft proposal reached COAP, Rodríguez made known his objections and Graham suggested that a special committee be set up within COAP to write a new law; this recommendation was supported by General Velasco and was approved.

The COAP committee drafting the legislation was made up of civilians and military officers; it met and deliberated largely in secret. Meanwhile General Benavides was forced to resign as agriculture minister in June 1969 after a verbal confrontation with President Velasco. Benavides was replaced by General Jorge Barandiarán who brought in his brother (General) Luis and the civilian Left-winger Carlos Delgado as asesores. These two took the initiative in converting Jorge to a radical viewpoint, the touchstone of which was the expropriation of the sugar haciendas of the north coast - the original power centre of the Peruvian oligarchy and still, despite some decline, assets of national economic importance.

COAP presented the draft of a radical agrarian reform to the Council of Ministers on 23 June 1969. Only military officers were involved at this meeting, which lasted fifteen hours. Meanwhile Luis Barandiarán carefully primed military officers in the Lima area with the information that a radical, but not Communist, agrarian reform law was now in prospect. The Council of Ministers received a copy of the draft law only a few hours before the meeting, as efforts were made to prevent civilian opposition from becoming aware of the law and mobilising against it. The agrarian society, the SNA, did however get hold of a copy of the law and began to discuss it. The SNA, however, was itself penetrated by military intelligence agents who reported back to the government. Thus, rather than waiting any length of time, the military government physically took over the north coast sugar haciendas within a few days of the passage of the agrarian reform.

In political terms, the agrarian reform law was a point of no return. It involved a major expropriation of landed property with compensation paid only in bonds. It gave the military control of one of the country's most important patronage resources, while opening an irreconcilable breach between the Velasco government and the country's major property-owners. Some moderate members of the military government expected that these would be replaced by a more respectable and less threatening group of medium-sized capitalists but this hope proved largely illusory and the state took over an increasing proportion of the Peruvian economy. In any case after June 1969 most big capital became solidly anti-government and the neo-liberals began to realise their mistake in calling so readily for military intervention. The Prado family had to wait until 1970, when the sale of the Banco Popular was again blocked and the whole Prado empire forced into bankruptcy, before they came to share this perspective with the rest of their class. At the same time, a step of this nature made it both apparently less necessary and certainly less possible to hand back power quickly to civilians. The military had become committed to a radical nationalist course which began to take on a momentum of its own.

By the end of 1969 it became clear that the military radicals had substantially consolidated their power within the government; outside the government, they had inflicted major setbacks on two rival power centres - the US presence in Peru and the land-owning oligarchy. Neither had been able to fight back in a way which threatened the political strength of the regime. While foreign companies and domestic capitalists continued to exist in Peru, and some even prospered under the military government, it was clear that neither could effectively veto policy.

It is clear in retrospect, however, that these early victories yielded fewer dividends than the regime had hoped; it was easier to break eggs than to make an omelette. The main problems which the military government faced stemmed from the logic of its organisation and strategy rather than from external adversaries. They became increasingly clear as the regime pressed ahead with an ambitious set of property reforms and efforts to stimulate popular mobilisation.[20]

Most observers have seen an ambiguity or lack of definition in the policies of the Velasco regime. This has been ascribed to an over-ambitious and potentially contradictory set of economic objectives[21], to a studied strategy aimed at preventing the mobilisation of opposition[22], to serious divisions within the government itself[23] and to a false military view that conflict-free patterns of social organisation could be established[24]. All of these explanations contain some truth and are for the most part complementary rather than contradictory. What is of particular interest here is the way in which the military government's policies related to an overall political strategy, and with what effect.

Velasco's political strategy can best be described as military populist. It involved extending political participation beyond the limits of pre-1968 politics. At the same time, this participation had to be kept within limits because the regime was unable or unwilling to dispose of the old order altogether. "The oligarchy and imperialism" were defined as enemies but not capitalism as such, nor the urban middle class. Consequently, the Velasco regime suffered many of the difficulties faced by earlier populist leaders in other countries; it had a policy of wealth distribution but no effective policy of wealth creation. The Peruvian economy was, in any case, a good deal weaker than (for example) the Argentinian economy in 1945 and the ability to distribute wealth was therefore far more circumscribed. The expropriations of IPC, large landholdings and a few corrupt business empires were spectacular in their way but they did not release many resources. An efficient state capitalism would have required much more investment in these areas, not less. The main resources which did become available to the government stemmed from the world commodity boom of 1969-74, the availability of abundant international lending during this period, and the prospect (though not the reality) of an oil boom based on discoveries in the Amazon area. Of those resources which would have been available to finance distribution, an excessively high proportion was wasted on subsidies to middle class consumer groups; this may have been political insurance of a kind, but also reflected some failure of political judgement and, probably, of economic understanding.

The government's participationist objectives, therefore, were heavily handicapped by an objective scarcity of resources aggravated by a chronic labour surplus and rapid population growth; land redistribution could help only a minority of peasants and industrial profit sharing provisions were of little concrete benefit to most urban wage labourers. A further handicap, not widely appreciated at the time, was the acute fragmentation of Peruvian society.[25] There was nothing in Peru resembling a homogeneous, mature working class - such as could perhaps be found, within Latin America, only in Buenos Aires. Instead there were a very large number of fragmented groups whose political loyalties were often calculated instrumentally. Such groups would only be impressed by a tangible redistribution of resources which, given the economic weakness already mentioned, would have required a determined form of zero-sum politics. Often groups whose support was being sought by the military government were in zero-sum conflict with each other.

Finally, apart from these unavoidable economic and social limitations, the regime also faced internal difficulties in its efforts to attract popular support. One problem was the degree of disunity within the government. This was always a latent problem but it worsened sharply when Velasco became seriously ill in February 1973. From then until his final overthrow in August 1975 rival factions manoeuvred for position and some of the most acute political rivalry was fought out within the government itself. Quite frequently, serious conflicts occurred between rival agencies each supporting different factions within the regime. Another handicap was the military approach to political participation. There was, of course, considerable variation between individuals some of whom showed an unsuspected talent for attracting popular support, but there were many cases of good intentions being spoiled by excessively bureaucratic procedures and an excessively authoritarian manner on the part of key military-political figures.

Given these weaknesses, it may seem remarkable that the Velasco government went as far as it did; in terms of property distributed, the Velasco regime was one of the most radical in South American history.[26] In the short-run, the main reason seems to lie in the weakness of its various potential antagonists. The neo-liberal Right had never seriously attempted to win a wide popular following in Peru, even to the extent of creating political parties of the kind existing in Chile and Colombia.[27] It preferred, instead, to rely on a congenial army officer - Benavides in the 1930s,

Odría during the 1940s and (so it thought) Velasco in the late 1960s. The Peruvian upper class had never seriously considered (as had the Chilean Right in 1932 or the Colombian Right after 1957) the need to contain an unpredictable and potentially hostile military institution. Nor was the economic power of the main domestic interests very considerable. In Peru during the 1960s most entrepreneurial dynamism was coming from foreign companies; there was some local entrepreneurial drive, particularly from some of the traditional mining families[28], but the most conspicuous oligarchic families were in evident decay by 1968. The main factor determining the success of the Peruvian economy in the short run was the state of international commodity markets which at first favoured the Velasco government. The main long-term factor was the willingness of big international companies to invest in, or at least finance investment in, very big oil and mineral ventures; these companies operate on a world scale, are mainly influenced by international market conditions and, provided that the terms of their own investments are right, are not greatly interested in the internal political systems of the countries in which they operate. A radical military regime which, as in Peru, was willing to negotiate bilaterally with big companies of this kind, had little to fear from the forces of international capitalism.

The political centre was scarcely stronger than the Right. Belaúnde's Acción Popular was clearly in a state of disintegration in October 1968; it was this which triggered the coup. Apra had been in opposition to military rulers for so long that it was known to pose little further threat. It had also undoubtedly weakened somewhat from its peak period of 1935-48. In 1962, after an open election campaign, Apra had failed to win the third of the vote necessary for outright victory. Its leadership was aged and many of its members, increasingly comfortable, were happy to work out local arrangements with the military. Apristas were able to undermine, to some extent, government efforts to spread the benefits of the land reform in the north beyond the already comparatively affluent permanent workers of the hacienda but this was a matter of deploying limited influence toward limited objectives. Apra was in no position either to subvert the loyalty of the military or to challenge it through mobilisation. The political Left was also weak in 1968. The defeat of the Castroist insurgency in 1965 had at least temporarily discredited the idea of an armed strategy. Until the mid-1970s the Left lacked serious electoral support. Thus, many prominent members of the Left, including some ex-guerrillas, moved to support the government.

Given these many sources of weakness, the military could survive for a considerable period even though its own success in creating popular participation of the right kind remained limited. The regime in fact made a number of such attempts, but these tended only to create harmful bureaucratic complexity and a good deal of confusion. The main efforts were the <u>Comunidades Industriales</u> set up in 1970 as part of the Industrial Law, Sinamos set up in 1971, the Social Property concept legalised in 1974 and a number of efforts to set up pro-regime trade unions and peasant leagues. There is not sufficient space to discuss all of these in detail. Briefly, however, the regime had more success in stimulating popular mobilisation than in channelling it. In the long run, it was the parties of the Left which benefited.

It is of course true that there was more to Peruvian politics than big capital, the old political parties and the Left. The regime expected that its own policies of nationalism, agrarian reform and domestic industrialisation would appeal to broad strata of the population. Perhaps even more important was its effort to retain the confidence of the officer corps which, as we have seen, was not universally sympathetic to radical policies. One important step which it took was greatly to extend government control over the economy. Prior to October 1968 there were few state companies in Peru and those that did exist were of very secondary importance. Subsequently, however, it became something of a national sport to decide how many state companies had been brought into existence; there were certainly more than fifty of some significance. This expansion was attractive to the military which (as we saw in chapter 6) did not have an economic power centre of its own prior to 1968. To give an idea of the scale of the change, there were in 1968 160 colonels and 39 generals in the Peruvian army. After 1968, there were nine cabinet posts for the army (the air force and navy had three each), a number of further positions in COAP, seven positions given to military officers or their close relatives in SINAMOS in 1972[29], five military officers in top management positions in Petroperú and a number of others in various state companies, and a number of military administrators of agrarian reform zones or properties. The effect was to provide new non-military jobs for perhaps one half of the senior officer corps. Many of the officers who took these postings were scrupulously honest (although all received double salaries) but others were not, and by 1977 there were many stories about military corruption.

It was, of course, not only the military which benefited from this expansion. Civilian technocrats, who had no place in the old oligarchic empires, were recruited into the new state companies. There were also commercial opportunities for at least some local capitalists. Moreover, even apart from those directly associated with the new state enterprises, firms in the consumer durables sector of the economy continued to enjoy heavy protection and cheap loans, just as they had done under Belaúnde.

It is almost axiomatic that those who benefit from a process of this kind are not anxious to see it reversed. For many nationalists, civil and military, the expulsion of some (by no means all) foreign companies and the destruction of much of the oligarchy were a source of opportunity to form a new establishment. This was centred more on the home market and on the public sector, and also on the military itself which in socio-economic terms had really come in from the cold after 1968. There was, no doubt, some consistency in an economic strategy which was based on state companies, new (rather than traditional) sources of foreign investment and domestic industrialisation. Yet such a strategy could still be pursued even if the objectives of popular mobilisation were curtailed and further radicalisation halted. By late 1973 a number of officers, eager to support the initial process of change, were now willing to support a quieter period of consolidation while others, who attached primary importance to popular mobilisation, were in danger of becoming seriously detached from majority thinking in the army.

THE SUCCESSION TO VELASCO

The no doubt somewhat precarious balance within the government was first disturbed in February 1973 when Velasco became seriously ill. Up until then, Velasco had played a crucial role in balancing the demands of the military radicals with a sense of what the rest of the military would accept, and he also enjoyed a purely military constituency of some significance. His illness, therefore, could not but be de-stabilising. He did stage a partial recovery but his own personal faculties were badly impaired; Velasco's illness also marked the beginning of a long and destructive battle for the succession. From then on, conflicts within the government became increasingly severe. These involved, on the one hand, rival groups of "mobilising" officers - the radicals such as Fernández Maldonado who retained some of their original idealism and the so-called La Misión group which was more opportunist and demagogic but perhaps also more realistic.[30] On the other hand, a number of moderate officers became increasingly unhappy about the fact of mobilisation and its possible consequences for controlled policymaking. This group had accepted the agrarian reform and other changes but now hoped that the shocks were over. Velasco himself, to the dismay of his radical supporters, became increasingly friendly with La Misión.

A second destabilising change was the military coup in Chile. The immediate effect of this was to encourage Right-wing opponents of Velasco. Just prior to the coup, various kinds of radical regime appeared in the ascendant throughout Spanish America; there was Allende in Chile, Campora in Argentina, a reformist military government in Ecuador and a rhetorically Revolutionary president in Mexico. After the Pinochet coup it no longer appeared so obvious that radicalism was the wave of the future. The Chilean coup was also important in a more direct sense. While it does not seem as if either Peru or Chile genuinely harboured aggressive designs on the other, both felt very threatened by the other's activities; Bolivia, meanwhile, was trying to play them off against each other in order to reopen its own claim for access to the sea. Consequently, beginning in 1974, the Peruvian military undertook a major rearmament programme which put further strains on an economy which was already beginning to suffer from export weakness and the start of world recession.

The press nationalisation of July 1974 was the first really serious political miscalculation of the Velasco regime. It seems to have had three major causes. One was Velasco's increasing sensitiveness to criticism of any kind (the result of his illness) and his unwillingness to put up with the muted attacks of El Comercio. The second was the desire both of the radicals and La Misión for political space in which to fight for the popular support with which to win the conflict for the succession. The third, related to the second, was the radicals' willingness to take more drastic measures in view of the relative failures, up until then, of attempts at stimulating the right kind of popular participation. Many serious officers, however, were profoundly unhappy at the press nationalisation; the more limited step of taking over El Comercio was considered but rejected by the government in 1973 after moderate officers had made their opposition known. In May 1974 Rear-Admiral Vargas Caballero, one of the leaders of the moderate faction, was sacked for making a speech indirectly opposed to further extension of government control over the press. This decisively alienated the navy and also created difficulties in the air force. However, Velasco was then able to get the necessary majority to carry through the press seizure.[31]

This takeover marked something of a breaking point for much of the Lima upper middle class. This had never really supported Velasco but was willing to tolerate him until the press seizure put an end to its apathy. The seizure triggered off anti-government rioting in Miraflores and San Isidro, the most desirable residential area of Lima. From then until the overthrow of Velasco just over a year later, riots and opposition rallies took on a new momentum. Increasingly it became clear to the military that something was going seriously wrong.

Between the press nationalisation and the coup of August 1975, the situation deteriorated across all fronts. Velasco's illness was affecting him increasingly, psychologically as well as physically, and even his political supporters were reluctantly coming to the conclusion that he needed to be removed. The economy, suffering from a variety of problems, was spinning increasingly out of control and it was clear that serious austerity measures would have to be applied. The civilian opposition, particularly in Lima, became increasingly aggrieved and militant. The government itself was becoming increasingly faction-ridden as the military radicals and La Misión battled increasingly openly for the succession, using the nationalised press and popular organisations in their conflicts with each other.

MORALES BERMUDEZ AND THE RETURN TO BARRACKS

When Morales Bermúdez overthrew Velasco in August 1975, his accession was greeted with relief. Morales was an adept military politician who had managed to make himself acceptable to most contending factions; the only clear losers in the coup were La Misión. Morales was a moderate officer whose acceptability to the radicals was due partly to some personal friendships and partly to Morales' general willingness to compromise on most contentious issues. Indeed, Morales was the radicals' own choice for president; they had been preparing to force Velasco's resignation in Morales' favour when they found, to their surprise, that Morales had launched a coup with a completely different set of supporters.[32] Morales Bermúdez came from a military family; his great grandfather had been a military president in the previous century and his father had been killed during an Aprista rising in 1939 when he was military governor of Trujillo. Despite this, he was never a hard-line anti-Aprista. Morales was not a member of the original coup conspiracy or even of the first military government. His cabinet experience consisted of a spell as finance minister under Belaúnde, which ended with his indignant resignation - but he was not the only finance minister to have had problems with Belaúnde. Under Velasco he served as finance minister, then as army chief of staff and finally as prime minister but it is not clear that he was ever committed to military government as an end in itself. It may well always have been his eventual aim, as a matter of personal preference, to hand back power to civilians.
Morales' initial task was a difficult one. By August 1975 it was clear that the time for fiscal expansion was over. Although the economic outlook

did not seem menacing, it was clear that at least some limited austerity would have to be introduced. This, however, was bound to exacerbate social conflict and would set back, at best, the military's long flirtation with popular participation. No less important was the psychological effect of austerity. Minds had to be concentrated on the balance of payments and on the need to sustain some domestic growth. The whole political agenda was changed from the time, only a year or so earlier, when it focussed on topics of expropriation and redistribution. The nationalisation of Marcona in May 1975, intended by Velasco as a support-winning move, fell completely flat largely for this reason. At the same time, the military radicals had by no means been defeated and they had also attracted something of a following from more junior officers. The clock could not just be turned back; conflict would have to be faced and the whole direction of policy laboriously put into reverse. Finally, the political conflicts during Velasco's illness had severely factionalised the military; the navy was alienated from the government, the air force was badly divided between supporters and opponents of Velasco and the splits in the army became increasingly open after the initial collective sigh of relief at the removal of Velasco.

During his first year in office, Morales gradually removed the leading <u>Velasquista</u> officers from positions of influence. General Graham did not appear at all in the first military cabinet. Subsequently Leonidas Rodríguez resigned in November 1975 after Morales had undermined his position in a dispute about promotions. Finally, after a good deal of pressure from within the army and (even more so) the navy, Fernández Maldonado and others were forced to resign at the end of July 1976.

Morales also gave a clear hint of the way in which his mind was working in May 1976. He went to Trujillo, the historic stronghold of Apra, and called for an end to the historic rivalry between Apra and the military. In July, the military traditionally celebrated the memory of the Trujillo garrison, killed in an Aprista rising in 1932. Morales made it clear that it was not to be celebrated in 1976 but Fernández Maldonado and a number of younger captains and majors in any case proceeded with the ceremony.[33] This drew attention to the increasingly apparent division between Fernández Maldonado and the president which culminated in the latter's removal at the end of July.

Peru went heavily into recession at the end of 1976 and did not emerge until 1979. This recession was certainly the most severe to have been suffered by Peru since the war and in some respects it was worse than the 1930s. Real wages, which had reached a plateau in 1974, fell heavily and unemployment rose alarmingly. The Peruvian government meanwhile came under strong pressure from the IMF and the banks to carry out even more drastic austerity measures; this pressure was for a time resisted and it looked briefly as if Peru might move into default on its rapidly increasing foreign debt. It did not help that the military, still concerned about potential conflict with Chile, was continuing to re-arm heavily. Relations between the military and a succession of civilian finance ministers were always uneasy; the resignation of one of these, Piazza, in July 1977, following a clash with the military, precipitated fears of a drastic deterioration of the situation. Le Monde at this time described Peru as "the IMF's Vietnam".

This recession succeeded in doing what the Velasco government's various participation measures had failed to do - it triggered off extensive popular mobilisation. A number of major strikes were declared in 1977 and 1978; a general strike in Lima ·declared on 19 July 1977 was extremely and unexpectedly successful. This, for the first time since the radical days of Apra, signalled the beginning of a serious Left-wing challenge in national politics.

Under these conditions, the military retreat from politics - if it was to take place at all - had to be well managed. Any serious error, either going too quickly or staying too long, could only strengthen the Left. At the same time, the recession finally killed a project, dear to the hearts of the military radicals, of revising the Constitution to entrench the reforms of the Velasco period; it also put an end to Morales Bermúdez' own hopes of emerging as the head of a civil-military electoral alliance. Handelman suggests that "the original transition scenario sketched by administration officials in 1976 called for appointment of a well-controlled commission which would draft a new constitution to be submitted to the electorate for approval in 1978."³⁴   By early 1977 it had become clear that the transition could not be managed in this way and that a far more open process of negotiation with political parties would be necessary. On the other hand, the possibility of a military retreat from power could be used as a bargaining counter to keep civilian politicians in line during a period of austerity; those who co-operated with the military in keeping social unrest at a minimum could be helped in various electorally significant ways.

Early in 1977, then, the military began formal negotiations with the political parties. Not all of these responded in the same way; Apra was, as so often, the most willing to deal with the military. The Left was, naturally enough, in opposition - but the government reserved its real venom, not for the Marxist Left, but for the PSR. This was a party formed by a coalition of civilians and ex-officers who had served with Velasco and it was pledged to continue with his programme; such a party would threaten to divide the military in a way that an uncomplicated Marxist party would not. Leonídas Rodriguez, a leading member of the PSR, was deported in 1978. The Communist Party itself, which had benefited considerably from military patronage during the Velasco period, continued in any case to support the government despite quite strong pressure from its members for a more aggressive line; this was one reason why the Communist Party lost its primacy within the Left, both in electoral terms and in its control over some important unions. However, the Communists continued to support Morales Bermúdez until the final transfer of power in 1980.

Belaúnde's Acción Popular was unwilling to co-operate with the military, but here the considerations were mainly tactical. Belaúnde's ultimate objective was electoral success (which was not necessarily the case with the Left) and he felt that any form of co-operation with the military government would be a liability; his tactic, like that of Sam Spade in The Maltese Falcon, was to be unhelpful but not excessively so for fear of provoking retaliation.³⁵

On 28 July 1977 Morales Bermúdez promised that elections would be held in 1978 for an assembly to draw up a new constitution and that presidential elections would be held in 1980. This gave the military what it wanted, a definite schedule toward civilian rule which would promise something to civilians and yet not so much as to be irrevocable. Three years would be enough to prepare a retreat fom office; meanwhile early elections for a constituent assembly, held in June 1978, would offer a guide to how the electoral land lay.

The announcement that elections would be held was followed by the gradual reorganisation of the political parties.[36] The military regime had earlier allowed them to remain in existence and had merely deprived them of their functions and from time to time deported some of their leading members. This political thaw went along with a continued worsening of the economic climate. Despite this, however, the 1978 elections went ahead with only a brief postponement. Their results were greatly influenced by the non-participation of Acción Popular. Apra polled convincingly, with just over 35% of the vote - a higher percentage than it had received in 1962 and from a much larger electorate. The PPC, formerly a small Right-wing party, also polled well with just under 24%. The Left as a whole, however, achieved the greatest moral victory with 36.25% of the vote divided, it is true, among a number of parties including the Communists who received 6%.

These results were reasonably acceptable to the military. The Right-wing parties within the Constituent Assembly were strong enough to head off Left-wing demands that formal business be abandoned in favour of attacks on the military and the government. A new constitution was in fact written and submitted to the government for approval in July 1979. It contained very few remarkable features.

Shortly after the new Constitution was presented to the military for approval, Haya de la Torre died at the age of 84. Haya had led Apra, often in autocratic style, from the foundation of the party in the 1920s. Although his leadership was not always consistent, he had maintained Apra as a major political force throughout this period. Every military coup between 1931 and 1968 was in some sense anti-Aprista, and every open election held out the possibility of an Apra victory. Apra was sometimes a polarising force, as in 1948, and at others appeared to provide a bulwark upon which a permanent political understanding could be built.

Morales Bermúdez' promise to return Peru to civilian rule in 1980 was part of an understanding with Apra which still seemed strong enough to ease the passage back for the military; Apra itself appeared to have much to gain from a return to the electoral arena. It is not clear whether Morales himself hoped that an Apra without Haya would call on him to lead the party into elections, but it was widely felt that Aprista support would be enough for victory. Apra had also been able to put into the new constitution a clause which stipulated that, in the event of the leading presidential candidate failing to receive 36% of the vote, the outcome would be decided by Congress where Aprista organisation could be expected to outweigh the personal charisma of any political rival.

Haya's death, however, was followed neither by the emergence of a clear successor from within the party nor by the adoption of Morales Bermúdez as candidate. Instead, rivals fought over the succession and the party looked for a time as though it might be falling apart. Meanwhile Belaúnde's refusal to participate in any association with the military seemed to have caught the public mood and, from late 1979, his star moved into the ascendant. What came to face the military, then, was not a managed transition to a collaborative civilian party but a moral defeat through the re-election of the president whom they had deposed in 1968.

In mid-1979, following the death of Haya, it seemed as though the military had second thoughts about the process of returning power. It had become politically isolated while, with the economy finally beginning to recover, its bargaining power had appeared to improve. 1979 was the best year for the economy since 1974, and certain officers began to flirt with the idea of a fresh move to the Left. Morales, however, was unwilling to connive at such a scheme ' which therefore aborted. Belaúnde meanwhile was willing to give the necessary guarantees that he would not enquire too closely into cases of mismanagement and corruption which occurred under the military regime; this made him at least minimally acceptable to the bulk of the military.

In May 1980 Belaúnde won a surprisingly comprehensive electoral victory with around 44% of the vote; his party also gained effective control of Congress. He returned to office in July. One

of the main reasons for his victory lay in the fact
that he was perceived as the most anti-military of
the main candidates. His victory marked the final
popular repudiation of the 1968 intervention and
subsequent military government. It also showed
clearly the inability of that government to manage
its own transition as it had originally hoped.

THE TWELVE YEARS OF MILITARY RULE

The Velasco regime in Peru was by far the most
radical military regime in South America since
1946. Its critics argue that it "did much but
achieved little" and there can be no doubt that
many of the regime's policies proved either
unsuccessful or seriously misconceived or both.
The severe economic setbacks which Peru faced in
1976-78 owed much to international conditions but
policy errors prior to 1975 (the over-subsidisation
of middle class consumers, excessive foreign
borrowing, the unintended discouraging of some
direct foreign investment, over-emphasis on
capital-intensive development projects with long
time lags) were important contributory factors.
Popular mobilisation was indeed encouraged, but not
as the government had wished. It failed to channel
its popular support and the Left benefited instead
from the generally unsettled social conditions.
Indeed, it appears that by destroying the
(admittedly unjust) social structure of rural Peru
the Velasco regime created the conditions or the
emergence of Sendero Luminoso - by far the worst
terrorist threat which Peru has faced this century.
Reform in this case did not head off insurgency;
instead it facilitated it. Finally, the Velasco
regime expired after a period of factionalisation
and decline which cruelly exposed some of its
earlier claims about the efficiency of military
rule and the moral superiority of military
officers. In contrast, the Morales Bermúdez
government failed less, but also attempted less.
It did succeed in a more-or-less orderly handover
of power to an elected government - though not the
government it would have chosen - but did little
else that was memorable. Its economic management
during the 1976-78 period also left a great deal to
be desired.
This is not a distinguished record,
particularly since Peru was relatively lucky with
the personal qualities of its two military

presidents. It is only fair, however, to point out
both that the Velasco regime did achieve some
genuine successes and that Peru is inherently a
very difficult country to govern well; most
Peruvian governments end in failure according to
some definition of the term. Thus the extension of
state control over the Peruvian economy, excessive
in places and self-serving though this may have
been, did confer undoubted benefits on particular
sectors.[37] The agrarian reform also had some
undoubted value and a positive, although limited,
effect on Peruvian income distribution. Moreover,
if one considers the fragmentation of Peruvian
society - ethnic and linguistic as well as
geographical - its high birth rate and limited
agricultural potential, its weak and highly
dependent domestic capitalist class, and its
dependence on a narrow range of exports all acutely
vulnerable to worldwide economic conditions, then
the shortcomings of military policy and policy-
making appear more understandable.[38]

What, then, was the specifically military
influence on the 1968-80 regimes? The fact that
the military in 1968 came into government from
"outside the system" made it possible for it to
carry out a much more sweeping reform plan than
would otherwise have been likely (just as Pinochet
was able to carry out what in his case were
measures of the radical Right); the Brazilian and
Argentine military institutions had by the 1960s
succeeded in entrenching themselves as elite groups
within civil society and so could far less
contemplate radical measures. However, by the mid-
1970s this entrenchment had also occurred in Peru.
A purely military constituency frustrated the
Morales Bermúdez government's stabilisation plans
in 1977 and, by pressing ahead with arms purchases
at a time of economic crisis, caused the burden of
adjustment to fall far more heavily upon the poor
than would otherwise have occurred. It is not at
all clear that the surplus available for investment
and redistribution which the military squeezed from
dominant civilian interests in 1969-70 was
significantly greater than that which the military
allocated to its own institution from after around
1974.

Moreover, the determined pursuit of reform
from above - while an undoubted asset in achieving
its self-targeted objectives - often had the effect
of isolating the government from quite reasonable

offers and suggestions from groups and interests whose co-operation was actually being sought. The Industrial Law of 1970, for example, frightened off far more private local capital than the government had intended. This strategy also had the effect of limiting support for the government from groups naturally sympathetic to the kinds of policy actually pursued.[39] It did, admittedly, also reduce hostility to the military regime - although after the press nationalisation of mid-1974 middle class hostility occurred in any case. The main disadvantage of this authoritarian strategy was that, with the demise of Velasco himself and his small group of military supporters, there was once again nothing of political significance between such basically conservative groupings as Apra and Acción Popular and the Marxist Left. As political strategy, therefore, reformism from above failed even though many of the reforms themselves were in fact carried out.

It is easy enough to trace out the political trajectory of the 1968-80 military government; it began as military populism and deteriorated into a period of factionalisation and impasse. Subsequently a slow return to barracks was promised and implemented. What is clear enough in retrospect, however, was not always so clear to contemporaries. During the period, a series of political groups and economic interests - the oligarchy and the Right in 1968-69, the Left in the early 1970s, Apra in the late 1970s - offered their support and gave their confidence to the military regime but received little or nothing in return mainly because they misread the actual political situation. What does seem clear is that the military tended throughout the period to act in what it perceived as a system-maintaining role in which its commitment to particular policies or interests was secondary. Thus the regime began by carrying through reforms which, it believed, would strengthen Peruvian development and also head off the danger of radicalism from below. Subsequently, when the reforms began to run into trouble and the regime factionalised, Morales Bermúdez first overthrew Velasco and then allowed policy to drift while a degree of military unity was re-established. He also sought to mend fences with the civilian parties and those who had been most aggrieved by the radicalisation of 1974-75. Later still, when the economy worsened sharply and society threatened to polarize, the strategy of a gradual return to barracks was devised to take some of the pressure off the military while also containing the Left. On occasion, however, these military perceptions were some way removed from Peruvian reality.

NOTES

1 D. Gilbert, "The Oligarchy and the Old Regime in Peru", (PhD, Cornell; 1977), pp. 154-155.
2 Ibid., pp. 154-155.
3 N. Gall, "Peru; the Master is Dead", Dissent, 1971, 280-320, p. 296.
4 See R. Thorp and G. Bertram, Peru 1980-1977; Growth and Policy in an Open Economy, (McMillan: 1978).
5 Gilbert, op. cit., p. 259.
6 Caretas, 14 October 1968.
7 Gilbert, "The Oligarchy ...", pp. 154-155.
8 For a more detailed discussion of forces and factors behind the 1968 coup see G. Philip, The Rise and Fall of the Peruvian Military Radicals 1968-76, (Athlone; 1978).
9 E. V. K. Fitzgerald, The State and Economic Development; Peru since 1968, (Cambridge U.P.; 1976).
10 For more detail on the IPC case see G. Philip, Oil and Politics in Latin America; nationalist movements and state companies, (Cambridge U.P.; 1982).
11 Quoted in R. Goodwin, "Letter from Peru", New Yorker, 17 May 1969.
12 L. Einaudi, "Peru", in A. Stepan and L. Einaudi, Latin American Institutional Development; changing military perspectives in Peru and Brazil, (Rand Corp; 1971), p. 20.
13 There is a difference of emphasis in G. Philip, The Rise and Fall as compared with A. Stepan, The State and Society; Peru in Comparative Perspective, (Princeton; 1978).
14 Interview with General Jose Graham, Lima, September 1981.
15 A detailed account of this incident is provided by A. Baella, el Septenato, (Lima; 1977).
16 Lisa North, "Ideological Orientations of Peru's Military Rulers", in C. McClintock and A. Lowenthal, The Peruvian Experiment Reconsidered, (Princeton; 1983).

[17] C. McClintock, "Velasco, Officers and Citizens; the politics of stealth", 275-309, in McClintock and Lowenthal, The Peruvian Experiment, p. 282.

[18] A. J. Pinelo, The Multinational Corporation as a Force in Latin American Politics; a case study of the International Petroleum Company in Peru, (New York; 1973).

[19] P. Cleaves and M. Scurrah, Agriculture, Bureaucracy and Military Government in Peru, (Cornell; 1980), on which this paragraph is based.

[20] For more detailed accounts, Philip, The Rise and Fall, and Stepan, State and Society.

[21] E. V. K. Fitzgerald, "State Capitalism in Peru: a model of economic development and its limitations", in McClintock and Lowenthal, The Peruvian Experiment Reconsidered.

[22] McClintock in McClintock and Lowenthal, Ibid..

[23] Philip, The Rise and Fall.

[24] Cotler, "Democracy and National Integration in Peru", in McClintock and Lowenthal, op. cit..

[25] A. Angell, Peruvian Labour and the Military Government since 1968, (ILAS Working Paper, London; 1980).

[26] Susan Eckstein, "Revolution nd Redistribution in Latin America" in McClintock and Lowenthal, op. cit..

[27] On which see F. Bourricaud, Power and Society in Contemporary Peru, (New York; 1970), and A. Angell, "The Difficulties of Policy-making and Implementation in Peru", in Bulletin of Latin American Research, Vol. 3, No. 1, January 1984.

[28] On Peruvian mining interests see D. Becker, Bonanza Development; the new bourgeoisie and the limits of development, (Princeton U.P.; 1983).

[29] D. Scott Palmer and K. Middlebrook, Military Government and Political Development; lessons from Peru, (London; 1975).

[30] For a fascinating insider account of conflicts over the nationalised press, see G. Thorndike, No Mi General, (Lima; 1976).

[31] For a full discussion of the press nationalisation, see D. Booth, "The Reform of the Press: Myths and Realities", 141-185, in D. Booth and B. Sorj, Military Reformism and Social Classes; the Peruvian Experience 1968-80, (McMillan, London; 1983).

32 Interview with General Jose Graham, Lima, September 1981.
33 <u>Latin America</u>, 30 July 1976.
34 H. Handelman, "Peru" in H. Handelman and T. Sanders, <u>Military Government and the Movement Toward Democracy in South America</u>, (Washington; 1980), p. 103.
35 "Spade too was all smiling blandness 'That's trick from my side', he said, 'to make my play strong enough that it ties you up, but yet not make you mad enough to bump me off against your better judgement'.", Raymond Chandler, <u>The Maltese Falcon</u>.
36 S. Woy-Hazleton, "The Return of Partisan Politics in Peru", 33-73, in S. Gorman, ed, <u>Post-Revolutionary Peru; the politics of transformation</u>, (Westview; 1982).
37 For a study of the mining industry see D. Becker, <u>Bonanza Development</u>, and on oil, G. Philip, <u>Bonanza Development? The case of the Selva Oil Industry in Peru</u>, (ILAS Working Paper; 1984).
38 Many of these points are made in Angell, <u>BLAR</u>, (Vol. 3, No. 1).
39 This point is well made by Cynthia McClintock, "Velasco, Officers and Citizens; the politics of stealth", in McClintock an Lowenthal, eds, <u>The Peruvian Experiment Reconsidered</u>, pp. 275-309.

Chapter 12

CHILE UNDER PINOCHET

The coup of September 1973 followed one of the most bitterly divisive periods in the political history of any South American country. Following the rather ignominious military retreat from power in 1932, the Chilean civilian elite had been concerned to strengthen the country's democratic structure. There had grown up something of a myth (in the sense of believed half-truth) of Chilean exceptionalism; most Chileans saw their country as law abiding and democratic - quite unlike their fractious Argentinian or Peruvian neighbours. Yet by 1970 Chile was undoubtedly experiencing a severe politics of frustration. On the one hand, "political development" was taking place in the shape of increasing popular mobilisation; the electorate, the strength of trade unions and the range of political organisations had all increased greatly since 1932. The economy, however, had performed disappointingly; Chile had become dependent on copper, and the copper industry, for various reasons, had not been doing well.[1] Meanwhile industry developed inefficiently and agriculture virtually stagnated. This dichotomy between a comparatively weak economy and a rapidly mobilising population led to quite severe struggles over income distribution which were in turn reflected in high rates of inflation.[2] These circumstances help to explain why the presidencies of Ibañez (1952-58) and Alessandri (1958-64) ended in failure. Neither Ibañez' populism nor Alessandri's open conservatism proved equal to the changes demanded by an increasingly insistent public opinion. By 1964 a consensus had grown up around the need for reform; the two main candidates for election that year were the

Christian Democratic (and very pro-US) Eduardo
Frei, who promised a "revolution in liberty" and
the Marxist Allende. Frei won but his efforts at
moderate reform proved divisive. A section of the
Christian Democrat party radicalised, while the
Right which had been willing to tolerate Frei would
not accept an accelerating reform programme under
the Christian Democratic Left. Consequently, the
Right, the Christian Democrats and the Left all put
up presidential candidates in 1970 and Allende was
narrowly the winner.

The Allende government has been exhaustively
analysed from almost every conceivable angle and
the ensuing bibliography is vast. It is worth just
noting here that during 1970-73 Allende's support
on the Left remained solid and perhaps even grew
slightly (although the Left as a whole was as
factionalised and divided as ever) but those who
were not for Allende in 1970 became, for the most
part, very strongly against him in 1973. In 1970
most opponents of Allende were reluctantly willing
to give him the benefit of the doubt, hoping that
constitutional guarantees and an opposition
controlled Congress would succeed in taming him.
Only a few extremists within Chile together with
the US government were at that stage plotting his
overthrow.

By September 1973, however, accelerating
inflation and a cumbersome system of price and
distribution controls, a progressively more
militant pattern of demonstration and counter-
demonstration and some relatively minor but nevertheless tension-creating acts of political violence
had combined to polarize the situation completely.
Very many Chileans greeted the military coup with
relief and a substantial number, including Eduardo
Frei and other more conservative leaders of the
Christian Democratic party, as well as the
Nationalist Party as a whole, gave it their active
support.

The military itself, precisely because it had
not been directly involved in politics for many
years, was very much an unknown quantity. Yet its
initial behaviour in power did much to dispel
uncertainty about its intentions. The coup was
extremely brutal. Many thousands were killed and
at the beginning there were as many as eighty
thousand political prisoners - some held in the
international football stadium in Santiago. This
degree of repression - in a country of some 11

million people - was quite disproportionate to the
threat posed by the armed Left. It is of course
true that the military, and much of the Right,
exaggerated the extent of the threat which they
were facing. At the same time, the military's
early behaviour strongly suggests that top military
leaders intended to pave the way for a long period
of authoritarian government. Their coup was
directed as much against the Left in general as
against the armed Left in particular. Apart from
direct repression through arrest and torture, the
military dissolved all left-wing parties (the
others were forbidden to operate) and the trade
unions were disbanded. The legislature ceased to
exist and the government ruled by decree. The
impression that a long period of dictatorship was
in prospect was reinforced by the considerable
amount of purging that took place within the
military itself after the coup; hard-line
supporters of the takeover were promoted and would
clearly not welcome either questions about their
repressive tactics or any threat to their careers
following subsequent amnesty for those who had been
removed.

It appears that the coup was originally
plotted by navy hard-liners. These approached
civilians early in 1973.[3] The first man whom
they approached was Hernan Cubillos; Cubillos was
an ex-navy officer, connected both with the CIA and
with some of the leading private sector groups in
Chile (notably the Edwards family which owned,
among other things, El Mercurio). Cubillos was
himself part of an anti-Allende group which
included some of the leading private employers. He
first contacted Saenz, the president of the
Association of Chilean Manufacturers, who used its
research department to contact the Catholic
University of Chile. From March 1973 a group of
Catholic University economists began, with the
navy, to plan the economic policy that would follow
the coup.

The political balance within the army swung
away from Allende during the course of 1973. A
crucial stage was reached in July 1973 when the
constitutionalist army commander, General Prats,
was forced to resign. However, anti-Allende forces
in the navy were by this time well ahead with their
plans. They were joined at a late stage by air
force commanders - the aerial bombardment of the
Moneda palace on 11 September played a crucial part

in the success of the operation - and by General
Pinochet at a later stage still. Thus, at the
beginning Air Force General Leigh and Admiral
Merina were the most confident and outspoken
members of the Junta. Leigh began by talking about
the introduction of some form of corporatism or
Fascism while the Naval commanders wanted a long
period of authoritarian neo-liberalism. Those
Christian Democrats who had supported the coup
meanwhile pinned their hopes on the army and,
particularly, on General Pinochet, who began by
talking about an eventual return to democracy.

As the son of a "political colonel", active
during the first Ibañez period, Pinochet came from
a more clearly anti-democratic background than most
Chilean officers. As long as he could maintain it,
his position as head of the army, no matter how
unglamorous his role in 1973, would eventually give
him the strongest position in the Junta as a
reflection of the army's own greater size and
importance. Thus he was designated president of
the Junta in June 1974 and in December 1974 he
assumed the title of President of the Republic.

PINOCHET'S CONSOLIDATION

Pinochet's personal power rested essentially
on three foundations - the DINA, the Chicago boys
and the army. He was careful to supplement this,
on occasion, by appealing in a carefully stage-
managed way to public opinion as a whole. One of
the crucial early steps taken by the military
regime was the setting up of a central military
intelligence and repression agency - later known
as the DINA - by secret decree in December 1973.
Up until then, Chile had five different
intelligence services which diffused much of their
limited energy in competing with each other.
DINA's head, Manuel Contreras, was a colonel in
September 1973; he was thus a man with no power
base of his own within the military and so
dependent on Pinochet who had appointed him. DINA
was financed through the government fishing company
and later earned some income from cocaine
smuggling. It recruited from various areas of the
military as well as from the extreme Right-wing
civilian group <u>Patria y Libertad</u>. It quickly
achieved an autonomous status within the government
and set up its own initiation procedures and
hierarchies.[4] Its techniques of operation were

the familiar ones - plain-clothes police in unmarked cars, "disappearance" of suspects, the routine use of torture and, often, of murder.

During 1974 Contreras, with help from the CIA, established DINA as a fully fledged agency and as a major power base within the military government. It was given official recognition in June 1974 by which time it had around 600 full-time agents. By 1977 DINA employed 9,300 and could also rely upon "a network of paid and volunteer informants several times as large, honeycombing all walks of life inside Chile and abroad."[5] By this time, DINA had become an important instrument in Pinochet's own hands; he had used it to penetrate the government bureaucracy as well as a number of other areas. As Dinges/Landau point out, "the DINA network functioned not only to control opposition but to influence policy on lines favoured by Contreras. DINA demanded, and received, a quota of top-level policy positions in each government ministry. The ministers themselves - many of them generals - began to feel threatened as DINA assumed the shape of a shadow government run personally by Contreras."[6] DINA at different times clashed with the Air Force intelligence agency, with General Bonilla (a general suspected of moderate political tendencies) and General Odlanier Mena who was subsequently posted to the Panamanian Embassy. In 1976 General Leigh withdrew air force personnel from the DINA in protest against its expanding range of activities.

DINA also, in mid-1974, set up an external sector which planned assassination attempts on various Chileans in exile. Civilian extremists were recruited to carry out these attacks which included the assassination of General Prats in Buenos Aires in 1974, the attempted murder of Bernardo Leighton in Rome in 1975 and, most dramatically of all, the murder of Carlos Letelier in Washington in 1976. By this time DINA had been successful in eliminating armed opposition to the regime (the death of Miguel Enriquez, the head of the MIR, in a gun battle with the police in October 1974 was a major success for the regime) and also in making inroads into the organisations of the unarmed Left - although the Communist Party retained an underground structure throughout the period.[7]

The DINA was a crucial element in guaranteeing Pinochet's own personal ascendancy. Another main pillar was the economics team with which Pinochet became associated - the Chicago boys. These both identified Pinochet with an intellectually coherent and temporarily successful set of economic policies and brought him into alliance with some of the most prominent capitalist groups in Chile; under the "Chicago" regime, agriculture and manufacturing industry suffered, but finance capital benefited enormously.

By the end of 1974 it had become clear that the Chilean economy was in even worse difficulty than the pessimists had suspected. Apart from the need to bring down inflation from the extremely high rates which it had reached by September 1973, it was also necessary to cope with the effect of sharply higher oil prices, falling copper prices (from the middle of 1974) and the economic consequences of Chile's international isolation following the revulsion felt in much of the world at the brutality of the 1973 coup.

The solution which the Chicago boys offered to these problems was necessarily drastic. In the long term, the strategy was to integrate Chile directly into the world capitalist economy and to eliminate the "distortions" caused by government control and intervention. New exports would be promoted from a major standardisation and reduction in tariffs; a large number of state companies were to be sold off to the private sector; organised labour was to be weakened, not simply as a repressive move but because labour was regarded simply as a factor of production. In the short-run the strategy involved "shock treatment" to bring down a rate of inflation which remained high. This shock involved a major cut in government spending and a heavy deflation of the economy. The policy was first advocated by El Mercurio in November 1974 and soon afterwards by the most prominent US "Chicago" economists - Milton Friedman and Harberger - on a visit to Chile early in 1975. It was announced as policy on 24 April 1975.[8]

This announcement marked the final break between the regime and the Christian Democrats; Christian Democrats were not economic liberals and, quite apart from the very severe social consequences of the deflation being proposed (about which the Catholic Church also became greatly concerned), it had also become apparent by then that the military regime was not planning to hold early elections. Ambitious programmes of long-run

311

reconstruction are not compatible with a quick military return of power to civilians. Apparently, the "shock" measures were scarcely discussed either in Cabinet or in the military. Their imposition did, however, lead to a clash with the Air Force which controlled the Labour Ministry and had begun to build a base among sectors of the labour movement with corporatist and "participationist" policies. In June 1975 the Interior Ministry carried out a series of arrests of trade union activists without reference to the Air Force or the Labour Ministry; in March 1976 a civilian took over as labour minister, and the ministry was downgraded.

Gradually the rest of the Chicago package was applied. The economic role of the state was heavily reduced; state expenditures fell from 25.8% of GDP in 1974 to 19.7% in 1979.[9] From 507 public enterprises at the time of the coup, only 15 remained in government hands in 1980. State investment on infrastructural projects was also greatly reduced. Public employment was reduced more than proportionately, falling by 21% between 1974 and 1978. Parts of the private sector benefited enormously from this set of policies, and also from the partial reversal of previous governments' agrarian reform. Important state assets were sold off at basement prices. According to Foxley, the subsidy element in this sale

> calculated on the basis of the market value of assets, turned out to be equivalent to 30% of the firms' net worth and up to 40% and 50% of the purchase value. The low sale prices was influenced by the state's urgency to sell and its doing so at a moment of deep recession and high interest rates... Given these circumstances, only those firms which had liquid resources or access to cheap foreign credit were in a position to buy the auctioned enterprises.[10]

This last point is a crucial one. The smaller Chilean capitalists, particularly those in the manufacturing sector, did not have the necessary flexibility to take advantage of these new measures; instead, they suffered badly from the "shock" treatment and the easing of tariffs. Bigger capitalists, on the other hand, had access to international borrowing and could buy state assets, and those of their bankrupted competitors, at rock-bottom prices. A group of financiers, known locally as the pirhanas, did indeed use their access to credit to greatly extend their involvement in the local economy. The fact that domestic interest rates were set high, in order to make the deflation effective, gave a further major advantage to those who could borrow internationally. A final factor working in the same direction was that private capital markets were deregulated; the private sector's share of financial deposits increased from 11.1% in 1970 to 64.7% in 1979.[11] In keeping with the same approach, almost all restrictions on private borrowing abroad were lifted.

The immediate effect of all of these changes was a huge recession starting with the application of shock treatment in April 1975. From June 1976 there began a moderate recovery. The exchange rate appreciated somewhat and real wages began to recover. The years between 1978 and 1980 were ones of moderate boom. However per capita income grew at no more than an average of 1.5% between 1974 and 1980, and total employment by no more than 0.9%. The average rate of unemployment increased from 6.5% to 13%, and income distribution deteriorated drastically; more positively, inflation did come down to almost nothing by early 1981 and non-copper exports did show considerable growth. By the end of 1981, for reasons which will be explored below, the whole Chicago experiment was hurriedly abandoned.

The third pillar of the regime was the army, far more than the navy or the air force. The fact that the army had not, prior to 1973, been able to acquire a major stake in Chilean industry (unlike their Argentine or Brazilian counterparts) ensured that there was no "nationalist" army objection to a reduction in the state's role in the economy. Instead, the army sought to improve its position via a larger budget. In fact, between 1973 and 1980 the army expanded in size from 32,000 men to 53,000, and the number of generals from 25 to 42.[11] In 1975, moreover, Pinochet set up a National Security Academy to train senior officers and selected civilians at Staff College level. Moreover, the political inexperience of the army made Pinochet's power of patronage greater than might otherwise have been the case. Immediately after the coup, the military committees which had

313

hitherto judged promotions were suspended and all army promotions were placed in the hands of Pinochet. In 1976 a decree allowed the president to postpone the retirement age for generals which he wished to keep on; this power, too, was used to its fullest extent.

Spending on the military was facilitated by the fact that Chile became involved seriously in border disputes after 1973. Between 1974 and 1977 there loomed the threat of war with Peru, which was rearming heavily (largely due to fear of Chile), as a consequence of Bolivian attempts to re-open the question of its access to the Pacific. In 1977-78 there was also a war scare with Argentina over the Beagle Channel dispute; this, in fact, came very close to ending in hostilities. The nationalist sentiments generated by these threats helped consolidate support for Pinochet while, more specifically, permitting a major increase in military spending. In 1979 Chile was spending an estimated 9.4% of its GDP on arms, and its military spending doubled between 1977 and 1980.[12]

Finally one must consider the role of Pinochet himself. There can be little doubt that a strong presidential system is an asset to stable authoritarianism. After all, one of the most de-stabilising features of any military (or other authoritarian) government is strong competition within the political elite. A strong individual leader can discipline contending factions in the interests of overall elite unity and - with the aid of carefully controlled mass media - maximise such popular support as is available for a government of this kind. The majority of Chileans who were opposed to Allende could now focus their positive support on an individual rather than simply acquiescing in the policies of an institutional military government. It should also be said that there were few competing charismatic individuals in post-1973 Chile with a strong attraction for the Right. The Christian Democratic Left was out of the question, Frei was discredited as "Chile's Kerensky" and Alessandri was too old to be a serious alternative ruler. (It is, however, worthy of some comment that the politicians of the Right - at any rate prior to 1982 - made little effort to assert a political role for themselves.) Pinochet himself was willing and able to fill the role of political leader of the Right; he has been a consistent traveller within the country, good at

public relations and at stage-managed events. Much
of his personal popularity appears to have been
genuine, as was subsequently confirmed by
plebiscite.

FROM DINA TO PLEBISCITE 1976-81

In 1976-78 a further process of political
definition occurred within the Chilean regime. The
"Chicago school" policies, as we have seen, had
involved the selling off of public sector companies
at recession prices to those few Chilean business
interests with the money to buy them. These
financial interests thus came to control an
increasing proportion of the Chilean economy and,
naturally, supported the regime even through the
recession when many less well-placed business
interests were expressing misgivings about the
radicalism of the programme. By 1976 the financial
elite had become solidly aligned behind Pinochet.
By then, however, they were coming to regard DINA
as an embarrassment particularly now that its main
repressive task seemed to have been accomplished.
Contreras' own rather confused economic nationalism
was a further cause of conflict. Finally, growing
US concern over the human rights situation in Chile
- following Letelier's murder and Carter's election
as president - helped to persuade the financial
elite that an improvement in Chile's international
image was in order. They had, in this, the support
of several senior military figures who remained
loyal to Pinochet. It is likely that Pinochet
himself could at this point see the advantages of
"cleaning up his act" even if only cosmetically,
and may also have wished to get rid of Contreras
who was now a certain embarrassment and a possible
rival. In any case, during 1976 and 1977 there
emerged within Chile a "civilised Right" which
broadly supported Pinochet but which was eager to
see a movement away from police-state repressive-
ness and toward a more positive form of
institutional definition.

In June 1977 <u>Ercilla,</u> which was owned by the
Edwards family, reported sensationally on the
tactics of the DINA - the first time that reporting
of this kind had been tolerated by the regime. The
Edwards' family stuck to its position despite some
reprisals from DINA itself. The following month
Pinochet gave a speech, written by one of the

Chicago boys, which called for the "institutionalisation" of the regime. He followed this by
various manoeuvres within the Junta in order to
isolate Contreras and in August 1977 DINA was
declared "dissolved" and replaced by a new security
organisation, the CNI. Contreras was allowed to
remain as head of the new agency for a few months
but was forced out in November 1977 after which the
CNI was downgraded. Meanwhile, the US
administration took a hard line against Chile and
human rights activitists caused considerable
difficulty with the regime's image abroad; on
7 December 1977 the United Nations General Assembly
voted to condemn Chile for violating human rights.
The resolution was co-sponsored by the USSR, Cuba
and the United States. Meanwhile within the USA,
the Letelier case was also being pursued with some
vigour by the FBI. In February 1978 this pressure
reached some kind of peak when Jorge Cauas, a
Chicago boy but a man with some concern with human
rights, resigned as Chilean ambassador in
Washington. According to Dinges/Landau, there
followed several meetings of the "civilised Right"
- including several key military figures as well as
civilians - who considered withdrawing support from
Pinochet; they decided against so drastic a step
but nevertheless insisted that the regime should
not protect Contreras in the face of demands from
the USA.[13] From these meetings there emerged a
strengthened blando, or soft-line, tendency among
regime supporters of which Harnan Cubillos emerged
as the natural leader. He was soon afterwards
appointed foreign minister to Pinochet.

Pinochet's response to this pressure was to
increase further the personal characteristics of
his rule. In some ways, late 1977 offered a
promising time for this. The Chicago treatment had
appeared successful, and Chile was enjoying both
falling inflation and economic recovery. Following
the UN vote, Pinochet decided upon a plebiscite
which asked Chilean voters whether

> in the light of the international aggression
> unloosed against the government of our
> patria, I support President Pinochet in his
> defence of the dignity of Chile, and I
> reaffirm the legitimacy of the government of
> the Republic to lead in a sovereign manner the
> process of institutionalisation of the
> country.

The plebiscite was held on 4 January 1978, some two weeks after the decision to hold it was made public.

Pinochet's decision aroused protests from the rest of the Junta (Admiral Merino and General Leigh) which feared that he was personalising the regime. The Christian Democratic party, which unlike the parties of the Left remained barely legal after September 1973, advocated a "no" vote and even the bishops advocated a postponement of the plebiscite. However, when the results were announced, Pinochet was seen to have won with around 75% of the vote.

These various developments marked a decisive stage in the political evolution of the regime. They were the culmination of a process seriously begun in April 1975 when the "shock treatment" had finally ruled out any possibility of an orthodox handback of power to civilians. By early 1978, with the repression largely accomplished (and the DINA used and disposed of) and with the economy apparently on the mend, the way was open for transition to a personalist authoritarian regime with a limited plebiscitary basis. Pinochet had won his internal power struggles and from then on would brook no public opposition; Leigh and Cubillos were both dismissed outright from the government as soon as Pinochet found the moment opportune. Leigh went in July 1978 after publicly criticising Pinochet in an interview with an Italian newspaper and Cubillos was sacked as Foreign Minister the following year after it had become clear that he had not succeeded in making the Pinochet regime internationally respectable. In 1980, the final stamp of approval was apparently set on Pinochet's ascendancy. A plebiscite was called, at one month's notice, to decide whether or not to approve a new constitution; this constitution introduced an eight year presidential term, starting in 1981, with Pinochet himself as the only candidate to be the first president; after 1989 a limited democratisation was foreseen but not until 1997 would the president again be popularly elected. Despite a spirited campaign against the Constitution, led by Eduardo Frei, the vote was said to be 65% in favour.

ECONOMIC COLLAPSE AND POLITICAL MANOEUVRES

The first serious signs that Pinochet's position was coming under threat occurred in late 1981 when his economic strategy first began to confront growing and increasing difficulty; there followed a drastic fall in Chilean GDP in 1982. One important step leading up to this disaster occurred in 1979 when the regime's monetarist approach was modified in an attempt simultaneously to bring down the inflation rate even further and to protect the financial allies of the regime (and the Chicago boys) from serious embarrassment. Many of the latter had borrowed heavily on the international market to invest in projects with a peso income yield; heavy devaluation would be a serious matter for them. It might perhaps charitably be said that the financial elite, which had never in the past been given this degree of economic freedom, lacked a tradition of sound banking and was therefore prone to make errors; less charitably, speculative fortunes were made at high cost to the long term development of the productive sectors of the economy. In any case, policy was changed in the direction of exchange rate stabilisation, along the lines of the experiment attempted in Argentina in and after 1979. It was announced that the peso would in future be pegged to the dollar; it was hoped that this would give a downward push to price expectations and that the need for greater competitiveness would cause a reduction in the price of tradable goods. This measure did have a short-run effect on inflation but in two crucial respects the economy failed to adjust. The tradable sector was not able to recover from lost competitiveness; instead, the problems of a worsening trade position were masked by the continued inflow of foreign loans, eagerly contracted now that the peso/dollar rate appeared to be guaranteed. At this point, international bankers seemed ready to lend to anything and their policies with respect to Chile were no exception. The Chilean government, true to its free market beliefs, did not prevent the contracting of loans abroad; high peso interest rates (part of domestic credit control) made such borrowing even more attractive. Chile's external problems grew worse when international interest rates started to increase in 1980; for Chile the position became

yet more difficult following a renewed fall in the
copper price in 1981 and also the second "oil
shock" of 1979-80. As a result of these
developments, the balance of trade went heavily
into deficit in 1981. This created the necessary
condition for a major financial crisis.[14]
The crash took a long time to come, but when
it came it developed swiftly. Early in 1981 one
major finance company broke and in November 1981
the government had to intervene in four banks and
four finance companies. These had borrowed heavily
from abroad, lent to domestic projects and, with
the near-collapse of the trading economy and the
general downturn in economic activity, could no
longer expect to recover the loans. There followed
both a drastic domestic recession and a major
crisis of confidence in the peso. This had to be
devalued heavily and at the end of 1982 was down to
40% of its previous parity. 1982 was a truly
horrendous year for the Chilean economy -
industrial output fell by 22%, imports by 46% and
employment was also drastically reduced. A wave of
bankruptcies followed and debt defaulters did much
to improve the social composition of Santiago gaol.
This collapsing economy gave a renewed impetus
to social and political protest against the
government. Monthly protests began in May 1983,
led by the copper workers union, and were repeated
regularly throughout the year. The protests often
became riotous and resulted in a number of deaths.
Meanwhile the "civilised Right", which had more-or-
less accepted the regime after the 1980 plebiscite,
began quietly looking for alternatives to Pinochet;
retired officers began to meet conservative
politicians and the familiar tactic of "knocking on
the doors of the barracks" began. Pinochet's
response was to affect a moderate liberalisation in
order either to bargain with the opposition or to
expose its divisions and discredit it. Despite
the seemingly complete failure of the regime's
economic policies, however, and the contrast
between its authoritarianism and the traditionally
democratic context of Chilean politics, Pinochet
remained in a stronger position than many had
expected. He did move towards the opposition in
certain respects; he sacked his Chicago boys from
the economics ministries, he lifted the state of
emergency (in effect since 11 September 1973) and
eased the censorship, and in August 1983 he
appointed Sergio Jarpa, a leading member of the

Nationalist Party, as his Interior Minister with a mandate to negotiate with the moderate opposition.

There were, however, at least three different opposition positions and no consensus at all on what the next step should be. Moderate conservatives, in the National Party and the Air Force, were uneasy with the personal power which had accrued to Pinochet and keen to reduce it. Against this, however, they accepted the validity of the 1980 Constitution and plebiscite vote. The main change which they sought was the calling of early Congressional elections (after the Constitution had first been amended by plebiscite) in order to put a limit on presidential power; they might also have welcomed the resignation of Pinochet and his replacement by a less controversial figure. Since the object of these changes would have been to reconcile Chilean public opinion to a continuation of conservative government, they could not easily have formed a basis for a comprehensive political settlement; without such a settlement conservatives preferred the status quo to a dangerous leap in the dark. The second position was adopted by the Christian Democratic Party and the moderate wing of the Socialist Party. These called for the resignation of Pinochet, the scrapping of the 1980 Constitution and a "democratic rupture" with the military government. A radical change in economic policy was also demanded. These demands, however, were obviously unacceptable to the regime and also to its moderate critics. The Christian Democrats were in fact caught, as they had been in 1970 and again in 1973, in the middle of a rapidly polarising situation. If they had joined forces with the National Party, they might have given sufficient reassurance to the regime's supporters to abandon Pinochet; to do this, however, would have been to become at least partially identified with a failed and increasingly unpopular economic status quo. This would have cost them support and such a decision might also have involved them in a game of political manoeuvering which they might have lost. The Christian Democrats were criticised, both within Chile and outside, for appearing to make a gradual transition of the regime more difficult and for relying excessively on highly publicised but ineffective forms of protest such as strikes and demonstrations - in short, for overplaying their hand. However, their alternative, more

conciliatory strategy was no less risky because it
would have handed the leadership of almost all
anti-government activity to the Left. The third
position was that of the MIR and the Communist
Party (which changed policy completely after the
1980 Constitution was approved[15]). This was
committed to the overthrow of the state by force.
Although there was relatively little genuine
terrorism (despite some activity by provocateurs),
this had the effect of heightening tension and
making a political settlement still more difficult.
Some members of the armed Left may have believed
naively that the regime really was vulnerable to
armed attack, but the strategy seems to have been
designed mainly in order to try to avoid letting
moderate politicians off the hook. A gradual
evolution from military dictatorship to a carefully
circumscribed form of democracy would have left the
Marxist parties out in the cold and would have
absolved most supporters of the 1973 coup from the
consequences of the economic failure and social
polarisation. The Communists and other Left-wing
parties, who had been savagely persecuted after
1973 by a regime initially supported by the
Christian Democrats, could not forgive and forget
so easily. The armed strategy, therefore, was
ultimately a spoiling role which aimed to prevent a
limited solution to the crisis by reinforcing the
hard-line Right at the expense of political
reformists.

Largely as a result of the incompatibility
between these different opposition strategies,
Pinochet's position appeared to strengthen during
the course of 1984. In September he completed
eleven years in office - an outcome which nobody
had expected at the time of the original coup. His
government's economic failure had tended not to
isolate him but rather to reproduce the lines of
cleavage (and some of the mobilisation) of the
early 1970s. This time, however, the hard-line
Right had direct access to the state and little
compunction about using its full force against
opponents. The Left, probably more popular than a
decade before, could not find a way of making its
pressure effective while the centre, as in 1973,
was being forced to choose between extremes.
Positions had become entrenched. In November
1984, therefore, Pinochet reimposed the state of
siege and announced that his political opening was
at an end.

THE PINOCHET DECADE

Much of the political behaviour of the Chilean regime can be explained in terms of the previous near-absence of military rule. Pinochet did indeed come down like a wolf on the fold. Because of its lack of interests within the socio-economic system, the Chilean military could accept an uncompromising monetarism in a way that the Argentine military could not. It is however unlikely, in view of the military's own accretion of institutional interests and the actual performance of the economy during the Pinochet decade, that another monetarist experiment will be attempted in the foreseeable future even in Chile. Moreover, unlike the regimes in Brazil, Uruguay and Argentina, the Chilean military set no limits to the presidential term and took few steps to establish its own relative independence from the personality of the dictator. As a result, the Chilean regime has been far more personalist than other recent military dictatorships in South America. Pinochet is the only military president to have held office for a decade since 1945 in any South American country except Paraguay.

Personalist regimes have their advantages at a time when the government is reasonably popular. It is easier to focus popular support on an individual than on a Junta, and easier also for the media to direct its attention to a particular figure. A personalist ruler may also arbitrate effectively on conflicts within the elite - as Pinochet appears to have done both in 1976-77 and again in 1983 - which might otherwise lead to factionalisation and decline. However, the difficulty of such regimes is that they leave the system almost without option in the event of serious economic and political failure. The Chilean elite - and, so far as one can judge, the officer corps - has been forced to cling to Pinochet because it has nowhere else to go. The result has been a process of political entrenchment which has undoubtedly protected property-owners from the Left but which has been damaging to them in almost every other way conceivable. The Right has now far less reason for confidence at the likely evolution of Chilean politics than it would have done had the regime been less personalist and less entrenched at the beginning of the 1980s than it actually was. If ever there were a political morality tale, the failure of the Pinochet regime in every respect save that of self-preservation must surely be it.

In 1973 Chile's main problems were a declining economy and intensifying political polarisation. Exactly the same is true at the end of 1984. A failed Marxist experiment was followed by a failed neo-liberal one whose social costs and long-term consequences seem if anything to be greater than the polarisation and violence of the Allende period. The direct violence and repression of the Pinochet regime is, of course, much worse than anything in Chilean history since independence. Underlying these failures has been Chile's inability to reconcile the emergence of mass politics since the 1950s with the limited performance of an economy whose main export - copper - is in secular decline. Pinochet's inability to resolve or supersede this underlying conflict will impose heavy costs on future governments as well as on those who have already suffered during his rule.

NOTES

1 T. H. Moran, Multinational Corporations and the Politics of Dependence; copper in Chile, (Princeton U.P.; 1974).
2 A. Hirschman, Journeys Toward Progress, (New York; 1963).
3 Latin American Bureau, The Pinochet Decade, (1983).
4 J. Dinges and S. Landau, Assassination on Embassy Row, (New York, Pantheon books; 1980).
5 Ibid., p. 132.
6 Ibid., p. 135.
7 C. Furci, "The Chilean Communist Party and its Third Underground Period 1973-80", in Bulletin of Latin American Research, Vol. 2, No. 1, (October 1982), 81-97.
8 LAB, The Pinochet Decade.
9 This account relies heavily on A. Foxley, Latin American Experiments in Neo-Conservative Economics, (U. of California; 1983).
10 Ibid., pp. 66-67.
11 P. Sigmund, "The Military in Chile", pp. 97-116, R. Wesson ed., New Military Politics in Latin America, (Hoover Inst.; 1982).

12 Angell, "The Soldier as Politician", p. 34.
13 Dinges and Landau, <u>Assassination</u>.
14 For an account of this crash, see T. Congdon's chapter on Chile in E. Duran ed., <u>Latin America in the World Recession</u>, (Cambridge U.P.; 1985).
15 Furci, in <u>Bulletin of Latin American Research</u>.

Chapter 13

SOME OTHER CASES; BOLIVIA, ECUADOR AND URUGUAY[1]

It is finally worth looking, in somewhat less
detail, at military regimes in some of the smaller
South American countries, Bolivia, Ecuador and
Uruguay. All of these countries are influenced in
their political behaviour to a greater or lesser
extent by the political situation in neighbouring
countries. The Velasco regime in Peru had an
influence in both Bolivia and Ecuador, while Brazil
and Argentina have always been influential in the
traditional buffer states of Bolivia, Paraguay and
Uruguay. It is indeed generally true in South
America that "models" of politics in one country
will influence the political behaviour of others;
the 1964 military coup in Brazil and the 1983
democratisation in Argentina had an impact far
beyond the borders of those countries. The three
countries considered in this chapter are subject to
a greater degree of influence from their neighbours
than are most others. Ecuador during the 1970s
underwent an experience in Peruvian-style military
populism, while the more conservative Brazilian-
style of military rule was attempted in Uruguay.
Bolivia has undergone virtually every imaginable
form of military government since 1964. All three
countries, however, experienced both military
interventions and de-militarisations between 1979
and 1984 and all now have elected civilian
governments.

MILITARY POLITICS IN BOLIVIA

The Bolivian revolution of 1952 surprised even
those who led it. It resulted in a heavy purge and
retrenchment of the military. General Ovando later
suggested that the officer corps was cut by around

20% and the size of the army as a whole by around 75%. Certainly only two officers who had been promoted colonel or above in the previous promotion list remained in the post-1952 army.[2] Civilian militias were also encouraged in order to provide a check on the army. Although the army lost men, money and prestige it remained in existence. Radical sections of the MNR did in fact call for its complete abolition but President Paz declined to put such a policy into effect. Instead the military was to some extent incorporated into the MNR structure; senior officers were required to join the MNR and attend political lectures. In return, they were able to use the MNR machinery to make contact with local civilian organisations and generally to extend their participation within society.[3]

After 1956 the fortunes of the military recovered considerably. The weakness of the Bolivian economy after the revolution encouraged the MNR leadership to turn to the US for support. This support included the imposition of an economically orthodox stabilisation process which aggravated conflicts within the MNR, particularly between the central government and the tin miners' leadership. President Siles Suazo (1956-60) down-graded the miners' and peasants' militias and the importance of the military again began to increase. Meanwhile the content of military training became increasingly technical and, after around 1960, included anti-guerrilla instruction. Bolivian colleges of higher military studies were set up in 1960 and 1961 and marked an increase in the autonomy of the military from the MNR. Moreover, the direct role of the United States in training Bolivian officers, whether in the country or in Panama, greatly increased after the Cuban Revolution. By the end of 1963 Bolivia had more graduates from the US army war school at Fort Bragg than any other Latin American country.[4] At a political level the army was also used increasingly to control the intense factional disputes which occurred in the aftermath of the Revolution; in 1960 for example Santa Cruz was placed under military control.

The MNR continued to factionalise and this gave Bolivia's military leaders an opportunity to return to power. By late 1963 a military coup was under active consideration.[5] By this time, shifts in US policy and a general disillusionment

with the MNR on the part of Washington made it
clear to the military that a coup would not be
opposed by the US, as would have been the case two
years earlier. As a major provider of aid,
Washington exerted considerable influence on
Bolivian politics.[6] Moreover, it was becoming
clear to military leaders that some sections of the
MNR were willing to accept a direct military
presence in government; specifically, the opponents
of Paz Estensoro greatly resented his decision, in
1963, to seek office for a third term and made it
clear that they were not averse to a military veto
of his candidacy. At a lower level the military
had increasingly come to control peasant leagues
nominally under the control of the MNR; in 1962
President Paz had asked the military to intervene
in troublesome peasant organisations in Cochabamba
- a request which enabled the military to extend
its control over them. This pattern of intervention gradually extended throughout the rest of
the country. Thirdly, as the need for repression
grew, the military was itself increasingly
unwilling to carry it out on behalf of a government
which it could not control; the use of troops in
the tin mines in 1963 was an important factor in
diminishing military respect for the government.
Finally, there was a degree of military frustration
with the MNR's evident inability to manage the
Bolivian economy with any degree of effectiveness.

Under pressure from the military, Paz in 1964
agreed to select Air Force General Rene Barrientos
as his Vice-President. A few months later a
military rising led Barrientos to demand Paz'
resignation.[7] Barrientos then emerged as
president although his own position was checked by
the power of the army commander Ovando, who had
played a major part in rebuilding the army after
1956 and took a very strong view of his institutional responsibilities. The government which
emerged could rely on some considerable bases of
support outside the military itself. There was the
United States government, solidly behind
Barrientos, as well as Gulf Oil, an increasingly
important presence in the country, which lent him
helicopters.[8] Barrientos was also able to
inherit the MNR rural patronage machine and, with
it, the guarantee of an electoral majority (which
would prove helpful later). The coup was also
generally welcomed by conservatives within the
country.

BARRIENTOS, OVANDO AND TORRES 1964-71

The officers who came to power in 1964 were of the post-1952 generation; they were at least verbal supporters of the Revolution. Barrientos, an accomplished military demagogue, reinforced the impression that little had changed when he organised elections in 1966 and won them convincingly. Rising tin prices (due to the Vietnam War) and the beginning of oil exports in 1966 also appeared to indicate that Bolivia could at last count on a little modest prosperity. However, the disintegration of the MNR and the even harder military line against the tin miners showed that Barrientos' government was basically confrontational and Right-wing.

In 1967 Bolivian politics reached a major watershed with the capture and killing of Che Guevara. Guevara had left Cuba sometime in 1966 to prepare the overthrow of the Bolivian government. News of his arrival and activity led to an energetic response from Washington. Various US agencies had already shown themselves to be particularly active in Bolivia, but CIA involvement with the Bolivian army now exceeded all previous limits. Washington quickly achieved its major objective, the capture and killing of Guevara, but the campaign also upset institutional arrangements within the Bolivian military; evidence of this lies in the decision of Barrientos' interior minister to break with the regime and to send Guevara's diary to Cuba. In early 1969 the Catholic newspaper **Presencia** published a whole series on CIA activities within Bolivia, forcing Barrientos to admit to its presence in the country. Moreover, after its victory over Guevara and faced with pressing concerns elsewhere, Washington looked to reduce its presence in Bolivia; it was helped to do so by an increase in international tin prices induced by the Vietnam War. By the same token, this increased the fiscal independence of the Bolivian government - for the first time since the early 1950s La Paz was largely free of dependence on US aid which had, in the past, been one of the most important sources of public finance.

Under these circumstances the emergence of the Velasco regime in Peru was regarded with very great interest by many Bolivian officers. It seemed to show that there was no necessary antagonism between military rule and socio-economic reform. Ovando, who continued to control the army, was in any case unhappy with the embrace between President Barrientos and Washington if only because it seemed to threaten Ovando's own aspiration to reach the presidency in 1970. The defeat of Guevara's insurgency gave him the opportunity to continue his strategy of pushing the Barrientos government in a nationalist direction. We will never know how Barrientos would have responded to this kind of pressure because in May 1969 he was killed in a helicopter accident.

By the time of Barrientos' death, the most obvious symbol of the US presence in Bolivia was Gulf Oil which had steadily been increasing its investments since its entry into Bolivia in the late 1950s and had begun exporting oil in 1966. Pressures against the company mounted quickly. Siles Salinas, Barrientos' civilian vice-president who took over as president after the helicopter crash, pressed the company for a renegotiation of the original 1955 oil code but Gulf refused; it did not adjust quickly enough to rapidly changing circumstances and proved unable to head off an increasingly threatening situation. In October 1969 General Ovando seized power and nationalised the company.

The nationalisation certainly owed more to the civilian advisers who had come to support Ovando than to the military establishment. Ovando, like Barrientos, had been able to form a team of civilian asesores who, well before 1969, were persuaded that Gulf had to be expropriated. Undoubtedly Ovando himself was motivated by concern that the Bolivian military had become dangerously factionalised during its period of rule; the aftermath of the Guevara campaign made this only too apparent. Anti-US nationalism seemed to be a way of re-establishing the identity of the military and broadening the base of social support for continued military rule. Moreover Ovando, who badly lacked Barrientos' demagogic skills, needed to look for support on a much more organised and programmatic basis. It is notable that the nationalisation of Gulf was called for and strongly supported by Juan Lechin who was head of the Bolivian labour confederation.

Ovando's economic nationalism, however, was a good deal less successful than that of Velasco in Peru. Much of the reason for this lay in the different nature of Bolivian society to that of

Peru. Bolivia had already experienced a Revolution which had involved widespread land-seizures and the nationalisation of the tin mines. The Bolivian tin miners were exceptionally militant and had challenged the comparatively reformist and flexible MNR before being put down harshly by the military in 1963, 1965 and again in 1967. Guevara's campaign, although in military terms quite unsuccessful, had also contributed to a sense of political radicalisation. In such a society, a few reformist gestures - such as the nationalis-ation of an American oil company - would not cut very much ice with the Left. Against this, the post-Revolutionary period had seen the rise of the eastern province of Santa Cruz which had been virtually unaffected by the original revolution. Santa Cruz quickly developed an independent and Right-wing political identity, greatly strengthened by the nationalisation of Gulf Oil which was located in the province. The cession of oil investment hit the regional economy hard, particularly since Bolivian provinces received a portion of the government's oil revenue directly.

Military efforts at reformist nationalism, then, quickly foundered between a radical Left and a militant Right. By mid-1970 Ovando was himself moving to the Right but nevertheless a number of military conservatives continued to seek his overthrow. The confusion following a failed coup in October 1970, however, allowed a more Left-wing general, J. J. Torres, to take office. Torres, unlike Ovando, showed some willingness to radicalise in order to maintain a Left-wing following. In January 1971 he was able to put down a coup and called a public rally to win support from workers and students. Yet Torres' efforts at mobilisation did more to unite his enemies than strengthen his friends. As Ovando had found earlier, the Left could be won over only by a direction of policy which would be totally unacceptable to the high command of the military because the whole existence of the institutional military would come under threat once again.

This dilemma could clearly be seen when, at the beginning of August 1971, a manifesto was published on behalf of the Vanguardia Militar del Pueblo.[9] This manifesto analysed the socio-economic conditions of the lower ranks of the Bolivian army in class terms; it called for a class war within the military and the dissolution of the command structure and its replacement by a popular army. The fact that it seems to have been signed both by NCOs and junior officers was a particularly disturbing sign; as already noted, NCOs are of particular importance in Bolivia because of the linguistic divide between most senior officers and most conscripts. Whitehead suggests that the radical young commissioned officers may have been influenced by student brothers or cousins.[10] The appearance of this manifesto led to determined efforts on the part of most senior officers to establish their own command positions and turned them against the main destabilising force which they faced - in this case the radical conditions of civil society as a whole.

In August 1971 the Torres government precipitated a rebellion by arresting General Banzer, who was engaged in a coup conspiracy. Banzer was a native·of Santa Cruz, from a land-owning family, and had acted briefly as Minister of Education under Barrientos and also as attaché in the Bolivian embassy in Washington. Banzer's arrest triggered a rising which was supported by the FSB, the main conservative party in Bolivia and particularly strong in Santa Cruz. The rising was also strongly supported from Brazil and, more cautiously, by Washington and Buenos Aires. By the end of the first day the rebellion was securely in control of Santa Cruz. It was then joined by the Ranger regiment under control of Colonel Selich, who had been a leading figure in the anti-Guevara campaign of 1967. Torres had never felt strong enough to purge the Ranger regiment and had merely posted it far from the capital where it now joined the developing rebellion. Once the rebellion succeeded in Santa Cruz, Torres' support in La Paz largely melted away although the commander of the Colorado regiment remained with Torres to the end. Civilian support for Torres only slightly affected the military balance, partly because of Torres' own reluctance to arm civilians but mainly because of the military's control of far more sophisticated weaponry than it had been able to command in 1952. By the end of August, Banzer was securely in the Presidency.

BANZER AND THE DECAY OF MILITARY RULE

Banzer headed a coalition of military and civilian opponents of Torres, and originally promised a gradual constitutionalisation of the new regime. Instead, however, he manoeuvred carefully to develop a limited constituency of his own while heavily promoting both purely military and generally conservative interests; in November 1974 he found himself in a position to launch an autogolpe, removing his allies and establishing a clearly military dictatorship. Although not generally as brutal as the Cono Sur dictatorships of the period, Banzer was careful to destroy potential opposition. Peasant disaffection was crushed after the massacre of a peasant demonstration in January 1974. After 1976 Banzer began installing troops directly within the mining districts of the country which thus found themselves under effective military occupation. Military interests were also promoted directly. In 1972 a military corporation (COFADINA) was set up in order to take a direct role in the arms industry. After 1974 a considerable part of the central government was also placed under the control of military officers; although Banzer himself stated that the number of officers with direct administrative responsibilities "did not amount to fifty"[11], this was still a considerable proportion of the senior Bolivian officer corps. Ironically, however, the most serious threat which Banzer faced in his first three years in office came from a coup attempt by junior officers in June 1974; these were opposed to the participation of the MNR in the government, insistent on a more nationalist foreign policy and anxious to see an extension of military control over the Bolivian economy.[12] Although defeating these officers, Banzer in fact stole much of their programme.

Banzer in fact showed himself adept at political manoeuvre throughout this period - there were a number of unsuccessful military conspiracies against him - and also proved capable of building a limited personal base within both the military and civil society as a whole. International events also helped; Bolivia enjoyed something of an economic boom during 1974-1977 due to a big increase in hydrocarbon prices and the increased willingness of the international banks to lend to Bolivia. Moreover, the Pinochet coup in Chile appeared to alter the regional balance of power in South America and Banzer fished energetically, although ultimately unsuccessfully, in these troubled waters in the hope of improving Bolivia's territorial position by playing Chile off against Peru. Renewed Bolivian access to the sea was a question put very firmly on the international agenda between 1974 and 1977.

In November 1977, however, Banzer declared his intention of calling elections for 1978; since he could not run himself while simultaneously retaining control of the armed forces, he nominated General Pareda to stand as a pro-regime candidate. There seem to have been a number of factors making for this somewhat surprising decision. Undoubtedly there was pressure from the United States, traditionally influential in Bolivian affairs; Carter had taken office in January 1977 with a resolve to help the democratic forces in Latin America and the Bolivian military was not well placed to resist US pressure. There may also have been pressure from within the army. Banzer had ruled in a very factional way, with the particular support of older officers (i.e. those of the pre-1952 generation); many of these had used government office to enrich themselves considerably and younger officers were either showing their disgust or, in some cases, becoming impatient for their turn. The increasing importance of the cocaine export trade, in which Bolivian generals were heavily involved, was a further factionalising influence. Banzer is likely to have realised also that, by November 1977, the immediate economic boom was coming to an end and that his foreign policy was in difficulty; he appears to have concluded, in any case, that it was better to take an initiative than be overtaken by events. He was also to some extent lulled into a false sense of security by the short-term success of his authoritarian regime, and he almost certainly underestimated the potential offered to the opposition by a programme of limited liberalisation.[13] By 1977 Banzer had established clientelist control over the main peasant unions and also used the labour ministry to build up a clientele in the less strongly organised areas of the economy. Many outside observers, in mid-1977 (including the present author) concluded that the regime was fairly secure.

Banzer's decision in November 1977, to allow an electoral opening, began the unravelling of authoritarian rule; more than five years of extreme instability (even by Bolivian standards) were to follow before full scale civilian rule was restored in 1982. Very briefly, the political opening which

Banzer offered quickly led to a hunger strike by four miners' wives begun on 28 December 1977 to demand an amnesty for imprisoned miners. This followed a very limited Christmas amnesty intended to pave the way for a broader political opening. The hunger strike, supported tacitly by the Church and actively by the country's human rights movement, quickly spread and achieved its objective at the end of January 1978. This weakened the regime and encouraged the miners union to press its demands on the government.

Elections went ahead during a political climate over which the regime progressively lost control. Siles Suazo won unsuspected support as the main opposition candidate and factionalism within the military undermined the efficiency of the pro-Pereda state machine. When the election results came in, it was clear that Pereda had obtained a tenuous victory only by rigging to an extent which completely deprived them of credibility. This, in turn, led to a split between Pereda and Banzer, and Pereda seized power in July 1978 promising to hold elections the following year. In November 1978 Pereda was in his turn removed by General Padilla. Padilla led a less Right-wing and more democratic group of officers which wanted elections so as to put an end to factional conflicts within the military and allow the strengthening of the military institution.

Elections were then held again in July 1979 but unfortunately resulted in stalemate. Siles led the poll but did not have enough votes for an outright victory. Paz, who had come second, appeared better placed to secure election once the decision had been referred to Congress. Banzer came a respectable third but would not deal with the other candidates. Congress in fact almost failed to make a choice of president but eventually, following growing military impatience, chose Walter Guevara Arce as a compromise president prior to yet another set of elections, scheduled for 1980. Guevara could not easily take any kind of decisive action in the face of a deteriorating economic situation or check various minority Left-wing parties from demanding the trial of Banzer and accountability and punishment for those who had abused their office during his presidency.

Guevara had been in office for only a few months when another military coup attempt occurred in November. This was an unusually violent affair although its leader General Natush had some reformist pretentions and his fortnight-long regime was warmly received by the Soviet Embassy.[14] Widespread opposition to the coup then led the military to hand power back quickly to civilians but, in order to disguise a complete defeat for the army, Guevara was replaced as president by Lidia Gueilier. It was confirmed that a further set of elections would be held in 1980.

Siles Suazo and the UDP did in fact win the July 1980 elections but the military again seized power before Siles had time to take office. This coup was openly opposed by the USA, a section of the army and almost all civilians. It was exceptionally brutal by Bolivian standards and clearly modelled on the "Southern Cone" coups earlier in the decade; and it was carried out with the support both of Argentine officers and of some European figures of the extreme-Right who had been attracted into Bolivia partly by the cocaine industry and partly to escape from the European police. The coup followed a number of acts of violence from the Right, calculated to set the stage for renewed military intervention. Its Bolivian leaders, moreover, were men quite openly involved in Bolivia's illegal narcotics industry which provided much of the financing of the coup.

It is, for obvious reasons, impossible to trace in detail the rise of the cocaine export industry in Bolivia and its connections with the military.[15] There is little doubt, however, that the military was heavily involved in this trade at least from around the middle of the Banzer period and that it has continued to play a major part in Bolivian politics. Corruption is, of course, nothing new in South American politics but the Bolivian narcotics trade is distinctive in several ways. First, the financial rewards which it brings are out of all proportion to the "official" revenues of the Bolivian state or military institution. In 1983 one of Bolivia's leading narcotics dealers offered to pay the country's entire foreign debt out of his own pocket in return for the right to operate unhindered for a period of three years. It is not a question of a military-political figure turning a blind eye to minor fortunes made by loyal military officers. The money available is so great (and Bolivian politics so unstable) that many officers would be tempted to remain a few months in power in order to guarantee a well paid retirement anywhere in the world; Dunkerley estimates[16] that the presidency was worth $40,000 a week to General Garcia Meza in 1981. Even this does not take account of direct military involvement in the trade below the presidential level. It is also quite obvious that military discipline and unity could not easily survive temptation on such a scale. Nor was it possible for the rewards to be shared out in an institutionally acceptable way. Narcotics money became, instead, a source of conflict between rival gangs which, with their links to the military and their own private armies, controlled and fought over the spoils. Secondly, Washington's opposition to the international narcotics trade is genuine and relatively constant; so, following the Garcia Meza coup, was its opposition to the political ambitions of military officers connected with the drugs trade. Washington was thus virtually bound to treat the Garcia Meza regime (1980-81) with hostility. Thirdly, the narcotics trade attracted certain figures connected with organised crime from other parts of the Continent and even from Europe; cocaine, political fanaticism and organised crime came together in a witches brew which had international repercussions. One key figure in the Bolivia narcotics trade was Klaus Barbie.

For these reasons, the 1980 coup, despite its brutality, was inconclusive. The officers who led it claimed to be following an institutionalist line. In the words of one "high official" they

> utilised the campaign which the Left-wing parties were waging against the armed forces at that time [accusations levelled against General Banzer, slashing the defence budget] to reverse the majority trend in the high command which favoured respecting the democratic process. They pointed out that the military institution could not tolerate such attacks on its prestige any longer and cleverly played on the fears that troop strength and salaries might be cut.[17]

Those politicians who had explicitly criticised the military were dealt with particularly harshly and several were murdered. The coercive structure of the state was further strengthened by the setting up of a new internal-security organisation, the SES, with the participation of experienced military

officers from Argentina. This was set loose on all
the main non-government organisations in Bolivia
(the parties, the Church, trade unions,
universities, peasant leagues etc.). By March 1971
it was believed to have around 11,000 members.[18]
However, a drug mafia, particularly one which was
in conflict with other drug mafias, could hardly
provide military unity and its political hold began
to slip only months after it took power.

One early blow was the refusal of the incoming
Reagan administration to reverse Carter's
opposition to the regime. Moreover, following
Reagan's rapprochement with Buenos Aires, the
Argentine government became less keen to support
its erstwhile clients in Bolivia. In March 1981
there was a rebellion at the military academy
directed against the growing factionalisation of
the regime and its increased use of the SES. This
failed, as did a number of other efforts until
August 1981 when a partially successful revolt
broke out in Santa Cruz. After scenes of unprecedented political confusion General Torrelio - an
officer acceptable both to Garcia Meza and his
opponents - was designated president. He presided
over another disorderly military retreat from
power. Originally Torrelio promised to hold
elections in 1983 but, under growing popular
pressure, simply abandoned this objective and in
October 1982 handed over power to Siles Suazo whose
1980 election victory had originally precipitated
the Garcia Meza coup.

ECUADOR

The Ecuadorian military, like most others in
Spanish America, went through a caudillo phase
before professionalising seriously.[19] Indeed the
beginnings of serious professionalisation occurred
late. An important milestone was reached in July
1925 when a junior officers' movement seized power.
Subsequently the Escuela Militar was established as
the primary source of recruitment for the officer
corps. This professionalisation was facilitated by
export-led economic growth which was most notable
during the 1890-1920 period; this gave the state
sufficient means to pay for a permanent military
establishment. This economic growth also increased
the social differentiation of Ecuadorian society.
Although Ecuador remained overwhelmingly rural,
there was a notable growth of cities and the

beginnings of the emergence of an urban middle
class. This class came to provide an increasing
proportion of recruits into the officer corps whose
growing size helped strengthen its professional
identity.

A further impetus to professionalisation was
Ecuador's severe defeat at the hands of Peru in
1941. This defeat partially upset the command
structure and led to a young officers movement
which was involved in several coups and counter-
coups in 1944 and 1947. After 1947 the military
withdrew from active politics to concentrate on
strengthening its own profession. A period of
post-war prosperity underlain by the banana boom
helped facilitate this transformation, while also
underpinning a period of successful civilian rule.
The extent of military education was expanded;
promotion from the ranks was restricted after 1950
and abolished altogether in 1961. The military
budget and size of the officer corps were both
expanded. Consequent on this increased
professional development, the military came to act
in politics more as an institution with its own
identity and less as a power centre which could be
co-opted by the civilian establishment.

There was a limited military intervention in
1961 when Velasco Ibarra was forced to resign in
favour of his vice-president, and a much more
definite one in 1963 when Carlos Julio Arosemena
was overthrown. Arosemena's excessive drinking was
a major cause in his overthrow; one important study
of this coup identifies this together with various
military-institutional concerns as the major
cause.[20] Fitch has subsequently argued that a
generalised fear of Communism also played its
part.[21] In any case, the 1963-66 government was
moderately reformist domestically (although very
pro-American in its foreign relations) and,
although somewhat ineffectual, did consider
seriously various ideas relating to national
planning, land reform and industrialisation.
However, the military government eventually fell
foul of the Guayaquil business community and, after
losing prestige following excessively severe
repression of student demonstrations in Quito,
decided to step down.

The coup of 1972 was a much more serious
affair. It followed a turbulent period of rule by
Velasco Ibarra who had been elected president - for
the fifth time - in 1968. Velasco Ibarra on this

occasion sought to build a personal political base
in the military, perhaps to guard against his
possible overthrow as had occurred in 1961 and on
earlier occasions. He used his Defence Minister
(and nephew) Jorge Acosta to promote supporters
into key positions. This tactic seemed to have
paid off in 1970 when Velasco Ibarra was able to
rely on military backing to close Congress and
govern by decree. In 1971, however, Acosta's
increasingly obvious violation of bureaucratic
procedures led to the mobilisation of a group of
young officers who successfully demanded Acosta's
resignation. Following this, Velasco Ibarra and
other politicians engaged in political manoeu-
verings prior to the elections scheduled for 1972
in an effort to block the candidacy of Assad
Bucaram, the populist mayor of Guayaquil.
These manoeuvres led to an increasingly complex
and polarised situation ended by military coup in
February 1972.

The nature of the post-1972 military
government highlights the influence of foreign
experiences upon Ecuador. The main tendencies of
officers were a group of peruanistas, mainly to
be found in the navy and among younger officers,
and Brazilianists, with a few senior army officers
- notably President Rodríguez Lara - holding the
balance. Another important influence was the
prospect, from the second half of 1972, of
considerable oil revenue stemming from the
beginning of serious production from Texas/Gulf's
Andean discoveries. Expectations were high that an
Ecuadorian military government, freed from
financial dependency by its oil income, would be
able to carry through significant social reforms.

Despite these expectations (or in some cases
fears) the resulting military regime was in many
respects weak and indecisive. It was neither as
repressive as the Brazilian nor as reformist as the
Peruvian. It contained some vigorous, able and
dynamic officers but lacked sufficient unity and
power of decision to make these qualities tell.
One reason for this was the extent of inter-service
rivalry in Ecuador. The navy was relatively more
powerful in the Ecuadorian military than in most
other South American cases. It had also been
radicalised by its conflicts with the United States
over fishing limits, and was far more nationalist
than the army. However, naval contacts with the
Guayaquil business community ensured that at least

some key naval officers, although nationalist, had little interest in social reform. General Rodríguez, who ultimately emerged as head of the junta, adopted at least a rhetorical nationalism himself, and relied for support on various younger army officers for support; within the army leadership, however, there was a more conservative old guard whose views also had to be taken into account. This tendency to nationalism tempered by indecision was strengthened by the very collegiate style of rule adopted. There were military officers posted in all government ministries and major public sector agencies and, as Hurtado points out, "the entire upper echelon" of the military was involved in decision making.[22]

The one area where military nationalism did quickly make itself felt was in the oil industry. During its first two years, the military government - and its Oil Minister (then) Captain Jarrín - set up a state oil company, made plans to build a state oil refinery, and evicted a number of private companies from their exploration territory in Ecuador. Ecuador also became a member of OPEC and began to change its foreign policy alignment in a "Third Worldist" direction. The increase in world oil prices meanwhile financed an economic boom in the country and so made it appear as if the government had been able to carry through these changes without significant cost. This even remained the case during 1974 when the regime moved into a state of open confrontation with the Texas/ Gulf consortium.[23]

If the regime was fairly determined in its oil policies, however, this marked the limit of its coherence. Land reform was promised but the 1974 statute proved to be very weak and was never seriously enforced. Despite some efforts at planning, the public sector remained highly inefficient and - outside the oil industry - there was no serious attempt at dirigisme. Nor did the regime bother with political organisation. It was not particularly repressive; political parties remained legal and, though individuals who criticised the military with excessive force were subjected to some harassment, these measures fell far short of common practice in Brazil, Chile or Argentina. On the other hand, no serious effort was made to mobilise support. Instead, the military seemed content to rely on informal support offered by the civilian Left including the

Communist Party. It also expected that the unprecedented economic boom which the country enjoyed during 1972-74 would moderate the tone of any criticism and enable the government to resist civilian pressure.

THE END OF REFORMISM

This ostensibly non-political pattern of military rule was rather similar to that adopted by the 1963-66 junta and had rather a similar result. In each case, military rule was tolerated for a time by most sections of the population due to the various earlier problems associated with civilian rule. It also helped that the first years of military government were ones of considerable economic prosperity. However, when the economic situation worsened, the junta had no defence against strongly-mounted civilianist movements; if it moved to repress, this seemed like over-reaction and discredited the regime, but if it did not, this seemed like weakness and encouraged further agitation and demands. In both 1966 and 1975-6, however, the military was at least able to delay its return to civilian government although its efforts to control the succession ultimately ended in failure.

1975 was a bad year for the Ecuadorian economy, as the world recession took its toll of the world oil market. Much of the business community blamed the military nationalists for having earlier taken an excessively hard line with the companies, leading them to cut back on their investments and produce only the minimum from their existing holdings. The government took some limited steps away from its earlier nationalism but these were not sufficient to revitalise the oil industry; the oil ministry was only too well aware that some US conservatives were looking to damage OPEC as a whole by breaking the price resistance of Ecuador, one of the weakest states in the organisation.

However, this determined nationalism was expensive in fiscal terms and the government needed to raise taxes to compensate.

This difficult situation offered an opportunity to the conservative civilian opposition. In May 1975 two ex-presidents, Camilo Ponce and Carlos Julio Arosemena, announced the formation of a <u>Frente Civico</u> and called for early

341

elections. In September an attempted <u>civilista</u>
coup failed after considerable fighting and a
number of casualties. However, the government was
unable to take advantage of this weakness in order
to shore up its position; its attempts at
repression came to appear as bullying and its
conciliatory gestures as weakness. Only three
months later, President Rodríguez Lara was forced
to resign in favour of another military junta.

The new regime, however, was also a coalition
of different groups. The senior officers,
particularly General Durán, were for the most part
moderate conservatives who intended to call
elections eventually. More junior officers,
however, were still attracted by reformist
nationalism. In 1976 these officers, led by the
oil minister Colonel Vargas and also by retired
Admiral Jarrín who had returned from a diplomatic
posting in London, tried to use oil nationalism as
a banner to win popular support for continuing
military reformism. Their position seemed
strengthened by the fact that one of the partners
in the consortium, Gulf Oil, had made no secret of
its unhappiness at continuing in Ecuador and wanted
to be expropriated with compensation. Gulf, for
its own reasons, became increasingly acrimonious in
its dealings with the government during 1976.
However, despite this apparent opportunity, the
more conservative military officers were able to
defeat the nationalist challenge; Gulf Oil was
nationalised but in a way which avoided any kind of
popular mobilisation. A cabinet reshuffle at the
end of 1976 reinforced Durán's control over the
government, and the main military nationalists were
moved. Early in 1977 the regime signalled its
intention to begin a slow hand-back of power to
civilians.

The isolation of the military by the beginning
of 1977 perhaps mattered less than it might have
done because the regime was already committed to
democratisation. During 1977 its popularity fell
further as it became involved in repressing various
labour disturbances. The military began its
delayed return to democracy, in time honoured
fashion, by drawing up a new constitution.
Meanwhile civilian political parties began
negotiations among themselves and at the end of
1977 a number of conservative parties put together
a "national constitutional front" whose main aim
was to frustrate the presidental ambitions of Assad

Bucaram. It appears, indeed, that some pact between these conservative parties and the military was under active consideration for a time; the interior minister Colonel Bolivar Jarrín was at this time discussing with the Liberal and Conservative leaders a plan to cancel the proposed 1978 elections.[24]

The first round of voting, to select a new constitution, took place in January 1978; turnout was high and few incidents were reported. In February, however, the government decreed that only Ecuadorians born of Ecuadorian parents could stand for the presidency - thus making Bucaram's candidacy ineligible. The first round of presidential elections were held in July 1978 and were surprisingly won by Jaime Roldós, Bucaram's nephew but a political figure with an identity of his own.

Roldós' victory was not at all to the liking of the military government which had by now established close links with the old civilian conservative parties. Some members of these parties did their best to promote a coup by denouncing these election results as fraudulent and there are indications that a number of senior army officers were conspiring. However, a combination of opponents of any threatened coup - the navy, junior officers, the press in both Quito and Guayaquil and the US embassy - together succeeded in averting it. Instead, the military decided to hold the second round of elections as late as it could, April 1979, in order to give the opposition as much time as possible to overturn Roldós' first round lead. The military also stated that the winning candidate would take office in August 1979.

Despite this, efforts persisted on the part of civilian politicians to hold off a possible Roldós victory. Conservative figures now began to call for the cancellation of presidential elections; instead, they declared, a constituent assembly should be elected and this should select an interim president. In November 1978, moreover, a leading Guayaquil political figure was murdered shortly after publicly supporting Roldós in the second round of the election. Initially the authorities declared that this murder had no political connection but action by the dead man's family quite soon led to the unravelling of a murder plot led by Bolivar Jarrín. Jarrín was removed from his post in late December 1978 and charged with murder in February 1979. He eventually served a prison sentence.

Roldós meanwhile began secret negotiations with the military. He promised not to pursue corruption investigations against those connected with the previous regime and eventually succeeded in convincing them that he was not the bogey figure, with horns and a tail, depicted by his opponents. Elections, therefore, did go ahead in April and Roldós (and his vice-president Hurtado) clearly emerged victorious. In August 1979 he took over the government.

The Ecuadorian military government in 1978-79, like many others in South America, proved unable to manage the transition to a party of its choice. This was no doubt partly because, in an open political environment, association with the previous military regime was an electoral liability. It was also because members and allies of an authoritarian regime had no easy means of knowing what public opinion actually was and were prone to indulge in various kinds of wishful thinking (as had happened in Bolivia in 1977-78). The decisive question became, what would happen when reality caught up? In Bolivia the surprise proved too much to take and there were a series of military retreats and returns before the voters' preference was respected. In Ecuador the military held back from a pre-emptive coup but it appears to have been a close thing. The transition to civilian rule was neither smooth nor, from the point of view of the regime, particularly successful.

URUGUAY

The military coup in Uruguay was a creeping affair rather than a direct military takeover of the state; most observers date the coup in June 1973 when Congress was suspended although one might equally well date it to February 1973 when the National Security Council was set up within the executive branch and became the effective locus of all decision-making. In fact the military did not replace the elected president until 1976. Whatever date is selected, however, the coup marked a new low point in the economic and political decline of a country which had once been known as "the

Switzerland of Latin America". It was also particularly brutal.

The underlying weakness was caused by economic failure; per capita income had gradually declined from a high point in the mid-1950s as a result of declining terms of trade and an inability to move away from dependence on the traditional commodities of meat and wool. Uruguay was far too small to sustain an efficient home-market based industry but the high levels of protection and government spending introduced during days of earlier prosperity had together made new economic departures very difficult to achieve. The political parties which dominated Uruguay, themselves dependent upon elaborate clientelist systems, and an extreme form of consociationalism which blurred the presentation of clear policies, could not easily carry out the necessary changes.[25] The electoral system also separated the immediate interests of politicians from those of key outside forces such as employers, trade unions and the military.

There was in any case a lack of consensus as to what changes were necessary to reverse Uruguay's economic decline, and as the decline became more pronounced so the radicalism of the various positions made each more repugnant to supporters of the others. Those on the Right called for the re-introduction of a market economy which would create incentives for export development; those on the Left, pointing to the relative inefficiency of Uruguayan agriculture and its concentrated pattern of ownership, called instead for land redistribution. Either of these strategies would necessarily involve pain - either for the landed interests or for the large, and mostly dependent, metropolis of Montevideo. The political parties were not well equipped to make such decisions. Indeed several government attempts to reform the economy foundered on the organised power of the various social groups which were affected - the urban working class, the bureaucracy and the landowners. Such efforts in the event only aggravated the situation by stimulating increased interest in group militancy without resolving any of the underlying problems.

Another damaging factor was the development of an urban insurgent movement, the Tupamaros, who in the late 1960s and early 1970s were posing an increasingly serious threat to the authorities. The Tupamaros began by attacking popular targets and exposing the corruption of certain businessmen and officials. Subsequently, however, they came into open conflict with the state. In 1972 the pro-landowner President Broadaberry (narrowly elected against the reformist candidate Wilson Ferreira) allowed the military a free hand in repressing the Tupamaros. This was accomplished in a brutal six months (May to November 1972) with the aid of mass arrest, torture and the complete suspension of civil liberties.

This counter-insurgency campaign brought the military into the centre of the political stage, which it had last occupied in 1942. In 1971 General Gregorio Alvarez organised and led a new organisation, the supreme military command (ESMACO).[26] This began by pressing Congress in order to head off any possible investigations into human rights abuses. The military also began to undertake certain corruption investigations and, for a time, certain members of the military seemed to be interested in radical reform as well as repression. In February 1973, President Broadaberry accepted complete loss of control over the military when he failed to have his choice of Defence Minister approved; he also had to accept military comuniques which called for the elimination of corruption and radical reforms of land tenure. In June 1973 the military went further and dissolved congress, although retaining Broadaberry as a figurehead president.

The armed threat posed by the Tupamaros was probably not very great. Nevertheless, the response has to be seen partly in terms of the activities of the armed or semi-armed Left in other parts of South America. In early 1973 the Peronist Left and the Argentine ERP were very active in a neighbouring republic while in Chile Allende's government was moving toward its final confrontation. In Brazil, a Left-wing urban guerrilla had been decisively defeated by a Right-wing military regime in circumstances which conservatives elsewhere on the Continent viewed as encouraging. Also encouraging to these conservatives, was the Brazilian "miracle" which, in the early 1970s, contrasted very sharply with the lack of economic success in Uruguay. The Brazilian military had also, at the ESG (see chapter 9), evolved a counter-insurgency doctrine which asserted that it was necessary to move, not just against active terrorists, but against their allies and their material and intellectual supporters. This should therefore involve a radical re-shaping of the state to remove any possible basis for insurgency.

Contemporary political observers tended to see the Uruguayan military as divided into a reformist wing (the "Peruvianists") and an authoritarian capitalist wing (the Brazilianists) as well as having a diminishing number of constitutionalist officers, mainly centred in the navy. This last group certainly did exist and it largely prevented the February 1973 confrontation turning into a coup, but it had tended to lose influence as the situation deteriorated.[27] The Brazilianists were committed to the doctrine of counter-insurgency and supported strong repression. Struck also with the "Brazilian miracle", they supported the dismantling of Uruguay's welfare state and bureaucratic controls and the implementation of a full scale capitalism. The so-called "Peruvianist" officers, however, were a good deal less reformist than this label implies. Much of the Uruguayan .Left, not least the Communist Party, placed their hopes on some kind of alliance with these officers but to no avail. The logic of counter-insurgency dictated priorities, along with a desire to create a strong central authority in place of the weak and clientelist (not to say corrupt) state structures which had existed prior to the coup. Thus during 1973 the power of organised labour in Uruguay was virtually destroyed. The "Peruvianists" including Generals Gregorio Alvarez and Abon Raimundez and Colonel Carlos Trabal, did not appear defeated by this adoption of determinedly authoritarian policies - their careers certainly did not suffer - and it is probable that their reformism did not go very deep. It merely had the effect of, for a time, reducing opposition to the military takeover as some who might otherwise have opposed it instead hoped to deal with military reformists.

The repression of the Left was fairly intense. There were not so many deaths in Chile or Argentina (the Uruguayan military did not go in for disappearances) but the degree of surveillance was even greater. Uruguay is a small political community and repression could be focussed far more directly than in such countries as Brazil or Argentina. Many Uruguayans emigrated, and public spending cuts (notably in the national university) also helped to rid the country of those whom the military regarded as undesirable but who had not committed any crime. The Left (which in Uruguay included the Christian Democrats) had polled only 18% in 1971 and it clearly had less of a potential social base in Uruguay than in some other countries. Trade unions were also repressed, however, more for economic reasons than because they represented a political threat to the status quo. In any case, the repression and violations of human rights in Uruguay, though perhaps less than those of the post-1976 Argentine military, was more than enough to arouse fears of revenge or of public trial should the political situation spin out of military control. This was a factor which further strengthened the military hard-line and tied the government even closer to the rural bourgeoisie which was its most (and after a time perhaps its only) important base of civilian support.

Following the military takeover, questions of long-term political development were put on one side while the military pursued its objectives of counter-insurgency and economic reform. The economic reforms were real enough but were Chicago-influenced rather than "Peruvian" in inspiration. They were carried through by a civilian, Vegh Villegas, who served as finance minister. Although checked in some ways by military opposition, Vegh did succeed in introducing a far more open kind of capitalism into Uruguay.[28] His aim, and that of the military, was less to impose the kind of radical deflation attempted in Chile than to re-dynamise an economy which suffered from historical weaknesses. Import quotas were dropped, tariffs gradually reduced and, at the same time, export subsidies were also phased out. Undoubtedly these measures did have some success - Uruguayan exports increased from $321.45m in 1973 to $1,059m in 1980 and, as a proportion of GDP, from 23.7% in 1973 to 32.8% in 1980. However, the social cost was high and there were major reductions in both employment levels and real wage rates.

In late 1975 the military did begin a process of political definition. From this point on, some of the more conservative civilian politicians hoped to be brought back increasingly into the political game. These hopes, however, were to be disappointed. In December 1975 Broadaberry circulated a memorandum among high level officials and military leaders which called for the banning of all political parties, cancellation of elections scheduled for 1976, and the creation of a corporatist state with Broadaberry at its head. This idea was emphatically rejected by the military - some of whom wanted an eventual return to democracy while others were jealous of their institutional autonomy - and Broadaberry was removed from office the following year. The 1976 elections were, as had been expected, cancelled and after a brief interim, Aparicio Mendez - a civilian with neither conspicuous merit nor a political base of his own - was nominated president to serve until 1981. In the same year an institutional act was passed which banned all previous civilian presidential candidates from holding office until 1991 at the earliest. This package was received as evidence of a victory by the hard-liners within the military. Vegh Villegas, a political moderate although an economic neo-liberal, resigned in protest and other civilians working for the regime registered their unhappiness. The failure of the "Constitutionalists" in Uruguay in 1976-77, like that of their Brazilian counterparts in 1965-68, was due to the progressive militarisation of the power structure. In Uruguay real power had come to be held, not by formal government leaders (as the selection of Aparicio Mendez made obvious) but by a group of army troop commanders with the rank of colonel or above. As Gonzales has explained, "the command structure of the Uruguayan armed forces may be a pyramid, but it is a 'truncated' pyramid."[29] The Ministry of Defence had little power over the troop commanders. These had less reason than anybody to support any kind of political opening which might have raised awkward questions of accountability for the repression.

By this time the Uruguayan regime was becoming internationally isolated. The US Congress terminated military aid to Uruguay in September 1976 (after which Aparicio Mendez accused the US Democratic Party of being part of the International Communist Conspiracy). Even the Brazilian government, which had been liberalising since 1974, was beginning to distance itself from Uruguay. Within Uruguay the press and opposition parties began to put some limited pressure on the government. The immediate military reaction was hard-line, but it indicated some pressures for democratisation from within the military; early in 1977 twenty officers were arrested for calling for a return to barracks. In the short-run, these liberalising pressures failed; there was, instead, a purge of the military moderates which left the hard-liners more securely in power than ever.

However, in response to this growing isolation, the Uruguayan military in 1977 announced plans to present plans for a new constitution to a plebiscite in 1980. This schedule was followed and a proposed constitution was drawn up. This would very much have prolonged the military stay in power. It would have allowed presidential and congressional elections in November 1981 but the military would remain in effective control behind the scenes. Indeed, the 1981 presidential candidate was to be unopposed and the military would in effect nominate both candidates in 1986. However, as the day of the plebiscite came closer, opposition parties met to join in calling for a "no" vote. Against all the odds, the plebiscite, held in November 1980, resulted in a defeat for the government by a margin of around 57%/43%.[30]

Publicly the military reacted with a certain insouciance. If the proposal for a new Constitution was defeated, some argued, this must prove that the voters were eminently satisfied with existing arrangements. Privately, however, there was a period of confusion and internal conflict; the majority of the military felt, however, that it was necessary to replace the existing figurehead with a "real" president and begin bargaining with the opposition so as to maintain as much control as possible over a gradual transition to democratic rule. Gregorio Alvarez was nominated president in 1981 but full elections were promised for 1984 (with the elected president taking over in 1985).

The first step towards civilianisation took place in 1982 with the reorganisation of the main political parties, the Blancos and Colorados. In November these parties were allowed to hold intra-party primaries to select nominees for an eventual presidential campaign. The turnout for these primaries was high and voters' desire for a return to democracy was clear. The candidate most identified with opposition to the military, Wilson Ferreira, won a decisive victory in the Blanco Party while the most pro-military candidate, Pacheco, polled badly among the Colorados.

Following this undoubted setback, which indicated that the military could not easily control the outcome of any subsequent elections, the government instead tried to bargain at arms length. It sought to win the agreement of the parties to a new constitution which would have entrenched certain military powers after an eventual return to civilian rule. These powers were not very different from those for which the military had sought approval in the 1980 plebiscite. Not surprisingly these negotiations failed and in August 1983 the regime banned party political activity and it seemed that the whole transition would be called into question. The victory of Alfonsin in Argentina and the curtailment of military privileges which followed (as well as the arrest of the most notorious military leaders and torturers) caused some fear in the Uruguayan military. However, the Uruguayan regime was unable to make its various threats credible; one factor here was the growing confidence and visibility of opposition, which made its presence felt in illegal rallies (in November 1983), successful strikes (in January 1984) and various protest marches. The military bluff had been called. Moreover one should mention that the economic situation in Uruguay was deteriorating sharply, largely for reasons over which the government had little control (the second oil shock, the major recessions in Brazil and Argentina) although there may also have been some errors of policy. Inevitably the Uruguayan people blamed the government for their falling living standards; while the regime was never truly popular it had during the 1970s been able to survive on an ample margin of public indifference. This had ceased to be the case by 1982 and President Alvarez was unable to summon up sufficient military enthusiasm for a new spell of repressive government. Instead, he reluctantly accepted the idea of a return to barracks while seeking to guard the military's flank.

In February 1984, a few weeks after the first general strike since 1973, the military reiterated its pledge to hold elections in November of that year and it began to negotiate its retention of some residual powers after these elections were held. Above all, it wanted to make sure that the Left could not win the elections, to prevent the trial of officers involved in torture and repression and (in what had now become a personal duel) to keep Wilson Ferreira out of the Presidency. In March the regime did, however, release Serengi, the leader of the Uruguayan

Communist Party, from prison although he remained forbidden to stand in the elections. In May the military went further and agreed that a new Constituent Assembly could be elected in November, at the same time as the presidential elections, and that the new Constitution could take effect in 1986. This meant that military residual powers would assuredly end by this date, and also opened the way for an amnesty and the full re-incorporation of all Uruguayans into political life. However, it became clear that there were limits to military conciliation when, in June 1984, Wilson Ferreira returned to Montevideo from exile despite warnings from the regime that he faced arrest upon his return. On this occasion Wilson Ferreira overplayed his hand; his arrest did spark off major demonstrations and a short-term political crisis but the Colorados and the Left soon made it clear that they were unwilling to jeopardise the election date purely on his behalf. In November elections went ahead, with all three parties but without Ferreira.

When the elections were held they were won by Julio Sanguinetti, a Colorado of essentially conservative orientation. Sanguinetti, although in some ways an authoritarian figure, had been careful to distance himself enough from the military to retain credibility as a leader of the transition. He had earlier served in the Broadaberry cabinet but had resigned at the time of the military takeover in June 1973 and campaigned for a "no" vote in the 1980 referendum. He was a strong opponent of the pro-military Pacheco whom he roundly defeated in the 1982 referendum, but he was careful to take a conciliatory stand and not to rock the boat when negotiations with the military took place in 1983-84. In private he made it clear that the military should not be repudiated openly and expressed the belief that they would be willing to relinquish power only if they did not suffer open rejection. For him, there would be no question of any serious calling to account of the military for its behaviour when in power.[31]

Sanguinetti's election victory was largely due to the fact that the two other parties were in competition for the same reformist vote - which comprised a majority of the electorate, but not so big a majority that it could afford to split its vote. The Left won some 20% of the vote, little more than in 1971. It was also apparent that the

Blancos' identification with a single individual, no matter how popular, was not enough to outweigh the desire of many voters for a trouble-free transition to democracy. Of all the candidates, Sanguinetti was perceived as the man most likely to permit a smooth return to civilian rule.

NOTES

1 There is, alas, insufficient material on Paraguay to make even a brief secondary account of the Stroessner regime worth undertaking. But see J. Painter, Paraguay in the 1970s: continuity and change in the political process, (Institute of Latin American Studies, London; 1983).

2 C. Corbett, The Latin American Military as a Socio-Political Force; case studies of Bolivia and Argentina, (Univ. of Miami; 1972), pp. 29-30.

3 See L. A. Whitehead, "Politics and the Military in Bolivia", in SLAS Bulletin, 26, March 1977.

4 Whitehead, Ibid., Corbett, The Latin American Military.

5 Gral Gary Prado Salmon, Poder y Fuerzas Armadas 1949-82, (La Paz; 1984), pp. 153, et seq..

6 On this topic see L. A. Whitehead, The United States and Bolivia; a case of neo-colonialism, (Haslemere; 1969), C. Blasier, "The United States and the Revolution", in J. Malloy and R. Thorn, eds, Beyond the Revolution; Bolivia since 1952, (Pittsburgh U.P.; 1971) and, for a first hand account, G. J. Eder, Inflation and Development in Latin America; a case study of inflation and stabilisation in Bolivia, (U. of Michigan; 1968).

7 For an account of these events see J. Dunkerley, Rebellion in the Veins; Political Struggle in Bolivia, (Verso, London; 1984).

8 For a discussion of the oil nationalisation, G. Philip, Oil and Politics.

9 Quoted in L. A. Whitehead, "Bolivia Swings Right", Current History, February 1972 and see also the account in Prado Salmon, Poder y Fuerzas Armadas.

10 Whitehead in SLAS Bulletin.

11 Quoted in Ibid..

[12] Prado Salmon, Poder y Fuerzas Armadas, pp. 337-345. Also Dunkerley, Rebellion in the Veins.

[13] The main sources for this period are J. Dunkerley, Rebellion in the Veins, and also Bolivia 1980-81; the political system in crisis, (Institute of Latin American Studies, London; 1982), and L. A. Whitehead, Bolivia's Failed Democratisation 1977-80, (Woodrow Wilson Paper 100, Washington 1981).

[14] Dunkerley, Bolivia 1980-81, p. 9.

[15] There are, however, some interesting passages in M. Linklater, I. Hilton and N. Ascherson, The Fourth Reich; Klaus Barbie and the Neo-Fascist Connection, (Hodder and Stoughton, London; 1984).

[16] Dunkerley, Bolivia 1980-81, p. 31.

[17] Quoted in Whitehead, Bolivia's Failed Democratisation, p. 16.

[18] Dunkerley, Bolivia 1980-81, p. 29.

[19] An important study of the military, and political society in general, is that of O. Hurtado, Political Power in Ecuador, (Univ. of New Mexico; 1980).

[20] M. Needler, Anatomy of a Coup d'Etat; Ecuador 1963, (Washington; 1964).

[21] J. S. Fitch, The Military Coup d'Etat as a Political Process, (Johns Hopkins; 1977).

[22] Hurtado, Political Power, p. 259.

[23] Philip, Oil and Politics.

[24] H. Handelman, "Ecuador" in Handelman and Sanders, eds, The Movement Toward Democracy in South America, (AUFS: 1980), p. 45, and Hurtado, Political Power, p. 301. Both of these accounts are helpful for the whole 1977-79 period.

[25] M. Finch, "Three Perspectives on the Crisis in Uruguay", Journal of Latin American Studies, Vol. 3, No. 2, (November 1971), and C. Gillespie, "From Suspended Animation to Animated Suspension; Political Parties and the Reconstruction of Democracy in Uruguay", (paper presented in Oxford, June 1984).

[26] Handelman, "Uruguay" in Handelman and Sanders, Movement Toward Democracy, p. 219.

[27] Ibid..

[28] Handelman, Ibid., pp. 228-9.

[29] Luis Gonzalez, "Uruguay 1980-81; an unexpected opening", Latin American Research Review, Vol. 23, No. 3, 63-76.

[30] More detailed work on the 1980 referendum is being done by C. Gillespie at the University of Yale.

[31] These comments are based on the author's impressions following a seminar given in London by Sanguinetti in May 1984.

Chapter 14

THE MILITARY IN SOUTH AMERICAN POLITICS

   One striking conclusion to emerge from this
study is that military outlook and behaviour do
matter for South American politics. The military
does not behave in any simple or one-dimensional
way which can be deduced a priori. There is
therefore no substitute for empirical analysis of
military institutions. A second conclusion, which
relates to the first, is that contemporary
observers have been strikingly wrong in their
expectations of military behaviour. The Communist
Party, for example, expected military reformists to
emerge in Uruguay in 1973 and Moscow strongly
supported the Natusch coup in Bolivia in 1979. The
CGT, moreover, was a strong supporter of the
Onganía coup in Argentina in 1966. A
structuralist might argue that these errors showed
that the connections between military behaviour and
dominant class interests (or capital logic) were
insufficiently appreciated at the time. Such an
answer, however, would fail to account for the fact
that the Peruvian Right completely misunderstood
the nature of the 1968 coup. Explanations have,
of course, been put forward for the emergence of a
radical regime in Peru in terms of some kind of
structuralist logic but it is hard to escape the
conclusion that, had the Right won their expected
victory within the Peruvian military in 1968-69,
structuralists would now be putting forward logical
explanations for the inevitability of a Right-wing
military coup in 1968. It is easier to come up
with neat ex post facto rationalisations of
particular events than to tackle harder questions
of real political motivation and behaviour.
   It is always useful to stress complexity and
variety in political behaviour. One might

plausibly conclude a book such as this by
questioning whether generalisation was worthwhile;
an important recent book on the military in Latin
American politics has indeed been content to
outline different patterns without seeking to
relate these to any particular system of logic.[1]
Cautious generalisation does appear to be possible,
however, since South American military institutions
do seem to demonstrate some consistent patterns of
political behaviour. These patterns emerge from a
comparative approach but are not well comprehended
either by a "modernisation" or by a Marxist-
structuralist perspective.

The point can best be put negatively.
Observers of other parts of the world have
displayed pronounced scepticism as to how far the
military could be expected to play an effective
system-maintaining role while ruling directly.
Military regimes . have been overthrown by
insurgencies (Cuba, Nicaragua) and have been
rescued by foreign intervention from imminent
overthrow (El Salvador, the Dominican Republic).
In other places military officers have led the
Revolution rather than defending the status quo
against it; the Ethiopian military has developed
into a Marxist party, the Syrian and Iraqi military
are barely distinguishable from their one-party
systems, and the Grenadan military provoked a US
invasion following a hard-Left coup in October
1983. In other cases, military institutions have
been completely split by rebellions or coups led by
very junior officers or even by NCOs; Cuba in 1933,
Ghana and Liberia more recently may serve as
examples. Finally in parts of Africa the military
identity is far less salient even to senior
officers than various forms of tribal or ethnic
loyalty. South America is one of the few parts of
the world, Turkey and Indonesia are perhaps others,
where the military can play an active political
role without losing its "discipline" or
organisational identity.[2] This fact surely
relates directly to another phenomenon which has
often puzzled observers; military rule has occurred
for long periods in even the most developed
countries of South America which enjoy levels of
"modernisation" far higher than the Third World
average. It is clear that military rule can be
made to stick. (It does not follow from this, of
course, that there is any particular "rationality"
about military rule in these various cases.)

Effective system-maintenance through military rule is comparatively rare worldwide, but happens commonly in South America. Why, then, is South America different? One key factor is surely the nature of social stratification which tends to be based on class rather than religion or ethnicity. Class factors tend to unite the South American officer corps, whereas race and religion have been divisive factors elsewhere. Where (as in Chile before Ibañez, and Peru before Velasco) the military establishment has felt alienated from a particular socio-economic order, it has become reformist rather than revolutionary - wishing to join the establishment rather than destroying it. Where, as in Brazil since 1955, the military has been a secure part of the socio-economic establishment, its political outlook has been more consistently conservative. Another key factor is the size of South American military establishments. It is surely not surprising that, of the small Central American countries, the most populous country - Guatemala - has the most coherent military institution while within South America the least populous countries - Bolivia and Paraguay - have the least. There seems to be a critical mass, and a level of access to resources, below which the creation of a professional identity becomes impossible. Almost all South American countries are now populous and affluent enough to be able to sustain a professional military establishment - and we have already seen that military professionalisation earlier in the century related directly to South American states' increasing command over resources.

South American military institutions are of course historical as well as environmental creations and we have already seen how professional development proceeded, at different speeds and with different political consequences, in the various countries. What has now been developed is a form of political professionalism which permits military rule without fatally undermining military discipline. The social _mores_ and political imperatives of these organisations are related to the need to avoid damage to the military institution which, as we have also seen, is an impressive resource in the hands of a small elite of colonels and generals who derive many other benefits from it beyond the pleasure of command and even access to political power.

A fourth general conclusion to emerge from this study is that the military has consistently used its access to political power in order to develop and extend its own institutional interests. The process can be seen clearly in Brazil from military development of heavy industry (oil and steel) under the <u>Estado Novo</u>, to the post-war Petrobras campaign, to the development of military-industrial links through the ESG and later IPES, to the "statisation" of the economy after 1964 and particularly after 1969, to the extensive role of the SNI in the Brazilian economy and finally to the direct military role in nuclear energy, arms manufacture and communications technology. In Argentina the extension of the military role was more uneven but scarcely less significant; at the end of 1983 the Argentine national ballet was controlled by a military officer. Elsewhere, the "Peruvian Revolution" saw an impressive extension of state (and therefore military) control over the economy, while the military budget has been expanded directly under the decidedly non-nationalist military governments of Chile and Uruguay. In Paraguay the military's main economic role is in smuggling, and in Bolivia cocaine. The upward trend during periods of military rule was the same in all cases. Only in countries which have had a long period of civilian rule is there no real sign of military interests having been extended in this way.

A final generalisation is that military rule, like that of civilians, has been an impermanent though often durable form of government in South America. There has, however, been a broad tendency for the durability of military regimes to increase since the mid-1960s - often to the surprise of those who originally called for the military intervention. Nevertheless, this increase in durability has not been matched by any increase in the military's ability to influence the long-term direction of the political system. In Peru, Argentina and Brazil the most anti-government candidate not associated with the far-Left benefited most from the eventual hand-back of power to civilians; this did not happen in Uruguay, but here the military lost its own plebiscite in 1980. In Chile the military still rules, but the political situation seems scarcely less polarised and intractable than was the case in the early 1970s. While the South American military can indeed play a system-maintaining role, its ability to play a system-transforming one can safely be discounted. Indeed, it appears that the strength of the professional-political military identity seems to be at work in both of these directions - working strongly against the success of "breakthrough" military regimes for example by regarding all attempts at popular mobilisation with suspicion.[3]

If these general features are important, it is not less significant to be able to point out where it is unprofitable to generalise about military behaviour. One of these areas concerns the actual mechanisms by which the military has exercised power. The military has at times played no more than a behind-the-scenes role, at other times it has used blackmail against civilian authorities, at other times it has ruled indirectly behind a civilian or retired officer, and at yet other times it has taken over direct "institutional" control of the government. Finer's attempt to relate these different forms of behaviour to differences in political culture does not work well for South America.[4] In Argentina since 1960 virtually every possible permutation of military-political behaviour has been attempted, and surely not because political culture has changed dramatically every few years. On the contrary, the nature of military-political behaviour has been a variable, contingent upon circumstances. Perhaps fortunately, South American militaries have not yet found a perfect way of reconciling effective government with institutional autonomy and the means of attempting this are likely to vary over time as new military rulers attempt to avoid previous mistakes.

Moreover, while one can safely assume that no military regime is immortal, no predictions can easily be made about how long a particular regime will remain in power. Almost nobody in Chile in September 1973 (certainly not those Christian Democrats who energetically called for a coup) expected that Pinochet would celebrate his eleventh anniversary in power. Nor did very many people in Brazil in 1964 (and certainly not the US Ambassador) foresee that military rule would last a generation. Conversely, the post-1972 military government in Ecuador promised to hold power for thirty years and handed back power, unwillingly, after seven; and when Galtieri announced to

cheering crowds the capture of Port Stanley, few
expected that the Radicals would win an election
victory just over eighteen months later. Too many
complacent civilians have played sorcerer's
apprentice to military regimes, while at other
times military officers have been over-confident of
their ability to hold on to power.

The most important negative conclusion,
however, is that there is no direct correspondence
between military rule as such and any particular
economic policy. Within limits, policy has varied
according to circumstance. Thus, while it would be
hard to sustain the view that military governments
are generally reformist, it remains true that the
most radical governments in Peruvian and Ecuadorian
history, and the second most radical government in
Chilean history (in 1932), were military; military
officers also played an important role in setting
up the Chilean Socialist Party. The Argentine
military has perhaps been more conservative than
many, but radicalised in 1943-46 with momentous
consequences; it was also an Argentine military
government in 1983 which arrested the head of the
Central Bank for dealing too generously with
foreign creditors. Perhaps more typically, the
1966-73 government pursued almost every possible
permutation of economic (and political) policy; it
would be hard to describe the 1970-73 period, in
particular, as one of economic orthodoxy. In
Brazil, there has been a certain consistency in the
post-1964 regime (although even here there was an
important "nationalist" rebellion in 1969), but
military populism/nationalism played an important
part in politics between 1945 and 1964.

It is of course true that there are certain
limits beyond which any government in a capitalist,
and a fortiori dependent capitalist, system cannot
go without suffering severe adverse consequences.
Certain military governments (Chile in 1932, Peru
in 1975-78) have certainly suffered from trying to
radicalise "excessively". However, this point is
equally, perhaps more, true of civilian regimes.
Furthermore the predictive power of a hypothesis
relating to "structural limits" is limited. It
states (correctly) that there are certain things
that a government cannot easily do, but this still
leaves many matters undecided - which those
involved will rightly regard as being of legitimate
concern. Moreover, governments do not always
calculate the odds correctly; they frequently fail

and suffer the consequences. Thus, while it may be quite valid to assert that the options facing any South American government are necessarily circumscribed, this insight is of very limited usefulness in trying to understand the behaviour of particular military regimes.

There is much to be said for the argument that the two forms of indeterminacy considered here - let us call them regime indeterminacy and policy indeterminacy - are necessary consequences of the determinate system-maintaining and, above all, institution-maintaining role of the military. It is precisely because the military is not invariably anti-trade union, or anti-Communist, or anti-business that trade union leaders, Communists and businessmen are willing to tolerate or support military rule. When the military regime fails, or disappoints, it is the individual military-political officers who take the blame, not the military institution as a whole. Next time things will be different; a friendly officer can always be found to assure credulous civilians that the next military regime will next time be more nationalist/pro-American/reformist/conservative or whatever the case may be. It is for this reason that Rouquie has observed that "nothing is stranger in Argentina than anti-militarism"[5]; this statement is no less true of other South American countries. From the military's own point of view, it is crucial that certain contacts with civilians are maintained. No military-political leader wants to be left like Somoza, blinkered and alone, to face a popular insurgency. It is a central part of military-political strategy in South America to ensure that this cannot easily happen. To this end, specific regimes and a fortiori economic policies are ultimately expendable. It is surprising that anybody studying (say) the 1966-73 period in Argentina should fail to realise this.

In sum, then, the South American military has an institution-maintaining role first, and a system-maintaining role as a necessary part of this. The reason why the military is widely (and in a sense correctly) perceived as a conservative force is that it is fundamentally anti-Revolutionary and anti-subversive; in a South American context, of course, this means anti-Marxist. The military's narrowly political strategy at any particular moment - its support for particular regimes and policies - is inherently very subordinate to this general consideration, and may not even prevail over its broader (i.e. economic and financial) institutional interests. Development strategies are probably among the least salient features of military consciousness, although they may well play a decisive role in determining the degree of support given to military regimes by the various groups and classes within civil society.

It is not being suggested here that the prevalence of military rule in South America can be explained wholly in terms of the structure, outlook and behaviour of the military establishment - although there is a sense in which the fact of power creates conditions convenient to its own use. In certain cases, Chile 1973, Uruguay 1973 and Argentina 1976 for example, a great deal of weight must clearly be placed on the breakdown of civilian government. It is of course not news that the military is likely to intervene under conditions of mass political upheaval, near civil-war or complete political breakdown. Conservatives have defended coups under these conditions by arguing that they were a necessary response to the threat of anarchy; Marxists have argued that such coups were designed to protect bourgeois hegemony. Both interpretations, if one accepts the values implicit in them, seem fair enough. It is important to note, however, that decisive military interventions have often occurred in societies where conflict has been far less intense than in these notorious cases - for example Peru in 1968 and Argentina in 1966. There is also a persuasive argument that the prospect of military intervention tends to aggravate social conflict and make it more difficult for civilian politicians to head off impending polarisation.

CIVILIAN CONFLICT AND MILITARY RULE

This point may be developed by identifying the key variable as the management of political conflict. All politics involves conflict and conflict involves uncertainty (what happens if the other side wins?). Yet many people, particularly those who enjoy prosperity or authority, find this uncertainty hard to take. In democratic systems, therefore, there exist a variety of informal as well as formal controls designed to manage levels of conflict, and therefore uncertainty, in public

life.[6]   In   authoritarian   (and   still   more
totalitarian) systems, certainty is sought by the
suppression   of   conflict.   In South   America,
military   officers   have sought to rationalise this
suppression   by   suggesting   that   the apparently
consensual   democracy of   the developed   countries
(what   General   Viola,   in   Argentina,   called
"democracy without ideology on the North American
model") would be acceptable, but that political
polarisation   requires   a   military   response.
However, the   fact   that conflict may under certain
circumstances be repressed reduces the   incentive,
on the part   of some social group and interests, to
seek to manage it.

      There is a famous hypothesis which states that
politics in a democracy is likely to move towards
the centre due to the fact that politicians are in
competition   for   the   popular vote.[7] If the votes
of extremists can be   taken for granted, then it is
the vote of electors in the centre who are crucial
to the outcome of any election.   There   is   thus an
automatic   penalty attaching to a party which
becomes   excessively   intransigent   or   self-
righteously   attached to its own policies and
unwilling to listen to what the voters want. Its
rival (or rivals) can then expect to win support
merely by a show of studied moderation.   The
probability that democratic parties will alternate
in   power   also   provides   an incentive toward
moderation and   at least a limited degree of
consensus between opposing parties. An opposition
has every incentive to be "loyal" because it hopes
that its own turn in power will come; it will have
nothing to gain from polarizing the system and
creating a crisis atmosphere.   Similarly a
government which anticipates the possibility of
election defeat will want at least a limited basis
of understanding with the opposition which may
replace it.

      There is also another series of hypotheses
according to which, in a stable electoral system,
face-to-face and informal social contacts are
likely to develop between members of opposing
parties   which will   reduce the intensity of
political   rivalry between them.   Some issues
perceived as being too unimportant or, conversely,
too dangerous to air openly will be decided on the
basis of a consensus of political insiders; there
is likely to be a greater degree of consensus among
political insiders than among party workers or

electors in general. Democracy, then, has defences against the divisive impact of mass politics. In sum, the effect of a stable democratic system will be, according to several different systems of logic, to head off extreme conflicts and to search for a basis of consensus.

When there is, or is perceived to be, a military alternative to universal suffrage then all of these factors making for moderation disappear. It is all too easy to think of mechanisms by which mutual trust and confidence between civilian politicians may break down, as each side accuses the other of resorting to undemocratic tactics and then resolves to get its retaliation in first. For example the threat that a regime may seek to prolong its stay in office by using military support and suspending the constitution, or that it may use military support in order to rig the ballot or otherwise destroy the meaning of an electoral process, is likely to induce the opposition (even when acting in good faith) to seek military involvement to prevent <u>continuismo</u>. Arguments of this kind were certainly used against Goulart in Brazil. Good faith is, however, not always to be assumed and there are obvious cases (e.g. the Chilean Right under Allende) in which civilians have deliberately sought to destabilise and undermine elected governments by creating a crisis atmosphere and triggering military intervention. Nor is it only genuinely radical civilian governments which have faced this threat; scare tactics were used by the Right to bring down the utterly inoffensive Illia government in Argentina. All too often, tactics of this kind have proved successful.

This amounts, then, to a paradox. The military is an institution committed, above all things, to the maintenance of order. There is no reason to doubt that most senior military officers sincerely deplore intense political conflict among civilians. Yet the mere fact that the military is indeed committed to order creates a strong incentive for civilian opposition groups and interests, under certain circumstances, to create disorder in the hope that this will be blamed on their opponents and not upon them. Similarly those who feel vulnerable to military veto may easily conclude that the only answers are subversion of the officer corps or the armed overthrow of the state. Such efforts, in turn, will intensify military intervention and repression. Examples include the emergence of the Montoneros under the Onganía dictatorship, and their later suppression under Videla/Viola and the decision of the Chilean Communist Party in 1981, after much persecution, to adopt an armed strategy against the Pinochet government. Dictatorship is as likely to provoke violent political conflict as it is to resolve it. Moreover, even the threat of a military veto may work in the same way. If democracy is seen as a sham, it will clearly not inspire primary or unconditional political allegiance. Thus the factors which, in stable democratic countries, make for the maintenance of political moderation and a measure of consensus, cannot apply in countries where a military coup remains a genuine possibility. Rather, the possibility of military restraint removes from civilian politicians much of the incentive for self-restraint.

When the military itself rules, conflict is not completely suppressed but rather played out in different locations. There is a degree of conflict within the military itself whose outcome is often very surprising to civilian observers - both in the direction of military economic policy and of military-political strategy. Civilian observers have often been wrong, and civilian politicians and interest groups disastrously wrong, about the future evolution of military regimes. It is true that military regimes do provide a minimal level of certainty for the Right, who can be sure that these will neither lead a Marxist Revolution nor succumb to one, but this has to be set against a variety of other considerations. These include the military's own increasing share of GNP, uncertainties over economic and foreign policy and the commonplace if dreary possibility that the military regime may simply fail to achieve its objectives. The Chilean Right may still feel that Pinochet was preferable to Allende, but it is doubtful that Argentine conservatives who supported the 1966 coup or Peruvian conservatives who supported the 1968 coup would feel that they had made a very good bargain. For reformist or radical civilian politicians or groups, the advantages of military rule are fewer still. Many Chilean Christian Democrats must bitterly regret their party's support for the Pinochet coup. Moreover, it is genuinely hard to see what the Uruguayan Communist Party had to gain from a military coup in 1973. Even when military

populists have come to power, their record offers
little to the parties of the Left. In Bolivia,
Ovando and Torres quite quickly went down to defeat
while in Peru, where military populism appeared
much more effective, the anti-military Left
profitted far more from the Velasco regime than did
Left-wing allies of the regime.

If one accepts that military rule is likely to
prove disappointing for most, if not all, of the
groups who might originally have welcomed it, then
new perspectives arise. We have already seen that
military rule has only a limited capacity to
survive without 'serious support from civilian
society and that military coups rarely succeed
without quite substantial civilian encouragement.
Military regimes since the mid-1960s have, it is
true, tended to be more autonomous of civil society
than their predecessors but this autonomy is by no
means absolute. Why, then, have at least some
regimes continued to enjoy significant social
support? One major factor is fear. Conservatives
consistently, and moderates and even reformists
occasionally, have supported military intervention
when civilian politics has tended to polarise and
civilian government break down - obvious examples
are Brazil 1964, Uruguay 1973, Chile 1973 and
Argentina 1976. Fear has also helped strengthen
entrenched military governments. Moderate
opposition has generally been far more effective
against military regimes than violent
confrontation. A second factor might be described
as greed or even as naivety. There has been a
view, widely shared among both conservatives and
Marxists, that military technocracies have a
superior record as economic policymakers or even
that military dictatorship is somehow functional to
a new stage of capitalist development. We have
already seen (in chapter 1) that neo-realist
theories of the superiority of military rule have
not been confirmed in macro or cross sectional
terms. Within South America, the notion of the
superior competence of military regimes should not
long survive contemplation of the records of
Pinochet, Videla/Viola/Galtieri or even Velasco;
nor, in an earlier era, did Pérez Jiménez or
Rojas Pinilla do much better. In all of South
America, the best-managed economy during the past
generation has probably been the Colombian - where
there has been no military regime.

It is unlikely that extreme conservatives could ever be dissuaded from calling for military intervention if their position were really threatened by the Marxist Left. Military rule, whatever its other shortcomings, is after all effective in "anti-subversive" terms. One might also admit that there are likely to be circumstances under which intense underlying social conflict may contribute to political polarisation; previous military rule may well be an aggravating factor in such cases. Several South American countries, most obviously Bolivia - perhaps now Chile as well - suffer from a mismatch between the level of popular mobilisation and degree of political consciousness (on the one hand) and inability of low productivity and essentially stagnant economies to meet even minimal popular demands (on the other). By no means all South American countries are economically stagnant or popularly mobilised to this degree, however, and this "Huntingtonian gap" will by no means provide a general explanation for military intervention in South America. There are many cases in which effective democratic arrangements, underpinned by widely held democratic values, should be sufficient to head off polarisation.

It is sometimes rather misleadingly asserted that democratic values are almost universally shared in South America. It would be fairer to say that these values have a potential for acceptance in South America. Discussions of political culture are inevitably impressionistic and lack enough empirical substance to be fully credible. Nevertheless, it has certainly been argued seriously that Latin America is heir to an "organic statist" political tradition which gives more weight to notions of social justice and strong government than to the formal notions of democracy and interest representation.[8] This argument has proved controversial and the present author does not wholly accept it; nevertheless, it is noteworthy that such an argument should have been put forward at all. Moreover if one looks at the works of various prominent political and juridical thinkers in South America, as well as active politicians, one finds that there have been, according to time and place, democrats, Marxist-Leninists, liberals, nationalists, and Fascists. Others such as Haya de la Torre in Peru, were unquestionably <u>sui generis</u> even if more than a trifle confused. What in fact seems most striking about South American intellectual life has been the absence of a firm sense of identity and, in consequence, a considerable willingness to follow international fashion. (Consider, for example, the wide variety of enthusiasms and influences to have affected the Chilean Socialist Party since the 1930s). The same trend can be seen in South American politics; no country has enjoyed more than fifty years of uninterrupted political stability, whether democratic or authoritarian, during the past century. Within the military itself, it is not difficult to find officers who differ considerably in their political opinions. Many genuinely believe in authoritarian rule and do not simply apply it faute de mieux. It can still come as a surprise to hear a military officer like Vargas Caballero in Peru, not by any means a hard dictatorial figure but a man sacked by Velasco for his moderation, reflect that

> A country which needs to change rapidly, needs a dictatorship. The bad thing is that there is no good dictator ... Hitler and Mussolini, in the beginning, did much good for their countries because they took them out of crises, but later they committed atrocities. Perhaps Franco is an exception to this rule.[9]

The point is not that there is any inherent authoritarian tradition in South America, but rather that ideas are malleable weapons in day-to-day politics. What really concerns elites - civil as well as military - is the maintenance of social rather than political systems. Oakshottians almost to a man, they are eager to keep the ship afloat the better to plunder its stores. Politics is conducted without an overriding sense of what is legitimate, but neither does this mean that systems will be allowed to fall into ungovernability and chaos. (If legitimacy is dead, everything is not necessarily permitted.) Instead there is a limited but real desire for international political respectability, comparatively little attachment to political institutions per se (which is not to say none), and widespread de facto understandings of how state power is likely to be used.[10]

The implications of this state of affairs for democratic rule are limited but by no means annihilating. The ever-present possibility of a military veto, and the lack of procedural scruple within civil society, does mean that civilian governments can afford to offend fewer people than might be the case in other circumstances. In order to succeed, they need to place far more emphasis on conciliation of those within the system than on strict interpretation of electoral mandates. Explicit forms of consociationalism have appeared to work well for a time in Colombia and Venezuela; less explicit forms of power-sharing have more generally proved necessary to maintain the system. This sharing of power must take in not just the formal parties but a wide variety of interests and social organisations (otherwise, as in pre-1973 Uruguay, the result may be simply to isolate the "political class" and deprive it of respect); it would be a foolish government which needlessly alienated the Church. Excessively factional rulers (Perón, Illia, Belaúnde, Velasco Ibarra) are vulnerable even when they are not radically reformist; they have very little prospect of success if they are radical as well as factional. Under these conditions, there is clear evidence that South American political parties are capable of acting to dampen social conflict and a number of political leaders, chastened by the experience of military rule, are willing to act in this way.

This may well seem an unexciting prospect. South American societies remain unjust and a strategy of conciliation means that relatively little (though this is not to say nothing) can be done in the way of social reform.[11] Democracy in Colombia and Venezuela has not been "exciting" in its consequences though it has been stable and reasonably effective. As with old age there may be many disadvantages with this state of affairs, but it still seems better than the probable alternative.

NOTES

[1] A. Rouquie, *L'Etat Militaire en Amerique Latine*, (Paris; 1982).
[2] For similar comparisons in more detail see C. Clapham and G. Philip, *Political Dilemmas of Military Regimes*, (Croom Helm; 1984).

3 Huntington's argument to this effect (in Political Order in Changing Societies) appears to work well in South America though not in other parts of the world.
4 The Man on Horseback, Ch. 11, and Postscript.
5 A. Rouquie, Pouvoir Militaire et Societe Politique, p. 342.
6 The classic statement here is that of Ralf Dahrendorf, Class and Class Conflict in Industrial Society, (London; 1959).
7 J. Schumpeter, Capitalism, Socialism and Democracy, (New York; 1942) and A. Downs, An Economic Theory of Democracy, (Harper and Row; 1957).
8 For arguments along these lines, H. Wiarda, "Toward a Framework for the Study of Political Change in the Iberic-Latin Tradition; the comparative model", World Politics, 25, No. 2, (January 1973), and C. Veliz, The Centralist Tradition of Latin America, (Princeton U.P.; 1979). For a critical discussion of Veliz, see P. Cammack's review in Durham University Journal, Vol. 75, No. 2 (1983).
9 Quoted in L. Pasara, "When the Military Dreams", in C. McClintock and A. Lowenthal, The Peruvian Experiment Revisited, (Princeton U.P.; 1983), p. 319.
10 Compare C. P. Anderson's discussion of power contenders and veto power in Politics and Economic Change in Latin America, (Princeton; 1967).
11 For an interesting discussion of politics and social reform, see W. Ascher, Scheming for the Poor; the Politics of Redistribution in Latin America, (Harvard Univ. Press; 1984).

REFERENCES

Aguilar, L.   Cuba 1933, (Stanford U.P.; 1972).

Almond, G. &   The Politics of the Developing Areas,
Coleman, J. S.   (Princeton U.P.; 1960).

Anderson, C. P.   Politics and Economic Change in Latin
                     America, (Princeton U.P.; 1967).

Angell, A.   "The Difficulties of Policy-Making and
                     Implementation in Peru", Bulletin of
                     Latin American Research, Vol. 3, No. 1,
                     (January 1984).

Arroyo, E.   "Elections and Negotiation; Democracy in
                     Venezuela", (Ph.D., London; 1983).

Ascher, W.   Scheming for the Poor; the Politics of
                     Redistribution in Latin America, (Harvard
                     U.P.; 1984).

Astiz, C.   "The Argentine Armed Forces; their role
                     and political involvement", Western
                     Political Quarterly, Vol. 5, No. 2,
                     (December 1969).

Ayer, A. J.   Philosophy in the Twentieth Century,
                     (Unwin; 1982).

Baella, A.   El Septenato, (Lima; 1977).

Baer, W.   "Import Substitution and Industrialisation
                     in Latin America; experiences and
                     interpretations", Latin American Research
                     Review, 7, No. 1, (Spring 1972), pp.
                     95-122.

Baran, P.   The Political Economy of Growth,
                     (Standford U.P.; 1957).

Barros, de A.   "Back to Barracks; an option for the
                     Brazilian Military", (Mimeo, IUPERGE, Rio;
                     1984).

Becker, D.   The New Bourgeoisie and the Limits of
                     Dependency; Mining, Class and Power in
                     "Revolutionary" Peru, (Princeton U.P.;
                     1983).

Berlin, I.   "The Hedgehog and the Fox", in Berlin,
                      ed, Russian Thinkers, (Pelican; 1979),
                      pp. 22-82.

Booth, D.   "The Reform of the Press; myths and
                      realities", in D. Booth and B. Sorj, eds,
                      Military Reformism and Social Classes;
                      the Peruvian Experience, (McMillan;
                      1983).

Booth, J.   The End and the Beginning; the Nicaraguan
                      Revolution, (Westview Press; 1982).

Bourricaud, F.   Power and Society in Contemporary Peru,
                      (New York; 1970).

Burggraaff, W.   The Venezuelan Armed Forces in Politics
                      1935-59, (Colombia U.P.; 1972).

Cammack, P.   "The Political Economy of Contemporary
                      Military Regimes in Latin America; from
                      bureaucratic authoritarianism to
                      restructuring", (mimeo, Manchester; 1984).

                      "Bureaucratic-Authoritarianism; a dissent-
                      ing note", Politics, 2, No. 1, (April
                      1982).

                      "Clientelism and Military Government in
                      Brazil", in C. Clapham, ed, Private
                      Patronage and Public Power; Political
                      Clientelism in the Modern State, (Frances
                      Pinter; 1982).

Campos Coelho, A.   Em Busca de Identidade; o Exercito e a
                      Politica na Sociedade Brasileira,
                      (Forense, Rio; 1976).

Canton, D.   La Politica de los Militares Argentinos
                      1900-71, (Buenos Aires; 1971).

Cardoso, F. H.   "Dependency and Development in Latin
                      America", New Left Review, July/August
                      1972.

                      "On the Characterisation of Authoritarian
                      Regimes", in D. Collier, ed, The New
                      Authoritarianism in Latin America,
                      (Princeton U.P.; 1979).

References

Cardoso, F. H. &
Faletto, E.
Dependencia y Desarrollo en America Latina, (Santiago; 1967).

Castro de Andrade, R.
"Brazil; the military in politics", in SLAS Bulletin, No. 26, (March 1977).

Clapham, C. &
Philip, G. eds,
Political Dilemmas of Military Regimes, (Croom Helm; 1984).

Cleaves, P. &
Scurrah, R.
Agriculture, Bureaucracy and Military Government in Peru, (Cornell; 1980).

Collier, D.
Squatters and Oligarchs; Authoritarian Rule and Policy Change in Peru, (Johns Hopkins; 1976).

Congdon, T.
"Chile" in E. Duran, ed, Latin America in the World Recession, (Cambridge U.P.; 1985).

Conniff, M.
"The Tenentes in Power; a New Perspective on the Brazilian Revolution of 1930", Journal of Latin American Studies, Vol. 10, No. 1, (May 1978).

Conrad, J.
Nostromo, (Penguin; 1973).

Corbett, C.
The Latin American Military as a Socio-Political Force; Case Studies of Bolivia and Argentina, (U. of Miami; 1972).

Cortes, C.
"Armed Politics in Rio Grande do Sul", in H. Keith and R. Hayes, Perspectives on Armed Politics in Brazil, (U. of Arizona; 1976).

Dahrendorf, R.
Class and Class Conflict in Industrial Society, (London; 1959).

Dinges, J. &
Landau, S.
Assassination on Embassy Row, (New York; 1980).

Downs, A.
An Economic History of Democracy, (Harper and Row; 1957).

Draper, T.
The Dominican Revolt, (Commentary, NY; 1968).

Dreifuss, R.

"State, Class and the Organic Elite: Formation of an entrepreneurial order in Brazil", (Ph.D., Univ. of Glasgow; 1980).

Dudley, W. S.

"Professionalization and Politicization as Motivational Factors in the Brazilian Army Coup of 15 November 1889", Journal of Latin American Studies, Vol. 8, No. 1, (May 1976), pp. 101-125.

"Institutional Sources of Discontent in the Brazilian Army 1870-1889", Hispanic American Historical Review, Vol. 55, No. 1, (1975).

Dunkerley, J.

Rebellion in the Veins, (Verso Press; 1984).

"Reassessing Caudillismo in Bolivia 1825-79", Bulletin of Latin American Research, Vol. 1, No. 1, (October 1981).

"The Politics of the Bolivian Army; Institutional Development 1879-1935", (D.Phil., Oxford; 1979).

Eckstein, S.

"Revolution and Redistribution in Latin America", in C. McClintock and A. Lowenthal, The Peruvian Experiment Reconsidered, (Princeton; 1983).

Einaudi, L.

"Peru", in A. Stepan and L. Einaudi, Latin American Institutional Development; changing military perspectives in Peru and Brazil, (Rand; 1971).

Erickson, K. P.

The Brazilian Corporative State and Working Class Politics, (UCLA; 1978).

Evans, P.

Dependent Development; An Allegiance of Multinational, State and Local Capital in Brazil, (Princeton; 1979).

Falcon, R.

"The Rise and Fall of Military Caciquismo in Revolutionary Mexico; the case of San Luis Potosi 1910-38", (D.Phil., Oxford; 1983).

References

Ferner, A.
"The Industrial Bourgeoisie and the Peruvian Development Model", (D.Phil., Sussex; 1977).

Ferrer, A.
Crisis y Alternativas de la Politica Economica Argentina, (Buenos Aires; 1977).

Finch, M. J.
"Three Perspectives on the Crisis in Uruguay", Journal of Latin American Studies, Vol. 3, No. 2, (November 1971), pp. 173-190.

Finer, S. E.
The Man on Horseback, (2nd Ed., Penguin; 1975).

"The Mind of the Military", New Society, 7 August 1975

Fitch, J. S.
The Military Coup D'Etat as a Political Process; Ecuador 1948-66, (Johns Hopkins; 1978).

Fitzgerald, E. V.
"State Capitalism in Peru; a Model of Economic Development and its Limitations", in C. McClintock and A. Lowenthal, The Peruvian Experiment Reconsidered, (Princeton U.P.; 1983).

Flynn, P.
Brazil; A Political Analysis, (Benn; 1978).

Fortin, C.
"The Relative Autonomy of the State and Capital Accumulation in Latin America; Some Conceptual Issues", D. Tussie, ed, Latin America in the World Economy, (Gower, 1983).

Foxley, A.
Neo-Conservative Experiments in Latin America, (Stanford U.P.; 1983).

Frank, A. G.
Capitalism and Underdevelopment in Latin America, (Penguin; 1970).

"The Sociology of Development or the Underdevelopment of Sociology?", in R. Rhodes et al, Politics and Underdevelopment, (Monthly Review; 1970).

Furci, C.

"The Chilean Communist Party and its Third Underground Period", Bulletin of Latin American Research, Vol. 2, No. 1, (October 1982).

Furtado, C.

Diagnosis of the Brazilian Crisis, (Berkeley; 1965).

Gall, N.

"Peru; the Master is Dead", Dissent, 1971.

Galeano, E.

Open Veins of Latin America, (Monthly Review; 1973).

Garcia Marquez, G.

A Hundred Years of Solitude, (Penguin; 1972).

Geller, D.

"Economic Modernization and Political Stability in Latin America", Western Political Quarterly, Vol. 18 (March 1982), pp. 33-50.

Gellman, F.

Good Neighbour Diplomacy; United States Policies in Latin America 1933-45, (Johns Hopkins; 1979).

Gilbert, D.

"The Oligarchy and the Old Regime in Peru", (Ph.D., Cornell; 1977).

Gillespie, R.

Soldiers of Perón; Argentina's Montoneros, (Oxford U.P.; 1983).

Gilmore, R.

Caudillism and Militarism in Venezuela 1810-1910, (Ohio U.P.; 1964).

Goes de, W.

O Brasil de General Geisel, (Nova Frontera, Rio; 1978).

Goff, I. & Locker, G.

"The Violence of Domination; US power and the Dominican Republic", in I. L. Horowitz, ed, Latin American Radicalism a Documentary Report on Left and Nationalist Movements, (London; 1969).

Goldwert, M.

Democracy, Militarism and Nationalism in Argentina 1930-66, (U. of Texas; 1972).

"The Rise of Modern Militarism in Argentina", in B. Loveman and T. Davies, The Politics of AntiPolitics, (U. of Nebraska; 1978).

Goodwin, R. "Letter from Peru", New Yorker, 17 May 1969.

Griffin, K. Underdevelopment in Spanish America, (Oxford U.P.; 1969).

Handelman, H. & Military Government and the Movement
Sanders, T. toward Democracy in South America, (AUFS, Bloomington; 1980).

Hansen, R. "Military Culture and Organisational Decline; a Study of the Chilean Army", (Ph.D., UCLA; 1967).

Hayes, R. "The Formation of the Brazilian Army and the Military Class Mystique 1500-1853", pp. 1-27, in H. Keith and R. Hayes, Perspectives on Armed Politics in Brazil, (U. of Arizona; 1976).

"The Military Club and National Politics in Brazil", in Keith and Hayes, Perspectives on Armed Politics.

Hersh, S. "The Price of Power; Kissinger, Nixon and Chile", Atlantic Monthly, December 1982.

Hilton, S. "Armed Forces and Industrialists in Modern Brazil; the Drive for Military Autonomy 1889-1954", Hispanic American Historical Review, Vol. 62, No. 4, (Nov. 1982), pp. 629-674.

Hirschman, A. "The Rise and Decline of Development Economics", in Hirschman, ed, Essays in Trespassing; Economics to Politics and Beyond, (Cambridge U.P.; 1981).

"The Political Economy of Import Substituting Industrialisation in Latin America", Quarterly Journal of Economics, 82, No. 1, (February 1968), pp. 2-32.

	Journeys Toward Progress, (New York; 1963).
Huntington, S. P.	Political Order in Changing Societies, (Yale U.P.; 1968).
Imaz de, J.	Los Que Mandan, (Buenos Aires; 1964).
Immerman, R.	The CIA in Guatemala; The Foreign Policy of Intervention, (U. of Texas; 1982).
Jackson, R. W.	"Politicians in Uniform; Military Governments and Social Change in the Third World", APSR, Vol. 70, No. 4, (September 1976).
Johnson, J.	"The Military in South America", in J. Johnson, ed, The Role of the Military in Underdeveloped Countries, (Princeton U.P.; 1962).
Karakartal, B.	"Turkey; the Army as Guardian of the Political Order", in C. Clapham and G. Philip, eds, The Political Dilemmas of Military Regimes, (Croom Helm; 1984).
Karl, T.	Petroleum and Political Pacts in Venezuela, (Woodrow Wilson Paper; 1981).
Keith, H.	"Armed Federal Interventions in the States During the Old Republic", in H. Keith and R. Hayes, eds, Perspectives on Armed Politics in Brazil, (U. of Arizona; 1976).
Kenworthy, E.	"Coalitions and Political Development in Latin America", in E. Goenings and others, eds, The Study of Coalition Behaviour; Theoretical Perspectives and Cases from Four Continents, (Free Press; 1970).
Kinzo, M.	"The MDB in São Paulo", Bulletin of Latin American Research, 3, 2, (July 1984).

References

Kornhauser, W.   The Politics of Mass Society, (Free Press; 1959).

Lamounier, B & Moura, A.   Politica Economica e Abertura Politica no Brasil 1973-33, (IDESP, Texto 4; São Paulo; 1984).

Lanusse, A.   Mi Testimonio, (Buenos Aires; 1977).

Levine, D.   "Venezuela since 1958; the Consolidation of Democratic Politics", in J. Linz and A. Stepan, Latin America; The Breakdown of Democratic Regimes, (Johns Hopkins; 1978).

Lieuwen, E.   Arms and Politics in Latin America, (Praeger; 1961).

"The Problems of Military Government", pp. 1-16, in R. Wesson, ed, New Military Politics in Latin America, (Stanford U.P.; 1982).

Mexican Militarism; the Political Rise and Fall of the Revolutionary Army 1910-40, (U. of New Mexico; 1968).

Linklater, M., Hilton, I & Ascherson, N.   The Fourth Reich; Klaus Barbie and the Neo-Fascist Connection, (Hodder and Stoughton; 1984).

Linz, J.   "An Authoritarian Regime; Spain", in E. Allardt and S. Rokkan, Mass Politics, (Free Press; 1970).

"The Future of an Authoritarian Situation or the Institutionalisation of an Authoritarian Regime; the case of Brazil", in A. Stepan, ed, Authoritarian Brazil; Origins, Policies and Future, (Yale U.P.; 1973).

Little, W.   "The Popular Origins of Peronism", in D. Rock, ed, Argentina in Twentieth Century (Duckworth; 1975).

Lowenthal, A.   The Dominican Intervention, (Harvard, U.P.; 1972).

"The Dominican Republic; the politics of chaos", in A. Van Lazar and R. Kaufman, eds, Reform and Revolution; Readings in Latin American Politics, (Allyn and Bacon, Boston; 1969).

Lowi, T.   Interest Group Liberalism, (U. of Chicago; 1970).

Lynch, J.   Argentine Dictator; Juan Manuel de Rosas 1829-52, (Clarendon Press; 1981).

McAllistair, L.   "Recent Research and Writings on the Role of the Military in Latin America", Latin American Research Review, Vol. 11, (Fall 1966), pp. 5-36.

McCann, F.   "The Brazilian Army and the Problem of Mission 1939-64", Journal of Latin American Studies, Vol. 12, No. 1, (May 1980).

McClintock, C.   "Velasco, Officers and Citizens; the Politics of Stealth", in C. McClintock and A. Lowenthal, eds, The Peruvian Experiment Reconsidered, (Princeton; 1983).

McDonough, P.   Power and Ideology in Brazil, (Princeton U.P.; 1971).

McKinlay, R. &   "Performance and Instability in Military
Cohen, A.   and Non-Military Regime Systems", APSR, Vol. 20, No. 4, (December 1976).

Masterson, D.   "The Peruvian Armed Forces in Transition 1939-63; the Impact of National Politics and Changing Political Perspectives", (Ph.D., Michigan; 1976).

Medeiros de, A.   "Politics and Intergovernmental Relations in Brazil 1964-82", (Ph.D., London; 1983).

Meyer, J. et al   Estado y Sociedad con Calles, (Colegio de Mexico; 1977).

Miliband, R.   The State in Capitalist Society, (McMillan; 1969).

References

Millett, R.	<u>Guardians of the Dynasty; a History of the US-created Guardia Nacional de Nicaragua and the Somoza Family</u>, (Orbis, NY; 1977).
Morgan, T. H.	<u>Multinational Corporations and the Politics of Dependence; Copper in Chile</u>, (Princeton U.P.; 1974).
Murilho de Carvalho, J.	"Elite and State Building in Imperial Brazil", (Ph.D., Stanford; 1975).
	"Armed Forces and Politics in Brazil", <u>Hispanic American Historical Review</u>, Vol. 62, No. 2 (May 1982).
Murmis, J & Portantiero, J. eds,	<u>Estudios Sobre las Origines del Peronismo</u>, (Siglo XXI; 1971).
Needler, M.	<u>Anatomy of a Coup D'Etat; Ecuador 1963</u>, (Washington; 1964).
Nordlinger, R.	"Soldiers in Mufti", <u>APSR</u>, Vol. 64, No. 4, (December 1970).
North, L.	"Ideological Orientations of Peru's Military Rulers", in C. McClintock and A. Lowenthal, <u>The Peruvian Experiment Reconsidered</u>, (Princeton; 1983).
Nun, J.	"The Middle Class Military Coup Revisited", in A. Lowenthal, ed, <u>Armies and Politics in Latin America</u>, (Holmes and Meier; 1977).
Nunn, F.	<u>The Military in Chilean History; Essays of Civil-Military Relations 1810-1973</u>, (U. of New Mexico; 1976).
	"Military Professionalism and Professional Militarism in Brazil 1890-1940; historical perspectives and political implications", <u>Journal of Latin American Studies</u>, Vol. 4, No. 1, pp. 29-54, (May 1972).
	<u>Yesterday's Soldiers; European Military Professionalism in South America 1890-1940</u>, (U. of Nebraska; 1983).

382

Chilean Politics 1920-31; The "Honourable Mission of the Armed Forces", (U. of New Mexico; 1970).

O'Brien, D. C. "Modernization, Order and the Erosion of a Democratic Ideal", Journal of Development Studies, Vol. 8, (1971-72).

O'Brien, P. "Dependency; the New Nationalism?", Latin American Review of Books, 1973.

O'Brien, P. & Roddick, J & others Chile; the Pinochet Decade, (LAB; 1983).

O'Donnell, G. Modernisation and Bureaucratic-Authoritarianism; Studies in South American Politics, (Berkeley; 1973).

"Permanent Crisis and the Failure to Create a Democratic Regime; Argentina 1955-66", in J. Linz and A. Stepan, Latin America; The Breakdown of Democratic Regimes, (Johns Hopkins; 1978).

"Reflections on the Patterns of Change in the Bureaucratic-Authoritarian State", Latin American Research Review, 12, No. 1, (Winter 1978), pp. 3-38.

"Tensions in the Bureaucratic-Authoritarian State and the Question of Democracy", in D. Collier, ed, The New Authoritarianism in Latin America, (Princeton; 1979).

"Modernization and Military Coups; Theory, Comparisons and the Argentine Case", in A. Lowenthal, Armies and Politics in Latin America.

Argentina 1966-73; El Estado Bureaucratico-Autoritario, (Belgrano, Buenos Aires; 1982).

References

Packenham, R. A.   *Liberal America and the Third World*, (Princeton U.P.; 1973).

Painter, J.   *Paraguay in the 1970s; Continuity and Change in the Political Process*, (ILAS Working Paper 9; 1983).

Palma, G.   "Dependency; a formal theory of development or a methodology for the analysis of concrete situations of underdevelopment?", *World Development*, 6, (July/August 1978), pp. 881-924.

Palmer, D. S. & Middlebrook, K.   *Military Government and Political Development; Lessons from Peru*, (London; 1975).

Pasara, L.   "When the Military Dreams", in C. McClintock and A. Lowenthal, *The Peruvian Experiment Reconsidered*, (Princeton U.P.; 1983).

Peres, W.   "La Estructura de la Industria Estatal 1965-75", in *Economia Mexicana*, (CIDE, Mexico; 1982).

Perez, L.   "Army Politics, Diplomacy and the Collapse of the Cuban Officer Corps; the 'Sergeants Revolt' of 1933", *Journal of Latin American Studies*, Vol. 6, No. 1, (May 1974).

Army Politics in Cuba 1989-1958, (Pittsburgh U.P.; 1976).

Perina, R.   *Ongania, Levingston, Lanusse; Los Militares en la Politica Argentina*, (Belgraño, Buenos Aires; 1983).

Perlmutter, A.   "The Comparative Analysis of Military Regimes; formations, aspirations and achievements", *World Politics*, Vol. 33, No. 1, (October 1980).

Philip, G.   *The Rise and Fall of the Peruvian Military Radicals 1968-76*, (Athlone; 1978).

Oil and Politics in Latin America;
Nationalist Movements and State
Companies, (Cambridge U.P.; 1982).

"Military Authoritarianism in South
America", Political Studies, Vol. 22,
No. 1, (March 1984), pp. 1-20.

"Military Rule in South America", in C.
Clapham and G. Philip, Political
Dilemmas of Military Regimes, (Croom
Helm; 1984).

"The Military Institution Revisited",
Journal of Latin American Studies, 12,
2 (November 1980).

"Argentine Politics and the Falklands
Issue", Brassey's Defence Yearbook,
(London; 1984).

Bonanza Development? The Case of the
Selva Oil Industry in Peru, (ILAS
Working Paper; 1984).

Pinelo, A. J.   The International Petroleum Company in
                       Peru, (Praeger; 1973).

Pizzorno, S., ed,   Political Sociology, (Penguin; 1975).

Pope Atkins, G.   Arms and Politics in the Dominican
                       Republic, (Westview; 1981).

Potash, R.   The Army and Politics in Argentina
                       1928-45, (Stanford; 1969).

                       The Army and Politics in Argentina
                       1945-63, (Stanford; 1982).

Poulantzas, R.   Political Power and Social Classes,
                       (New Left Books; 1973).

Prado Salmon, G.   Poder y Fuerzas Armadas 1949-82, (La
                       Paz; 1984).

Premo, D.   "The Colombian Armed Forces in Search of
                       a Mission", in R. Wesson, ed, New
                       Military Politics in Latin America,
                       (Stanford U.P.; 1982).

References

Przeworski, A.

Some Problems in the Study of the Transition to Democracy, (Woodrow Wilson Paper No. 61; 1982).

Remmer, A. & Merckx, G.

"Bureaucratic-Authoritarianism Revisited", Latin American Research Review, Vol. 17, No. 2, (1982), p. 7.

Rock, A.

Politics in Argentina 1890-1930; the Rise and Fall of Radicalism, (Cambridge U.P.; 1975).

Rouquie, A.

Pouvoir Militaire et Societe Politique en Republique Argentine, (Paris 1976).

L'Etat Militaire Dans Amerique Latine, (Paris; 1982).

"Argentina; the Departure of the Military", International Affairs, 59, (4), Autumn 1983.

Roxborough, I.

Theories of Underdevelopment, (McMillan; 1979).

Ruhl, J. M.

"Civil-Military Relations in Colombia; a societal explanation", in Journal of Inter-American Studies, Vol. 23, No. 2, (May 1981), pp. 123-147.

Sater, W.

"The Abortive Kronstadt; the Chilean Naval Mutiny of 1931", Hispanic American Historic Review, Vol. 60, No. 2, (May 1980).

Santos Dos, T.

"The Crisis of Development Theory and the Problem of Dependence in Latin America", reprinted in H. Bernstein, ed, Under-development and Development in the Third World Today, (Penguin; 1973).

Schiff, W.

"The Influence of the German Armed Forces and the War Industry of Argentina; German Co-operation with the Argentine Military", Hispanic American Historical Review, Vol. 52, No. 3, (August 1972), pp. 436-456.

Schmitter, P.   Interest, Conflict and Political Change
                 in Brazil, (Stanford U.P.; 1971).

Schneider, R.   The Political System of Brazil;
                 Emergence of a 'Modernizing' Authorit-
                 arian Regime 1964-70, (Columbia U.P.;
                 1970).

Schumpeter, J.   Capitalism, Socialism and Democracy,
                 (New York; 1942).

Serra, J.   "Three Mistaken Theses Regarding the
                 Connection between Industrialisation and
                 Authoritarian Regimes", in D. Collier,
                 ed, The New Authoritarianism in Latin
                 America, (Princeton; 1979), pp. 99-
                 165.

Sigmund, P.   "The Military in Chile", in R. Wesson,
                 ed, New Military Politics in Latin
                 America, (Hoover Inst; 1982).

Simmons, C.   "Military Leaders in National Politics
                 1853-1889", pp. 27-51, in H. Keith and
                 R. Hayes, Perspectives on Armed
                 Politics in Brazil, (U. of Arizona;
                 1976).

Skidmore, T.   Politics in Brazil 1930-64, (Wisconsin
                 U.P.; 1967).

Smith, P.   Argentina and the Failure of Democracy;
                 Conflict among Political Elites 1904-
                 55, (Wisconsin U.P.; 1974).

Stein, S.   Populism in Peru; the Emergence of the
                 Masses and the Politics of Social
                 Control, (Wisconsin U.P.; 1980).

Stepan, A.   The Military in Politics; Changing
                 Patterns in Brazil, (Princeton U.P.;
                 1971).

                 The State and Society; Peru in
                 Comparative Perspective, (Princeton;
                 1978).

"The New Professionalism or Internal Warfare and Military Role Expansion", in A. Stepan, ed, Authoritarian Brazil, (Yale U.P.; 1973).

Stumpf, A & Pereira, M.
A Segunda Guerra; Sucessao de Geisel, (São Paulo; 1979).

Tambs, L.
"Five Times Against the System; Brazilian Foreign Military Expeditions and their Effect on National Politics", pp. 171-207, in H. Keith and R. Hayes, eds, Perspectives on Armed Politics in Brazil, (U. of Arizona; 1978).

Tavares de, M. O.
"The Growth and Decline of Import Substitution", Economic Bulletin for Latin America, 9, (March 1964), pp. 1-65.

Tella Di, T.
"Working Class Organisations and Politics in Argentina", Latin American Research Review, Vol. 16, No. 2, (1981).

Thompson, E. P.
"The Poverty of Theory", in E. P. Thompson, ed, The Poverty of Theory, (Merlin Press; 1979).

Thorndike, G.
No. Mi General, (Lima; 1977).

Thorp, R. & Bertram, G.
Peru 1890-1977; Growth and Policy in an Export Economy, (McMillan; 1978).

Timerman, J.
Prisoner without a Name; Cell without a Number, (Penguin; 1982).

Torre, J. C.
"Sob as Origines do Peronismo", Estudios CEBRAP, 16, (April-June 1976).

Veliz, C.
The Centralist Tradition of Latin America, (Princeton U.P.; 1979).

Viana, L.
O Governo Castelao Branco, (Forense, Rio; 1975).

Villanueva, V.
El CAEM y la Revolucion de la Fuerza Armada, (IEP, Lima; 1972).

Cien Anos del Ejercito Peruano, (IEP, Lima; 1973).

Apra y el Ejercito 1940-50, (Lima; 1977).

Un Ano Bajo el Sable, (Lima; 1963).

Whitehead, L. A.

"Bolivia Swings Right", Current History, February 1972.

The United States and Bolivia; A Case of Neo-Colonialism, (Haslemere; 1969).

Bolivia's Failed Democratisation, (Woodrow Wilson Paper 100; 1981).

Wiarda, H.

"Toward a Framework for the Study of Political Change in the Iberic-Latin Tradition; the Comparative Model", World Politics, 25, No. 2, (January 1973).

Wilde, A.

"Conversations among Gentlemen", in J. Linz and A. Stepan, Latin America; The Breakdown of Democratic Regimes, (Johns Hopkins; 1978).

Woods, R. B.

"Hull and Argentina; Wilsonian Diplomacy in the Age of Roosevelt", in Journal of Latin American Studies and World Affairs, Vol. 16, No. 3, (August 1974), pp. 350-371.

Woy-Hazleton, S.

"The Return of Partisan Politics in Peru", in S. Gorman, ed, Post-Revolutionary Peru; the Politics of Transformation, (Westview; 1982).

AAA (Triple-A Argentina) 189, 261
Acción Democrática 2, 113, 136, 141, 142
Alessandri, Jorge 99, 100, 118, 131, 132, 134, 135, 306, 314
Albuquerque Lima, Afonso 221, 222, 224
Alfonsín, Raul 269-270, 351
Allende, Salvador 259, 292, 307, 314, 346, 365, 366
Alsogaray, Alvaro 247, 251, 255
Alvarez, Gregorio 19, 346, 347, 350-352
Alvear, Marcelo 105, 118, 125, 202
APRA 118, 136, 137-138, 139, 140, 280, 289-290, 294, 295-296, 298, 299, 302
Aramburu, Pedro 67, 188, 193, 255
Arbenz, Jacobo 61, 112
ARENA (later PDS) 220, 235, 236
Argentina 6, 7, 8, 12-13, 15, 17, 18, 19, 28, 32, 34, 35-36, 47, 48, 54, 55, 66-69, 73, 85, 88, 95, 101-106, 109, 111, 116, 117, 118, 124-131, 135, 143, 144, 155, 157-163, 166, 168, 170, 173, 174, 178-179, 181, 183, 186, 188, 189-190, 191, 193, 194, 195, 196, 202, 204, 206, 210, 246-274, 287, 306, 313, 314, 318, 322, 325, 335, 340, 347, 356, 359, 360, 361, 362-363
Azules (Argentina) 161, 162, 202, 247, 248, 256

Balaguer, Joaquim 59, 61
Banzer, Hugo 331-334, 335, 326
Barrientos, René 327, 328-329
Barros, Adhemar de 213, 217, 218, 230
Batista 1, 48, 70, 71-72, 73, 119, 208
Belaúnde, Fernando 167-168, 275, 276, 278, 289, 291, 294, 297, 299-300, 370
Beltrán, Pedro 141, 277
Benavides, Oscar 19, 138, 141, 146
Benavides, José 277, 284-285, 288
Betancourt, Romulo 108, 139
Blanche, Bartolome 133, 145
Bolivia 74, 85, 87, 106-107, 110, 111, 112, 127, 135-137, 146, 182, 188, 193, 292, 314, 325-337, 358, 367, 368
Bosch, Juan 58, 59
Brazil 11, 14, 15, 117, 18-19, 27, 28, 29, 32, 34, 35, 36, 44, 47, 48, 54, 55, 57, 73, 84, 85-86, 90-96, 98, 100, 101, 109-110, 111, 112, 116, 118-124, 129, 130, 131, 135, 141, 143, 144, 149-157, 162, 164, 166, 168, 173, 174, 177, 178, 179, 180-181, 183, 186, 187, 192-193, 195, 196, 201, 204, 205, 206, 210, 213-245, 250, 254, 266, 281, 301, 313, 322, 325, 340, 346, 347, 349, 359, 365
Brizola, Lionel 222, 239
Broadaberry 346, 348-349
Busch, German 136
Bustamante, Jose 139, 140

Campora 259, 260, 262, 292
Carter, Jimmy 266, 315, 333, 337
Campos, Roberto 183, 219
Castello Branco, Humberto 124, 213, 217, 218, 219, 220-222, 242
Castro, Cipriano 107
Caudillismo 84, 85, 86-88, 110
Caxias, Duque de 86, 92
Centro de Altos Estudios Militares (CAEM) 163-166, 180, 184, 278, 280
CGT (Argentina) 159, 247, 249, 251-252, 256, 272, 356
Chaco War 107, 135
Chaves, Aureliano 238, 239, 240
Chile 6, 8, 11, 13-14, 15, 33, 35, 36, 37, 55, 57, 73, 84-85, 86, 96-101, 102, 106, 111, 113, 116, 129, 131-135, 137, 144, 145, 168, 172-173, 178, 181, 183, 184, 185, 189, 191, 193, 196, 202, 203, 205, 206, 207, 260, 264, 266, 288, 292, 296, 306-324, 332-333, 340, 359, 361, 363, 365, 366, 367, 368
Christian Democrats (Chile) 307, 309, 311, 314, 317, 320-321, 360, 366
Church, Catholic 57, 65, 142, 160, 185, 204, 224, 227, 233, 235, 251, 311, 327
Colombia 1, 7, 84, 89, 110, 168-170, 172, 188, 288, 367, 370
Colorados (Argentina) 161, 196, 202, 247
El Comercio (Peru) 165, 181, 280-281, 284, 293
Communist Party
(Brazil) 150, 222
(Chile) 310, 321, 361

(Peru) 297
(Ecuador) 340-341
(Uruguay) 347, 351-352, 356, 366
(general) 349, 362
Contreras, Manuel 181, 309-310, 315-316
Cordeiro de Farias 124, 151, 213
Cordobazo 253-254, 255
Costa e Silva 217, 218-219, 221, 222-224, 233, 242
Cuba 1, 29, 48, 57, 69-74, 72, 73-74, 193, 328, 357
Cuban Revolution (effect of) 26-27, 151, 156, 326
Cubillos, Hernan 308, 316, 317

Davila 133-134
DINA 181, 189, 309-310, 315-316, 317
Dominican Republic 1, 14, 29, 57-61, 63, 65, 247, 357
Dutra, Gaspar 119, 122, 149, 150, 151, 155

Ecuador 12, 18-19, 110, 122, 138, 141, 178, 181, 182, 202, 207, 292, 325, 337-344, 360
El Salvador 11, 357
ERP (Argentina) 252, 262, 346
Escola Superior de Guerra 150, 151-154, 162, 163, 164, 180, 213, 218, 281, 346-347
O Estado de São Paulo 217, 227, 235
Estado Novo 121, 124, 192, 214, 219, 359

Fabricaciones Militares 126, 130, 158, 163, 186, 272
FEB 124, 149, 150
Fernández Maldonado, Jorge 292, 295, 296

Figueiredo, Joao 229, 233, 234-238, 243
France 17, 36, 89, 137, 165, 246, 271
Franco, Francisco 66, 251, 271
Frei, Eduardo 307, 314, 317
Frondizi, Arturo 161, 247, 248, 271

Garcia Meza 326, 337
Galtieri, Leopoldo 48, 266-268, 269, 360-361, 367
Geisel, Orlando 19, 223, 224-225, 226
Geisel, Ernesto 19, 184, 203, 213, 223, 225, 227-236, 239, 242
German Military Missions 94, 97, 101, 102-103, 106, 124, 126, 143
Golbery do Couta e Silva 152, 154, 189, 213, 215, 222, 223, 228, 229, 230, 234, 235, 236, 237, 242
Goes Monteiro, Eduardo 119, 120, 122
Gomez, Juan Vicente 65, 107-108, 195
GOU 128, 129
Goulart, Joao 153, 156-157, 187, 191, 201, 214, 215, 222, 365
Graham, Jose 280, 284, 285, 295
Grove, Marmaduke 101, 207
Guatemala 60, 61, 358
Guevara, Che 328, 329, 331
Guevara Arce, Walter 334-335
Gulf Oil of Bolivia 182, 327, 329

Haiti 48, 58, 63
Haya de la Torre, Victor Raul 137, 139, 140, 191-192, 298, 299, 368

Ibañez, Carlos 99, 100, 131-133, 135, 144, 145, 174, 207, 306
Illia, Arturo 246, 247-248, 271, 365, 370
International Petroleum Company (Peru) 184, 278, 279, 282-283, 287

Jarpa, Sergio 319-320
Jarrín, Bolivar 343-344
Jarrín, Edgardo 182, 340, 342
Justo, Agustin 105, 125

Körner, Emil 97
Kruel, Amaury 124
Kubitischek, Juscelino 153, 155, 202, 218, 220, 221

Lacerda, Carlos 213, 217, 219, 220, 221, 242
Lanusse, Alejandro 247, 250, 253-254, 255, 256, 257-260
Larazábal, Wolfgang 142, 145
Leigh, Gustavo 309, 317
Letelier, Orlando 310, 315
Levingston, Roberto 256-257
Leguía, Augusto 146, 195
Leoni Raul 108
Lonardi, Eduardo 67, 159
López Contreras, Eleazar 108
López Rega 258, 259, 261

Magalhâez Pinto, 213, 216, 217, 218, 222, 223, 234
Maldonado Yanez, Alberto 277, 283, 284
Maluf, Paulo Salim 239, 240, 241
Martínez de Hoz 183, 269
MDB (later PMDB) 220, 238, 240-241
Medici, Emilio 222, 224, 225-228, 229

Medina Angarita, Isaias 109, 141
Menéndez, Benjamín 19, 159, 160
Mercado Jarrín, Edgardo 164, 281
El Mercurio (Chile) 132, 181, 308, 311
Mexico 18, 32, 43, 46, 57, 74-79, 209, 236, 266, 271, 292
Montagne, Ernesto 19, 167, 281
Montoneros (see also Peronism) 252-253, 255, 257, 262, 346, 366
Morales Bermúdez, Francisco 19, 167, 284, 294-299, 301
Movimiento Nacional Revolucionario (Bolivia) 136-137, 146, 326-327, 332
Mussolini 105

Netto, Delfim 183, 222, 223, 224, 226, 230, 236
Neves, Tancredo 240-241
Nicaragua 43, 57, 58, 62-66, 74, 357

Odría, Manuel 4, 19, 66, 141, 167, 206, 276, 277, 281, 282, 289
Onganía, Juan Carlos 34, 161, 162, 247, 249, 250-256, 272, 274, 356
Ovando, Alfredo 325-326, 327, 328-330, 367

Panama 58, 165, 326
Paraguay 43, 91, 127, 187-188, 195, 267, 322, 325, 358, 359
Pareda, Jose 333, 334
Paz Estensorro, Victor 326, 327, 334
PDS (Brazil) 238, 239, 241
Pérez Jiménez, Marco 4, 108, 141, 142-143, 144-145, 170, 173, 189, 203, 205, 208, 367

Perón, Juan 4, 13, 66-69, 117, 127-129, 157-160, 161, 162, 167, 185, 192, 196, 208, 209, 210, 247, 248, 253, 254, 256, 257, 258-260, 272, 370
Perón, Isabel 259, 260
Peronism (see also ERP and Montoneros) 45, 207, 246-247, 249, 250-260, 264, 271
Peru 2, 11, 12, 13, 19, 54, 66, 73, 85, 111, 112, 116, 135, 137-141, 143, 146, 163-168, 173, 177, 181, 182, 186, 187, 189, 193, 194, 195, 196, 202, 206, 208, 275-305, 306, 329, 356, 358, 359, 360, 361, 363, 366
Petrobrás 155, 215, 225, 228, 229, 359
Pinochet, Augusto 4, 19, 36, 185, 195, 206, 210, 292, 301, 309-324, 332, 366
PMDB (see MDB)
Portales, Diego 84
Portugal 8, 11, 206
Prado, Manuel 138
(Prado family) 167, 187, 275-277, 286
Prestes, Luis Carlos 96, 101

Quadros, Janio 155, 156, 215

Radical Party (Argentina) 103, 105, 112, 118, 125, 127, 158, 256, 258, 361
(UCR) 161
Roca, Julio 101
Rodríguez Figueroa, Leonidas 285, 295
Rodríquez Lara, Guillermo 339-342
Rojas Pinilla 169, 206, 367
Roldós, Jaime 342, 343, 344
Rosas, Juan Manuel de 88

Sánchez Cerro, Luis 137, 138, 146, 167
Sanguinetti, Julio 352-353
Sâo Paulo 92, 94, 96, 110, 119, 121, 122, 123, 213, 216, 220, 222, 223-224, 226, 228, 230-232, 233, 235, 236, 241
Siles Salinas, Luis 329
Siles Suazo, Hernán 326, 334, 337
SNI (Brazil) 189, 222, 224, 225, 232, 233, 234, 359
Somoza, Anastasio 63-64, 208
Somoza, Anastasio Jnr. (Tacho) 64-65, 73
Sorbonne Group (Brazil) 213-214, 218, 223, 228
Soviet Union 192, 266, 356
Spain 6, 8, 206
Stroessner 65, 66, 188, 195, 205

Tavora, Juarez 96, 122, 213
Tenentes 73, 95, 119, 120, 123, 132, 149-150
Toro, David 136
Torres, Jose 60, 328, 330-331, 367
Trujillo, Rafael 2, 58, 60, 65
Tupamaros 345-346

Uniâo Democratico Nacional (UDN) 149, 150, 155, 216, 220
United States 17, 58, 62-63, 65, 69, 72, 124, 127, 139, 153-154, 157-158, 185, 214, 219, 224, 267, 278-279, 283-284, 326-327, 328, 329, 343
Uriburu, Jose 124-125
Uruguay 6, 8, 11, 14, 15, 17, 28, 33, 35, 36, 55, 84, 127, 130, 183, 205, 206, 322, 325, 344-353, 356, 359, 363, 366
USSR (see Soviet Union)

Valle, Juan Jose 160, 193
Vandor 252, 253, 254
Vargas, Getulio 4, 117, 118, 143, 144, 149, 153, 155, 195, 201, 214
Vargas Caballero, Luis 293, 369
Vasena, Kreiger 183, 251-252, 254
Velasco, Juan 19, 166, 167, 185, 196, 207, 208, 210, 276-294, 295, 296, 300, 302, 325, 328, 329, 367
Velasco Ibarra, Jose Maria 338-339, 370
Venezuela 2, 4, 7, 8, 12, 57, 87, 89, 107-109, 110, 13, 116, 141-143, 144, 146, 168, 170-172, 188, 189, 191, 203, 370
Videla, Jorge 4, 261-266, 367
Villalba, Jovito 108
Villaroel 146
Villegas, Vegh 183, 348
Viola, Roberto 261, 263, 266, 364, 367

Yrigoyen, Hipolito 104-105, 124

Zimmerman, Augusto 280-281, 284

For Product Safety Concerns and Information please contact our EU
representative GPSR@taylorandfrancis.com
Taylor & Francis Verlag GmbH, Kaufingerstraße 24, 80331 München, Germany